Social Policy for Development

ANTHONY HALL AND JAMES MIDGLEY
with
chapters by
Jo Beall, Mrigesh Bhatia
and Elias Mossialos

SAGE Publications
Los Angeles • London • New Delhi • Singapore

First published 2004
Reprinted 2006, 2007

SAGE Publications Ltd
1 Oliver's Yard
55 City Road
London EC1Y 1SP

SAGE Publications Inc
2455 Teller Road
Thousand Oaks, California 91320

SAGE Publications India Pvt Ltd.
B1/I 1 Mohan Cooperative Industrial Area
Mathura Road, New Delhi 110 044
India

SAGE Publications Asia-Pacific Pte Ltd
33 Pekin Street #02-01
Far East Square
Singapore 048763

British Library Cataloguing in Publication data

A catalogue record for this book is available
from the British Library

ISBN: 978-0-7619-6714-9 (hbk)
ISBN: 978-0-7619-6715-6 (pbk)

Library of Congress Control Number: 2003109261

Typeset by C & M Digitals (P) Ltd., Chennai, India
Printed and bound in Great Britain by Athenaeum Press Ltd., Gateshead, Tyne & Wear.

Contents

List of Tables

List of Figures

Preface

It is over 20 years since the publication of *The Social Dimensions of Development* (London: John Wiley, 1982), written by Margaret Hardiman and James Midgley as the first basic textbook to systematically consider the development of social policy outside of the industrialized nations. That volume was aimed at students of social policy and planning in developing countries at the London School of Economics and elsewhere, on postgraduate programmes that by then had already existed for almost a decade. Since those pioneering days, courses in social policy, social planning and social development have multiplied. In parallel, development organizations at all levels, from the grassroots to the global, have steadily expanded their professional capacity to deal with these social dimensions, many having sought training for their staff in UK academic institutions. There has also been a wealth of literature on specific social sectors that has played a key role in sensitizing development policy-makers and practitioners to these issues. However, we felt that at this juncture there was the need for an updated core text for students that would review rapidly evolving theoretical and practical debates on social policy in the context of the South.

Although this volume is aimed primarily at students of social policy, we hope that it will have a much broader appeal. We would like to think that it will serve as a reference point for academics in related disciplines as well as policy-makers and practitioners in government, international and non-governmental organizations. Thanks are due to several cohorts of students at the London School of Economics on the MSc *Social Policy and Planning in Developing Countries* who have acted as sounding boards for many of the ideas expressed in these pages. Thanks also to Jo Beall, Mrigesh Bhatia and Elias Mossialos for authoring two of the book's chapters. We are grateful to everyone at Sage Publications who worked on the book; and particularly to Lucy Robinson and David Mainwaring, who supported the project from the beginning; and to Fabienne Pedroletti who saw the book through production. We hope that the book will make a modest contribution towards consolidating the evolution of social policy as a central concern of development organizations around the globe, to be placed on an equal footing with economic and environmental policy in the continuing struggle to promote people's well-being.

Anthony Hall
James Midgley

List of Abbreviations

ADB	Asian Development Bank
AfDB	African Development Bank
AIDS	Acquired immune deficiency syndrome
CBO	community-based organization
CSO	civil society organization
DAC	Development Assistance Committee
DALY	disability-adjusted life year
DFID	Department for International Development
ECLAC	Economic Commission for Latin America and the Caribbean
ED	essential drugs
EFA	Education For All
EU	European Union
GATT	General Agreement on Tariffs and Trade
GDP	gross domestic product
GNP	gross national product
HDI	human development index
HIV	Human immunodeficiency virus
IBRD	International Bank for Reconstruction and Development
IDA	International Development Association
IDB	Inter-American Development Bank
IDC	international development cooperation
IFAD	International Fund for Agricultural Development
ILO	International Labour Organization
IMF	International Monetary Fund
ISSA	International Social Security Association
MDG	Millennium Development Goal
NAFTA	North Atlantic Free Trade Area
ND	neglected disease
NGO	non-governmental organization
ODA	overseas development assistance
ODI	Overseas Development Institute
OECD	Organization for Economic Cooperation and Development
PHC	primary health care
PRSP	Poverty Reduction Strategy Paper
SAL	structural adjustment loan
SLF	sustainable livelihoods framework
SWAP	sector-wide approach

UNCED   United Nations Conference on the Environment and Development
UNCHS   United Nations Centre for Human Settlements
UNDP   United Nations Development Programme
UNESCO   United Nations Educational, Scientific and Cultural Organization
UNICEF   United Nations Children's Fund
UNRISD   United Nations Research Institute for Social Development
UPE   universal primary education
VET   vocational education and training
WB   World Bank
WCD   World Commission on Dams
WCED   World Commission on Environment and Development
WDR   *World Development Report*
WHO   World Health Organization
WTO   World Trade Organization

Glossary

Agrarian transition   The evolution and position of the agrarian sector during the process of economic modernization and development.

Agroforestry   A combination of short-cycle and perennial tree crops that is meant to discourage slash-and-burn farming in the quest for more sedentary, sustainable production models.

Allocative efficiency   A theory developed by economist Theodore Schultz, maintaining that, despite their poverty, poor farmers in developing countries are efficient allocators of the scarce resources at their disposal.

Basic education   Primary and non-formal education that provides basic academic and productive skills.

Basic human needs (BHN)   The minimum material and non-material needs required for a decent standard of living, also used as targets for development interventions.

Bilateral aid   Government-to-government foreign aid.

Capitalism   An economic and political theory that places primary importance on the individual ownership of property and stresses the role of capital investments in the creation of wealth.

Charity Organization Society   An association established in London in the mid-nineteenth century to provide social services to the poor whose approach led to the emergence of professional social work.

Civil society   Those groups and institutions that do not form part of government, including non-governmental organizations, the church, local communities, trades unions, social movements and the private sector.

Class   *See* social class.

Colonialism   The advocacy of establishing colonies of settlers from one society in another society. Colonialism is closely linked to imperialism.

Community development   A process by which local communities collaborate with government and voluntary organizations to enhance their well-being.

Community participation   The participation of local community members in local economic and social programmes sponsored by government and voluntary organizations.

Conscientization   A literal translation from the Portuguese *conscientização*, meaning a process through which people are made aware of their surroundings and the forces which affect their daily lives.

Cultural suitability   The suitability of social policies to the cultural realities of societies.

Dependency theory   A set of theories alleging that the development of the South is conditioned by, and dependent upon, development of the industrialized nations.

Development   A process of economic, social and political change that produces improvements in standards of living, social well-being and political participation.

Developmental social welfare   Social policies and human service programmes that contribute positively to economic development.

Employer mandates   Social security benefits that governments require employers to provide to their employees.

Empowerment   The acquisition of power to control or influence the course of events, often assumed to be a *sine qua non* of authentic development, especially at grassroots level.

Extractive reserves   A new type of land unit created in Brazil in 1990 in which land is collectively leased from the government by local associations of natural resource users as part of a longer-term plan for conservation and development.

Foreign aid   Defined by the OECD as international financial assistance, bilateral or multilateral, which contains a subsidy (concessional) element of at least 25 per cent and has economic development and welfare as its main aims.

Globalization   A process of international integration involving increased economic exchanges and communications.

Green Revolution   The huge increase in grain production experienced during the post-war period as a result of the development of new hybrid, high-yielding varieties of rice, wheat and corn.

Gross national product (GNP)   The total domestic and foreign output claimed by a country.

HIV/AIDS HIV is the virus that causes AIDS (acquired immune deficiency syndrome), attacking the body's immune system and leaving it vulnerable to opportunistic infections.

Human capital The productive capacity of human beings in the process of economic development supported by investments in education, health and other programmes.

Human services Organized programmes provided by government and non-profit organizations with the purpose of improving people's welfare.

Imperialism The exercise of political and economic power by one society over others.

Incremental welfare The expansion of social service and welfare provision in response to demands exerted by the most politically influential social groups such as the urban middle classes and labour unions.

Inequality The unequal and inequitable distribution of income, wealth and political power in a society.

Integrated rural development The integration of agricultural and other productive activities together with the provision of complementary social and infrastructure investments considered essential for successful development.

Keynesianism Named after the British economist John Maynard Keynes (1883–1946), this approach advocates government intervention to correct market failure and generate employment. Keynesianism stands in contrast to the neo-liberal belief that markets are self-regulating and prosperity is inevitable in the long run.

Liberalization The withdrawal of government interference (regulation) in financial markets, capital markets and trade.

Livelihoods The activities, assets and access to resources that jointly determine the living gained by an individual or household.

Micro-credit Loans provided by government or voluntary organizations to fund micro-enterprises.

Micro-enterprise Small businesses usually owned and operated by low-income people with assistance from government or voluntary organizations.

Modernism The advocacy of modernity.

Modernity A historical period beginning in the eighteenth century associated with industrialization that emphasizes the importance of rationality in social life.

Modernization The process of becoming modern and of promoting modernity through industrialization.

Multilateral assistance Financial assistance channelled through multilateral institutions such as the World Bank, the IMF and the UN.

Neo-liberalism A resuscitation of nineteenth-century *laissez-faire* political theory advocating capitalism and limited government intervention in economic and social affairs on the grounds that markets are self-regulating in the long run. *See also* capitalism, liberalization, Washington Consensus.

Non-formal education (NFE) Education for academic or vocational purposes that is not provided through the formal school system. *See also* basic education.

Non-formal social security Institutionalized social security practices that operate in the traditional cultures of societies.

Non-formal welfare Institutionalized welfare practices that operate in the traditional cultures of societies.

Oppression Domination and subjugation of individuals and groups by powerful elites.

Participation A catch-all term widely used to denote any form of beneficiary involvement in development project or programme activities. Such participation ranges from minimalist cost sharing and consultation to active empowerment.

Political capital The capacity of households or communities to mobilize collectively in defence of their interests.

Poor Laws A series of statutes enacted in Britain to provide services to poor people and to control vagrancy and begging.

Popular education Literally 'education for the people', it refers to group- or community-based non-formal education activities geared primarily towards local development. *See also* conscientization.

Post-modernism The advocacy of post-modernity.

Post-modernity A historical period beginning in the twentieth century that stresses the role of uncertainty, local identity and non-rationality in social life.

Poverty A condition of material and social deprivation in which people fall below a socially acceptable minimum standard of living or in which they experience deprivation relative to others in a society. *See also* basic human needs.

Poverty line A monetary measure of poverty that establishes a socially acceptable minimum standard of living.

Poverty Reduction Strategy Paper (PRSP) A strategy prepared by national governments in the South at the request of aid donors that outlines policies for poverty reduction as a precondition for debt relief. It is sometimes referred to as an instrument of 'social conditionality'.

Primary health care Health care that emphasizes preventive and public health measures based on low-cost techniques to reach the maximum number of people, as opposed to expensive, hospital-based secondary health care.

Privatization The process of transferring State-owned enterprises and services to private ownership. The term is also used to refer to the contracting of government services to commercial firms.

Provident Funds Mandatory savings funds managed by governments to provide income benefits to workers when they retire.

Relative poverty A condition of social deprivation in which people experience deprivation relative to others in a society.

Residual welfare An approach to social policy based on delivering or targeting basic services to deal with social pathologies and extreme poverty, relying heavily on the voluntary sector and with a minimum of direct State intervention.

Rural non-farm economy (RNFE) Agricultural processing and non-agricultural productive activities based in the countryside that provide an alternative income to traditional farming.

Safety net Economic and social programmes designed to assist or 'catch' the poorest in society so that they do not fall through the 'net' of a basic minimum income.

Sector-wide approach (SWAP) The funding of economic and social sectors by foreign donors in an attempt to influence broader policies through reforms and training. The SWAP may be contrasted with the more traditional approach of concentrating on individual, freestanding projects.

Social allowances Universal social security programmes that provide benefits to certain categories of people such as the elderly, children and families irrespective of their incomes or means.

Social assistance Means-tested social security programmes designed to target benefits to poor people.

Social capital Social relationships and networks that bind people together and facilitate coordinated action.

Social change Changes over time to the culture, organization and social structure of a society.

Social class Hierarchical arrangements in societies by which people are categorized according to their income, wealth, status and ability to exercise influence over others.

Social development A process of planned social change designed to improve the welfare of the population as a whole in conjunction with economic development.

Social exclusion The exclusion of certain groups from an acceptable standard of living or basic level of social and political participation.

Social funds Financial resources provided by international organizations such as the World Bank for short-term projects to help alleviate poverty arising from structural adjustment programmes.

Social indicators Measures of standards of living, both quantitative and qualitative.

Social insurance Contributory social security programmes that pool resources to provide benefits when needed.

Social policy Measures that affect people's well-being, whether through the provision of welfare services or by means of policies that impact upon livelihoods more generally.

Social progress A process of social improvement involving positive economic, social and political change.

Social protection *See* social security.

Social security Social programmes designed to protect people's income during times of economic adversity. In some countries, the term also includes health services.

Social services *See* human services.

Social work A profession concerned with promoting the welfare of individuals and their families, as well as groups and communities.

Socialism   An economic and political theory that places primary importance on the ownership of property by the community and stresses the role of cooperation in the creation of wealth.

South/North   The 'South' refers to those countries once labelled 'Third World', which is nowadays considered a pejorative term. Correspondingly, the 'North' denotes the industrialized nations.

Stakeholder   A person, group or organization with a direct or indirect interest or involvement in a project or programme.

Structural adjustment   The process through which countries are meant to undertake structural changes to their economy as a precondition to qualify for loans from the IMF and World Bank.

Sustainable livelihoods framework   An analytical framework designed to analyse how people's livelihoods are constructed and to identify possible development options.

Third Way   An economic and political theory that seeks a middle ground between capitalism and socialism.

Underclass   A group of people living in deprived conditions, usually in inner-city areas, whose lives are marked by high rates of crime and other social problems.

Universal primary education (UPE)   Access by all children to primary (elementary) education.

Universal social services   Human services provided by governments to all citizens who fall into designated demographic and need categories irrespective of their income.

Voluntary organizations   Non-governmental organizations providing human services on a non-profit basis.

Washington Consensus   A term coined by economist John Williamson to denote a set of neo-liberal policies imposed since the 1980s by Washington-based international financial institutions, notably the IMF, as a precondition for providing financial assistance to debt-strapped developing countries. These comprise trade liberalization, privatization and fiscal austerity.

1 SOCIAL POLICY FOR DEVELOPMENT: LOCAL, NATIONAL AND GLOBAL DIMENSIONS

Summary

Conceptualization and application of social policy in a development context has evolved significantly in recent years. Notions of what constitutes social policy have moved from the statutory provision of social services, either under a minimalist, residual model or through a more systematic, institutional-incremental approach. Narrow, targeted interventions of a residual type have become popular since the 1980s as a short-term response to the poverty generated by structural adjustment, including safety net devices such as social funds. Yet in order to address long-term issues of poverty and social deprivation in the South, it is increasingly recognized that a more comprehensive, holistic and cross-sector livelihoods analysis is more appropriate. The goals of social policy have broadened to include poverty alleviation, social protection, social inclusion and the promotion of human rights. Implementing these goals requires not just a strong State, but also the actions of civil society, the private sector and international development institutions. The increasing 'globalization' of social policy through development banks, UN bodies, regional and supranational organizations raises important issues about where the locus of social policy-making now lies. In dealing with these fundamental questions, traditions of representative, analytical and normative theory should be borne in mind. Normative theory in particular enables a distinction to be made amongst three major schools of thought and value systems that determine social policy: the statist, institutional-welfarism model, the individualist, free market enterprise approach and populist or community development strategies. All have contributed elements to an emerging hybrid and holistic model of social policy for developing countries that will prove useful in identifying the most appropriate interventions to address the specific needs of diverse groups.

Rethinking social policy for development

The time is ripe for a re-examination of social policy and its role in the development process. Past development paradigms and related social policy approaches have proved to be of limited effectiveness in addressing mass poverty and promoting human welfare in the South. Arguably, this criticism is as valid for neo-liberal economic growth theories as it is for targeted and other more radical strategies. Intellectually, the unilinear, blueprint and universal solutions of the modernization and Marxist approaches have been challenged by post-modern and post-structuralist critiques. The latter, in their turn, have been criticized for adopting too incremental and piecemeal an approach that does not address structural barriers to promoting more equitable patterns of economic growth. Furthermore, it could be argued that one of the major reasons for the shortcomings of conventional development strategies has been their inability to recognize and take due account of social complexity and its interface with other key development dimensions such as the economic, the political and the environmental. These lacunae have undoubtedly helped to perpetuate serious problems of poverty, vulnerability, powerlessness and exclusion.

However, while policy itself tends to evolve slowly, the perceptions and practices that generate policy change have advanced markedly over the past decade. Interventions have become more targeted and tailored to meet the specific economic and social needs of diverse groups. At the same time, development planners have become increasingly aware of the need to systematically integrate social analysis and social policy into the mainstream of development policy design and implementation. There is a growing consensus that inclusion of the social dimension, while no panacea for the above problems, is one of the major prerequisites for more successful development. Reflecting this evolution, development institutions at both domestic and international levels have begun to incorporate and institutionalize social policy, social planning and social development into their mainstream activities.

The literature on social policy and development has also expanded considerably over this period and, together with related academic courses, has played a key role in sensitizing development policy-makers and practitioners to these issues. There have been many books published on specific social sectors including health, education, rural development and urban housing as well as related areas such as the environment and gender. There have also been landmark texts cutting across the social development and social welfare spectrum (Conyers, 1982; Hardiman and Midgley, 1982; MacPherson, 1982; MacPherson and Midgley, 1987; Booth, 1994; Midgley, 1995, 1997). Those early publications, among the first to address economic and social development within a more holistic vision, have been instrumental in advancing the frontiers of international social policy. They have extended its legitimate sphere of concern beyond narrow conceptions of social service provision by national governments towards inclusion of much broader livelihood issues. In particular, threats to human welfare arising from the internationalization and globalization of economic, social and political forces have generated new pressures that require a rethinking of how social policy reforms can most effectively respond to these changes.

It is important to stress, however, that re-examining the role and scope of social policy in development does not signify a rejection of all past practices, nor is it an exercise in reinventing the wheel. In other words, we seek to identify the best of these practices and combine them with new experiences and analyses in appropriate applications suitable for diverse and changing circumstances. We wish in this volume to review how conceptions of social policy have evolved, how such ideas and linked strategies have been applied to promote human well-being, and how they may be improved to better address critical development problems in the South.

Redefining social policy: from welfare to livelihoods

The above opening remarks suggest that defining 'social policy' is not as straightforward a task as it once seemed. The term is nowadays fraught with potential ambiguity and confusion. It therefore needs to be carefully set out and employed appropriately. In the first instance, a basic distinction should be made between social policy as (a) an applied policy arena relating to governmental and other institutional interventions that affect people's welfare and (b) an academic field of enquiry. These two aspects are closely related since theory feeds directly into practice.

Historically, for example, the writings of early utopians and advocates of scientific social planning such as Auguste Comte, one of the founding fathers of sociology, were relevant for the emergence of social policy as an applied field. Early socialistic ideas were applied by pioneering industrialists such as Robert Owen, who in the early 1800s established the community of New Lanark in Scotland. Poverty surveys conducted by Charles Booth, Paul Kellogg and Seebohm Rowntree exposed the harsh and brutal conditions under which many ordinary people lived and fuelled pressures for social reform by pioneers such as Sidney and Beatrice Webb in the UK and Jane Addams in the US (Midgley et al., 2000). Anti-slavery movements in the US, Latin America and England during the nineteenth century can also be regarded as early intellectual expressions of progressive social policy. Social security and welfare policies introduced during the 1930s in the US under the New Deal, as well as publication of the Beveridge Report in the UK, were both underpinned by pioneering academic enquiry and the application of normative principles of social science for the improvement of society. Subsequently, social policy as an academic subject acquired its own identity in the UK with the appointment in 1950 of Richard Titmuss to the first such professorial position at the London School of Economics. In this discussion of emerging social policies, however, it should not be forgotten that societies have always evolved their own informal mechanisms for dealing with the needs of the elderly, sick and frail amongst their numbers. As will be seen in the following chapters, there is much to be learned from indigenous systems of social support and much to be gained from incorporating such lessons into modern practice.

Conceptions of social policy have thus evolved to reflect historical priorities and changing attitudes towards the causes of social problems and solutions perceived as being most appropriate. These definitions overlap with, and should be considered alongside, the theoretical paradigms of normative social policy discussed in a later section of this chapter in which statist, enterprise and populist approaches are outlined.

Social policy as welfare services

Conventionally, applied social policy has been considered synonymous with government intervention to provide social services. Until the early twentieth century, this signified minimal State action to address the immediate needs of the poor and destitute. Comprehensive and systematic public social policy provision came to the fore in the European post-war conception of the 'welfare state', in which government was perceived as having a duty to ensure certain fundamental living standards for all its citizens, literally 'from the cradle to the grave'. Alongside economic planning based on Keynesian principles of employment-generating public investment, this involved government funding for key social sectors such as health, education and housing. In addition, complementary support would be provided to the socially disadvantaged and the needy through statutory regulation, including a range of unemployment and social security benefits. Taken together, such government measures are based on normative principles that are commonly understood to form the basis of a 'civilized' and 'modern' society. They include, for example, the economic, social and political rights and freedoms that comprise 'citizenship' (Marshall, 1950).

In the developing world also, social policy has tended to become equated with government intervention. During the 1950s, according to mainstream economic theories of the time, it was expected that central planning would stimulate modernization and growth through urban-based industrialization, generating employment while alleviating poverty. It was generally held that the benefits of growth would inevitably 'trickle down' to the wider population, automatically improving their welfare. At the same time, public spending on social sectors was considered a wasteful diversion from the business of economic growth. According to this 'residual model' of social welfare, introduced by many colonial authorities before independence, government intervention to meet social needs was to be minimized (Hardiman and Midgley, 1982). Government would restrict its actions to dealing with social pathologies such as crime and prostitution, as well as helping those who could literally not help themselves, such as the disabled, the old and infirm or orphans. Social needs would be met through individual effort in the market place, with support from the family and community, and via charitable or voluntary organizations such as the church. This minimalist approach, echoing nineteenth-century European and American Poor Laws, was commonly incorporated into the policy agendas of Ministries of Welfare in newly independent developing countries.

However, the residual welfare model proved unworkable for several reasons. Firstly, even where economic growth did take place, it by no means guaranteed improved standards of living and welfare for the poorer classes. Residual social policy was evidently not equipped to cope with mass poverty. Secondly, social demand for basic services such as health, education and housing grew emphatically, especially from the 1960s onwards. The populations of newly independent nations were understandably anxious to gain access to social services and enhance their life chances, which they saw as their right after years of colonial domination. Responding to pressure from urban middle classes in particular, governing elites have expanded social service provision by building new schools, houses and hospitals in the competition to secure electoral support and political legitimacy. Thus, the 'incremental welfare' model was put in place, in which social sectors are expanded in a piecemeal, expedient fashion in response to political pressures rather than to social need as such (Hardiman and Midgley, 1982). This gave rise, for example, to accusations of 'urban bias' on the grounds that the pressing needs of the majority rural poor were simply ignored by most governments (Lipton, 1977). Arguably, this incremental approach is still characteristic of social sector planning in most of the developing and much of the industrialized world.

Deciding upon the means by which to achieve social policy goals has been a matter of growing political contention. During the 1980s, Keynesian economics together with the hitherto central role of the State in implementing public policy came under fire. The administrations of Ronald Reagan and Margaret Thatcher, supported by the Friedmanite stance of the New Right, raised serious doubts about the viability of the comprehensive welfare state (Friedman and Friedman, 1980). Other analysts, notably Charles Murray (1984), questioned the effectiveness of public assistance and social welfare programmes in the industrialized nations, alleging that they merely exacerbated the problems they were meant to solve and lead to the creation of a permanent, poor 'underclass'. The post-war welfare ethos was thus undermined by several factors. Firstly, by ideological mistrust of the allegedly paternalist and repressive State machine, coupled with the proposal to strengthen individual freedom of choice. Secondly, by the need to contain public spending and shift a larger share of the cost burden to service consumers themselves. To meet these two goals, economic liberalization and deregulation have meant the growing privatization of public services along with reliance on the creation of markets and internal quasi-markets to boost efficiency in the allocation and spending of resources in Europe's 'welfare' states. Some countries such as France, Sweden and Germany retain a strong belief in the responsibility of central government to fund and manage basic welfare provision and public utilities, while others such as the UK have resorted increasingly to assistance from the private commercial and voluntary sectors as service providers.

Social policy as safety nets

This free market ideology was transferred to the developing world through programmes of economic stabilization and structural adjustment from the mid-1980s onwards. In order to strengthen indebted economies and their repayment capacity, their productive potential would be enhanced through a combination of economic and social measures. The so-called 'Washington Consensus' thus emerged to preach market deregulation and competition (Williamson, 1990). This ideology also embraced measures including withdrawal of the State machine from monopolistic positions such as agricultural marketing boards, the reduction of public expenditure, incentives for foreign investment, restrictions on imports and the provision of export incentives. The adverse social impacts of these policies have been documented at length (Cornia et al., 1987; Ghai, 1991; Stewart, 1995). Far from being self-rectifying under adjustment, as had originally been predicted, poverty and vulnerability were exacerbated in many countries and, for many groups, social indicators worsened. Welfare provision was heavily compromised, with basic sectors such as health and primary education often bearing the brunt of spending cutbacks, as detailed in Chapter 9 of this volume (Graham-Brown, 1991; Kanji and Manji, 1991).

There has for some time been discussion of medium- and long-term policies for dealing with the adverse social impacts of structural adjustment. Even in the initial stages, 'adjustment with a human face' was advocated in order to deal not just with short-term problems but also to address deep-seated cross-sector and structural obstacles to balanced development (Cornia et al., 1987). In practice, however, the emphasis has been on the creation of social safety nets using social funds to target scarce resources at poorer, more vulnerable groups (Narayan and Ebbe, 1997; Subbarao, 1997; Conway, 2000). However, the minimalist and selective nature of this approach as well as its reliance on the voluntary sector for implementation is somewhat reminiscent of the residual welfare model. Yet the havoc caused by adjustment has led to the realization amongst policy-makers that a longer-term perspective is also necessary to address deep-seated social problems within a more systematic analysis of poverty, its causes and appropriate policy solutions. These issues are taken up in Chapters 2 and 9.

Social policy and livelihoods

The above perspectives consider social policy as being concerned primarily with either, (a) social and welfare services of one kind or another, or (b) safety nets to alleviate immediate crises. However, a third definition views social policy in a much broader sense as encompassing any planned or concerted action that affects people's lives and livelihoods. In this conceptualization, social policy is concerned essentially with more fundamental questions of sources and stability of employment, support institutions, processes and structures that determine people's well-being as well as broader natural and political factors which encourage and constrain human development. Thus, in the words of one observer, social policy in this wider vision may be defined as, 'collective interventions directly affecting transformations in social welfare, social institutions and social relations ... [and] ... access to adequate and secure livelihoods and income' (Mkandawire, 2001: 1).

The switch in emphasis towards a cross-sector, integrated and holistic livelihoods approach involving participatory planning to address people's specific needs is mirrored in other recent attempts to reformulate the social policy agenda (de Haan, 2000; Devereau and Cook, 2000). This evolution in thinking has been inspired by several factors. Firstly, there are evident shortcomings in Northern concepts of social policy when applied to the profound social problems and extreme poverty of developing countries. Secondly, a generally more comprehensive notion of interdependent economic and human development has emerged during the 1990s. Thirdly, the 'sustainable livelihoods framework' (SLF) has emerged as an analytical and operational tool. During the 1980s, the SLF was developed to facilitate a more integrated approach to dealing with poverty and deprivation. Moving away from single-sector strategies, this analytical framework allows livelihood strategies to be analysed within their wider environment, and context-specific solutions to be devised based on local capacities and needs. This framework is explored at greater length in Chapter 3 (Chambers and Conway, 1992; Scoones, 1998; Farrington et al., 1999). In this holistic view of social policy, welfare services and safety nets are likely to play a minor role in poverty alleviation strategies except under special circumstances such as targeted projects for the very poor and/or in emergency relief situations.

Although it will always be necessary to address crisis situations through social fund-type emergency solutions, longer-term development requires investment in people. Followers of the neo-liberal, residual approach take the view that there is necessarily a trade-off between social and economic development and that such social investments are a drain on national resources. However, traditions of political economy from the Enlightenment onwards caution against such simplistic conclusions (Myrdal, 1984). In the 1960s, Adelman and Morris (1965) underlined the importance of social and political variables in accounting for economic performance. Such views have regained their popularity more recently. Stewart et al. (2000) note that countries adopting a human development approach tend to enjoy higher rates of economic growth along with improved social indicators. It has for some time been recognized by major international development institutions that strengthening key social sectors such as basic education and health are instrumental, yielding not only direct productivity gains but also high social returns (UNDP, 1990; World Bank, 1991). Furthermore, the notion that the acquisition of basic human rights and fundamental freedoms forms an integral welfare need essential for balanced human development has gained wide if not universal acceptance (UNDP, 2000).

Most critically, the livelihood approach acknowledges the fact that 'the poor' are not a homogenous mass nor are they always merely weak, passive recipients of government handouts. It emphasizes the fact that they also have strengths, assets and capacities that may be mobilized for pro-active participation in the development process (Ellis, 2000; Helmore and Singh, 2001). Indeed, so-called 'empowerment' of the poor, once the exclusive prerogative of radical non-governmental organizations, has now been seized upon – some would say hijacked – by multilateral development banks as a fundamental prerequisite for tackling poverty (World Bank, 2001). Development thus increasingly becomes a multi-institutional challenge in which the State, international development agencies and donors, NGOs, the private sector and grassroots communities must combine forces to design and implement locale-specific solutions to particular problems. In this sense, social policy is necessarily concerned with taking due account of people's expressed needs and with making sure that project or programme design fits and is compatible with the social reality of affected groups (Cernea, 1991). The growing professionalization of social policy and planning as a discipline in its own right within international and domestic institutions, both academic and development-based, bears ample witness to this growing demand for specialist social planning skills.

Another important dimension of social policy embraced by this more holistic approach concerns what could be called its 'scope'. Social policy has conventionally been treated as a macro-level set of issues viewed in national and, more recently, in global terms. Yet analysis, policy prescription and implementation need to be disaggregated by levels of intervention and impact. The social policy expert must apply social science skills to appropriate units of analysis, whether socially or spatially determined. In gauging the impacts and policy implications of a development scheme, for example, it would be crucial to distinguish between its effects on key social units such as groups differentiated by social class, gender, age or ethnicity. In other circumstances, the household may be the most appropriate unit of analysis, while further disaggregation to the level of the individual may reveal additional nuances unperceived at higher levels.

The scope of social policy as it pertains to different institutional contributions is also relevant, as the respective roles of the State and civil society change and social regulation becomes a multi-organizational phenomenon. Cutting across social divisions, spatial or geographical characteristics may reveal key factors relating to local and regional dimensions as well as to national and international aspects. In a development climate that sets much store by decentralization of decision-making and on local participation, such distinctions become crucial. Yet another element of scope relates to the issue of time, since social consequences and policy prescriptions may vary considerably over the short, medium or long term. Thus, social policy analysis and prescription must necessarily take due account of differential scope on the basis of social, spatial and temporal dimensions.

The goals of social policy

The broadening of the social policy agenda described above, from charitable works and welfare service provision to a more encompassing concern for strengthening livelihoods, necessarily implies a multiplication both of policy objectives and of the types of institutions required in order to achieve them. The goals of social policy have thus become multi-faceted, embracing an ambitious array of ideals towards which, some argue, development organizations seem to be converging at least in part. This package includes poverty reduction, social protection, fighting social exclusion, promoting human rights and even con-serving the natural resources that form the basis of many people's livelihoods in the South.

Poverty alleviation

Poverty reduction sits on top of the social policy agenda for practically all devel-opment agencies and governments, at least rhetorically. However, important differences exist in terms of how poverty is defined and, consequently, how it may be most effectively tackled (see Chapter 2). Definitions of poverty range from reference to an absolute poverty line expressed in US dollars, to inequality in terms of relative poverty and deprivation and, more recently, to multi-dimensional concepts combining material and non-material needs. Poverty lines remain a popular tool with governments due to their simplicity and, arguably, the ease with which they can be manipulated for political purposes to show greater or lesser degrees of suffering by merely adjusting the poverty threshold. Relative poverty and inequality are concepts that have become increasingly unpopular with official development organizations due to their politically sen-sitive and operationally problematic nature. Associated in particular (although not always) with the radical left and centralized planning, policies that prescribe compulsory asset redistribution such as massive land reform in order to eradi-cate poverty have lost favour. If redistribution takes place at all, it is in response to locale- or identity-specific crises in which grassroots organizations and social movements take the initiative to secure livelihood assets, a case in point being Brazil's Movement of the Landless (see Chapter 3). Furthermore, such restruc-turing is increasingly likely to be facilitated by a market-based approach. In order to defuse potential conflicts, for example, land may be transferred not by expropriation but rather on the basis of willing buyer/willing seller through land banks or similar funding mechanisms.

Associated with the idea of alleviating the absolute poverty of particularly vulnerable groups, another social policy goal to have emerged during the 1990s is that of social protection. According to the World Bank (1990, 2001), the economic priority in development should remain that of maximizing the potential of the poor by increasing labour productivity. In addition, basic social services in health care, education, family planning, nutrition and primary education have to be provided. These two approaches are reputed to have brought about a significant reduction in poverty in Indonesia and Malaysia during the 1980s (World Bank, 1990). However, these measures may not be adequate to protect the very weak and vulnerable. In such cases, targeted transfers and safety nets such as social funds are seen as an essential complement in order to protect those who may not benefit directly from economic growth or social service provision. Emergency measures such as feeding programmes may be necessary, but social protection departs from the mere provision of charity since it is intended to support people's own livelihood strategies in the longer term during times of vulnerability or high risk. A variety of policy responses has thus arisen in the wake of structural adjustment such as employment generation, micro-credit and social insurance schemes (see above and Chapters 7–9).

It has been recognized during the 1990s, perhaps rather tardily, that in addition to poverty and inequality, social disadvantage can be perpetuated through mechanisms of social exclusion. Many factors may combine to exclude or marginalize large sectors of the population from participating fully in mainstream economic, social or political life. These factors may be associated with social class, caste, ethnicity, religion, culture, age or gender, for example. It remains a controversial issue whether concepts of social exclusion constructed in the industrialized nations in relation to minorities have the same applicability in the South where problems of mass poverty and structural marginalization are the norm (see Chapter 2). However, the goal of promoting greater social integration and inclusion into the mainstream of substantial groups which have been actively discriminated against, trapping them in situations of poverty and vulnerability, has become an increasingly important social policy objective. Improving the plight of many women, indigenous populations, the old and those at the bottom of the social ladder such as scheduled castes and street children are increasingly evident on the social policy agenda as specialized areas of investigation and intervention.

Social policy and human rights

Poverty reduction, social protection and livelihood strengthening as well as combating social exclusion have thus emerged as legitimate social policy goals in addition to the more conventional preoccupation with welfare service provision. Since the mid-1990s, the issue of human rights and the promotion of social justice have also entered the social policy agenda. In the post-war period, there have been a number of human rights instruments expounding fundamental freedoms. *The International Bill of Rights* comprises the *Universal Declaration of Human Rights* (1948), the *International Covenant on Civil and Political Rights* (ICCPR) (1966) and the *International Covenant on Economic, Social and Political Rights* (ICESPR) (1966). There followed several other conventions on discrimination against women: CEDAW (1979); against torture: CAT (1984); and on the rights of the child: CRC (1989). The ICESPR entered into force in 1976 with 142 state parties to this covenant and it introduced a rights-based perspective on development issues.

The early focus on civil and political liberties has been complemented by a concern for economic, social and cultural rights, providing a link with development and social policy discourses. Human rights have in the past tended to be seen as the domain of international relations and legal expertise with social scientists following a parallel but separate path in their concerns with promoting fundamental freedoms. Major international organizations such as the World Bank and UNDP have long emphasized the importance of providing education, adequate health care and other basic necessities. Yet these policy recommendations have often been couched in rather instrumentalist terms, justified because they contribute to improving economic and social development indicators rather than because they intrinsically constitute a fundamental human right. Such concerns were, however, formalized in the *UN Declaration on the Right to Development* (1986) that placed economic, social and cultural rights on a par with civil and political rights. More recently, the notion of 'environmental human rights' has gained ground, based on the right to a clean and safe environment as well as people's freedom to take part in environmental decision-making (IIED, 2001).

These legal and developmental discourses are now converging so that the strengthening of people's basic rights is increasingly seen as an integral and essential part of the development process. 'Human rights express the bold idea that all people have claims to social arrangements that protect them from the worst abuses and deprivations – and that secure the freedom for a life of dignity' (UNDP, 2000: 2). A human rights approach brings to development the notion that people are entitled to have their basic needs met, and that those in power have a duty and a moral obligation to facilitate this process. By attributing culpability to those who fail to duly deliver these benefits, a rights-based approach thus introduces an element of accountability that can be a powerful tool in the hands of civil society groups lobbying for change. In the final analysis, therefore, achieving comprehensive social policy goals in terms of reducing poverty and inequality, providing basic services, combating exclusion and strengthening people's livelihoods can only be achieved within a political environment that simultaneously seeks to address the issue of human rights for all citizens.

The institutions of social policy

Four major institutional sets of players may be identified in the social policy field: the State, civil society, the business sector and international development or financial agencies. Traditionally, the State has been seen as the major architect of social policy constructs and the main driving force behind social reform. This perception applies in particular to the narrower conception of social policy as providing either for residual needs associated with 'curing' pathologies such as crime and delinquency, or for government-funded incremental expansion of social services to meet the demands of growing urban populations. Yet this picture has become rather more complicated since the 1980s as social policy goals have broadened to encompass a wider range of human development concerns, including poverty alleviation and livelihood support.

Expansion of this social policy agenda has to a significant extent been driven by a diverse range of institutions previously confined to the margins of development policy-making and implementation, which was dominated overwhelmingly by central government. They include civil society entities such as non-governmental organizations, grassroots associations, social movements, trade unions, the church and in some cases even the private sector. They have pressured the larger international development and financial institutions such as the World Bank and the IMF, as well as bilateral aid agencies, to adopt a more sensitive and responsive attitude towards people's needs. These international bodies have, at the same time, articulated a more comprehensive social and economic policy agenda that requires the active involvement of many public and civil society collaborators in policy design and execution in the drive towards poverty alleviation, social justice and sustainable development. In addition to the State, civil society and international development institutions, the business sector is also becoming an increasingly important participant in social issues and policy dialogue.

The State

Arguably, however, the State remains the single most crucial social policy institution despite its failure in many contexts and despite the growing pressure upon internal affairs by international financial organizations. Central government expenditure in developing countries grew from 15 per cent of GDP in 1960 to some 25 per cent in 1990 (World Bank, 1997). Central government is still primarily responsible for basic social services such as education and health, for example, which together account for over 6 per cent of public expenditure in developing countries as a whole (UNDP, 2000). Aside from social-sector spending, and far more significantly, governments determine development policy priorities and, hence, the social impacts and social policy implications to which such interventions give rise. For example (as discussed in Chapter 3), the social consequences and resettlement policy implications of large-scale population displacements associated with hydropower development can have major repercussions not just upon the populations directly affected but also on national policies towards those evicted. Similarly, official plans to develop and 'modernize' frontier zones such as the Amazon rainforest in the pursuit of economic progress and national integration have massive social impacts which policy-makers must take due account of in designing more appropriate responses to meeting people's livelihood needs.

During the post-independence period until the 1970s in most developing countries, centralized government planning was seen as the key to promoting economic development. The national plan was seen as a model scientifically crafted by experts to guarantee progress, and seemed during the 1950s and 1960s at least to have '… joined the national anthem and the national flag as a symbol of sovereignty and modernity' (Waterston, 1965: 28). Centralized planning met with limited success and failed by a long way to live up to expectations. During the 1960s and 1970s, supported by agencies such as the World Bank, there was a move towards project planning as the major vehicle through which governments implemented and shaped policies (Rondinelli, 1983). By the 1980s, other factors had further called into question the effectiveness of the State apparatus in promoting comprehensive economic and social development. The politics of the 'New Right' with its twin philosophy of liberalization and privatization as elements of the so-called 'Washington Consensus' was followed by the collapse of Communism in the USSR and Eastern Europe. During the 1980s, neo-liberal agencies such as the World Bank and the IMF called for the rolling back of the State and condemned virtually any form of central planning.

Yet during the 1990s, for all the rhetoric of the Right, the limitations of these market-based policies became all too evident, especially in the context of structural adjustment and worsening poverty in developing countries (see Chapter 9). Proponents of the Washington Consensus, especially the IMF, have come under heavy criticism for allegedly exacerbating the woes of indebted nations through the imposition of free market economic and social policies (Stiglitz, 2002). The World Bank soon called for a balance to be struck between State and market, each with its own distinctive and mutually supportive contribution to make to the development process, forming a social-democrat-style middle ground or, as it later became popularly known, a 'Third Way' (World Bank, 1991; Giddens, 1998). The key developmental role of the State was thus resurrected but redefined in the process.

According to the new wisdom, the central State should be less interventionist and act more as a facilitator of balanced development, providing a favourable context and concentrating on those fundamental areas in which government has a unique role to play. These areas of government priority include establishing a conducive legal framework, guaranteeing macro-economic stability, investing in basic social services and infrastructure, protecting the poor and vulnerable with safety nets, conserving the environment and promoting sustainable development policies. In addition, alternative controls to top-down government regulation should be explored, such as encouraging effective market-based tools to promote more efficient resource allocation. These include public–private partnerships and the creation of internal 'quasi-markets' in the provision of services such as education and health (see Chapters 5 and 6), as well as public participation to encourage greater accountability of public servants (Turner and Hulme, 1997; World Bank, 1997, 2002; Stiglitz, 2002).

There are different levels of government intervention, from central or federal level through to state and provincial authorities down to local or municipal administration. Many developing countries have large and impenetrable areas of terrain comprising jungle, mountain or desert, whose isolation is often reinforced by a systematic neglect of rural development on the official policy agenda and a poor communications infrastructure. Frequently, the central State may be poorly represented and have only a weak presence. In such cases, although national policies may be set centrally, their execution is very much conditioned by the constellation of regional and local political forces and bureaucratic structures. Government based in the capital is often perceived as being out of touch with local people and their wishes, with heavily centralized decision-making procedures and funding practices leading to the inefficient and ineffective use of resources.

Increasingly, therefore, the decentralization of responsibilities and resources within the State apparatus both territorially and functionally has been seen as a major tool for streamlining development, including social policy. The term 'decentralization' can be interpreted in many ways (Rondinelli, 1983; Turner and Hulme, 1997). In most cases, it signifies some degree of 'deconcentration', namely, the transfer of authority from central to local government agencies, parastatals and quangos in terms of planning, control over budgets and related decision-making, including a degree of accountability. Purists would argue, however, that authentic decentralization should involve full 'devolution' of power to sub-national governments accountable to their local electorates. Recently, debates on decentralization have become closely entwined with that on the privatization of devolved social services functions such as contracting out of the State system and the introduction of voucher schemes in health and education.

Decentralization within the State, rather like the related notion of 'community participation', was heralded as something of a panacea for development problems and it is portrayed as having many potential advantages. These benefits include: (a) enhanced responsiveness to local needs and the preparation of locally specific, tailor-made plans; (b) stronger motivation and capacity of local field personnel given their greater responsibilities; (c) a reduced workload for agencies at the centre as local representatives take over many delegated tasks; (d) greater inter-agency coordination at the local level; and (e) greater government accountability through local participation (Rondinelli, 1983; Turner and Hulme, 1997).

However, there are also many dangers inherent in decentralization which is mere window-dressing or which contains no effective mechanisms of accountability. It has been forcefully argued, for example, that decentralization policies in many post-independence African countries such as Kenya, Uganda and Tanzania, were masks to disguise the retention of power at the centre by essentially authoritarian, neo-populist regimes (Kitching, 1982). Some success has been achieved with the Indian *panchayati raj* system of local government and in the case of the Philippines (Turner and Hulme, 1997). There have also been notable achievements in improving social service provision when the right balance has been struck between federal and local roles and responsibilities, as in the case of health care in Brazil's northeastern state of Ceará (Tendler, 1995). However, the effectiveness of decentralization policies in Latin America in promoting equity and efficiency has in general been undermined. This has been due either to persistent traditions of centralized government, or to the grip on power of local elites, which usually continue to exercise control over local resources either through the use of force or through the system of clientelistic politics. As discussed below, however, this monopoly has increasingly been challenged by civil society organizations in defence of their livelihoods.

Civil society

The partial rolling back of the State and the modification of its role from sole provider to partner in development has been accompanied by the rapid expansion of civil society organizations (CSOs). 'Civil society' is an arena embracing a range of entities that have become key actors in the design and implementation of social policy. These include non-governmental organizations (NGOs) at both domestic and international levels, grassroots or community-based entities such as village associations, trade unions and the church as well as social movements that may bring together one or more CSOs in the pursuit of specific goals. Religious or 'faith-based' organizations are an increasingly important sub-category within this group. In Latin America, for example, Catholic entities were instrumental in spearheading radical community action and political protest during the years of military dictatorship in the 1970s and 1980s. More recently, Protestant and evangelical churches have greatly expanded their influence in the region through spiritual and community works. The private business sector is sometimes considered part of civil society but here it is treated separately.

Non-governmental organizations are perhaps the vital link since they are so critical for a number of reasons. They bring together a number of key ingredients for change: popular mobilization at the grassroots, wider political support at national and global levels for important causes and, critically, financial backing where such resources are scarce or non-existent. From occupying a relatively insignificant position in the early 1970s, usually as relief agencies, NGOs are now major contributors to social policy and social development. As a mark of their importance, some 12 per cent of all Western aid is channelled through NGOs (Clark, 1991; UNDP, 2000). In net transfer terms, NGOs contribute more resources than the World Bank. Arguably, the development and policy impact of NGOs is proportionately far greater than even these figures suggest. Clark (1991) identifies six major types of domestic and international development NGO functions, which are by no means mutually exclusive.

- *Relief and welfare agencies* such as Catholic Relief Services and missionary societies undertaking emergency and charitable works.
- *Technical innovation organizations* that operate their own pioneering projects such as the Intermediate Technology Development Group (ITDG) or the Aga Khan Foundation.
- *Public service contractors* working closely with government and official aid agencies, hired to provide services such as health, basic education and micro-credit, where government capacity is limited; for example, CARE and various social funds. Some NGOs are now so heavily dependent on such government funding that their ability to act autonomously is often, arguably, seriously undermined.
- *Popular development agencies* that operate community-based projects and may also become involved in lobbying for wider policy change as their role expands. Examples include Oxfam, ActionAid, Save the Children, the Bangladesh Rural Advancement Committee (BRAC) and FASE in Brazil.
- *Grassroots development organizations*, local, community-based southern NGOs which often have links with popular development agencies in their livelihood struggles and may receive external funding. They are often very small-scale but may expand considerably to embrace a web of connected grassroots actions. This would include well-known examples such as SEWA in India, the Grameen Bank in Bangladesh and Brazil's Movement of the Landless. Policy changes may also spring from such grassroots

initiatives and their NGO links, such as the spread of sustainable agriculture for small farmers (Farrington and Bebbington, 1993; Blauert and Zadeck, 1998).

- *Advocacy groups and networks* have no field projects of their own but exist, either at the domestic or international level, for education and lobbying purposes to bring about policy reform. There are many examples of cases in which such CSO/NGO action has had a marked influence on policy formulation and implementation. These include, for example, the introduction of comprehensive resettlement policy guidelines by the World Bank and other development organizations during the 1990s. Other achievements include the campaign against the use of powdered milk as a substitute for breast-feeding and environmental pressure groups working in both the North and South pursuing a range of objectives from sustainable forest management to the campaign against global warming. Other action includes campaigns for debt relief as well as the anti-globalization movement (Keck and Sikkink, 1998).

The relationship of NGOs with the State is a major determinant of their development contribution, depending upon whether voluntary organizations act in parallel with government, in direct opposition or as a vehicle for strengthening the representation and bargaining power of weaker groups in society. In this sense, there has been a broad move from a 'supply-side' (technical, delivering projects) to a 'demand-side' (politicized, demanding reforms) approach (Edwards and Hulme, 1992; Clark, 1995), but globally speaking the picture is still very mixed. In some areas of the world such as the Indian sub-continent, it has been argued that NGOs work much more closely with government, possibly compromising their independence in the process. In other regions such as Latin America, NGOs have tended to be far more confrontational and in open opposition to mainstream government policy, such as on the environment and indigenous affairs, for example, while the situation in Africa is mixed (Turner and Hulme, 1997).

NGOs have some advantages over the public sector. They are in theory based on principles of voluntarism and local participation rather than top-down control. They are task-oriented and their members dedicated to achieving social or development goals as ends rather than as means of achieving political domination. NGOs are attributed with greater sensitivity to people's livelihood needs and often have greater technical skills. At the same time, their smaller scale and lack of red tape should make them more flexible and responsive, with the freedom to challenge official development priorities as appropriate.

More recently, words of caution have been expressed regarding the extent to which NGOs have lived up to expectations. Despite their virtues, NGOs are not the panacea for solving social development problems they were once held up to be. Their contractual role as service providers and project implementers can make NGOs heavily dependent on financial support from government and international agencies, compromising their traditional autonomy, bringing them 'too close for comfort' to the State and weakening their links with the grassroots (Hulme and Edwards, 1997). One of the major criticisms of NGOs is that, unlike most governments, they are almost totally unaccountable to the wider public (Edwards and Hulme, 1995). The strength of NGOs in terms of their heterogeneity may also be a weakness, as their sheer diversity and contrasting philosophies can make coordination problematic if not impossible at times. Competition and rivalry rather than collaboration are, unfortunately, often the order of the day. In many countries, NGOs are able to offer better salaries and work conditions than government agencies, leading to a drain of qualified personnel from the public sector.

Turner and Hulme (1997) suggest that in future NGOs must recognize their limitations and acknowledge the fact that, although they have certain comparative advantages, they cannot replace the State. Rather, they argue, NGOs should help strengthen civil society to make it more effective and cohesive in articulating people's needs to negotiate with the State apparatus, while demanding greater public accountability. This is especially pertinent in debates about social spending allocations and the need for transparency in order to lessen the danger of misappropriation. Whether through the use of adversarial or collaborative tactics, NGOs still have a major role to play in making sure that government responds effectively to the needs of the poorer, deprived sectors of society which have conventionally been neglected in the policy-making process.

The private sector

Discussions of social policy often concentrate almost exclusively on the role of the State and NGOs, ignoring the increasingly crucial impact of the business sector on people's lives. The private sector comprises at least three major areas of activity: (a) the formal economy of firms and enterprises; (b) the informal sector, so significant in the South; and (c) international business and transnational corporations (TNCs). All have social policy implications to the extent that they create employment and unemployment, generate wages, salaries and other benefits, and engage in activities that may have other profound economic, social and environmental impacts. Indeed, the private sector is arguably the single most important actor on the stage, especially in nations where the State is relatively weak and ineffectual and/or closely controlled by business interests. The stereotypical example of such domination would be certain primary commodity-exporting countries of Central America (Burbach and Flynn, 1980). This potential corporate power is illustrated by the fact that the top 500 corporations account for 30 per cent of the world's gross product, 70 per cent of world trade and 80 per cent of world investment (Griesgraber and Gunter, 1996).

Liberalization and privatization within the context of economic stabilization and adjustment have provided the context for a more obvious and direct link between business and social policy, with mixed results. The sale of State assets to private business in the transport, telecommunications and other sectors in Latin America during the 1990s, for example, may yet prove to be in the public interest by providing more efficient and cost-effective services (Whitehead, 2000). Privatized health provision and pension schemes as well as expansion of internal markets and private university education such as those in Chile and Brazil may help expand access to basic services at least for some sectors of society. The contracting out or 'tertiarization' of health and education services from the State to the private sector has become a well-established trend. In rural areas, the appropriation of common property by private commercial interests such as cattle ranchers, logging enterprises and oil companies has had strong adverse impacts on the livelihoods of local and indigenous populations in the Andean highlands and Amazon Basin. This process has stimulated massive popular reaction and the generation at grassroots level of alternative policies for more sustainable forms of development, which are gradually being mainstreamed (Hall, 2000a).

Yet socially and environmentally sustainable development must be underpinned by economically sound practices. For example, if extractivism and agroforestry are to replace destructive slash-and-burn farming practices, thus reducing deforestation rates, markets must be developed for non-timber forest products that can yield an income to support such endeavours. Otherwise, projects will collapse once external support ceases, along with the livelihoods of those producers involved (see Chapter 3). The private commercial sector therefore clearly has a key role to play in helping to generate and sustain environmentally sound markets, a case in point being the expansion of 'green' certified timber produced under managed conditions with no harmful social or ecological impacts.

With some 50,000 companies operating at the multinational level, in addition to steadily expanding domestic business sectors in the South, the issue of 'corporate social responsibility' (CSR) has grown considerably in importance over recent years. The social responsibility of the private sector, 'concerns the relationships of a company not just with its clients, suppliers and employees, but also with other groups, and with the needs, values and goals of the society in which it operates' (UN, 2000a: 2). Many leading companies now attest to their public transparency and accountability through systems of 'social reporting' or 'social accounting'. Such preoccupations have been driven in part by growing pressure from civil society, especially powerful international campaigns designed to 'name and shame' large companies accused of social and environmental abuse. A well-known example is the campaign against child labour in the rug-making industry in India. Major protests and legal challenges have also been made against the socially and ecologically calamitous exploration activities of oil companies, including Texaco and BP, on indigenous territories in the Amazon jungle of Ecuador and Peru as well as Shell on Nigeria's Ogoni lands (Vidal, 1999; Kimerling, 2000). Aside from fear of public approbation, companies also have an incentive to declare their social credentials due to publication of the FTSE4Good and Dow Jones Sustainability indices, which screen enterprises in terms of socially responsible investment practices. Research indicates that corporate social programmes may also often have the side-effect of attracting and retaining socially conscious staff, especially in the wake of 11 September 2001 and the desire of individuals to personally contribute more to society which has been engendered (Murray, 2001).

There are various dimensions to CSR that should be distinguished: (a) *Legal:* this involves complying with local laws and following international guidelines on matters such as labour, human rights and the environment. (b) *Philanthropic:* companies often donate money, staff time and other resources to benevolent causes as high-profile proof of their commitment to social responsibility, poverty alleviation, etc. (c) *Corporate citizenship:* going beyond legal compliance and charitable works, corporate citizenship implies becoming directly involved in dialogue and action on social issues with company stakeholders (employees, suppliers and markets). In a globalizing world especially, companies' social contracts must extend far beyond the immediate community in which the enterprise is situated.

There is thus increasing pressure for the adoption by companies of international guidelines to regulate activities and ameliorate their social impacts. In 1999, the Secretary-General of the United Nations launched the 'Global Compact' initiative, centred on a set of nine principles based on globally acknowledged human and social rights. Endorsed by sectors of the business community, the Global Compact is designed to stimulate greater commitment to basic social issues such as eliminating child labour, the right to collective bargaining, the elimination of forced and compulsory labour (slavery), discrimination in employment and environmental responsibility (UN, 2000a). These aims were underlined at the sequel to the *World Summit on Social Development* held in Geneva in June 2000, which stressed the need for '... increased corporate awareness of the interrelationship between social development and economic growth' (UN, 2000b; 2000c: 16). Efforts are under way to establish cross-sector partnerships between development NGOs, the private sector and local communities in an attempt to increase the poverty-alleviating potential of business activities. The 'Business Partners for Development' (BPD) network, for example, focuses on the social impacts of oil, gas and mining, while the Atlanta partnership based in Sailkot, Pakistan, has campaigned to regulate child labour in the football manufacturing industry (RCD, 2001).

Critics argue that social reporting is motivated more by companies' preoccupations with their public image than by a genuine commitment to social justice or sustainable development, effectively an exercise in 'corporate gloss' (Cowe, 2001). They allege that social reporting appears to have become something of a bandwagon with corporate transparency more illusory than real. It has been pointed out, for example, that three-quarters of the UK's top 100 listed companies that provide such reports supply no quantitative data to back up their claims, even on straightforward issues such as the gender composition of their labour force (Cowe, 2001). Yet generally accepted standards and principles are being developed all the time, such as the AA1000 Framework for accountability monitoring of the Institute of Social and Ethical Accountability (ISEA, 2001) as well as those standards set by the United Nations (UN, 2000a). There can be little doubt that the business sector will play an increasingly important role in the formulation and implementation of social policy at all levels.

International development institutions

Having considered the State, civil society and private business sectors as major players in the social policy arena, a fourth major set of actors encompasses the international development institutions (IDIs) and related bodies. This collectivity is made up of several distinct groups of influential organizations: (i) multilateral agencies such as the World Bank and IMF; (ii) the regional development banks – IDB, AfDB and ADB; (iii) bilateral aid donors; (iv) UN agencies such as UNICEF, UNDP, WHO and UNRISD amongst others; and (v) regional and supranational actors such as the EU, NAFTA, the OECD, ILO, WTO and ECLAC. These bodies, together with the activities of major NGOs and transnational corporations as well as the internationalized responses of civil society, have created a relatively new global dimension to the social policy debate. Yet, as several authors have pointed out (Deacon, 1997; Mishra, 1999), unlike in other academic disciplines such as political science, in the social policy field globalization remains under-theorized and under-researched, although this situation is changing fast.

These groups of institutions impinge on social policy in distinctive and sometimes overlapping (although often contradictory) ways. Their influence will be considered at greater length in Chapter 9 but some major issues can be highlighted here. Undoubtedly the highest-profile of these are the World Bank and the IMF, largely as a result of their policies of stabilization and structural adjustment. In the case of the World Bank, structural adjustment loans (SALs) increased from 2 per cent of its total loan portfolio in 1996 to 39 per cent by 1999 (Randel et al., 2000). As already mentioned, the social policy implications of adjustment have been reflected in diverse ways such as public spending cuts affecting basic social services, unemployment and changing employment patterns (for example, expansion of the informal sector) affecting livelihoods, and the creation of social safety nets using devices such as social funds.

However, the World Bank's influence upon the social agenda is arguably much broader than this. It involves sector policy work in education, housing and health amongst others. In addition, the Bank's 'safeguard' policies in the areas of involuntary resettlement, indigenous and cultural affairs attempt to establish basic criteria for incorporating social dimensions into project design and implementation. Furthermore, this influence on social issues is underpinned by the formal prioritization of poverty alleviation alongside economic growth and targeting of the poorest, while enlisting the help of the NGO sector in this process (World Bank, 1991, 2000). The Bank has also been working towards a unified set of social policy principles and 'Social Development Strategy', although this process was still in its formative stages at the time of writing in 2003.

Bilateral aid institutions have traditionally been far more concerned with promoting their own commercial, political and strategic interests than with social policy matters. Japan and the USA, respectively the world's first and second largest donors, accounting for 37 per cent of OECD overseas development assistance (ODA), have been notorious in this respect. Overall, about two-thirds of bilateral aid is still tied to the purchase of donor country goods and technical services (Randel et al., 2000). Yet some donor countries have in recent years emphasized pro-poor policies and have attempted to mainstream a concern with social dimensions in their aid policies and projects. These include

Sweden, Denmark, Norway, the Netherlands and the UK through the DFID's Social Development Division. Regional development banks in Latin America (IDB), Africa (AfDB) and Asia (ADB) tend to take their policy cues from the World Bank in terms of addressing poverty and basic needs alongside encouraging economic growth. However, decisions tend to be less transparent and more heavily influenced by the political agendas of recipient countries rather than by technical considerations. Social policy dimensions remain poorly defined in most instances and the social policy agenda remains ambiguous or unclear. These issues are explored in more detail in Chapter 9.

Since it was established in 1919, the ILO has been instrumental in setting global labour and social standards. Based on the principle of tripartism (the notion that good governance must involve consensus amongst industry, workers and government), some 200 ILO conventions in the post-war period have been formulated, many of which have been ratified by significant numbers of nations. These cover employment policy, social security, social policy, wage-fixing machinery and working conditions as well as the protection of women, children and indigenous peoples. This European welfare policy orientation based on organized labour, corporatist social security structures for the formal labour sector has in recent years been challenged by the neo-liberal thinking of the IMF and World Bank. They view the ILO approach as inappropriate for developing countries on the grounds that it excludes the poor and those who remain outside of the formal labour sector. The OECD, in contrast, has developed a balanced set of economic and social policies, although fears have been expressed that mean-tested targeting could soon be introduced which would challenge the European notion of universal social support (Deacon, 1997).

Social policy has become prominent in discussions about the apparent contradiction between promoting free trade on the one hand and, on the other, guaranteeing basic labour and social rights. The ILO's role in support of international social standards has come to the fore in debates on 'social dumping', or the shedding of social costs by producer nations in order to become more competitive in world markets. Attempts by industrialized nations under the GATT and later the WTO to introduce social clauses in trading agreements in order to guarantee minimum labour standards have been resisted by some developing countries, who see this as an attempt by the North to impose a cost/price disadvantage. EU member states have attempted to give preferential treatment to trading partners that adhere to certain social practices, such as the non-use of forced labour, but such social clauses have come up against WTO rules and this remains a contentious issue.

At the sub-global, regional level, organizations such as the EU, the North American Free Trade Association (NAFTA) and the Economic Commission for Latin America and the Caribbean (ECLAC) illustrate contrasting approaches to social policy matters. In Europe, the Social Chapter of the Maastricht Treaty of 1992 and the redistributive Structural Fund established in 1979 laid the foundation for attempts to build a regional social policy. Despite resistance from some member-states with their own political agendas, the dominance of the social-democratic centre has continued to move towards common social policies which provide for minimum standards while maintaining economic competitiveness (Deacon, 1997; Hutton, 2002). In Latin America, the growth in conventional statutory social policy has had very little impact on overall poverty (Abel and Lewis, 2001). ECLAC thus takes a broad approach to tackling poverty and deprivation in the region, seeing the attainment of greater equity through a combination of economic and social policy. It emphasizes investments in basic education, health and nutrition as well as strengthened political participation and a robust legal system rather than social security as the key to providing appropriate social policies for the region. This sentiment is well captured in the title of its policy document, *Equity, Development and Citizenship* (Ocampo, 2000). This contrasts strongly with NAFTA's approach, which envisages no redistributive mechanisms and seems not to recognize that its activities might possess any kind of social dimension.

Of the UN agencies, the UNDP and UNICEF have been especially prominent in developing a social policy agenda. In 1978, UNICEF and the WHO convened the path-breaking International Conference on Primary Health-Care at Alma-Ata in the Soviet Union (see Chapter 6). During the mid-1980s, long before the World Bank had expressed concern over the social impacts of structural adjustment, UNICEF specialists were prominent in denouncing the negative costs of adjustment. Annual publication of *The State of the World's Children* (from 1980) as well as via other seminal works such as *Adjustment with a Human Face* (Cornia et al., 1987) had a decisive influence on the Bank and IMF, obliging them to reconsider earlier narrow views. From 1990, the UNDP started publishing the *Human Development Report*, its multi-dimensional 'human development index' (HDI) constituting a new measure of economic and social progress. The HDI combines conventional GDP levels with other indices of life expectancy and educational achievement. In addition, international comparisons are made within the annual report in terms of country performance in related key areas such as gender, the environment and human rights (UNDP, 2000). The UN research institute, UNRISD, has also been increasingly active in examining social policy issues through its programme 'Social Policy in a Development Context' (UNRISD, 2001a, 2001b; Mkandawire, 2001, 2003). This adopts a broad approach to social policy and seeks to promote developmental goals, democracy and social inclusion, while questioning the neo-liberal privatization orthodoxy of the WTO.

A number of UN summit meetings throughout the early 1990s helped to highlight social development goals. These included the *World Conference on Education for All* (Jomtien, Thailand, 1990) and the follow-up *World Education Forum* (Dakar, Senegal, 2000), the *World Summit for Children* (1990), the Rio *Earth Summit* or UNCED (1992), the *World Conference on Human Rights* (Vienna, 1993) and the *International Conference on Population and Development* (1994). The *Social Summit* held in Copenhagen in 1995, to which the major UN agencies and many NGOs contributed, '… represented the most significant global accord on the need to tackle issues of poverty, social exclusion and social development' (Deacon, 1997: 87). As Deacon notes, it also clarified the battle lines between the World Bank/IMF anti-poverty and safety net social policy vision for the South and Eastern Europe on the one hand and, on the other, an alliance of European and some developing countries that oppose social regulation. The sequel *World Summit on Social Development* held in Geneva in 2000 underlined the need to integrate social development with macro-economic growth and noted, '... a growing awareness of the positive impact of effective social policies on economic and social development' (UN, 2000b: 7).

The internationalization of social development issues through the policies and actions of overseas development assistance organizations, supranational NGOs and the business sector has lent support to the notion that national social policy is increasingly moulded by external agents. 'Strong' globalization theory views the powers of individual nation-states as having been eroded and national sovereignty undermined by the pressures of having to conform with the needs of globally influential institutions converging towards a neo-liberal consensus. This view has been criticized by others as unduly reductionist, underestimating the autonomy of nation-states and other domestic political forces in their dialogue with global actors on economic and social issues (Yeates, 2001). Indeed, it is argued that the social risks associated with global-ization could force States to intervene more actively in order to expand social protection mechanisms. The above-mentioned clash of perspectives on the nature and scope of social policy between, for example, the EU, ILO and OECD on the one hand and, on the other, the World Bank, illustrates this tension very clearly. The former organizations subscribe to a social policy agenda centred around comprehensive, statutory welfare provision based on redistributive principles of the mature welfare state. The Bank, on the other hand, has endorsed a more selective, residual, targeted anti-poverty approach involving means-testing and much greater private provision which mirrors US domestic policy to a large extent (Hutton, 2002).

Despite ideological and institutional differences in perspective on this issue, there have been moves to try and define a common global standard for social policy. Deacon has identified five elements of a 'global social reformist project' or 'global governance discourse' (1997: 202–3). These consist of: regulating global competition, making the Bank and IMF more accountable, reforming the UN, strengthening global human rights and empowering international civil society. More specifically, at the request of the Development Committee of the World Bank/IMF and prompted by the East Asia financial crisis, the Bank produced a set of guidelines for 'good practice in social policy' (World Bank, 1998, 1999a). Drawing heavily on the 10 basic principles outlined at the Copenhagen Social Summit in 1995, the Bank outlined four major areas or goals: universal access to basic services, securing sustainable livelihoods, providing social pro-tection for the weakest and fostering social integration. The Bank places a strong emphasis on social policy to deal with short-term hardship and speaks unequivocally of 'managing the social dimensions of crisis' through good social practices via safety nets, basic education, health and labour market policies (World Bank, 1999a, 1999b).

However, serious doubts have been raised about the feasibility of applying and monitoring such a common global standard. Arguably, any global principles should refer to long-term policy and not just to dealing with situations of financial crisis. Furthermore, even if a measure of common agreement could be reached, it is unlikely that such universal principles could be applied to all countries. In the final analysis, the practical application of any set of global principles is likely to be undermined by a '... lack of structures of power, authority and accountability capable of dealing with issues of this scope and scale' (Norton, 2000: 4).

Theoretical perspectives in social policy

The preceding sections of this chapter have discussed definitions of social policy, its goals and major implementing institutions. As an academic textbook, the present volume also seeks to identify major cross-cutting theoretical debates that underpin the design and practice of social policy. Since social policy is concerned primarily with the best ways of promoting people's welfare, it has tended to concentrate on practical issues. For many years, these were at the forefront of social policy thinking and theory was not regarded as very important. Many social policy experts believed that their profession should be primarily concerned with identifying social needs and social problems, formulating policy options and implementing appropriate solutions, neglecting theoretical issues in the process. However, it is more widely accepted today that theory plays a major role in shaping social policy decisions. It is also recognized that theoretical ideas have, in fact, always influenced social policy. Although these ideas were often implicit, social policy has always been based on assumptions about how social problems and needs could best be dealt with. Although it was previously argued by some that social policy is a technical field based on a scientific assessment of what works best, such opinions are heavily influenced by values and ideological beliefs.

Today, the influence of theory on social policy decisions is widely acknowledged. By recognizing the importance of theory, social scientists have been able to understand the ideological assumptions underlying different social policy approaches. An appreciation of theory has also helped explain why social policy decisions have been made and it has facilitated an analysis of the wider forces that have influenced the emergence of social policy. Theory has also helped to classify different types of social policy approaches, and this has resulted in the construction of different models of social policy that provide a better understanding of the field. This section is concerned with the role of theory in social policy. It describes and illustrates the different types of theory that characterize social policy. Special emphasis is placed on normative theory, which provides a value base for social policy. Generally, three types of social policy theory can be identified: (1) representational theory; (2) explanatory or analytical theory; and (3) normative theory.

Representational theory

This is concerned with classification. It seeks to reduce very complex social policy phenomena to more manageable categories and, in this way, to promote a better understanding of different social policy approaches. These categories are also known as typologies or models. One of the first attempts to construct a typology of social policies was Wilensky and Lebeaux's (1965) residual–institutional model. This model divided social policies into two categories. The first category, which the authors called the 'residual model', consists of social policies that are limited and meagre, and are referred to in previous discussions in this chapter of colonial social policy and of structural adjustment. They are used to supplement the family, voluntary sector and market when these institutions are unable to meet social needs. The second type, which they called the 'institutional' model, consists of social policies that play a frontline role in society and promote universal coverage and extensive social service provision. The residual–institutional model was subsequently expanded by Titmuss (1974), who added a third model that he called the 'industrial achievement–performance model'. This model, he believed, linked social policy to the economy and provided welfare services on the basis of merit, work performance and productivity. While Wilensky and Lebeaux's model sought to classify two major social policy approaches in the United States, Titmuss used his model to identify the dominant social policy approaches being used in different countries.

Since then, numerous models of social policy have been developed. One of the most widely cited is Esping-Andersen's (1990) 'three worlds' model. Like Titmuss' model, Esping-Andersen also groups countries in terms of their social policy approaches. However, the models developed by Wilensky and Lebeaux, Titmuss, Esping-Andersen and other scholars refer to the industrialized countries and, as MacPherson and Midgley (1987) showed, few attempts have been made to construct models that incorporate the developing countries of the South.

Explanatory or analytical theory

Such theory seeks to answer a variety of questions about the nature of social policy, its functions in society and the reasons social policies have evolved. This approach has generated a substantial body of knowledge that has given interesting answers to many questions. For example, different theoretical approaches have been used to explain the reasons governments around the world expanded social programmes during the middle decades of the twentieth century. As Midgley (1997) revealed, some theories emphasize the role of industrialization in motivating governments to extend social welfare provisions, while others believe that interest groups played a vital role in fostering social policy expansion. Yet others have concluded that social policies were expanded because governments genuinely wanted to improve social conditions and promote the welfare of their citizens. In turn, others have contended that governments adopted social policies because they realized that social programmes could prevent political unrest and maintain order. Unfortunately, as will be recognized, these different theories have not produced answers that are universally accepted, and explanatory social policy theory is still marked by sharp disagreements. Sharp disagreements also characterize a third type of social policy theory known as normative theory.

Normative theories

Normative theories are used to provide a value framework for social policy. They help to identify desirable social policies in terms of different sets of values, ideologies and political objectives. Normative social policy theory is closely associated with political ideologies. People on the political right will be committed to quite different social policies than those on the political left. But normative theory is linked not only to these familiar political ideologies. People of different religious points of view, people with strong nationalist beliefs, and people who believe that the best society is one based on free market principles take very different normative social policy positions.

Normative theories play a vital role in social policy. They influence the social policy decisions of political parties, governments, non-governmental organizations, popular social movements and official international bodies. These different groups prefer different normative theories and give expression to these theories in their social policy decisions. Normative social policy theory often evokes strong feelings. Many people have a strong commitment to their beliefs and they will oppose social policies that contradict their deeply felt views. Traditionalists oppose social policies that appear to undermine cultural beliefs or weaken the traditional family. Nationalists oppose social policies that appear to favour social groups who do not belong to the nation. Free marketeers challenge the extension of government provisions, and statists will oppose the privatization of social services. It is obvious that social policy is infused with normative convictions. This is why it is important to understand different normative theories in social policy and to appreciate their role in shaping social policy decisions.

Studying normative theory

It was noted earlier that many social policy experts previously believed that social policy is a purely technical subject concerned with the practical aspects of solving social problems and meeting social needs. These experts believed that social policy should transcend ideological differences. This view reflected what has been called the 'welfare consensus' of the post-World War II years when political parties of different ideological beliefs seemed to agree that the government should be responsible for health care, education, housing, social security and other social programmes. Many social policy writers at the time believed that ideology was not a very important factor in explaining the reasons for government involvement in social welfare. They claimed that governments expanded social programmes because of the forces of industrialization, the activities of interest groups and other non-ideological factors.

During the 1970s and 1980s, this belief was shaken by the strident arguments of those on the political right who insisted that social expenditure was causing economic stagnation, sapping the industrial countries of their economic vitality and creating a huge underclass of indolent people who were totally dependent on government. Economists associated with the political right published influential papers claiming that social security was harming economic growth (Feldstein, 1974). They also argued that the proportion of the population who were not working and who received generous social benefits from the government had increased substantially. This had, they argued, imposed an intolerable burden on the few producers who continued to work (Bacon and Eltis, 1976).

At the same time, Marxist writers were popularizing the idea that social welfare was incompatible with capitalism (Gough, 1979; Offe, 1984). They argued that the governments of the Western capitalist countries were not altruistic but had used social policy to exercise social control and promote the interests of capitalism. However, they claimed that these countries would soon face a crisis of legitimacy in which the fiscal burden of providing extensive social services in an attempt to pacify working people would prove to be unsustainable (O'Connor, 1973). It was at this time that the first systematic attempts were made to identify the major normative approaches to social policy. Initially, these attempts identified the major ideological orientations in social policy. The first account of ideology in social policy was published by George and Wilding in 1976. Although it was narrowly concerned with Britain and its political ideologies, it facilitated more sophisticated analyses in which political ideology was linked to major social science theories such as structuralism, functionalism and critical theory (Taylor-Gooby and Dale, 1981; Hewitt, 1992).

These efforts have now resulted in a much more extensive appreciation of the role and importance of normative theory in social policy. They have also shown just how complicated the study of normative theory in social policy has become. While George and Wilding identified four major normative positions in social policy, it is now recognized that there are many more. In addition, it is also accepted that the elemental positions they identified can be combined and linked to each other to form a very complex normative system. However, studies of normative social policy theory have focused primarily on the industrialized countries. Although little research into non-Western normative systems and their relevance to social policy has been undertaken, some social policy scholars have attempted to examine the role of indigenous normative systems on social policy in the South. For example, some scholars have claimed that social policy in the East Asian countries is based on Confucian beliefs (Jones,

1993). Although opinions are divided on this subject, this discussion suggests that, in future, more attention will be paid to the role of indigenous values and beliefs in social policy.

Varieties of normative theory

Although it is very difficult to classify and analyse the bewildering variety of normative positions in social policy today, social policy scholars have built on George and Wilding's seminal contribution to extend the spectrum of ideological beliefs that have influenced social policy thinking. As was noted earlier, some writers have also sought to combine an account of ideology with social science positions that are not overtly ideological but which nevertheless provide a normative basis for social policy thinking. For example, Taylor-Gooby and Dale (1981) developed a classification in which they identified three groups of social scientists that have exerted a strong normative influence on social policy. The first group, which they called the 'individualists', includes Milton Friedman and Frederick von Hayek. The second group, which they called the 'reformists', includes William Beveridge, John Maynard Keynes, Richard Titmuss and Kenneth Galbraith. The third group, or 'structuralists', includes Fred Hirsch, Jürgen Habermas and Michel Foucault. The writings of these social scientists obviously transcend the ideological categories identified by George and Wilding, which have nevertheless exerted an influence on social policy thinking.

Another approach to understanding the role of normative theory in social policy comes from Midgley's (1993, 1995) analysis of key social development strategies. His analysis is based on what he calls the three dominant ideological traditions in Western social and political thought. These are 'individualism', 'collectivism' and 'populism'. These three traditions give rise to distinctive approaches that respectively emphasize the role of the market, the State and communities in social development. Midgley suggests that these ideological positions have provided a normative basis for many different social development policies and programmes. Sustainable development, the promotion of micro-enterprises, centralized development planning, community participation and many other interventions are all derived from these basic orientations, although in complex ways that sometimes involve the amalgamation of different orientations. The three ideological traditions are, therefore, the building blocks that are used to construct more complex normative systems and to inspire particular social development strategies.

(1) The statist approach. Social policy has historically been strongly influenced by statism. Indeed, the evolution of social policy in many parts of the world during the twentieth century owed much to the idea that governments could bring about significant improvements in social conditions by introducing a range of social services to meet social needs and raise the living standards of ordinary people. Statism is inspired by a collectivist ideology suggesting that the best society is one in which people cooperate to meet their common needs. Under the influence of collectivism, they form a variety of associations or

collectives and share their resources for the good of all its members. The ultimate collective is the State that is not, in collectivist thinking, a remote and bureaucratic organization but a body comprised of all citizens, which is answerable to the citizens and which serves their interests.

These ideas inspired nineteenth-century liberal reformers, social democrats and Marxists alike who believed that the State's power and ability to control and direct resources could be used to promote the well-being of all. Of course, their goal was to secure political office and ensure that comprehensive social services were introduced. While Marxists believed that it would only be possible to take control of the State through revolution, social democrats were optimistic that they could persuade the electorate to vote for them and that they would secure political power in this way. The success of social democratic parties in Europe during the middle decades of the last century resulted in a massive expansion of government social service provisions and, for this reason, these countries were often described as 'welfare states'. The normative ideas that influenced this expansion were not, at first, explicated, and as was noted earlier, many social policy experts paid little attention to the assumptions on which social policy expansion was based. The lack of awareness of theory was encouraged by the 'welfare consensus' of the time, which downplayed the role of ideology in social policy.

However, as noted above, the normative ideas attending social policy were subsequently recognized and formalized. The dominant position, which favoured government social welfare provision, became known as 'institutionalism' or 'welfarism'. Its leading exponents included Wilensky and Lebeaux (1965) whose famous typology already referred to above not only classified social policies but also took a normative position by asserting the superiority of the institutional over the residual approach. Titmuss (1968, 1971, 1974) developed this idea and in many eloquent publications offered a powerful moral justification for State welfare stressing its role in giving expression to people's altruistic feelings, promoting social integration and creating a caring and just society. Marshall's (1950) discussion of rights also informed the development of institutional theory. He argued that the notion of citizenship had slowly evolved in European countries through a process of struggle to secure civil and political rights for all. In the latter half of the twentieth century, these struggles had culminated in the recognition that people also had social rights. By ensuring that all citizens were educated, properly housed, adequately fed and provided with health and other social services, the welfare state embodied the ideal of social rights.

These normative ideas had a powerful influence on social policy in the decades following World War II. Many governments embraced the notion of social rights and many signed international treaties and conventions that guaranteed the provision of social services. Many accepted the role of social welfare in promoting social solidarity and believed that it was the duty of the State to ensure that the basic needs of all citizens were met. These ideas were not confined to the industrial countries of the North but were promoted internationally by the United Nations and other organizations as well as, of course, by many governments in the developing world. Yet by the 1970s institutional–welfarist theory was being widely challenged. As mentioned above, Marxists argued that governments were hardly motivated by altruism to care for their citizens and that they cynically used the social services to exert social and political control (Gough, 1979; Offe, 1984). Populists agreed, arguing that the State was out of touch with ordinary people and that social services were being administered by an indifferent and insensitive bureaucracy that had little real interest in helping those in need (Kitching, 1982; Midgley, 1995).

But by far the most forceful criticism of the institutional approach came from neo-liberal economists and others on the political right who claimed that government provisions were seriously damaging the economy and fostering indolence and irresponsibility (Feldstein, 1974; Friedman and Friedman, 1980; Murray, 1984). Although right-wing critics had been actively opposing government intervention for many years, it was only in the 1980s that their opposition resulted in retrenchments in social programmes. With the election in the 1980s of political parties with radical right-wing commitments not only in Britain and the United States, but in other parts of the world as well, the welfare consensus and the dominance of the institutional–welfarist approach was effectively ended.

Despite the demise of institutionalist theory, various attempts have been made to revitalize the statist approach and several forms of neo-institutionalism in social policy have been promoted. These include Giddens' 'Third Way' theory and Midgley's developmentalist theory. Other neo-institutionalist theories have also been proposed but these two examples are indicative of the ways social policy scholars are trying to reformulate earlier statist ideas. Third Way theory (Giddens, 1998) has provided a normative basis for the British Labour Party's approach to social policy. It emphasizes the need for a more pluralist welfare system in which the State seeks to promote greater individual responsibility, community involvement, market participation and voluntary provision in social welfare. The Third Way thus offers a new position on the ideological spectrum between the radical advocacy of free markets by neo-liberals (the new right) and the old statism of traditional social democrats (the old left) such as Titmuss who believed that the State should be the sole provider of social services.

Developmentalism is based on social development thinking that first emerged in the South and has been actively promoted by the United Nations and other international organizations (Midgley, 1995, 1999). Developmentalism offers a macro-perspective on social policy and seeks purposefully to link social and economic policies within a comprehensive, State-directed development process, involving both civil society and business organizations in promoting development goals. It regards economic development as a desirable and essential element in social welfare, and proposes that social programmes support the developmental commitment. Developmentalism urges the adoption of macro-economic policies that promote employment, raise incomes and attain other 'people-centred' economic development outcomes. It also recommends that social programmes be 'productivist' and investment-oriented by promoting economic participation and generating positive rates of return to the economy.

By linking productivist social investment programmes to a comprehensive development process that is sustainable and people-centred, developmentalism offers a universalistic and interventionist approach that is committed to progressive social change. No lesser an institution than the World Bank has also reaffirmed the crucial role of an efficient and reformed State in guiding the development process, providing appropriate regulatory frameworks and a supportive policy environment within a Comprehensive Development Framework (World Bank, 1997, 2000). Research from many countries from Brazil to South Korea clearly shows that successful social policy formulation and implementation is a multi-institutional process in which public institutions commonly play a central role in directing progressive change (Grindle, 1980; Grindle and Thomas, 1991; Tendler, 1995; Mehotra and Jolly, 1998; Stiglitz, 2002).

(2) *The enterprise approach*. The enterprise approach is based on individualist ideology that stresses the fundamental importance and centrality of the individual in social life. Its roots have been traced to the Protestant reformation, the rise of rationalism during the Renaissance and the successful assertion of individual liberties over traditional feudal authority during the French and American revolutions and the English civil war. Individualism also finds expression in utilitarianism and, in its economic form, in the doctrine of *laissez-faire* and in free market economics.

As noted earlier, the enterprise approach previously exerted little influence in social policy. However, following the electoral successes of the Thatcher and Reagan administrations in the 1980s, it now shapes social policy thinking in many parts of the world. Under the influence of individualist ideology, many governments, including those in the political centre, have abandoned institutional welfarism and now appear to favour a minimal role for government in social welfare. With the imposition of strict public budget limits, the social services have been retrenched and they are increasingly contracted out to commercial providers. Social policy has been subordinated to the interests of free market capitalism and it now seems that residualism dominates social policy thinking.

The enterprise approach stresses the primacy of the market in social welfare. Neo-liberals believe that social policies should be compatible with the market economy and reinforce market relations. This means that social policies should never undermine the working of the market by imposing excessive taxation, or by facilitating the exit of people from the market unless they are genuinely unable to work through illness or disability. Social policies should encourage individual responsibility and hard work. Social needs should, as far as possible, be met through the market. This requires the creation of viable markets in the social services. Private commercial firms should be encouraged to provide health, education, social security and other services previously supplied by government. Government health programmes should be replaced with private medical care and social insurance should be abolished and replaced with commercially managed retirement accounts. Similarly, education and housing should be obtained through the market.

As a result of the influence of enterprise theory in social policy, governments around the world are increasingly contracting out the social services to commercial providers. While non-profit organizations are also encouraged to bid for contracts, commercial firms have been very successful in assuming responsibility for managing prisons, children's services, substance abuse clinics, homes for the elderly and many other programmes that were previously administered by government agencies. However, the use of commercial providers has been very controversial and many social policy writers have been critical of this trend.

The enterprise approach also finds expression in efforts to integrate the poor and the recipients of social benefits into the capitalist economy. A leading advocate of this approach is Stoesz (2000) who is very critical of government social programmes. He believes that these programmes marginalize poor people and keep them out of the productive economy. Instead of solving the problem of poverty, institutional welfarism has created a culture of welfare dependency and other ills that perpetuate deprivation. But, he contends, poor people and welfare clients are not lazy or unwilling to work. Rather, they lack the opportunities to participate in the market economy and enjoy the benefits that capitalism can bring. Stoesz argues that the oppressive weight of the welfare system must be lifted and welfare recipients and the poor must be given opportunities to participate in the market economy and learn to function within it. Mechanisms for promoting market integration include wage supplements, asset building and community capitalism. These mechanisms are comprised of policies and programmes that Stoesz describes as 'bootstraps capitalism'. If poverty is to be ended, he argues, welfare reform must itself be reformed to promote a dynamic process of bootstraps capitalism that integrates the poor into the market.

Stoesz's advocacy of market integration finds expression in 'welfare-to-work' programmes, which have become an important ingredient in social policy in the countries of the North. These programmes promote employment among those who previously received government social benefits. For example, the national welfare-to-work programme established in the United States in 1996 compels welfare clients to accept part-time employment as a condition for receiving benefits. As they adapt to employment, they are encouraged to work full-time and, indeed, the length of time they can continue to receive benefits is limited to five years.

The American legislation is based on the ideas of Mead (1992, 1997) who believes that governments must deal firmly with those who are dependent on welfare. Unlike Stoesz, Mead believes that the poor do not want to work and that they prefer to receive government benefits. Therefore, governments must actively promote employment and even use sanctions to ensure that this goal is achieved. Government should not waste resources trying to train or educate welfare clients or counsel or help them to cope with their problems. Instead, a firm, paternalistic approach that promotes 'work first' should be employed.

Since the number of people receiving benefits in the United States has fallen dramatically in recent years, the new welfare-to-work programme is widely viewed as a major success. However, many studies of the new American system are not optimistic that those who no longer receive welfare benefits will be able to raise their incomes to acceptable levels and permanently escape poverty. Nevertheless, many other countries are also adopting programmes of this kind in the belief that the 'work first' approach will be successful (Lodemal and Trickey, 2001). The popularity of the workfare approach in the North has led scholars such as Jessop (1994) to conclude that the institutional welfare state has now been replaced by a workfare state. In developing countries, the use of social funds to encourage individual productive enterprise through micro-credit and similar schemes mirrors something of this work ethic ideology.

(3) The populist approach. A third normative approach in social policy is based on populist ideology that emphasizes the involvement of 'the people' and their common values, beliefs and culture in social welfare. Although the concept of 'the people' is poorly defined, advocates of the populist approach believe that the people rather than individuals or collectives form the core of society and that the best society is one that recognizes and gives expression to their lifestyles and beliefs. Populist leaders often contrast the virtues of ordinary people with the interests of big business and government that, they contend, conspire to thwart the people's welfare. Many populist political leaders effectively use anti-establishment rhetoric to secure electoral support and they often advocate the expansion of social programmes that serve the needs of the people. Often, they promote nationalist sentiments and sometimes engage in anti-immigrant and other forms of negative ethnic rhetoric that appeals to the wider public.

Populist ideas also inform social movements, which emerge from time to time to gather widespread popular support for social and political causes. These movements are often comprised of loosely formed social groups and organizations, but they can be very effective in promoting social change. Many populists, also known as 'communitarians', believe that the community is the prime locus for people's activities and they stress the importance of communities in promoting a sense of belonging, fostering integration and meeting social needs. According to Etzioni (1994), for example, local groups may improve social conditions through their potential for strengthening individuals' entitlements and responsibilities as members of 'communities'. Together, populism and communitarianism comprise a very important normative perspective that has exerted a powerful influence in social policy thinking, particularly in the developing countries of the South.

Indeed, several scholars have written about the way the concept of development itself reflects strong populist tendencies (Kitching, 1982). Populism has certainly been a powerful theme in electoral politics in many developing countries and, in the form of nationalism, has exerted widespread influence. It has also provided a normative basis for social policy. For example, populism was an obvious factor in the expansion of the social services in Argentina during the time of President Juan Peron and it still exerts some influence on social policy in the country and in other Latin American countries as well. Populist ideas also informed the social policies of President Lyndon Johnson in the United States in the 1960s and, earlier, it had fostered the introduction of social programmes under Governor Huey Long and his brother Earl K. Long in Louisiana.

Social policy has also been influenced by radical populist ideas associated with social movements and revolutionary groups in many parts of the world. Radical populists have used confrontational tactics to pressure governments to address wrongs, introduce social reforms and expand social provisions. In the United States, campaigners like Saul Alinsky (1946, 1971) drew in their experiences of political organizing to formulate proposals that community organizers could use to bring about social change. His ideas have been widely adopted in many parts of the world. They have also been extended by numerous social activists who today advocate empowerment and 'conscientization' in organizing ordinary people to fight social injustice and improve social welfare conditions. Most notably, the Brazilian educationalist Paulo Freire (1972) advocated radical adult literacy training techniques as a tool for wider political action by the grassroots to press for economic and social justice (see Chapter 5). Of course, not all forms of populist engagement are based on conflict, and some organizers such as Mahatma Gandhi and Dr Martin Luther King have been strong advocates of non-violent resistance.

Social movements have brought about significant changes over the years and, as a result of their efforts, social policies in many countries have been substantially modified or expanded. The women's movement has played a major role not only in challenging traditional patriarchal arrangements and improving the status of women but in changing conventional social policy approaches towards education, health care, child welfare and family life. While it cannot be claimed that these gains have ended women's oppression, much has been achieved. Similarly, the environmental movement has not only drawn attention to the degradation of the natural world through industrialization, commercialization and consumerism but has secured important policy reforms that have improved the well-being of millions of people.

Community-based social programmes are now well established and form an integral part of the social service system. Previously, governments made extensive use of residential facilities to care for people in need. People in poverty, those with disabilities, neglected and abandoned children, the elderly and many other needy groups were housed in institutions and segregated from society. Today, services are more likely to be provided to needy people in their homes and in their communities. In addition, communities are now more frequently involved in the provision of social services. The developing countries have given international leadership in showing how local people can be actively involved in partnership with governments in creating community-based educational, health, housing and social service programmes. Often, these programmes adopt a productivist approach that links social programmes to economic development activities. Indeed, it was the formative involvement of local people in community-based schemes of this kind that created the community development model which is now so widely used around the world not only to promote social welfare at the local level but to enhance local community economic development (Brokensha and Hodge, 1969; Dore and Mars, 1981).

Community development initiatives have also embraced more radical action approaches that incorporate ideas such as 'conscientization' and people's empowerment in the provision of community social programmes (Freire, 1972; Kane, 2001). Departing from the State-directed, traditional community development model, these programmes are organized by local people themselves or with the support of local activists and non-governmental agencies. While they may seek support from the government and international funding institutions, they stress the need for local governance and people's involvement in service delivery.

However, it is important to recognize that populism also offers a normative basis for social welfare approaches that may not be commended by all progressive social policy thinkers. For example, nationalism, as a form of populism, emphasizes the role of government social services in creating national cohesion and strengthening the people's capacity to resist external threats. During the 1930s, the Nazi government in Germany expanded social provisions to promote the health, vitality and well-being of what it called the Aryan nation. Those who were excluded from the government's definition of national citizenship, such as Jews, Romany people, Slavs, gays and others were not only denied access to these services but were eventually subjected to the genocidal horrors of exclusion. Tang (2000) has also noted, for example, how social welfare provision in the case of the East Asian 'tigers' has in the opinion of some been driven in part by nationalistic political goals.

Populist and nationalist ideology is often linked to the advocacy of the people's traditional values and beliefs. In more recent times, with the resurgence of Islamic movements, traditionalism has become an important normative influence in social policy. The governments of Iran, Pakistan and several other Muslim countries have modified their social policies by replacing established Western approaches with Koranic provisions. Perhaps the most extreme example was the Taliban government in Afghanistan. Traditionalism has transcended social service provisions and informed other dimensions of social policy in these countries as well. Policies relating to marriage and divorce, the education of women and other family matters are, increasingly, being shaped by Islamic teaching. Of course, social policy in some countries such as Saudi Arabia has historically reflected traditional beliefs (Dabbagh, 1993).

Similar tendencies that reaffirm traditional values in social policy can be identified in other countries such as India where Hindu beliefs are being more vigorously promoted by popular social movements. In East Asia, it has been argued that the economic success of the four 'tigers' (Taiwan, South Korea, Singapore and Hong Kong) may be attributed to the traditional values of hard work, thrift and family cohesion associated with Confucianism (Jones, 1993; Tang, 2000). In Latin America, traditional Catholic teachings have, under heavy Vatican pressure, again been emphasized since the late 1980s. This has helped to reduce the impact of the radical church and its Liberation Theology, so influential during the 1970s and early 1980s, and critical in the formation of contemporary 'popular education' movements (Kane, 2001).

In the United States, traditionalism has found expression in the writings of several social policy scholars such as Olasky (1992) and Tanner (1996) who believe that government should abolish social services because these are supposedly incompatible with traditional American cultural values. Olasky argues that the churches and charities have historically functioned to help those in need and that the government should take steps to encourage them to once again play their traditional role. These ideas have been very appealing to President George W. Bush who has created a new Federal government agency known as the Office of Faith-Based Services that, it is hoped, will revitalize religious charity.

Towards a holistic social policy

The three major normative approaches discussed above have all contributed to the emergence of a broader and more all-embracing notion of social policy. Thinking in this field retains the provision of safety nets and social services as central and important components of social policy. Some critics argue, indeed, that policy-makers continue to over-stress residualism because it enables them (especially international donors) to 'projectize' social policy (Tendler, 2003). However, the notion of social policy has clearly expanded substantially to include livelihoods and rights-based approaches to the alleviation of poverty and satisfaction of basic needs. 'Holistic' social policy thus incorporates elements of the statist, enterprise and populist paradigms. From statism comes recognition of the continued importance of pro-active government to make economic and social investments and regulate the private sector while meeting people's basic needs and guaranteeing fundamental freedoms. The enterprise approach stresses the need to protect vulnerable groups with tailored anti-poverty measures and to improve the efficiency of service provision via the use of economic incentives. Increasingly, the adoption of economically sound, market-based strategies is seen as an essential element within income-generating projects to strengthen livelihoods. Populist development traditions underline the centrality of active community mobilization mediated via a range of institutions as a means of articulating people's needs and enhancing their participation in the process of policy design and implementation.

There is no doubting the fact that these approaches continue to represent ideologically contrasting, and often contradictory, stances to the challenge of addressing poverty and deprivation. While they share some middle ground, they represent frequently conflicting perceptions of how the world works and how its problems are best tackled. Yet be that as it may, it can also be argued that there is nowadays in development discourse and action a greater acceptance of social policy as a versatile actor performing diverse roles in accordance with different scenarios. There is, arguably, a more common understanding of social policy as a multi-dimensional notion aimed at addressing diverse social needs in diverse ways. While it may be premature to speak of a 'globalized' social policy, there has undoubtedly been a marriage of sorts in terms of theory, policy and practice of social policy. Some of these basic ideas are brought together in Table 1.1 in terms of normative theories and their implications for defining the leading players, target audiences and the combination of policies considered appropriate for tackling the problems within a given context.

Be that as it may, however, the ultimate test of new social policy formulations resides in how effective such approaches prove to be in effectively addressing poverty and deprivation. In the final analysis, no matter how policies are redefined and repackaged, political commitment is required at the domestic and international levels to seriously tackle these social issues and allocate resources accordingly. In the case of Latin America, for example, a brand of neo-liberal 'New Social Policy' involving a 'pragmatic blend of State provision, self-help solutions, private initiative and NGO assistance' was successful during the 1990s in neutralizing critics. Yet it has not faced up to basic problems of inequities in the distribution of power and wealth or persistent poverty, generating political tensions which have exploded into violence in countries such as Venezuela, Mexico, Bolivia and Ecuador (Abel and Lewis, 2002).

The remainder of this volume will explore in more detail various dimensions of social policy for development. Chapter 2 will examine concepts of poverty and social exclusion and the policy implications for addressing these issues in the South. Chapter 3 considers changing approaches to rural development in the evolution from modernization towards a sustainable livelihoods policy approach, while Chapter 4 analyses urban development and social policy. The links between basic education and social development are discussed in Chapter 5, while Chapter 6 looks at changing health policies and the gradual demise of primary health care in the context of economic liberalization. Chapters 7 and 8 respectively examine social work and social security policies in the developing world. Finally, Chapter 9 explores the specific contributions of overseas development assistance to advancing the social policy agenda.

Recommended Reading

The following sources offer a discussion of major themes within the evolving field of social policy in developing countries.

- Mkandawire, T. (ed.) (2003) *Social Policy in a Development Context*. Geneva: UNRISD. This brings together a series of papers arising from the research project of the same title, running from 2000–05. Its main themes are social policy in relation to macroeconomics, late industrializing countries, democratization, globalization and gender.

Table: 1.1 Normative theories and their social policy implications

Social policy traditions in normative theory	Main actors	Target groups/goals	Social policy implications
(1) *Statist Approach*	Central State (top-down)	Household welfare	Incrementalism (South) Welfare state (North) Statutory social services Citizenship rights
(2) *Enterprise Approach*	Market	Individual support	Residualism Safety nets/social funds Means-testing Privatization/quasi-markets Welfare-to-work
(3) *Populist Approach*	The people (bottom-up)	Community advancement	Community development Communitarianism Conscientization Social movements Indigenous knowledge/values

HOLISTIC SOCIAL POLICY

Actors	Target groups/goals	Policies
• State (central, decentralized) • Civil society (NGOs, communities, social movements) • Private business sector (domestic, supra-national, transnational) • International development institutions (multilateral, bilateral, UN agencies, regional bodies)	Individual, household, community Enhancement of well-being for all, enhancement of human capital, international competitiveness of labour, building social cohesion and combating exclusion (by class, gender, ethnicity)	Basic social services (health, education, housing, social security) Safety nets/social funds Sustainable livelihoods support Cross-sector approach Entitlements, social rights, capabilities Participatory/inclusive Accountability

- Midgley, J. (1997) *Social Welfare in a Global Context*. London: Sage. This book provides a comprehensive overview of social welfare policies and programmes in the international context. It contains chapters dealing with applied international social welfare paying attention to the contribution of social work and social development.
- Midgley, J. (1995) *Social Development: The Developmental Perspective in Social Welfare*. London: Sage. A discussion of the social development approach to harmonizing economic and social policies in the development process.
- Yeates, N. (2001) *Globalization and Social Policy*. London: Sage. A succinct and readable analysis of globalization, its impact on social policy formulation and implementation, set against the continuing power of the State.
- Kennett, P. (2001) *Comparative Social Policy: Theory and Research*. Milton Keynes: Open University Press. Intended as a textbook, this useful volume offers an insightful account of globalization, social policy and social development around the world.

References

Abel, C. and Lewis, C. (eds) (2002) 'Exclusion and engagement: a diagnosis of social policy in Latin America in the long run', in C. Abel and C. Lewis (eds) *Exclusion and Engagement: Social Policy in Latin America*. London: Institute of Latin American Studies, University of London, pp. 3–53.

Adelman, I. and Morris, C. (1965) *Economic Growth and Social Equity in Developing Countries*. Stanford, CA: Stanford University Press.

Alinsky, S. (1946) *Reveille for Radicals*. Chicago, IL: University of Chicago Press.

Alinsky, S. (1971) *Rules for Radicals*. New York: Random House.

Bacon, R. and Eltis, W. (1976) *Britain's Economic Problems: Too Few Producers*. London: Macmillan.

Baer, W. and Love, J. (eds) (2000) *Liberalization and its Consequences: A Comparative Perspective on Latin America and Eastern Europe*. Cheltenham: Edward Elgar.

Blauert, J. and Zadek, S. (eds) (1998) *Mediating Sustainability: Growing Policy from the Grassroots*. West Hartford, CT: Kumarian Press.

Booth, D. (ed.) (1994) *Rethinking Social Development*. London: Longman.

Brokensha, D. and Hodge, P. (1969) *Community Development: An Interpretation*. San Francisco, CA: Chandler.

Burbach, R. and Flynn, P. (1980) *Agribusiness in the Americas*. New York: Monthly Review Press.

Cernea, M. (ed.) (1991) *Putting People First: Sociological Variables in Rural Development*. New York: Oxford University Press.

Chambers, R. and Conway, G. (1992) 'Sustainable rural livelihoods: practical concepts for the 21st century', *IDS Discussion Paper* 296. Brighton: Institute of Development Studies.

Clark, J. (1991) *Democratizing Development: The Role of Voluntary Organizations*. London: Earthscan.

Clark, J. (1995) 'The State, popular participation and the voluntary sector', *World Development*, 23 (4): 593–601.

Conway, T. (2000) *Social Protection: New Directions for Donor Agencies*. London: DFID.

Conyers, D. (1982) *An Introduction to Social Planning in the Third World*. London: John Wiley.

Cornia, G., Jolly, R. and Stewart, F. (1987) *Adjustment with a Human Face*. Oxford: Clarendon Press.

Cowe, R. (2001) 'Inside track: corporate gloss obscures the hard facts', *Financial Times*, 11 December.

Dabbagh, A. (1993) 'Ideology and non-Western culture: an Islamic perspective', *Social Development Issues*, 15 (1): 17–18.

De Haan, A. (2000) 'Components of good social policy: lessons emerging from research', *mimeo.*, Department for International Development.

Deacon, B., with Hulse, M. and Stubbs, P. (1997) *Global Social Policy: International Organizations and the Future of Welfare*. London: Sage.

Devereau, S. and Cook, S. (2000) 'Does social policy meet social needs?', *IDS Bulletin*. 31 (4): 63–73.

Dore, R. and Mars, Z. (eds) (1981) *Community Development*. London: Croom Helm.

Edwards, M. and Hulme, D. (eds) (1992) *Making a Difference: NGOs and Development in a Changing World*. London: Earthscan.

Edwards, M. and Hulme, D. (eds) (1995) *Non-Government Organizations: Performance and Accountability: Beyond the Magic Bullet*. London: Earthscan.

Ellis, F. (2000) *Rural Livelihoods and Diversity in Developing Countries*. Oxford: Oxford University Press.

Esping-Andersen, G. (1990) *Three Worlds of Welfare Capitalism*. Cambridge: Polity Press.

Etzioni, A. (1994) *The Spirit of Community: The Reinvention of American Society*. New York: Touchstone.

Farrington, J. and Bebbington, A., with Wellard, K. and Lewis, D.J. (1993) *Reluctant Partners? Non-Governmental Organizations, the State and Sustainable Agricultural Development*. London: Routledge.

Farrington, J., Carney, D., Ashley, C. and Turton, C. (1999) 'Sustainable livelihoods in practice: early applications in rural area', *Natural Resource Perspectives*, No. 42, June. London: Overseas Development Institute.

Feldstein, M. (1974) 'Social security, induced retirement and aggregate capital accumulation', *Journal of Political Economy*, 83 (4): 447–75.

Freire, P. (1972) *Pedagogy of the Oppressed*. Harmondsworth: Penguin.

Friedman, M. and Friedman, R. (1980) *Free to Choose: A Personal Statement*. New York: Avon.

George, V. and Wilding, P. (1976) *Ideology and Social Welfare*. London: Routledge and Kegan Paul.

Ghai, D. (ed.) (1991) *The IMF and the South: The Social Impact of Crisis and Adjustment*. London: Zed Books.

Giddens, A. (1998) *The Third Way: The Renewal of Social Democracy*. Cambridge: Polity Press.

Gough, I. (1979) *The Political Economy of the Welfare State*. London: Macmillan.

Graham-Brown, S. (1991) *Education in the Developing World: Conflict and Crisis*. London: Longman.

Griesgraber, J. and Gunter, B. (eds) (1996) *Development: New Paradigms and Principles for the Twenty-First Century*. London: Pluto Press.

Grindle, M. (ed.) (1980) *Politics and Policy Implementation in the Third World*. Princeton, NJ: Princeton University Press.

Grindle, M. and Thomas, J. (1991) *Public Choices and Policy Change: The Political Economy of Reform in Developing Countries*. Baltimore, MD: Johns Hopkins University Press.

Hall, A. (ed.) (2000a) *Amazonia at the Crossroads: The Challenge of Sustainable Development*. London: Institute of Latin American Studies, University of London.

Hall, A. (2000b) 'Privatizing the commons: liberalization, land and livelihoods in Latin America', in W. Baer and J. Love (eds), *Liberalization and its Consequences: A Comparative Perspective on Latin America and Eastern Europe*. Cheltenham: Edward Elgar, pp. 232–61.

Hardiman, M. and Midgley, J. (1982) *The Social Dimensions of Development*. London: John Wiley.

Helmore, K. and Singh, N. (2001) *Sustainable Livelihoods: Building on the Wealth of the Poor*. London: Kumarian Press.

Hewitt, M. (1992) *Welfare Ideology and Need: Developing Perspectives on the Welfare State*. Hemel Hempstead: Harvester Wheatsheaf.

Hulme, D. and Edwards, M. (eds) (1997) *NGOs, States and Donors: Too Close for Comfort?* London: Macmillan and New York: St Martin's Press.

Hutton, W. (2002) *The World We're In*. London: Little, Brown.

IIED (2001) 'Environmental and human rights: a new approach to sustainable development', *Opinion: World Summit on Sustainable Development*. London: International Institute for the Environment and Development.

ISEA (2001) 'The accountability challenge' (www.accountability.org.uk).

Jessop, B. (1994) 'The transition to post-Fordism and the Schumpeterian workfare state', in R. Burrows and B. Loader (eds) *Towards a Post-Fordist Welfare State?* New York: Routledge, pp. 13–27.

Jones, C. (1993) 'The Pacific challenge', in C. Jones (ed.) *New Perspectives on the Welfare State in Europe*. London: Routledge. pp. 198–217.

Kane, L. (2001) *Popular Education and Social Change in Latin America*. London: Latin America Bureau.

Kanji, N. and Manji, F. (1991) 'From development to sustained crisis: structural adjustment, equity and health', *Social Science and Medicine*, 33 (9): 985–93.

Keck, M. and Sikkink, K. (1998) *Activists beyond Borders: Advocacy Networks in International Politics*. Ithaca, NY: Cornell University Press.

Kimerling, J. (2000a) 'Oil development in Ecuador and Peru: law, politics and the environment', in A. Hall (ed.), *Amazonia at the Crossroads: The Challenge of Sustainable Development*. London: Institute of Latin American Studies, Institute of London, pp. 73–96.

Kitching, G. (1982) *Development and Underdevelopment in Historical Perspective*. London: Methuen.

Lipton, M. (1977) *Why Poor People Stay Poor: Urban Bias in World Development*. London: Temple Smith.

Lodemal, I. and Trickey, H. (eds) (2001) *An Offer You Can't Refuse: Workfare in International Perspective*. Bristol: Policy Press.

MacPherson, S. (1982) *Social Policy in the Third World*. London: Wheatsheaf.

MacPherson, S. and Midgley, J. (1987) *Comparative Social Policy and the Third World*. Brighton: Wheatsheaf.

Marshall, T.H. (1950) *Citizenship and Social Class and Other Essays*. Cambridge: Cambridge University Press.

Mead, L. (1992) *The New Politics of Poverty*. New York: Basic Books.

Mead, L. (ed.) (1997) *The New Paternalism: Supervisory Approaches to Poverty*. Washington, DC: Brookings Institution Press.

Mehotra, A. and Jolly, R. (eds) (1998) *Development with a Human Face: Experiences in Social Achievement and Economic Growth*. Oxford: Oxford University Press.

Midgley, J. (1993) 'Ideological roots of social development strategies', *Social Development Issues*, 15 (1): 1–13.

Midgley, J. (1995) *Social Development: The Developmental Perspective in Social Welfare*. London: Sage.

Midgley, J. (1997) *Social Welfare in Global Context*. London: Sage.

Midgley, J. (1999) 'Growth, redistribution and welfare: towards social investment', *Social Service Review*, 77 (1): 181–8.

Midgley, J., Tracy, M.B. and Livermore, M. (eds) (2000) *The Handbook of Social Policy*. Thousand Oaks, CA: Sage.

Mishra, R. (1999) *Globalization and the Welfare State*. Cheltenham: Edward Elgar.

Mkandawire, T. (2001) 'Social policy in a development context', *Social Policy and Development Programme*, Paper No. 7. Geneva: UNRISD.

Mkandawire, T. (ed.) (2003) *Social Policy in a Development Context*. Geneva: UNRISD.

Murray, C. (1984) *Losing Ground: American Social Policy, 1950–1980*. New York: Broadway Books.

Murray, S. (2001) 'Social responsibility, a lure for recruits', *Financial Times*, 13 December.

Myrdal, G. (1984), 'International inequality and foreign aid in retrospect', in G. Meier and D. Seers (eds) *Pioneers in Development*. New York: Oxford University Press. pp. 151–65.

Narayan, D. and Ebbe, K. (1997) *Design of Social Funds*, Discussion Paper 375. Washington, DC: World Bank.

Norton, A. (2000) 'Can there be a global standard for social policy? The "social policy principles" as a test case', *ODI Briefing Paper* 2, May. London: Overseas Development Institute.

Ocampo, J. (2000) *Equidad, desarrollo y cuidadanía*. Santiago: CEPAL/ECLAC.

O'Connor, J. (1973) *The Fiscal Crisis of the State*. New York: St Martin's Press.

Offe, C. (1984) *Contradictions of the Welfare State*. Cambridge, MA: MIT Press.

Olasky, M. (1992) *The Tragedy of American Compassion*. Washington, DC: Regnery.

Randel, R., German T. and Ewing, D. (eds) (2000) *The Reality of Aid 2000*. London: Earthscan.

RCD (2001) 'Partnerships – how do they impact poverty alleviation?', *Resource Centre Discussion Forum*, 23 October. London: Resource Centre for the Social Dimensions of Business Practice.

Rondinelli, D. (1983) *Development Projects as Policy Experiments*. London: Methuen.

Scoones, I. (1998) 'Sustainable rural livelihoods: a framework for analysis', *Working Paper* 72. Brighton: Institute of Development Studies.

Stewart, F. (1995) *Adjustment and Poverty: Options and Choices*. London: Routledge.

Stewart, F., Ranis, G. and Ramirez, A. (2000) 'Economic growth and human development', *World Development*, 28 (2): 197–219.

Stiglitz, J. (2002) *Globalization and its Discontents*. London: Penguin.

Stoesz, S. (2000) *Poverty of Imagination: Bootstraps Capitalism, Sequel to Welfare Reform*. Madison, WI: University of Wisconsin Press.

Subbarao, K. (1997) *Safety Net Programs and Poverty Reduction: Lessons from Cross Country Experience*. Washington, DC: World Bank.

Tang, K. (2000) *Social Welfare Development in East Asia*. Basingstoke: Palgrave.

Tanner, M. (1996) *The End of Welfare: Fighting Poverty in the Civil Society*. Washington, DC: Cato Institute.

Taylor-Gooby, P. and Dale, J. (1981) *Social Theory and Social Welfare*. London: Edward Arnold.

Tendler, J. (1995) *Good Government in the Tropics*. Baltimore, MD: Johns Hopkins University Press.

Tendler, J. (2003) 'Why social policy is condemned to a residual category of safety nets and what to do about it', paper prepared for the UNRISD project on, *Social Policy in a Development Context*. Geneva: UNRISD.

Titmuss, R.M. (1968) *Commitment to Welfare*. London: Allen and Unwin.

Titmuss, R.M. (1971) *The Gift Relationship*. London: Allen and Unwin.

Titmuss, R.M. (1974) *Social Policy: An Introduction*. London: Allen and Unwin.

Turner, M. and Hulme, D. (1997) *Governance, Administration and Development: Making the State Work*. Basingstoke: Macmillan.

UN (2000a) *Development of Guidelines on the Role and Social Responsibilities of the Private Sector: Report of the Secretary-General*. Geneva: United Nations.

UN (2000b) *Twenty-Fourth Special Session of the General Assembly entitled 'World Summit for Social Development and Beyond: Achieving Social Development for All in a Globalizing World': Report of the Secretary General*. Geneva: United Nations.

UN (2000c) *Resolution Adopted by the General Assembly. S-24/2. Further Initiatives for Social Development*. Geneva: United Nations.

UNDP (1990) *Human Development Report 1990*, United Nations Development Programme. New York: Oxford University Press.

UNDP (2000) *Human Development Report 2000: Human Rights and Human Development*. New York: Oxford University Press.

UNRISD (2001a) *UNRISD Research Programme: Social Policy in a Development Context*. Geneva: UNRISD.

UNRISD (2001b) *Social Policy in a Development Context: Report of the UNRISD International Conference 23–24 September 2000, Tammsvik, Sweden*. Geneva: UNRISD.

Vidal, J. (1999) 'Shell fights fires as strife flares in delta', *The Guardian*, 15 September.

Waterston, A. (1965) *Development Planning: Lessons of Experience*. Baltimore, MD: Johns Hopkins University Press.

Whitehead, L. (2000) 'Privatization and the public interest: partial theories, lopsided outcomes', in W. Baer and J. Love (eds), *Liberalization and its Consequences: A Comparative Perspective on Latin America and Eastern Europe*. Cheltenham: Edward Elgar, pp. 262–92.

Wilensky, H. and Lebeaux, C. (1965) *Industrial Society and Social Welfare*. New York: Free Press.

Williamson, J. (1990) 'What Washington means by policy reform', in J. Williamson (ed.) *Latin American Adjustment: How Much Has Happened?* Washington, DC: Institute for International Economics.

World Bank (1990) *World Development Report 1990: Poverty*. Washington, DC: World Bank.

World Bank (1991) *World Development Report 1991: The Challenge of Development*. Washington, DC: World Bank.

World Bank (1997) *World Development Report 1997: The State in a Changing World*. Washington, DC: World Bank.

World Bank (1998) *Communiqué of the Development Committee*, 5 October. Washington, DC: World Bank.

World Bank (1999a) *Principles and Good Practice in Social Policy: Issues and Areas for Public Action*. Washington, DC: World Bank.

World Bank (1999b) *Managing the Social Dimensions of Crisis: Good Practices in Social Policy*, September 14. Washington, DC: World Bank.

World Bank (2000) *World Development Report 1999/2000*. Washington, DC: World Bank.

World Bank (2001) *World Development Report 2000–2001: Attacking Poverty*. Washington, DC: World Bank.

World Bank (2002) *World Development Report 2003: Sustainable Development with a Dynamic Economy*. Washington, DC: World Bank.

Yeates, N. (2001) *Globalization and Social Policy*. London: Sage.

POVERTY, INEQUALITY AND DEVELOPMENT: THE CHALLENGE FOR SOCIAL POLICY

Summary

This chapter is concerned with the problems of poverty and inequality and their relation to development. The chapter contends that social policies that directly address the poverty problem in the context of development are needed. The chapter is divided into four sections. The first section is concerned with the way poverty has been conceptualized and defined. It examines absolute and relative poverty lines and discusses the role of social indicators in understanding poverty. Attention is given to definitions of poverty that stress inequality and oppression and to behavioural definitions that employ the notion of social exclusion and the under-class. The section concludes with a discussion of recent debates attending the definition of poverty. The chapter's second section examines income studies as well as studies of the quality of life to determine the extent of global poverty. An account of the incidence of poverty in different world regions is provided. This material is related to historical trends that show that, while the incidence of poverty has declined in some parts of the world, it remains a problem of huge and serious proportions for hundreds of millions of people. The final section deals with strate-gies for poverty eradication. It contends that poverty alleviation strategies are linked to wider values and beliefs. The section outlines several of these strategies from a historical perspective, showing that quite different approaches for poverty eradication have evolved over the last 50 years. These different strategic approaches are outlined and assessed. They are the modernization approach; the develop-mentalist state planning approach; the critical approach; the community participa-tion and local development approach; and the neo-liberal approach. The chapter's final section contends that the social development approach as articulated at the United Nations World Summit provides the most useful framework for dealing with the challenge of poverty and inequality today.

Acknowledging poverty

There has been a tendency in the academic literature and in social policy circles in recent years to avoid terms such as poverty and inequality. Instead it is more fashionable to talk about 'social exclusion' and the 'capabilities' of poor people. But, poverty and inequality remain central issues in both development and social policy. The fact that millions of people in the world today live in appalling conditions of material deprivation while others enjoy unprecedented prosperity suggests that concepts such as poverty and inequality remain highly relevant.

The avoidance of these terms reflects the dominance of neo-liberal ideas about the nature of poverty. Many political leaders and social scientists today believe that poverty has little to do with wider issues of privilege or structural inequality and they argue instead that the poverty problem can be solved when countries promote economic growth by creating free markets, reducing government regulations and social services, attracting foreign investments and permitting entrepreneurs to pursue profits. By adopting a vibrant form of free market capitalism, governments create employment opportunities, and, in this way, raise the incomes of the poor.

The problem with this strategy is that many countries that have recorded high rates of economic growth still have a high proportion of the population in poverty. While development is indeed needed to reduce poverty, development has no meaning if it does not increase the incomes and well-being of all. Economic growth that fails to raise standards of living for all on an equitable scale cannot be described as development. Unfortunately, economic development in many parts of the world has not achieved this goal. It is for this reason that many development experts today talk about a 'crisis' or 'impasse' in development. After more than half a century of organized development effort, many hundreds of millions of people in the South continue to live in abject poverty and deprivation.

It is here that development and social policy interface. It will be argued in this chapter that the best hope of raising standards of living and eradicating poverty lies in an approach that combines a commitment to economic development with the introduction of social policies that specifically and directly address the poverty problem. This idea is at the core of the social development approach and the theme of the United Nations World Summit that was held in Copenhagen in 1995.

However, social development is only one of many different approaches for addressing the problem of poverty. Indeed, proposals for poverty eradication – as well as the poverty issue as a whole – are controversial. It will be shown that social scientists even disagree about the definition of poverty, and that attempts to measure the extent of poverty are complicated by these disagreements. The idea that poverty is closely associated with inequality is particularly controversial. Another source of contention is whether poverty can best be analysed with reference to income and consumption or in terms of qualitative factors reflecting lifestyles, culture and values.

Despite these disagreements, the stark realities of poverty today are readily apparent. News reports of starvation in Africa, slum dwellers in Asia, child beggars in Latin America and homeless street people in the United States project powerful images that evoke compassion and understanding and transcend academic debates about definitions. That abject poverty persists for hundreds of millions of people at a time that others enjoy unprecedented wealth and prosperity remains a cruel and depressing contradiction.

Understanding poverty

Although poverty has been the subject of popular speculation and religious interpretation for centuries, it was only in the nineteenth century that the first systematic attempts were made to define, measure and understand poverty. Among the earliest were qualitative accounts that described the lives of the poor. An example is Henry Mayhew's voluminous work, *London Labour and London Poor*, published in 1851. The first quantitative studies of poverty, which were based on census data, also emerged at this time. These studies used census reports to estimate the prevalence of poverty but they were subsequently superseded by household surveys that used direct interviews to obtain more detailed information about incomes, expenditures, housing conditions, family size and other relevant factors. One of the first poverty surveys was undertaken by Charles Booth in London at the end of the nineteenth century.

These early studies laid the foundations for the subsequent emergence of quite different definitions and interpretations of poverty. Quantitative studies that define poverty as a lack of adequate income are widely used today but they have been complemented by studies that define poverty in terms of lifestyles, attitudes and behaviours. These approaches have also been augmented by conceptualizations that do not use the term 'poverty' and instead make use of other concepts such as 'social exclusion', 'underclass', 'standard of living', 'livelihood', 'inequality', 'relative deprivation', and other terms that are, nevertheless, closely associated with poverty. This has resulted in a great deal of confusion and disagreement. However, the problem is not merely one of semantics. As will be shown, the way poverty is defined is closely linked to policy proposals for poverty eradication, which are, in turn, rooted in different values and beliefs. To properly understand these issues, different approaches to defining poverty need to be comprehended.

Poverty, income and deprivation

Definitions of poverty based on income reflect the idea that human beings require a minimum level of consumption of food, water, shelter and clothing to survive. By defining these minimum needs, and linking them to prices, it is possible to construct an absolute minimum poverty line which can then be used in social surveys to determine how many people have incomes that fall below this line. This approach was pioneered by Charles Booth in London and subsequently refined by Seebohm Rowntree in his studies of poverty in the

English city of York. In the early decades of the twentieth century, numerous poverty studies based on the minimum income criterion were undertaken not only in Britain but in the United States, India and South Africa.

Many of these studies supported social reform efforts. Rowntree's findings informed proposals for the introduction of social insurance and other social programmes in Britain after World War II (Bruce, 1961) while poverty studies undertaken by Paul Kellogg in the United States (Chambers, 1971) were used to persuade the federal government to introduce social security. Poverty line research also helped to establish the means-tests that were used to determine eligibility for social benefits. It is not surprising that social assistance means-test standards are often used by governments today to define and determine the incidence of poverty.

However, the use of poverty lines based on absolute survival minima have been widely criticized. One difficulty is that absolute poverty lines are very meagre and, therefore, unrealistic. Even Rowntree pointed out that his minimum poverty line was not realistic because people could not survive on the minimum standards he had used (Stitt and Grant, 1993). Another problem is that they engender a degree of complacency. As incomes rise, and the incidence of absolute poverty falls, many have concluded that the problem of poverty has been solved. This happened in Britain when subsequent studies of poverty in York in 1936 and 1951 undertaken by Rowntree revealed that the incidence of absolute poverty had declined significantly since his first study was undertaken in 1899. This conclusion was hotly contested by Townsend (1974, 1979), who argued that it made no sense to talk of absolute survival minima in affluent societies. Poverty in societies such as Britain should not be defined in terms of absolute survival minima but in terms of relative criteria based on social expectations and the standards of living that most people enjoy. A relative definition, he argued, showed that poverty remained a major social problem in Britain.

Townsend's critique has been widely accepted and relative criteria are now widely employed to define poverty in the North. Usually, the poverty line is determined by taking average incomes into account and often they are linked to social security eligibility standards. For example, this is currently the practice in the European Union, which defines poverty as 50 per cent of the median income of a country's population. As will be appreciated, this approach makes explicit reference to the distribution of incomes and raises the issue of inequality and its association with poverty. The concept of 'relative deprivation' has been used to promote this idea (Runciman, 1972).

Nevertheless, absolute poverty lines continue to be useful, particularly in the South where survival needs remain relevant to an understanding of poverty. Perhaps the best known is the one dollar a day poverty line which is widely used by international agencies such as the World Bank and the United Nations. This approach emerged from studies undertaken in the 1970s for the World Bank by Montek Ahluwahlia (1974, 1976) who used two arbitrary poverty lines of $50 and $75 per capita per annum at 1971 prices to estimate the incidence of poverty in a number of developing countries. Ahluwahlia's methodology was also employed to make estimates of the incidence of global poverty. In the

World Bank's 1990 *World Development Report*, two poverty lines of $275 and $370 per capita per annum were used. The former denoted the 'extremely poor' while the latter referred to the 'poor'. Following the 1995 World Summit on Social Development, the one dollar a day (or $365 per annum) poverty line has been widely employed by international agencies including the World Bank, the United Nations and the Organization of Economic Cooperation and Development (OECD) not only to estimate the incidence of global poverty but also to set targets for poverty alleviation.

Poverty, social indicators and the quality of life

Income poverty lines are a useful way of measuring poverty but they focus on minimum consumption needs and provide little information about the health, education, housing and other conditions that characterize the lives of poor people. In an attempt to address this problem, the United Nations in the 1960s promoted the study of social indicators. It was believed that these could provide useful insights into social conditions in different countries. It was also hoped that social indicators would provide more useful insights into social well-being than per capita gross national product (GNP), then widely regarded as a useful measure of both economic and social development. Critics pointed out that per capita income was not only an economic measure but that it produced highly skewed results. A country with a relatively high per capita GNP could still have a high rate of poverty and poor social conditions. For example, Ahluwahlia (1974) showed that South Africa's per capita income was twice as high as Zambia's, but that South Africa had almost twice as many people in absolute poverty.

Social indicator research has now become very sophisticated. Governments now routinely collect data about births, deaths, the incidence of infectious diseases, housing conditions, literacy, educational attainments and many other facets of life. As Midgley (1984) noted, these data are both measures of specific conditions such as health or housing or education but they also allude to, or 'indicate', wider social conditions. For example, it is generally agreed that infant mortality and life expectancy are good 'indicators' of a country's standard of living. Indeed, both correlate highly with many other measures including GNP per capita. Using social indicators, a great deal of data about social conditions around the world have been collected, and detailed profiles of social conditions in different nations have been published.

Another important development has been the construction of 'aggregate' or 'composite' indicators. These indicators combine different discreet measures such as life expectancy, school enrolments and access to safe drinking water into a single index which also gives an indication of wider social conditions. The first composite indicators were developed at the United Nations Research Institute of Social Development (UNRISD) in the 1970s (Baster, 1972) but many others have since appeared. They vary in complexity. For example, the OECD (1976) constructed a development index that amalgamated no fewer than 100 separate indicators. A similarly ambitious measure, known as the Index of

Social Progress (ISP), was developed by Estes (1985). On the other hand, Morris (1979) introduced a simpler index known as the Physical Quality of Life Index or PQLI. This was based on only three measures: namely, life expectancy, literacy and infant mortality. Perhaps the most widely used composite indicator today is the Human Development Index (HDI) that was constructed by the United Nations Development Programme (1990). The HDI features in its annual Human Development reports and has more recently been accompanied by the Gender-Related Development Index (GDI).

The social indicator approach shares similarities with the income poverty line approach in that it is based on quantitative data. It also facilitates a relatively straightforward conceptualization of poverty. However, the social indicator approach expands the definition of poverty. It augments the idea that poverty is a matter of low income by demonstrating that poverty is associated with a set of negative social conditions manifested in the form of ill-health, inadequate shelter, poor nutrition, low educational attainments and illiteracy, low life expectancy, and limited access to health and other services. Most accounts of the incidence of income poverty are now accompanied by accounts of the extent of these conditions as measured by social indicators.

However, some experts are critical of the social indicator approach because it is primarily concerned with the material conditions associated with poverty neglecting non-material aspects. While it is important to ensure that people have access to schools or immunization or food it is equally important, they contend, to stress the need for political participation, opportunities for self-expression, freedom from economic exploitation and the other dimensions of a wholesome life that transcend income. This issue has attracted increasing attention in recent years and it is now more widely recognized that poor people are disproportionately affected by discrimination, crime, violence and oppression and other problems that transcend a narrow preoccupation with income. Today, poverty is increasingly viewed in both material and non-material terms.

Poverty, inequality and oppression

Attempts to define poverty with reference to social inequalities have also become more cognizant of non-material aspects. Originally, inequality was narrowly defined in terms of income distribution but today inequality is more frequently related to issues of discrimination, exploitation and oppression, differential access to resources and an inability to exercise power effectively and to resist those who oppress. This wider concern does not, of course, negate the importance of income and wealth inequality and their role in creating and maintaining poverty.

Studies of income inequality have long informed the understanding of poverty. It has been shown that countries with high rates of inequality often have high rates of poverty. But, as research undertaken many years ago by Kuznets (1955) revealed, very poor countries with a large subsistence agricultural economic sector are not highly unequal. This is because the vast majority of the population in these countries is poor. However, in countries experiencing economic development, income inequality often increases sharply. Kuznets argued that inequality increases because the incomes of those who are drawn from the subsistence sector into the modern, wage employment sector rise rapidly in comparison with those who remain in agrarian occupations. However, he also postulated in his 'U-curve' hypothesis that income inequalities fall as economic development proceeds. As a result of increased wage employment, the incomes of most people rise and inequalities decline.

Kuznets' pioneering studies facilitated a good deal of subsequent research into income inequality in the South. Many studies used household surveys to show that there were marked differences in the income shares of the highest and lowest earners. In many countries, the richest 20 per cent of the population often earned more than one-half of total income. The Gini coefficient was widely used to represent these inequalities. A Gini coefficient of zero represents maximum equality while a Gini coefficient of one represents maximum inequality. One contested finding, which emerged from this research, was the absolute impoverishment hypothesis developed by Adelman and Morris (1973). Their research revealed that economic development was not only accompanied by high inequality but that it resulted in an absolute decline in the incomes of the poorest groups. They reached the startling conclusion that the poor would have been better off if there had been no economic growth at all.

During the 1960s and 1970s, the issue of income inequality was hotly debated in social policy and development circles. Kuznets' findings were used to justify high income inequality in countries experiencing rapid economic growth on the ground that income inequality would resolve itself and did not require government intervention. Although Kuznets' work engendered a degree of complacency in development circles, studies of gender oppression, the treatment of ethnic minorities and particularly indigenous peoples and other forms of oppression by military and political elites challenged the idea that greater equality would inevitably result from economic progress. Human rights activists, feminist writers and representatives of minority communities such as Rigoberta Menchu have effectively publicized the pervasiveness of oppression around the world. Many other mainstream development writers argue that government intervention is needed to redress these inequities as well as wider income disparities. They contend that inequality, poverty and development are inextricably linked. However, this contention is summarily rejected by those who believe that poverty has little to do with wider structural inequalities in society or even with low income. They argue instead that poverty is a matter of lifestyle, cultural disposition, attitudes and ultimately of choice.

Behaviour and poverty: social exclusion and the underclasss

Henry Mayhew's book, which was referred to earlier in this chapter, focused in some detail on the most disreputable and disagreeable types of poor people in

London in the middle decades of the nineteenth century and his vivid portrayal of drunkenness, immorality, indolence, prostitution, violence and criminality in the city's slums was a precursor to many subsequent depictions of poverty as a behavioural issue. Like Mayhew's book, subsequent accounts of poverty based on behavioural interpretations have paid little attention to income poverty lines or the use of Gini coefficients. Poverty, they argue, should be defined as an undesirable and deviant lifestyle.

This approach reflected popular views about the poor. By the mid-nineteenth century, the expanding wage employment opportunities created by industrialization had attracted many poor rural migrants to the cities but few found the riches they hoped for, and many lived in run-down tenements in unsanitary conditions, working sporadically and earning incomes that were, as Booth and Rowntree discovered, often below subsistence minima. The crowding of poor people in the slums and the high rates of crime, illegitimacy, substance abuse and violence that characterized these areas was regarded by the 'respectable' middle and upper classes of the Victorian era as a matter for grave concern. Their image of the poor was denoted by the widely used phrase 'dangerous and perishing classes'. The poor were not only to be pitied but also feared. In his famous denunciation of the poor, Karl Marx evoked both dimensions when he wrote about the 'lumpenproletariat' as including not only 'vagabonds and criminals' but 'pauper children, the sickly, the widows ...' (Herkommer and Koch, 1999: 102).

This imagery has persisted for many decades and although many new terms have been invented to characterize the poor, their lives and the areas in which they live, contemporary notions such as 'the underclass' and 'social exclusion' are the direct descendants of nineteenth-century representations of poor people as immoral, indolent, violent and deviant. However, before the idea of the underclass became popular, the negative behaviours of the poor have been interpreted in many different ways. In the early twentieth century, the eugenics movement attributed the negative lifestyles of poor people to low intelligence or 'feeblemindedness'. In the 1920s, prohibitionists in the United States were persuaded that poverty was closely associated with alcohol abuse. In the 1950s, social workers focused attention on what were called 'multi-problem' families who required intensive casework if child abuse, drug addiction, mental illness and many other personal pathologies were to be addressed. In the 1960s, 'culture of poverty' explanations pioneered by Lewis (1966) were used to argue that poverty was transmitted between the generations, and that cultural traits which engendered complacency, a lack of ambition, infantile demands for instant gratification, and a lack of foresight and planning, would persist.

In the 1970s, these ideas were interwoven with racist interpretations. Riots in many American cities in the late 1960s reinforced popular white middle-class stereotypes about poverty, and resurrected older ideas about the dangerous and perishing classes except that the poor were now overwhelmingly believed to be comprised of people of colour. These stereotypes were combined with claims that poverty, race and low intelligence were inextricably linked. Herrnstein's (1973) early work linked poverty to low intelligence and this idea has since been notoriously restated in association with Murray (Herrnstein and Murray, 1994). Although scientifically discredited, these notions have been widely accepted because they express what many ordinary people actually believe. More recently, popular beliefs about the behaviour of the poor in the industrial countries have been reinforced by linking poverty and race with the receipt of welfare benefits (Murray, 1984; Mead, 1992). In these accounts of poverty, poor people are not only predominantly people of colour but they are believed to be exploiting the social welfare system.

The association of poverty and race has been augmented by the addition of a spatial dimension. Poverty has been viewed not only as a lifestyle, but as a lifestyle lived within an area of concentrated deprivation known variously as the ghetto, inner city, slum or squatter settlement (Clark, 1965; Banfield, 1968). The popularization of the term 'underclass' to characterize poor people who live in these areas (Auletta, 1982), solidified this link and recapitulated nineteenth-century images of the urban poor. Subsequent explanations of the underclass phenomenon such as those of Wilson (1987, 1993) and Denton and Massey (1993) have not only emphasized the spatial dimensions of poverty but have sought to explain it in terms of spatially linked causative factors. In Wilson's writing, the absence of employment opportunities and the mismatch of job skills caused by de-industrialization have been stressed. On the other hand, spatial segregation is given high etiological importance in Denton and Massey's work.

However, in both cases, the underclass phenomenon is no longer attributed to low intelligence or culturally transmitted negative behavioural traits but to wider social causes. Poor people are not held responsible for their deviant actions but are viewed as the victims of extrinsic forces. This factor is especially important in understanding the origins of the concept of 'social exclusion' which, despite its ambiguity, has become very fashionable in social policy circles in Europe today. Littlewood and Herkommer (1999) point out that while the idea of social exclusion has only become popular in recent years, its origins are rooted in notions of social solidarity which have historically characterized continental European social policy thinking. The idea of social exclusion accompanied growing concern about the way de-industrialization, global competitiveness and other economic difficulties emanating from the 1970s had produced a large number of unemployed people who were increasingly marginalized from mainstream society. Policy-makers in European countries that value social solidarity began to stress the need for interventions that would address this problem. The idea of social exclusion was in turn adopted by the European Union and, following the election success of the Labour Party, was incorporated into British social policy.

Social exclusion is now one of several key themes in New Labour's advocacy of a 'Third Way' approach to social policy. This approach rejects what the Labour leadership regards as the excessive statism of its predecessors, as well as the radical individualism of Thatcherism. Instead of viewing poverty as the result of the personal failings of poor people, poverty is now attributed to wider exclusionary processes such as inadequate education, de-industrialization and social isolation. However, in several policy statements by Labour officials, the link between the old-fashioned underclass approach and social exclusion is made clear. For example, Geoff Mulgan, a senior government policy adviser, stressed the need to target the 8 to 10 per cent of the population whose lifestyles are characterized by crime, drug addiction, truancy and illegitimacy and who are, as he put it, 'the chronic losers' (Lund, 2002).

New approaches to defining poverty

The British Labour Party's approach to poverty has been significantly influenced by the writings of Giddens (1998, 2000) who is critical of the traditional 'welfare state' which provides services and income benefits to passive recipients. The purpose of his 'positive welfare' approach, which is an integral component of 'Third Way' thinking, is to help people negotiate risk and manage their own problems within a dynamic social and economic environment shaped by globalization and new, powerful forces of change. The excluded, who function on the margins of society and are often dependent on state aid, must be taught how to participate actively in this environment so that they too can function effectively as autonomous actors in the new and volatile world of risk.

However, the idea that poverty can be solved by inculcating attitudes and behaviours that facilitate autonomous functioning and help people to assume responsibility for their own welfare is not a new one. Indeed, it is central to the neo-liberal belief that poverty can be eradicated when free markets thrive and when people have opportunities to pursue their own enlightened self-interest. But while the Third Way promotes individual choice and responsibility, these ideas are encapsulated within a wider context of social care, reciprocity and other communitarian ideals (Newman and de Zoysa, 2001). By linking individualism to communitarianism, the Third Way straddles the collectivism of statism and the radical individualism of free market capitalism.

Sen (1992, 1999) has also attempted to synthesize these traditions. He has criticized both the absolute and relative notions of poverty and argued that poverty has less to do with income deficiency than with people's abilities to choose what they want to do and be. In Sen's rather obtuse terminology, functionings refer to different states of existence that people may value. They range from basic states of existence, such as being adequately fed, to more complex states involving lifestyles and cultural choices. To achieve different combinations of functionings, people must have capabilities which are, in turn, determined by wider opportunities, freedoms and entitlements. Freedom, Sen argues, is essential if people are to realize their functionings. Freedom is an intrinsic feature of societies where hunger is eliminated, where educational opportunities abound and where diseases are controlled. But compared to neo-liberal writers such as Friedman (1962, 1980), who have also emphasized the need for freedom, Sen's concept transcends the notion that freedom is the absence of restraint. Instead, action is needed to create positive freedoms that enhance people's capabilities and permit them to realize their functionings.

Sen's work has become influential in development circles and has provided a conceptual basis for much current United Nations thinking on social development. This is reflected in the way definitions of poverty in both UNDP and World Bank documents now transcend income lines. While the incidence of global poverty is still ubiquitously measured in terms of the dollar per day criterion, these accounts are augmented by notions of 'opportunities', 'empowerment', 'security', 'participation' and many other terms that reflect non-material lifestyle issues (World Bank, 2001). However, concepts such as social exclusion and the underclass have not yet been incorporated into definitions of poverty in mainstream development thinking, and it is doubtful whether they have much value in conceptualizing poverty in the developing countries. On the other hand, they remain fashionable and will probably find their way into discourses about poverty and development in the future. Indeed, it seems that the notion of social exclusion has already been introduced into the language of development. Francis (2002) reports that the International Labour Office has begun to use the term to emphasize the increased marginalization of poor people in the South. However, he also points out that the concept remains ambiguous and of limited value. The problem is compounded by the tendency to use social exclusion as a synonym for poverty with the result that the majority of a country's population may be classed as 'socially excluded'. This was the case at a recent conference on social development where a South African scholar (Conradie, 2001) reported that as many as 50 per cent of her country's population were 'socially excluded'.

The extent of global poverty

As was noted earlier in this chapter, disagreements among scholars about the definition of poverty complicate attempts to measure its extent. Because poverty is defined differently by different social scientists, their accounts will highlight different dimensions of poverty. While some will discuss global poverty in terms of income data and use income poverty lines to examine its incidence, others will place more emphasis on inequality and refer to Gini coefficients, income shares and other pertinent data. Yet others will be concerned with the way poverty is manifested in low life expectancy, illiteracy, high rates of infant mortality and other problems that are usually measured by social indicators. Yet others will use qualitative information to focus on the behavioural dimensions of poverty. Although these different approaches compound the task of providing an account of the extent of global poverty, all provide insights into the challenges facing the hundreds of millions of people who live in conditions of poverty and deprivation today.

The incidence of poverty and inequality

Absolute poverty lines are now widely used to report the global incidence of poverty. Using this approach, the World Bank (2001) estimates that about

Table 2.1 Incidence of absolute poverty by world region, 1998

Region	Numbers in poverty (millions)	% of poor	Proportion of population in poverty (%)
East Asia and Pacific	278.3	23.2	15.3
Eastern Europe and Central Asia	24.0	2.0	5.1
Latin America and Caribbean	78.2	6.5	15.6
Middle East and North Africa	5.5	0.5	1.9
South Asia	522.0	43.5	40.0
Sub-Saharan Africa	290.9	24.3	46.3
Global South	1,198.9	100.0	24.0

Source: World Bank (2001).

1.2 billion people or 24 per cent of the world's population of about 6 billion people had incomes of less than one dollar per day or ($365 per person per annum) in 1998. The World Bank also uses the two dollars per day poverty line. Using this measure, 2.8 billion people, or approximately 46 per cent of the world's population, had an income of less than two dollars per day (or $730 per annum) in 1998. Although the one dollar per day poverty line is an arbitrary one, it is intentionally used by the World Bank to dramatize the fact that poverty remains a problem of grave proportion in many parts of the world and, indeed, in the world as a whole. It is an absolute minimum subsistence poverty line and, as the Bank notes, those living below the one dollar a day line are considered destitute.

Almost all of the world's extremely poor people, as measured by the one dollar a day poverty line, live in the South. Table 2.1 summarizes the World Bank data on absolute poverty for these developing countries. The World Bank also provides poverty data for 'transitional' economies, comprising the former communist countries of Eastern Europe and Central Asia. No data are provided for the industrial nations of Western Europe and North America or for Japan, which have very small numbers of people in absolute poverty.

Table 2.1 shows that absolute poverty in the developing countries is not equally distributed among the major world regions. In 1998, fully 43 per cent of the poor in the South, or 522 million people, lived in South Asia. Another 24 per cent, or 291 million, were to be found in sub-Saharan Africa, and 23 per cent, or 278 million, lived in East Asia and the Pacific. Much smaller proportions of the world's poor live in Eastern Europe and Central Asia and the Middle East. Less than 1 per cent of the world's poor are in the Middle East and North Africa, while 2 per cent are to be found in Eastern Europe and Central Asia. About 6.5 per cent live in Latin American and Caribbean countries.

The concentration of the largest number of poor people in South Asia is obviously related to the fact that the region contains the largest share of the world's population. South Asia includes very sizeable countries such as India, Indonesia and Pakistan. On the other hand, a large proportion of the world's population is also to be found in East Asia and the Pacific, which includes China, but here the proportion of the population with incomes below the one dollar a day line is far lower than in South Asia. While 15.3 per cent of the population in East Asia and the Pacific lived below the poverty line in 1998, no less than 40 per cent of South Asia's population has an income of less than one dollar per day. However, the incidence of poverty expressed as a share of the total population is highest in sub-Saharan Africa where no less than 46 per cent of the region's population lives in absolute poverty. However, only 5.5 per cent of people in Eastern Europe and Central Asia have incomes below this amount. In Latin America and the Caribbean, the proportion of the population in poverty is about the same as in East Asia and the Pacific – roughly 15 per cent. Of course, these regional data mask differences between countries within these regions. For example, the World Bank reported that there were significant variations between poor African countries. Using national poverty data, it reported that the incidence of poverty in Ghana was about 29 per cent while in Nigeria it was 65 per cent. Differences were also to be found between more prosperous regions such as Eastern Europe. While the incidence of absolute poverty in Hungary was less than 5 per cent, the comparable figure in Russia was 19 per cent (World Bank, 2001).

Although the dollar a day poverty line shows that the incidence of absolute poverty remains high, it understates the extent of the problem in those countries where absolute survival minima have been met. While very few people in Europe, North America and other industrial nations have incomes of less than a dollar or even two dollars a day, poverty remains a problem. For example, in the United States, the world's most powerful and, many would contend, wealthy nation, about 12 per cent of the population lived below the poverty line in 1998. This figure translates into 32 million people – equal to about the total population of California, the country's largest state (Burtless and Smeeding, 2001). Similarly, World Bank estimates of poverty in high-income developing countries such as Algeria, Argentina, Jordan and Thailand based on the one and two dollar a day lines are very low when compared to estimates based on national poverty lines. For example, the World Bank estimates that the proportion of people earning less than one dollar a day in Jordan is under 2 per cent. However, studies undertaken by Jordanian researchers revealed that 11.7 per cent of the population live below the country's own poverty line.

For this reason, many researchers prefer to use relative poverty lines based on national criteria which they believe provide a more realistic assessment of the incidence of poverty. In an effort to obtain a more accurate assessment, the World Bank (2001) has also calculated relative poverty lines for many developing countries by estimating the proportion of the population earning one-third or less of the national average. Information about the incidence of relative poverty is provided in Table 2.2. Using this poverty line, the Bank found that in some regions of the world where the incidence of absolute poverty is comparatively low, relative poverty remains a serious problem. In Latin America, for example, more than a half of the population is below the relative poverty line even though the incidence of absolute poverty is only 15.6 per cent. In the Middle East and North

Table 2.2 Relative poverty by world region, 1998

Region	Proportion of population below $1 per day poverty line (%)	Proportion or population earning less than one-third average income (%)
East Asia and Pacific	15.3	19.6
Eastern Europe and Central Asia	5.1	25.6
Latin America and Caribbean	15.6	51.4
Middle East and North Africa	1.9	10.8
South Asia	40.0	40.2
Sub-Saharan Africa	46.3	50.5
Global South	24.0	32.1

Source: World Bank (2001).

Africa, the figure was 10.8 per cent. This is considerably higher than the numbers falling below the absolute one dollar a day poverty line.

As noted earlier in this chapter, the relative poverty line is also a measure of inequality. Although few people in the Latin American countries fall below the absolute poverty level, income distribution is highly skewed. For example, in Brazil the highest income earners (top 10 per cent) receive about 47 per cent of total income. In Mexico, the top one-tenth of income earners receive 42 per cent of income, while in Colombia and Guatemala the top 10 per cent earn 46 per cent of total income. Similar income inequalities are to be found in other regions. In South Africa, the top one-tenth receive about 45 per cent of total income, while in Nigeria the figure is 41 per cent. Income inequalities are considerably lower in the industrial nations. In Denmark, the top 10 per cent earn just 20 per cent of total income, while in Germany the figure is 23 per cent. Income inequality is somewhat higher in Britain and the United States where the top one-tenth earns 27 per cent and 30 per cent respectively of total income. But even here, income inequality is considerably lower than in the Latin American countries mentioned earlier (World Bank, 2001).

Studies of income inequality at the global level have produced some particularly striking conclusions. For example, Mayor and Binde (2001) report that the poorest 20 per cent of the world's population (or more than a billion people), earn approximately 1 per cent of the world's income. To make matters worse, this 'derisory amount', as they call it, is lower than it was in 1960 when the poorest 20 per cent earned 2.3 per cent of the world's income. On the other hand, the richest 20 per cent, who live mostly in the North, now earn about 82 per cent of the world's income. This is a significant increase since 1960 when the comparable figure was only 30 per cent. The concentration of income and wealth is also revealed by the significant increase in the number of very wealthy individuals. As Mayor and Binde (2001) report, the number of billionaires has increased from about 150 in the late 1980s to about 450 by the mid-1990s. They also note that the three wealthiest people in the world today have a joint income that exceeds the combined GDP of the world's 48 poorest countries.

Table 2.3 **GNP per capita by world region, 1999**

Region	GNP per capita (US$)	Growth in GNP per capita per annum 1998–99 (%)
East Asia and Pacific	1,000	6.0
Eastern Europe and Central Asia	2,150	−0.1
Latin America and Caribean	3,840	−2.4
Middle East and North Africa	2,060	Not known
South Asia	440	4.2
Sub-Saharan Africa	500	−0.3
Global South	1,240	1.4
Global North	25,730	2.1
World	4,890	1.3

Source: World Bank (2001).

Inequality among countries and groups of countries within the different world regions is also very marked. Although it was noted earlier that GNP per capita is a crude measure of social well-being, it provides some indication of the differences in standards of living of people in different parts of the world. The GNP per capita data summarized in Table 2.3 show that there are huge regional disparities. While the high-income industrial nations reported a GNP per capita income of about $25,000 in 1999, the comparable figure for the developing countries of the South was only $1,240. However, within the industrial nations of the North, per capita incomes were not uniform but diverged from a high of $38,000 in Switzerland to a low of $10,600 in Portugal. Significant differences are also to be found among the regions of the South. The Latin American and Caribbean region reported the highest per capita income of $3,840 followed by Eastern Europe and the Middle East that had per capita incomes of $2,150 and $2,060 respectively. Yet per capita incomes in South Asia and sub-Saharan Africa were only $440 and $500 respectively. Within these two regions, per capita incomes were generally very low in the sub-Saharan African countries ranging from $3,240 in Botswana and $3,160 in South Africa to as little as $100 in Ethiopia, $120 in Burundi and $190 in Malawi. Several South Asian countries including Bangladesh, Cambodia, Laos, Nepal and Vietnam had per capita incomes of less than $500 in 1999.

Poverty and the quality of life

These GNP data translate into real differences in the quality of life and in the experience of well-being among people in different parts of the world. As Demery and Walton (2000) point out, it is not difficult to grasp the implications of the fact that an engineer in Frankfurt earns 56 times as much as a woman worker in a textile factory in Kenya and that she, in turn, earns many times more than the country's street vendors and small farmers. While the textile worker's income is far below that of the European engineer, she receives a steady monetary wage and can meet her basic needs and enhance the welfare of her family. Even on her low wage, she is able to enjoy certain comforts and can use her income to secure educational opportunities for her children. On the other hand, for most informal sector and agricultural workers, poverty is a grinding, daily reality that transcends a lack of income. The problem is exacerbated by the risk of losing income. If the textile worker loses her job or if her factory closes she faces destitution. The street vendor and farmer are equally vulnerable. However, the European engineer is supported by a social service safety net of unemployment, sickness and disability insurance programmes. Furthermore, because of his high educational qualifications, he may well find alternative employment if his firm ceases to operate. He has more choices, and his 'functioning', as Sen calls it, is safeguarded.

These real life examples transcend faceless statistical reports on the incidence of poverty and link them to actual human experiences. By revealing the way poverty is linked to ill-health, illiteracy, infant and child mortality and low educational attainment, social indicators also serve this function. They dramatically illustrate the way poverty is associated with social deprivation, disadvantage and suffering and how it affects hundreds of millions of people in the world today. The United Nations Development Programme (2001: 9) reports that 2.4 billion people lack basic sanitation, nearly a billion drink unsafe, polluted and infected water, 850 million are illiterate, 325 million children do not attend school and about 11 million infants a year die from preventable diseases.

While these social indicators reveal the extent of the problem, they are all the more poignant when compared with the social indicators of affluence. For example, World Bank (2001) social indicators reveal that life expectancy at birth is 75 years for men and 81 years for women in the world's high-income countries, but that it is only 59 years for men and 61 years for women in the low-income countries. While the adult literacy rate in low-income countries is only 40 per cent, it is about 99 per cent in the industrialized nations. In low-income countries, more than 100 children per 1,000 die within the first 5 years of life, while in the high-income countries the figure is about 6 per 1,000. As these indicators reveal, the quality of life is closely related to the harsh inequalities that pervade the global community.

The social indicators listed in Table 2.4 show that social conditions in South Asia and sub-Saharan Africa compare very unfavourably with the other world regions. Life expectancy in sub-Saharan Africa is only 51 years while the child mortality rate is about 151 per 1,000 per annum. In South Asia, the rate is 89 per 1,000, which is lower than that in Africa but considerably higher than in other regions. Furthermore, life expectancy in South Asia at 63 years is significantly higher than in Africa. Female literacy is lowest in South Asia where only 41 per cent of adult women can read and write. In Africa, in the Middle East and North Africa just over one-half of adult women can read and write.

Within most countries, the worst health, educational and nutritional standards are concentrated in the poorest communities. Although communicable diseases have the potential to infect everyone, they are disproportionately

Table 2.4 Key social indicators

Region	Life expectancy (years)	Female literacy (% of women)	Child malnourishment (per 1,000 deaths)	Child mortality (% under five)
East Asia and Pacific	69	78	43	22
Eastern Europe and Central Asia	69	95	26	8
Latin America and Caribbean	70	77	38	8
Middle East and North Africa	67	52	55	15
South Asia	63	41	89	51
Sub-Saharan Africa	51	51	151	33
Global South	65	67	79	29

Source: World Bank (2001).

concentrated among the poor. The World Bank (2001) reports that in India, tuberculosis is far more prevalent among the poorest families. Similarly, the child mortality rate in Brazil is three times higher among poor families than among higher-income families. Similar disparities exist for literacy and educational attainments in many countries. Disparities in income inequality between men and women and between people of different ethnic and religious groups also persist on a huge scale not only in the developing countries of the South but in the industrial nations as well where women still earn less than men even when employed in similar occupations. Even in egalitarian Sweden, men in industrial employment earned approximately 16 per cent more than women in the 1990s.

In all regions of the South, the most disadvantaged people are concentrated in rural areas. In some countries, disparities in social indicators and in the poverty rate between rural and urban areas are striking, and in some places they are exacerbated by rapid economic growth in the cities. For example, the World Bank (2001) reports that China's recent impressive rates of economic growth have been concentrated in urban areas with the result that urban–rural income inequalities have increased. As in many other countries, poverty rates are highest in the most remote regions. In China, the most mountainous provinces have the highest poverty rates and the worst social indicators. This is equally true of other countries. In Peru, two-thirds of the poorest households live in the mountain regions, while in Thailand the poverty rate in the country's rural North-East region was twice as high as the national average (World Bank, 2001). A different picture emerges in many industrial countries where poverty is often higher in urban than rural areas. For example, the United Nations (2001) reports that the poverty rate in Washington DC is about 23 per cent while in rural New Hampshire it is only 8 per cent.

Women, children and minorities are over-represented among the poor and socially disadvantaged. The literacy rate among women is generally lower than among men, and primary school enrolment rates among girls are frequently but not always lower than for boys. In some countries, including low-income ones such as Madagascar, Zambia and the Philippines, gender differences in school enrolment are negligible, while in others, such as Benin, Nepal and Pakistan, the gap in enrolment rates between boys and girls is about 20 per cent (World Bank, 2001). In India, for example, members of the lower castes and the indigenous tribal people are the most disadvantaged, having lower literacy and school attendance rates and poorer health status than the rest of the population. Indigenous people in Latin America face similar disadvantages. In Guatemala, for example, indigenous people have an average of 1.8 years of schooling while the average for the rest of the population is about 5 years (World Bank, 2001).

Poverty, deprivation and social progress

These indicators reveal that poverty and social deprivation remain widespread and that the situation for many hundreds of millions of people in the world today is desperate. However, despite these gloomy realities, there is ground for optimism. In an attempt to garner support for global poverty eradication, the international development organizations have redoubled their efforts to enhance awareness of the problem. Although some governments in the North (and particularly the current administration in the United States) remain sceptical, poverty eradication targets have for the first time been adopted by the international organizations. At the Millennium Summit in September 2000, the United Nations committed member-states, as its first Millennium Development Goal (MDG), to halving the number of people living on less than one dollar per day by 2015.

In addition, there is evidence to show that significant social progress has been made, particularly in some regions of the world. For example, the World Bank (2001) reports that the incidence of absolute poverty in the world, as measured in actual numbers, declined by about 80 million people between 1990 and 1998. Although this is not a large decrease in absolute numbers (from 1.27 billion to 1.19 billion), the proportion of the world's population living below the one dollar a day poverty line has fallen from 29 per cent to 24 per cent. These trends are summarized in Table 2.5. The fact that the absolute numbers of people living in poverty remains high is due primarily to continued population growth. The World Bank also points out that the current rate of decline is not sufficiently rapid to meet the global poverty reduction targets set by the international organizations.

Nevertheless, the fact that the absolute number as well as the proportion of the world's population living in absolute poverty has fallen since 1990 is encouraging. Table 2.5 shows that there were regional gains as well. The proportion of the population in absolute poverty in East Asia and the Pacific declined significantly from about 28 per cent to 15 per cent during the 1990s. Rising incomes in China contributed disproportionately to the overall decline in absolute poverty in the region and, indeed, in the world as whole. Smaller declines were recorded in Latin America and the Caribbean, the Middle East

Table 2.5   Change in the incidence of absolute poverty by world region, 1990 and 1998

Region	Numbers in poverty (millions)		Proportion of population in poverty (%)	
	1990	1998	1990	1998
East Asia and Pacific	452.4	278.3	27.6	15.3
Eastern Europe and Central Asia	7.1	24.0	1.6	5.1
Latin America and Caribbean	73.8	78.2	16.8	15.6
Middle East and North Africa	5.7	5.5	2.4	1.9
South Asia	495.1	522.0	44.0	40.0
Sub-Saharan Africa	242.3	290.9	47.7	46.3
Global South	1,276.4	1,198.9	29.0	24.0

Source: World Bank (2001).

and in sub-Saharan Africa. In South Asia, the proportion of the population in poverty fell from 44 per cent to 40 per cent during this time. Yet the proportion of people in absolute poverty in Eastern Europe and Central Asia increased significantly during this period. There were more than three times as many poor people in this region in 1998 as in 1990. The problem is also acute in sub-Saharan Africa where the proportion of the population in poverty declined by only 1.4 per cent during this time. It should also be noted that, despite a decline in the proportion of the population living in poverty, the absolute numbers of poor people actually increased by almost 50 million.

When social indicators are taken into account, the trend is also mixed but there are some encouraging signs. For example, the United Nations Development Programme (2001) reports that many more people today live a longer and healthier life, are better nourished and better educated than ever. There has been progress towards greater gender equality and environmental sustainability. Improvements in human rights and democratic participation have also been recorded. The organization notes that children born at the turn of the twenty-first century can now expect to live to the age of 68 years – eight years longer than those who were born in 1970. The global infant mortality rate has fallen from about 97 per 1,000 in 1970 to about 52 per 1,000 today. The number of undernourished people has declined from over 900 million to about 820 million during the same time period. The literacy rate among adults rose from 47 per cent in 1970 to 73 per cent in 1999, and the number of rural households which now have access to safe drinking water has increased by about 500 per cent since 1970.

The World Bank (2001) reports that progress has been made even in the low-income developing countries. For example, average infant mortality rates have declined from around 97 per 1,000 in 1980 to 68 per 1,000 in 1998 in these countries. In the middle-income developing countries, average infant mortality declined from 60 per 1,000 to 31 per 1,000 during the same time period. Primary school enrolment rates in the low-income developing countries also improved from 66 per cent to 76 per cent during this time. In the middle-income developing countries, the primary school enrolment rate rose from 86 per cent to 97 per cent. Yet, as pointed out in Chapter 5, this achievement should not be allowed to obscure the fact that the quality of education leaves much to be desired, a fact which is reflected in continuing high rates of primary school non-completion.

As the United Nations Development Programme (2000) put it, these gains are 'impressive' and they suggest that it is possible to bring about real improvements in standards of living and even to eradicate poverty. On the other hand, there is little room for complacency. The organization notes that in certain regards, conditions have worsened. AIDS is claiming many more lives today than before; conflicts within and between nations have produced many more refugees and internally displaced people; criminal activity associated with the drug trade and prostitution has increased and in some parts of the world, democratic institutions have been undermined. In addition, as was noted earlier in this chapter, income and wealth inequality has increased significantly. The unevenness of social progress is particularly marked in some regions of the world. The absolute poverty rate in Eastern Europe and Central Asia has risen significantly largely because of economic and social disruption following the collapse of the Soviet Union which, as the UNDP (2000: 13) put it, 'extracted a heavy toll on human lives with adverse effects on income, school enrolment and life expectancy, particularly of males'. The rise in the number of people in absolute poverty in sub-Saharan Africa has been accompanied by endemic wars and internal conflicts that have caused enormous suffering. The rapid spread of AIDS in the region has also exacerbated adverse social conditions. In 1999, more than 5 million people in the region were infected with HIV, and more than 20 sub-Saharan African countries recorded declines in life expectancy because of AIDS. About 13 million African children were AIDS orphans (United Nations Development Programme, 2000). In a similar vein, Midgley (1995) argues that the development process has been highly distorted, creating conditions of prosperity for some but continued deprivation for many.

Because of marked differences in social progress among the world's regions and countries, some development writers are extremely pessimistic when interpreting trends over the last four decades and in projecting future developments. For example, Sachs (1992: 1) notes that, 'The idea of development stands like a ruin ... delusion and disappointment, failures and crime have been the steady companion of development'. Similarly, anti- or post-development writers contend that development has failed to address the pressing problems facing the world's poor countries (Escobar, 1995; Rahnema, 1997). Although they present a more balanced account, Kothari and Minogue (2002) conclude that post-war development strategies have failed to reach the goal of improving the standards of living of people in most parts of the world. They argue that, instead, these strategies have produced unevenness and perpetuated the continued coexistence of development and deprivation.

Even optimists will find it hard to disagree with Kothari and Minogue's conclusion about the unevenness of the development experience and the continued coexistence of poverty and prosperity. Certainly, the optimism that characterized development thinking in the middle decades of the twentieth century, when many previously colonized peoples secured independence from European imperial rule, has dissipated. Also, many past projections of development trends have not been realized. For example, in 1978, the World Bank incorrectly estimated that the incidence of global poverty in the year 2000 would fall to about 600 million people. In its widely discussed 1990 *World Development Report* that dealt with poverty, the World Bank also projected poverty declines that were not achieved (United Nations, 2001). Similarly, the World Bank's data concerning improvements in infant mortality and school enrolments in low-income developing countries, which were reported earlier, need to be considered with reference to the fact that these trends reveal average rates for these countries. While average infant mortality rates for the low-income countries as a whole may have declined to 68 per 1,000, many of these countries still have infant mortality rates well in excess of 100 per 1,000.

Strategies for poverty eradication

The goal of eradicating poverty was discussed and articulated at the United Nations World Summit in 1995. Previously, development writers talked about poverty 'alleviation' or poverty 'reduction'. Now, by adopting the *Copenhagen Declaration*, the world's governments declared a commitment to eradicate poverty, and to achieve other social goals such as full employment, social integration, gender equity and the attainment of universal and equitable access to education and health (United Nations, 1996). The Millennium Development Goals (MDGs), articulated by the United Nations in September 2000, included the halving of absolute poverty by 2015, along with other aims such as universal primary education, greater gender equity, reduced child mortality and improved maternal health, amongst others.

However, neither the 1995 nor the 2000 Summit answered the critical question of *which* strategies are the most effective for eradicating poverty. While it may be possible to agree on poverty reduction targets, it is far more difficult to agree on the policies and programmes that are needed to achieve these targets. This is a very controversial topic not only among social scientists but also among politicians, aid officials, community workers, economists and development activists. As Cox and Healy (2000) revealed, there are major differences of opinion on how poverty can be reduced even among the development assistance agencies of the governments of the industrial nations. Similar differences are to be found among the major multilateral donor bodies. The United Nations agencies favour greater government intervention and social provisions than the International Monetary Fund and the World Bank, which have consistently argued that rapid economic growth through the creation of a free market economy is needed.

The complexity of the issue is compounded when specific anti-poverty interventions are linked to wider strategies for development. In the development context, poverty and development are closely associated. Ultimately, development is about raising standards of living, enhancing the quality of life of all and improving social conditions. Therefore, to address the problem, specific anti-poverty interventions must be related to the overarching development strategies that are so passionately debated in the field. In turn, these development strategies and their prescriptions for poverty eradication must be considered within the wider context of values and ideologies.

While many would agree that employment-generating projects, village health clinics, food-for-work programmes, technical assistance to farmers, the promotion of small-scale informal-sector enterprises, micro-credit, cooperative savings accounts and a host of other programmatic interventions can help to reduce poverty, there are sharp disagreements about how these interventions relate to wider development initiatives involving governments, private enterprise and local responsibility. For example, should micro-credit be managed by governments or private banks or local village self-help cooperatives? How do micro-credit schemes fit in with other anti-poverty programmes, and how do they give expression to wider goals such as promoting individual responsibility and self-reliance or, on the other hand, cooperation and equality? Once these wider questions are asked, strong differences of opinion emerge and these, in turn, reflect very different ideological preferences about how poverty and social need can best be addressed and indeed about how the goals of development can be realized.

The remainder of this chapter will discuss the major strategies that have been proposed for promoting development and achieving significant improvements in the incomes and livelihoods of the world's poor. Although they are rooted in what are essentially Western values and ideological beliefs, they have general relevance to current debates on poverty and social welfare in many different countries. However, as will be shown, some development writers reject the relevance of these values and beliefs to non-Western societies.

Modernization, capitalism and economic growth

In the years following World War II, when many colonized territories in the South secured independence from European imperial rule, many social scientists believed that poverty could be eradicated by the adoption of a development strategy that modernizes the economy (as well as social and political institutions) and generates rapid economic growth through industrialization and capitalist development. These social scientists became known as the modernization theorists and they exerted a strong influence on development thinking at the time. While some emphasized the importance of free markets in promoting growth, others of a Keynesian persuasion took the view that governments had an important role to play in directing or 'guiding' the modernization process.

Modernization theorists believe that poverty is an original condition which has characterized human societies since ancient times. Although there were periods of rapid economic growth when people living in the urban civilizations enjoyed comparatively high standards of living, poverty has been pervasive for most of human history. This situation began to change when the nations of Western Europe experienced rapid economic growth as a result of industrialization and were able to raise incomes and standards of living for the vast majority of their populations. The modernization theorists argued that rapid economic growth could achieve the same results in the newly independent developing countries that were dominated by subsistence agriculture and informal sector economic activities. Many pointed out that these countries had a dual economy comprised of a large, impoverished agrarian sector and a small but vibrant modern, urban sector located in the colonial capitals (Boeke, 1953; Nurkse, 1953; Lewis, 1955; Higgins, 1956). The task for policy-makers was to expand the modern sector so that it would draw labour out of the subsistence into the modern sector.

This, they suggested, could be achieved through massive investments in industrial enterprises. Industrialization, they argued, creates employment on a large scale, transferring labour out of the impoverished subsistence and informal economy into the modern, urban industrial sector. As people enter wage employment, incomes and standards of living rise, resulting eventually in the eradication of poverty. Drawing on the experience of the European nations that had undergone industrial development in the eighteenth and nineteenth centuries, they argued that capital to fund industrial development should be mobilized either through domestic sources, foreign investment or international aid.

These ideas were articulated by numerous development economists at the time. Rosenstein-Rodan's (1943) research into economic growth in Southern Europe suggested that governments needed to adopt a 'big push' policy of industrialization which required that priority be given to mobilizing funds for industrial investments. Nurkse (1953) agreed that it was only through industrial development that the vicious cycle of poverty could be broken but argued that governments also needed to promote investments in infrastructure and complementary industries to ensure that balanced growth took place. A major report for the United Nations (1951), prepared under the chairmanship of Arthur Lewis, urged governments to give high priority to securing capital for industrial development, and in his widely cited book Rostow (1960) formulated a precise set of policy prescriptions by which capital formation would create the conditions for growth, and result subsequently in economic 'take off' and sustained industrial development. Most favoured the deferral of consumption. Governments should, as far as possible, limit spending, and particularly social spending, and promote capital formation instead. Most also suggested the creation of domestic industries which would produce goods to replace imports from the industrial countries. Import substitution became an important element of the modernization approach.

Sociologists and other social scientists argued that modernization also involves non-economic processes and that, to properly understand poverty and deprivation in the developing countries, attention should be paid to the non-economic factors that contribute to economic 'backwardness'. They drew attention to the way traditional cultural beliefs and practices maintain poverty and economic underdevelopment, and how they impede economic modernization. For example, Goode (1963) argued that the extended family in the developing world imposed cultural obligations on its members that were inimical to economic development. These obligations prevented young people from pursuing their own ambitions, from moving to places where jobs were being created and from saving. His writings implied that it was desirable that the extended family be replaced by a Western, nuclear family formation. Hagen (1962) and McClelland (1964) believed that traditional attitudes and beliefs were responsible for poverty and economic stagnation. The traditional culture needed to be replaced with modern values that rewarded competition, achievement motivation and ambition. Lerner (1958) took the view that the authoritarian political structures that characterized the developing countries needed to be replaced with modern, liberal democratic institutions if development was to take place. Hoselitz (1960) agreed, arguing that traditional forms of social stratification would impede rapid economic growth.

By linking social and cultural factors with economic explanations of the causes of underdevelopment, the modernization theorists offered an account that stressed the role of subsistence production, primitive technology, traditional culture and an apathetic personal disposition in the etiology of poverty. Mass poverty, they believed, is a function of an archaic and traditional socio-economic system that needs to be replaced with a dynamic, industrial economy. Together with the emergence of modern attitudes, beliefs and institutions, industrialization would promote rapid growth and bring about prosperity for all.

As was noted earlier, some modernization theorists argued that the task of promoting industrialization and rapid economic growth could be best achieved if a capitalist, free market style of development was adopted. However, others were persuaded that government direction of the economy was needed. At the time, many governments adopted centralized economic planning which set economic growth targets and produced five-year development plans (Waterston, 1965). Although planning was viewed with scepticism by modernization theorists and many Western development experts, they did not reject the need for government policies and programmes that would promote rapid economic growth. It was in this context that State intervention gradually increased and, by the 1960s and 1970s, began to dominate development policy in the South.

The modernization theorists seemed to be unaware of the extent to which they were incorporating a highly biased Western approach into their analyses, and it was not surprising that they were heavily criticized for being culturally insensitive and even imperialistic (Frank, 1971). Although many of the nationalist leaders of the developing countries favoured the high-growth economic prescriptions of modernization theory, its socio-cultural implications were given little attention and, in any case, were hardly amenable to policy interventions. Even if they wanted to, it was hardly possible for political leaders to legislate against the extended family or other highly valued cultural institutions. Similarly, few were attracted by the tenets of Western liberal democratic thinking. In addition, few countries successfully adopted industrialization strategies and significantly reduced the incidence of poverty by expanding the modern, wage employment sector. With the exception of the East Asian nations that adopted export-led rather than import-substitution industrialization policies, the modernization approach could claim few successes. For these and other reasons, its influence gradually waned and, by the 1960s, a more vigorous statist approach that advocated extensive government involvement in poverty eradication became popular.

Planning, welfare and the State

The idea that poverty eradication and development could best be achieved through the active engagement of governments in economic planning and in the provision of social services and development programmes was actively promoted by a group of social scientists and policy-makers who are sometimes described as the 'developmentalists'. They agreed with the modernization theorists about the need for rapid economic growth and industrialization, but urged governments to transcend their economic development agendas by allocating resources for social programmes. When accompanied by economic growth, social welfare programmes would have a major impact on the poverty problem. While the modernization thinkers urged governments to limit social expenditures in order to mobilize resources for industrial investment, the developmentalists believe that economic planning combined with social expenditures is highly desirable.

Like modernization theorists, the developmentalists contend that poverty is an endemic condition associated with subsistence agriculture and informal sector activities that should be addressed through industrialization and economic growth. However, they argue that economic growth engendered by industrialization does not automatically result in prosperity for all. In fact, economic development has disproportionately benefited those in the modern sector, and the poor have often been left behind. The ubiquity of 'uneven' or 'distorted' development as they called it, must be addressed through a comprehensive range of policies and programmes that promote economic growth and, at the same time, target the poor and raise their incomes.

Developmentalist ideas appealed to many of the independence leaders who had lived and studied in Europe and who were inspired by social democratic and other forms of interventionist thinking. The United Nations also played a key role in promoting these ideas. The organization called on its member-states to adopt social policies that would focus on the problem of mass poverty in the South and improve social conditions. These issues were extensively debated at various meetings of the Economic and Social Council. In addition, numerous expert groups were appointed to assist in the formulation of social policies of this kind. One of the most important addressed the need for redirecting economic planning so that it focused more explicitly on social goals. With the assistance of economists such as Myrdal, Singer and Higgins, the United Nations formulated what became known as the unified socio-economic planning approach that paid equal attention to economic growth and social welfare (United Nations, 1971).

At about this time, several development economists began to criticize the excessive emphasis that had been placed on industrialization and economic growth in development thinking. In a famous paper, Seers (1972) challenged the view that economic growth was synonymous with development. He pointed out that a country that had significantly increased its rate of economic growth but had failed to reduce the incidence of poverty or to improve the quality of life for ordinary people could not claim to have experienced development. Myrdal (1968) had previously made the same point in his voluminous study of Asian development which, he contended, had recorded positive rates of economic growth but had failed to significantly reduce poverty. Myrdal explicitly urged the adoption of redistributive policies that would address the underlying problem of inequality. Inequality, he argued, was closely associated with poverty.

In the 1970s, international efforts to promote greater government engagement with the problems of poverty, social deprivation and inequality increased. In addition to the United Nations, other international agencies such as the World Health Organization, the United Nations Children's Fund (UNICEF), and the International Labour Organization, urged the adoption of specific health, housing, educational, sanitary, rural development, nutritional and other social policies. Together with many developing-country governments, the World Health Organization embarked on campaigns to eradicate communicable diseases such as smallpox and polio and it promoted the incorporation of health-sector policy-making into national development planning. In the late 1960s, the International Labour Organization sponsored major studies into the problem of unemployment that, it concluded, was closely linked to poverty. Industrial development policies would not, its experts argued, create wage employment on a sufficiently large scale to reduce the incidence of mass poverty. For this reason, policies that target the poor and effectively reduce social deprivation were urgently needed. These ideas resulted in the adoption of the Basic Needs approach to development at the 1976 World Employment Conference (International Labour Office, 1976). Basic needs placed high priority on policies and programmes that would ensure that the poorest people of the developing countries had access to clean drinking water, nutrition, adequate shelter, heath care, education and security. Rather than waiting for economic growth to solve the problems of poverty and social deprivation, Basic Needs advocates urged governments to seek to address these problems immediately (Streeten and Burki, 1978; Streeten et al., 1981; Stewart, 1985).

UNICEF adopted a similar approach. Instead of stressing the need for conventional child welfare services provided by professional social workers, the organization began to promote community-based interventions that introduced preschool education, nutrition, women's programmes, micro-enterprise and other poverty eradication interventions at the local level (Midgley et al., 1986). Poverty alleviation was also given high priority by the World Bank during the presidency of Robert McNamara. His widely reported speech to the

World Bank's governors in Nairobi in 1972 proposed that the Bank's lending policies should be refocused to assist governments to address the needs of the poorest 40 per cent of the population of developing countries. Following this speech, the Bank produced numerous influential policy papers outlining how this goal might be achieved.

The emphasis on poverty reduction through direct government intervention and the provision of social services also raised the issue of inequality. Many developmentalists stressed the need to address the serious inequalities that characterized the developing countries and they proposed the adoption of redistribution and other reforms to create more egalitarian societies. As noted previously, Myrdal (1968) had argued that poverty in Asia was closely tied to inequality. If the incidence of poverty is to be reduced, policies that address the problem of inequality would be needed. This view was countered by the argument that redistributive policies will impede investment, entrepreneurship and the other requirements for rapid economic growth (Bauer, 1976; Lal, 1983). If governments adopt policies that deter investors and impose punitive taxes on entrepreneurs, growth would be impeded.

However, a major study by a group of economists led by Hollis Chenery of the World Bank (Chenery et al., 1974) refuted this point of view, claiming instead that redistributive policies are not antithetical to economic growth but that they would, in fact, promote growth. These policies remove obstacles to the participation of the poor in economic development, and increase their consumption and thus their demand for goods and services. For example, Griffin (1976) showed that land concentration has a negative effect on agricultural production because it dampens the incentives of sharecroppers to raise production, and that land redistribution to those who work it creates production incentives.

Exploitation, oppression and radical change

During the post-World War II years, when the Cold War between the Soviet Union and the United States and its allies gathered momentum, the leaders of the previously colonized societies became increasingly critical of the two superpowers. Nationalism and populism were dominant ideological themes in the South at the time, and the superpowers were frequently accused of trying to usurp the hard-won sovereignty of the independence movements. The leaders of many developing countries sought to adopt a non-aligned position, and the idea that they comprised a 'third force' in global politics was popular. It was at this time that the neologism 'Third World' emerged. Although the term is now avoided, it was originally intended to assert the autonomy and self-determination of the newly independent nations and to connote their collective efforts to counteract the powerful geo-political influence of the two superpowers.

It was in this context that development was increasingly defined as a neo-colonialist project designed to promote the interest of the Western industrial nations. Many non-aligned leaders, including Mao, Nasser, Nehru, Nkrumah, Nyerere, Sukarno and Tito sought to promote an indigenous and autarkic form of development which would end the economic dependency of their nations on Western imports and expertise and promote self-reliance. While many nationalist leaders favoured import substitution policies that would promote domestic industrialization, some such as Mao and Nyerere gave priority to the promotion of self-reliant agriculture and rural development.

As was noted earlier in this chapter, many of the nationalist independence leaders were inspired by the democratic socialist and welfare interventionism that were then so prominent in Europe and many were in favour of activist government policies that would address the problem of poverty. However, many were also inspired by Marxism. Although few were avowed communists, the rhetoric of Marxism provided a basis for analysing the causes of poverty and for criticizing superpower hegemony. It was also used with considerable effect in the late 1960s and 1970s by a group of scholars known as the international structuralists or dependency theorists (Frank, 1967, 1969; Sunkel, 1969; Furtado, 1970; Cardoso, 1972; Rodney, 1972; Amin, 1974). Originating in Latin America, the '*dependentistas*' argued that poverty was closely related to international capitalist exploitation. They were avid critics of modernization theory, which they condemned as little more than a cloak for Western neo-imperialism. It also legitimated the continued economic exploitation and political manipulation of the previously colonized nations.

For the dependency theorists, poverty is not an original condition but a direct consequence of European imperialism and colonialism. Writers such as Frank (1967, 1969) and Rodney (1972) argued that the developing nations had previously been wealthy and prosperous. Before European conquest, many were technologically advanced and many had sizeable urban capitals with sophisticated cultures. However, because of internal conflicts and the military superiority of the Europeans, these nations were readily subjugated. European imperialists destroyed their political and administrative systems, oppressed their peoples, demeaned their cultures and rapaciously expropriated their assets. With the enslavement of their people, poverty became widespread. The dependency writers also contended that poverty is not a static condition but the result of an ongoing, dynamic process by which the metropolitan powers continue to exploit and impoverish the nations and peoples of the South. A complex network of metropolitan–satellite relationships continues to transfer surplus from the poorest peasants and urban informal-sector worker through to landlords, merchants and factory owners to the elites of the Western capitalist nations. So-called 'development' will not eradicate but, in fact, increase poverty.

To end mass poverty in the South, the process of exploitation must be ended. Frank (1969) argued that this could only be achieved through a world revolution to end capitalist exploitation and oppression. The first step requires domestic revolutions and the overthrow of capitalism in the dependent nations. Other dependency writers disagreed with Frank's idea that revolutions were a requirement for poverty eradication and suggested instead that the developing countries should limit or terminate their relationships with the industrial nations. They believed that it is possible to 'de-link' the developing countries from the global economic system and to attain economic independence through political struggle and 'Third World' solidarity. For example, Mandel (1976) was quite adamant that poverty and exploitation can only be ended through a radical break with international capitalism.

However, some dependency writers questioned the desirability as well as the possibility of radically de-linking the periphery from the metropole. Cardoso and Faletto (1979) disagreed with Frank's characterization of underdevelopment as an ongoing process of impoverishment claiming instead that while the developing nations had indeed been exploited, they had also benefited from the development process. Despite their disadvantageous links with the centres of capitalism, they had in fact, experienced industrialization, economic growth and improvements in standards of living. It was more appropriate to talk about 'dependent development' than underdevelopment. Wallerstein (1980) agreed, pointing out that the developing nations were part of a global capitalist economic system that is extremely volatile and which, therefore, offers new opportunities for these nations to improve their position in the global economy. In a prescient commentary, he suggested that they can use their comparative advantage to attract international investments and in this way, promote industrialization, create wage employment and raise the incomes of their peoples.

These ideas were compatible with policy thinking in international development circles. In addition to adopting import substitution policies, the nationalist leaders urged that aid programmes be more generous, and that lending be more cognizant of the unique needs of the developing countries. They asked for improved terms of trade for poor nations and greater international social and economic justice. These ideas laid the foundation for subsequent efforts to promote a more just and equitable international order. Various international efforts ranging from the Dag Hammarskjold Foundation's (1975) manifesto and the Brandt Commission (Brandt, 1980) to popular campaigns against the International Monetary Fund and the World Trade Organization exemplify these activities. They have increasingly involved large-scale street protests in the industrial nations in which activists supported by students, trade unions and middle-class sympathizers, have drawn widespread attention to the injustices of the capitalist global economy.

The idea that poverty can only be eradicated through an analysis of the existing economic system and by radical change has been accompanied in development circles by other forms of critical thinking. One very significant contribution has come from feminists, who have succeeded in placing gender exploitation and oppression at the forefront of development discourse. Feminist scholars have argued that conventional development approaches are designed to serve the interests of men, and have reinforced the patriarchal structures that exploit and oppress women. What Shiva (1989) describes as 'maldevelopment' is a direct result of these development strategies. To address this problem, as well as the wider problem of poverty, which affects women disproportionately, a radical change in existing development thinking is needed. This involves more than a welfarist approach designed to provide services to women, or even a gender equity approach that seeks to enhance the status of women. It requires the adoption of an empowerment approach that is determined by women themselves and is, therefore, truly liberating (Moser, 1989).

More recently, critical approaches have been extensively informed by post-modernist ideas. Post-modernist scholars regard development as an integral part of the failed project of Enlightenment thought (Midgley, 1999). In their view, development comprises a 'grand narrative' of the Enlightenment that seeks to impose its world-view on peoples of diverse cultures, interests and commitments (Lyotard, 1984; Bauman, 1992). Like other grand narratives, development is imposing and oppressive, stultifying the aspirations of communities, groups and individuals whose perspectives and beliefs are different from those of Western rationalists and the optimistic advocates of progress. For the anti- or post-development school, which has drawn extensively on post-modernist thinking, the very idea of progress is anathema (Escobar, 1995; Rahnema and Bawtree, 1997; Munck and O'Hearne, 1999). Anti-development thinkers believe that the problem of poverty must be solved by the poor of the South themselves within the context of their own struggles for self-determination and liberation.

Communities, participation and local development

Critical approaches are appealing and they obviously inform the efforts of activists who seek to remedy the political and social causes of poverty, but they are not always readily translated into policy terms. This is not to deny the role of critical thinking in supporting human rights campaigns or efforts to reform the international economic system. In addition, they have made a significant contribution to community-based poverty eradication and development strategies. The idea that the poverty problem can be solved by mobilizing local people and involving them in various development projects which will raise standards of living and improve the quality of their lives, has become exceedingly popular in development circles. This approach offers an appealing alternative to both modernization and developmentalist poverty eradication strategies.

Although often idealized, the local community has long been regarded as a vital resource for development effort. In the early decades of the twentieth century, colonial development projects were often focused on local communities. In Africa, village people were mobilized to build feeder roads, water supply systems, community centres, clinics and schools (Brokensha and Hodge, 1969) and, in India, the utopian communities established by Ghandi and Tagore laid the foundations for a nationwide community development programme (Bhattacharyya, 1970). As Midgley (1995) reported, the notions of community development and social development evolved out of these formative efforts.

Community development is based on the idea that local people, supported by external resources, can implement programmes that significantly reduce the extent of poverty and social deprivation. In the 1950s, these programmes were usually administered by governments and involved para-professional community workers who assisted local village leaders to identify need, obtain external funds and materials and then involve local people in community projects. These projects focused on infrastructure development as well as cooperative productive activities such as vegetable gardening, the manufacture of local crafts and poultry raising. Often credit associations were established. Although community development was primarily associated with rural life and traditional agrarian institutions, it was, in time, extended to urban communities as well. Originally, urban squatter and slum communities were viewed in negative terms, but they were subsequently regarded as centres of cooperation and mutual support, and of developmental potential.

Community development was compatible with the populism of the nationalist independence movements and with the mutual aid traditions of indigenous cultures in the developing world. Many governments claimed that community development exemplified participatory ideals and gave expression to traditional democratic decision-making. It built on local associational institutions and permitted ordinary people to decide the nature and course of development for themselves. It seemed appropriate, therefore, that community development programmes were usually managed by government ministries or departments and they were largely funded by national governments (Brokensha and Hodge, 1969; Dore and Mars, 1981; Campfens, 1997). Community self-determination and national development were believed to be compatible ideals.

Critics were less enthusiastic about government responsibility for community development. They claimed that these programmes were bureaucratic, inefficient, wasteful, poorly funded and often corrupt (Mayo, 1975; Marsden and Oakley, 1982). Although they relied on the participation of local people, particularly to provide labour, community development officials were accused of being insensitive to the wishes of local people and more concerned with implementing the mandates of national planning agencies and regional authorities. Contrary to the claim that community development gave expression to local needs and preferences, critics argued that it actually amounted to little more than attempts to persuade and cajole local people to donate their time and labour to government road, water supply, sanitation and irrigation projects. Often, these projects were poorly conceived and, in many cases, expensive projects were not completed or otherwise so badly constructed that they were of little value.

Critics also claimed that government community development projects were being used for political and electoral purposes. Villages that supported the ruling political party were more likely to receive funds for community development, and in many cases these projects favoured local leaders, landlords and wealthy farmers. The needs of the poorest and most vulnerable groups, particularly women, were often ignored. This is not to deny that genuine efforts were made to engage local people in decision-making and to foster local enthusiasm for community development. But community development was part of a national, centrally directed effort to promote local economic and social development, and funding decisions were usually based on predetermined national goals.

As national resources became increasingly strained, community development programmes were often given low priority and popular support for these programmes declined.

As criticisms of community development programmes intensified in the 1970s, many development scholars came to the conclusion that conventional 'top-down' approaches were largely ineffective in addressing the needs of poor people. These criticisms resonated with international donors and aid officials and gradually more aid resources were allocated to non-profit organizations working with local communities and other groups. In addition, international agencies such as the United Nations Children's Fund (UNICEF) and the World Health Organization (WHO) were persuaded that local non-governmental organizations and local community groups in the developing countries were better able to address the needs of poor people than governments. Together with NGOs, both organizations began to promote what became known as community participation. This new approach stressed the importance of an activist style of intervention that relied less on the provision of services than on the active involvement of the poor in these projects (Midgley et al., 1986). Rural development was equally infused with these ideas (Oakley, 1991; Burkey, 1993).

The new community participation approach was influenced by the writings of the dependency theorists as well as populist radicals such as Saul Alinsky (1946, 1971) whose writings provided practical guidelines for effective social action at the local level. Also relevant is the influence of liberation theology and the writings of Paulo Freire (1972) in Brazil. Freire's theory of popular education stressed the need for awareness-raising ('conscientization') as a technique for raising the political awareness of the poor and oppressed. By engaging the poor and oppressed in a dialogue about power, inequality and oppression, they would appreciate their position in the social structure, and be empowered to engage in radical collective action to remedy their situation and overcome the conditions of poverty in which they lived. Feminist and ecological critiques provided further impetus for these ideas.

In addition to promoting empowerment and self-determination, community-based poverty eradication programmes now place greater emphasis on economic activities to raise the incomes and standards of living of the poor. Many studies have shown that rural community development programmes make a major contribution to agricultural production and that small-scale agriculture supported by public investments and appropriate rural development policies are more efficient than the large-scale agricultural programmes favoured by modernization theorists. Summarizing this literature, Mafeje (2001) argued that a 'trickle-up' strategy of development is a much more effective strategy for poverty eradication than conventional 'trickle-down' strategies based on industrial development and large-scale government intervention. In a similar vein, many have claimed that organized informal sector activities supported by appropriate public interventions can generate income and raise standards of living. Some writers, such as de Soto (1989), contend that the poor are able to engage in these activities without government aid and that government efforts to direct informal sector activities are likely to fail.

Small-scale community development projects also contribute to poverty eradication because they generate human capital through the development of skills, literacy and job experience. They also generate social capital in the form of networks that promote economic engagement. These programmes are compatible with micro-enterprise and micro-credit projects that facilitate the development of small-scale businesses owned and operated by people with low incomes or groups from impoverished communities. The Grameen Bank, established in Bangladesh in 1983 by Mohammed Yunus (Yunus, 1991; Wahid, 1994; Holcombe, 1995) is just one of many micro-finance development initiatives which have attracted widespread international attention. The Grameen Bank approach uses peer lending by which groups of individuals from a community combine efforts to create cooperative enterprises and to guarantee loans.

These community-based strategies are placing increasing emphasis on the role of local enterprise in the eradication of poverty. Although inspired by populist and communitarian ideas, they are today more frequently associated with the creation of local commercial initiatives which encourage greater personal responsibility, risk-taking and individual effort. While much community development effort previously emphasized cooperative activities among communities, the compatibility of local economic development effort with market-based development strategies has become increasingly apparent.

The neo-liberal revival

The ubiquitous emphasis which is placed today on the importance of free markets, entrepreneurship and profit-seeking today is indicative of the dramatic changes which have taken place in development thinking since the 1980s. Neo-liberal proponents of capitalist development argue that poverty will be eradicated if governments create the conditions in which profit-seeking entrepreneurs establish new enterprise, creating mass employment and raising the incomes of millions of people. The neo-liberal approach not only revives nineteenth-century *laissez-faire* economic theories but recapitulates many of the prescriptions of modernization thinking. The major difference is that neo-liberalism requires that the State reduce taxation, curtail public spending, and refrain from economic regulation. Instead, neo-liberals urge governments to actively facilitate market activities and promote the interests of the commercial sector. What is good for business, they argue, is good for everyone and particularly the poor. These ideas now dominate international development thinking. Since the collapse of the Soviet Empire, and the embrace of market 'reforms' by the government of the People's Republic of China, they have become the new international economic orthodoxy.

Various factors contributed to the neo-liberal revival. One factor was widespread disillusionment with development planning and State welfarism. By the late 1960s, development policy had become highly interventionist and, in many parts of the world, governments had adopted directive economic planning and Keynesian policy prescriptions. Many governments also engaged in large-scale social service expansion in an effort to extend education, health, nutrition, housing and other social welfare provisions to their populations. The result was a growing 'State welfarist' approach to development which critics such as Lal (1983) claimed was harming efforts to promote economic growth and eradicate poverty.

Despite the claim that extensive government intervention would impede development, many countries experienced rapid economic growth during the 1950s and 1960s. The economies of the Western industrial nations grew at an average annual rate of 4.4 per cent during the 1950s and at 5.5 per cent between 1960 and 1973, the time of the first oil shock (Midgley, 1997). During this time, the economies of the developing countries grew at a rate of about 3.4 per cent per annum, exceeding even the most optimistic economic growth predictions (Morawetz, 1977; Midgley, 1997). As was shown earlier in this chapter, these trends were accompanied by significant improvements in standards of living and social conditions in many parts of the world.

However, by the mid-1970s, the global economy was in recession. The decision of the Organization of Petroleum Exporting Countries (OPEC) to increase the price of crude oil during the Yom Kippur War between Israel and its neighbouring states in 1973 caused havoc, and many economies were plunged into recession. These recessionary trends were exacerbated by substantial interest rate increases, causing a massive debt crisis in the South and the problem of stagflation in the Western countries. To make matters worse, OPEC imposed a second price increase on the world economy in 1979, further impeding the prospect of recovery. During this time, the incidence of poverty in many countries increased and government expenditures on social programmes were curtailed causing further hardship and deprivation. These developments had a serious impact on the development efforts of the countries of the South slowing and, in some cases, reversing the gains of previous decades. However, the Western industrial countries and the communist countries of Eastern Europe were also affected. In the communist countries, and particularly the Soviet Union, increased military expenditures and shortages of commodities further exacerbated the problem.

These problems also caused widespread political resentment in the industrial nations and voters were increasingly persuaded that falling living standards, high unemployment and inflation were caused by high taxes, excessive government interference in the economy and an overly generous welfare system that had sapped the economy of its vitality. The ideas of leading neo-liberal scholars such as Milton Friedman and Friedrich von Hayek were effectively used by radical right political leaders such as Mrs Thatcher in Britain and President Reagan in the United States to persuade the electorate that radical economic reforms were needed to revitalize the economy. With the electoral successes of these leaders, new policies that favoured privatization, deregulation and reduced taxation were introduced.

Few governments in the developing nations enthusiastically embraced the neo-liberal orthodoxy. They were not persuaded that abandoning economic planning and social interventions would promote rapid economic growth and social progress. One exception was General Pinochet's military government in Chile. The general and his advisers, many of whom had been trained in neo-classical economics at the University of Chicago (Borzutsky, 1991), believed that the economic and social policies adopted by previous governments, and particularly by the Marxist government of President Allende, had destroyed the country's economy and social system. The advocacy of free market capitalism by General Pinochet's regime was accompanied by a new strand in thinking about development that asserted the need for coercion and authoritarianism. In addition to repression and widespread human rights abuses, the government used its power to ruthlessly eradicate interventionism and collectivism. Although not as overt, the proponents of neo-liberalism in Europe and North America expressed similar ideas, contending that development would occur more rapidly if the State used its authority to enforce marketization and the integration of the poor into the capitalist economy (Midgley, 1991). Despite their frequent use of *laissez-faire* rhetoric, neo-liberals have been anything but 'liberal', urging the State to use its coercive power to deregulate the economy, privatize its assets, reduce taxes on the rich, retrench the social services and actively promote the marketization of the economy and other aspects of social life.

Many governments opposed to neo-liberal doctrines were faced with huge debts following the economic crises of the 1970s. Few were able to obtain credit on commercial markets and most were compelled to seek emergency financial aid from the International Monetary Fund and the World Bank. These organizations imposed conditionality policies that required governments to adopt economic liberalization or 'structural adjustment' programmes (Danahar, 1994; Chossudovsky, 1997). These programmes involved a new form of economic planning in which officials from the IMF assumed control of economic policy-making in many countries. They set about dismantling economic planning agencies and abolishing government regulations that were disadvantageous to the business community. They required governments to reduce taxation, slash public spending, terminate thousands of civil service jobs, remove subsidies on food and other commodities, abandon land reform and other redistributive policies, retrench rural development and informal sector investment policies and privatize nationalized industries and government-owned utilities. The privatization of schools, clinics, hospitals and other social service facilities was promoted, and where this was not possible, charges for health care and other social services were introduced. The privatization of Chile's social insurance system was a major development which was subsequently emulated by other Latin American countries (Borzutsky, 1997). Governments were also required to abandon import substitution and open their economies to investment and global competition. Neo-liberal economic policy-makers claimed that integration into the global capitalist economy would attract capital and provide access to global markets, promoting economic growth and prosperity.

Despite the promise that these 'reforms' would spur economic growth and reduce poverty, the neo-liberal record has not been impressive. Although economic growth rates in some parts of the world have indeed accelerated, bringing substantial benefits to industrialists, businessmen and political elites, the problem of distorted development has been exacerbated, resulting in increased inequality, conspicuous poverty, homelessness and deprivation. In others, economic liberalization policies have been a complete disaster. Latin American countries such as Argentina, which enthusiastically adopted these policies, have experienced serious economic difficulties resulting even in the impoverishment of the formerly prosperous middle class. In 1997, several East Asian countries found that increased global economic integration could have serious consequences. In the 1960s, these countries had adopted highly interventionist policies which brought about sustained growth and significant improvements in standards of living for the majority of their people. They were now faced with capital flight, debt and rising unemployment. Although some have managed to recover, the legacy of the 1997 fiscal crisis continues to linger, affecting millions of people.

The imposition of neo-liberal policies through structural adjustment in the poorest indebted countries has had serious repercussions. In many low-income African and Asian countries, the incidence of absolute poverty has increased as structural adjustment programmes have siphoned off agricultural surpluses to finance debt repayments and as government investments, subsidies and social programmes have been curtailed. These trends have been accompanied by political instability, increased conflict and massive human suffering. As the IMF and the World Bank were subjected to increasing criticism, palliative measures such as social funds were established to address the problem. The role of these safety net programmes, which function as an essentially residual approach to poverty eradication, were discussed in Chapter 1 of this book. Chapter 7, dealing with the human services and social work, also discusses the role of social funds. The introduction of Poverty Reduction Strategy Papers (PRSPs) as a precondition for debt relief, discussed in Chapter 9, represents the latest attempt by the international donor community to leverage 'pro-poor' policies. However, it is clear that these programmes will not, of themselves, solve the poverty problem and, as this chapter has shown, poverty and deprivation remain problems of huge proportions in the developing countries of the South.

Towards poverty eradication

The idea that poverty can be totally eradicated is a noble one but, as has been shown, the adoption of major anti-poverty and development strategies by governments and international development agencies over the last 50 years has not achieved this goal. Despite the commitment of the world's leaders at the 1995 World Summit in Copenhagen, absolute poverty remains a massive problem. In June 2000, when the United Nations General Assembly met in Geneva to review progress in implementing the *Copenhagen Declaration*, the results were uneven. Poverty remained a serious problem, and ethnic and other forms of conflict have continued in many parts of the world, impeding efforts towards social integration. The global economy has experienced recession, financial crises wracked East Asia and South America, and violence and conflict has increased in many parts of the world.

Yet many would argue that progress has been made and that many millions of people around the world are better off today in material terms than they would have been if no development had taken place. Few development scholars agree with the pessimism of anti-development writers who claim that development has been an unmitigated disaster. Many would also argue that the adoption of specific targets is a useful mechanism that can be used to galvanize action and assess progress. The *Copenhagen Declaration* has, they point out, created an agenda for social policy at the global level. Indeed, as the United Nations Development Programme (UNDP) (2000: 22) reveals, progress has already been recorded on a number of indicators which have been linked to the *Copenhagen Declaration*. The UNDP also reports that the majority of the world's nations are 'on track' in meeting targets such as improving gender equality in education, achieving universal primary enrolment and promoting hunger alleviation.

It may be argued that countries that have adopted a social development approach have made impressive progress towards realizing these goals. By combining a commitment to economic growth with social policies, countries such as Botswana, Costa Rica, Mauritius, Taiwan, Singapore and others have reduced poverty significantly. Through effective economic planning, they have stimulated economic growth and created new employment opportunities for many people. Economic policy-making has been combined with social policies that have invested in education, health, community development and other human services programmes. Above all, they have attempted to address the glaring inequalities that characterize the process of distorted development.

As these examples suggest, social development is not only about growth and human services; it is also about an egalitarian development strategy that is concerned not with the prosperity of the few but with raising incomes and standards of living among the population as a whole. Social development also involves a total commitment to poverty eradication that harnesses the resources of the State, market and community (Midgley, 1995). Although the anti-poverty strategies discussed in this chapter are rooted in ideology and thus tend to evoke passionate commitments, the social development approach seeks pragmatically to combine their disparate elements into a heterodox set of prescriptions for poverty eradication. The prospect of synthesizing market, State and community approaches to poverty eradication deserves much more debate and discussion in both development and social policy circles.

Recommended Reading

The following books provide a discussion of major topics in the field of poverty and inequality in the context of development.

- Townsend, P. and Gordon, D. (eds) (2002) *World Poverty: New Policies to Defeat an Old Enemy*. Bristol: Policy Press. This useful book offers an international perspective on poverty and inequality covering numerous important issues relating to these topics. Townsend's call for the creation of an international welfare state based on human rights ideals offers a challenging alternative to current anti-poverty thinking.
- United Nations (1996) *Report of the World Summit for Social Development: Copenhagen, 6–12 March 1995*. New York: UN. United Nations (2001) *Report of the World Social Situation*. New York: UN. These two documents by the United Nations are essential reading for an understanding of the contribution the organization has made to anti-poverty thinking over the last 15 years. The *Report of the World Social Summit for Social Development* is especially important for the policy proposals it contains.
- Halvorsen-Quevedo, R. and Schneider, H. (eds) (2000) *Waging the Global War on Poverty: Strategies and Case Studies*. Paris: OECD. This collection discusses poverty eradication policies in the light of the international community's goal of reducing the incidence of absolute poverty by 50 per cent by the year 2015. The book examines the poverty reduction strategies adopted by international donors and provides case studies of the implementation of these strategies in several developing countries.
- World Bank (1990) *World Development Report, 1990: Poverty*. Washington, DC: World Bank. World Bank (2001) *World Development Report, 2000/2001: Attacking Poverty*. Washington, DC: World Bank. These two reports outline the World Bank's approach to anti-poverty policy in the developing world which, since 1990, has favoured high growth rates engendered by a free market development strategy with human capital investments and safety net programmes for the most vulnerable and for those affected by structural adjustment programmes. Both reports should be consulted to gain a better understanding of the Bank's approach.
- Chossudovsky, M. (1997) *The Globalization of Poverty: Impacts of IMF and World Bank Reforms*. New York: Zed Books. Professor Chossudovsky believes that the so-called 'reforms' which have been promoted by the World Bank and International Monetary Fund over the last 20 years have not achieved their goal of creating vibrant economies and reducing the incidence of poverty in the developing countries and in the countries that formerly comprised the Soviet Union. His scathing attack on these organizations and their policies may be regarded by some as exaggerated but his critique deserves to be read and understood.
- Danziger, S. and Haveman, R.H. (eds) (2001) *Understanding Poverty*. New York: Russell Sage Foundation, pp. 27–68. This book covers the topic of poverty and anti-poverty policy in the United States in great depth, paying attention to the question of how and why poverty persists in the world's most wealthy and powerful nation. Although the book is exclusively concerned with poverty in the United States, it locates the American situation in the international context.

References

Adelman, I. and Morris, C.T. (1973) *Economic Growth and Social Equity in Developing Countries*. Stanford, CA: Stanford University Press.

Ahluwahlia, M. (1974) 'Income inequality: some dimensions of the problem', in H. Chenery et al. (eds), *Redistribution with Growth*. Oxford: Oxford University Press, pp. 3–37.

Ahluwalia, M. (1976) 'Inequality, poverty and development', *Journal of Development Economics*, 3 (4): 309–42.

Alinsky, S. (1946) *Reveille for Radicals*. Chicago, IL: University of Chicago Press.

Alinsky, S. (1971) *Rules for Radicals*. New York: Random House.

Amin, S. (1974) *Accumulation on a World Scale*. New York: Monthly Review Press.

Auletta, K. (1982). *The Underclass*. New York: Random House.

Banfield, E. (1968) *The Unheavenly City: The Nature and Future of Our Urban Crisis*. Boston, MA: Little, Brown.

Baster, N. (1972) *Measuring Development*. London: Frank Cass.

Bauer, P.T. (1976) *Dissent on Development*. London: Weidenfeld and Nicolson.

Bauman, Z. (1992) *Imitations of Post-Modernity*. New York: Routledge.

Bhattacharyya, S.N. (1970) *Community Development: An Analysis of the Programme in India*. Calcutta: Academic Publishers.

Boeke, J. (1953) *Economics and Economic Policy in Dual Societies*. Haarlem: Willink.

Borzutsky, S. (1991) 'The Chicago boys, social security and welfare in Chile', in H. Glennerster and J. Midgley (eds), *The Radical Right and the Welfare State: An International Assessment*. Lanham, MD: Rowman and Littlefield, pp. 79–99.

Borzutsky, S. (1997) 'Privatizing social security: relevance of the Chilean experience', in J. Midgley and M. Sherraden (eds) *Alternatives to Social Security: An International Inquiry*. London: Auburn House.

Brandt, Willy (1980) *North–South: A Programme for Survival*. London: Pan Books.

Brokensha, D. and Hodge, P. (1969) *Community Development: An Interpretation*. San Francisco, CA: Chandler.

Bruce, B.T. (1961) *The Coming of the Welfare State*. London: Batsford.

Burkey, S. (1993) *People First: A Guide to Self-Reliant, Participatory Rural Development*. London: Zed Books.

Burtless, G. and Smeeding, T.M. (2001) 'The level, trend and composition of poverty', in S.H. Danziger and R.H. Haveman (eds) *Understanding Poverty*. New York: Russell Sage Foundation, pp. 27–68.

Campfens, H. (ed.) (1997) *Community Development Around the World: Practice, Theory, Research, Training*. Toronto: University of Toronto Press.

Cardoso, F.H. (1972) 'Dependency and development in Latin America', *New Left Review*, 74: 83–9.

Cardoso, F.H. and Faletto, E. (1979) *Dependency and Development in Latin America*. Berkeley, CA: University of California Press.

Chambers, C. (1971) *Paul U. Kellogg and the Survey: Voices for Social Welfare and Social Justice*. London: Oxford University Press.

Chenery, H., Ahluwalia, M., Bell, C., Duloy, J.H. and Jolly, R. (1974) *Redistribution with Growth*. Oxford: Oxford University Press.

Chossudovsky, M. (1997) *The Globalization of Poverty: Impacts of IMF and World Bank Reforms*. New York: Zed Books.

Clark, K. (1965) *Dark Ghetto: Dilemmas of Social Power*. New York: Harper and Row.

Conradie, I. (2001) 'Developmental social welfare in South Africa: the search for strategic direction', in P. Salustowicz (ed.) *Civil Society and Social Development*. Berne: Peter Lang, pp. 277–92.

Cox, A. and Healy, J. (2000) 'Poverty reduction: a review of donor strategies and practices', in R. Halvorsen-Quevedo and H. Schneider (eds) *Waging the Global War on Poverty: Strategies and Case Studies*. Paris: Organization for Economic Cooperation and Development, pp. 23–60.

Dag Hammarskjold Foundation (1975) *What Now? Another Development*. Uppsala: DHF.

Danahar, K. (1994) *50 Years is Enough: The Case Against the World Bank and the International Monetary Fund*. Boston, MA: South End Press.

Demery, L. and Walton, M. (2000) 'Are poverty and social goals for the 21st century attainable?', in R. Halvorsen-Quevedo and H. Schneider (eds) *Waging the Global War on Poverty: Strategies and Case Studies*. Paris: Organization for Economic Cooperation and Development, pp. 61–88.

Denton, N. and Massey, D. (1993) *American Apartheid: Segregation and the Making of the Underclass*. Cambridge, MA: Harvard University Press.

de Soto, H. (1989). *The Other Path: The Invisible Revolution in the Third World*. New York: Harper and Row.

Dore, R. and Mars, Z. (eds) (1981) *Community Development*. London: Croom Helm.

Escobar, A. (1995) *The Making and Unmaking of the Third World*. Princeton, NJ: Princeton University Press.

Estes, R. (1985) *The Social Progress of Nations*. New York: Praeger.

Francis, P. (2002) 'Social capital, civil society and social exclusion', in U. Kothari and M. Minogue (eds), *Development Theory and Practice: Critical Perspectives*. New York: Palgrave, pp. 71–91.

Frank, A.G. (1967) *Capitalism and Underdevelopment in Latin America*. New York: Monthly Review Press.

Frank, A.G. (1969) *Latin America: Underdevelopment or Revolution?* New York: Monthly Review Press.

Frank, A.G. (1971) *Sociology of Development and Underdevelopment of Sociology*. London: Pluto Press.

Freire, P. (1972) *Pedagogy of the Oppressed*. Harmondsworth: Penguin Books.

Friedman, M. (1962) *Capitalism and Freedom*. Chicago: University of Chicago Press.

Friedman, M. with Friedman, R. (1980) *Free to Choose*. London: Secker and Warburg.

Furtado, C. (1970). *Economic Development of Latin America: A Survey from Colonial Times to the Cuban Revolution*. Cambridge: Cambridge University Press.

Giddens, A. (1998) *The Third Way: The Renewal of Social Democracy*. Cambridge: Polity Press.

Giddens, A. (2000) *The Third Way and its Critics*. Cambridge: Polity Press.

Glennerster, H. and Midgley, J. (eds) (1991) *The Radical Right and the Welfare State: An International Assessment*. Lanham, MD: Rowman and Littlefield.

Goode, W.J. (1963) *World Revolution and Family Patterns*. New York: Free Press.

Griffin, K. (1976) *Land Concentration and Rural Poverty*. London: Macmillan.

Hagen, E. (1962) *On the Theory of Social Change*. Homewood, IL: Dorsey Press.

Herkommer, S. and Koch, M. (1999) 'The "underclass": a misleading concept and a scientific myth?', in P. Littlewood et al. (eds), *Social Exclusion in Europe: Problems and Paradrgms*. Brookfield, VT: Ashgate, pp. 89–111.

Herrnstein, R. (1973) *IQ in the Meritocracy*. London: Allen Lane.

Herrnstein, R. and Murray, C. (1994) *The Bell Curve*. New York: Free Press.

Higgins, B. (1956) 'The dualistic theory of underdeveloped areas', *Economic Development and Cultural Change*, 4 (1): 22–115.

Holcombe, S.H. (1995) *Managing to Empower: The Grameen Bank's Experiment of Poverty Alleviation*. London: Zed Books.

Hozelitz, B.F. (1960) *Sociological Factors in Economic Development*. New York: Free Press.

International Labour Office (1976) *Employment, Growth and Basic Needs: A One World Problem*. Geneva: ILO.

Kothari, U. and Minogue, M. (2002) 'Critical perspectives on development: an introduction', in U. Kothari and M. Minogue (eds), *Development Theory and Practice: Critical Perspectives*. New York: Palgrave, pp. 1–15.

Kothari, U. and Minogue, M. (eds) (2002) *Development Theory and Practice: Critical Perspectives*. New York: Palgrave.

Kuznets, S. (1955) 'Economic growth and income inequality', *American Economic Review*, 45 (1): 1–29.

Lal, D. (1983) *The Poverty of Development Economics*. London: Institute of Economic Affairs.

Lerner, D. (1958) *The Passing of Traditional Society*. New York: Free Press.

Lewis, O. (1966) 'The culture of poverty', *Scientific American*, 214 (1): 19–25.

Lewis, W.A. (1955) *The Theory of Economic Growth*. London: Allen and Unwin.

Littlewood, P. and Herkommer, S. (1999) 'Identifying social exclusion', in Littlewood et al. (eds), op. cit., pp. 1–21.

Littlewood, P., Glorieux, I., Herkommer, S. and Jonsson, I. (eds) (1999) *Social Exclusion in Europe: Problems and Paradigms*. Brookfield, VT: Ashgate.

Lund, B. (2002) *Understanding State Welfare: Social Justice or Social Exclusion?* London: Sage.

Lyotard, J. (1984) *The Postmodern Condition: A Report on Knowledge*. Minneapolis, MN: University of Minnesota Press.

Mafeje, A. (2001) 'Conceptual and philosophical predispositions', in F. Wilson, N. Kanjhi, and E. Braathen (eds) *Poverty Reduction: What Role for the State in Today's Globalized Economy?* London: Zed Books.

Mandel, E. (1976) *Late Capitalism*. London: New Left Books.

Marsden, D. and Oakley, P. (1982) 'Radical community development in the Third World', in G. Craig, N. Derricourt and M. Loney (eds) *Community Work and the State*. London: Routledge and Kegan Paul, pp. 153–63.

Mayo, M. (1975) 'Community development: a radical alternative?' in R. Bailey and M. Brake (eds) *Radical Social Work*. London: Edward Arnold, pp. 129–43.

Mayor, F. and Binde, J. (2001). *The World Ahead: Our Future in the Making*. London: Zed Books.

McClelland, D. (1964) 'A psychological approach to economic development', *Economic Development and Cultural Change*, 12 (2): 320–4.

Mead, L. (1992) *The New Politics of Poverty*. New York: Basic Books.

Midgley, J. (1984) 'Social indicators and social planning', in J. Midgley and D. Piachaud (eds) *The Fields and Methods of Social Planning*. New York: St Martin's Press, pp. 34–54.

Midgley, J. (1991) 'The radical right, politics and society', in H. Glennerster and J. Midgley (eds), *The Radical Right and the Welfare State: An International Assessment*. Lanham, MD: Rowman and Littlefield, pp. 3–23.

Midgley, J. (1995) *Social Development: The Developmental Perspective in Social Welfare*. London: Sage.

Midgley, J. (1997) *Social Welfare in Global Context*. London: Sage.

Midgley, J. (1999) 'Postmodernism and social development: implications for progress, intervention and ideology', *Social Development Issues*, 21 (3): 5–13.

Midgley, J., Hall, A., Hardiman, M. and Narine, D. (1986) *Community Participation, Social Development and the State*. New York: Methuen.

Morawetz, D. (1977) *Twenty Five Years of Economic Development: 1950 to 1975*. Baltimore, MD: Johns Hopkins University Press.

Morris, D.M. (1979) *Measuring the Conditions of the World's Poor*. Oxford: Pergamon.

Moser, C.O.N. (1989) *Gender Planning and Development: Theory, Practice and Training*. London: Routledge.

Munck, R. and O'Hearne, D. (eds) (1999) *Critical Development Theory: Contributions to a New Paradigm*. New York: Zed Books.

Murray, C. (1984) *Losing Ground: American Social Policy 1950–1980*. New York: Basic Books.

Myrdal, G. (1968) *Asian Drama: An Inquiry into the Poverty of Nations*. Harmondsworth: Penguin.

Newman, O. and de Zoysa, R. (2001) *The Promise of the Third Way: Globalization and Social Justice*. New York: Palgrave.

Nurkse, R. (1953) *Problems of Capital Formation in Underdeveloped Countries*. London: Oxford University Press.

Oakley, P. (1991) *Projects with People: The Practice of Participation in Rural Development*. Geneva: International Labour Office.

Organization for Economic Cooperation and Development (1976). *The Use of Socio-Economic Indicators in Development Planning*. Paris: OECD.

Rahnema, M. (1997) 'Towards post-development: searching for signposts, a new language and new paradigms', in M. Rahnema and V. Bawtree (eds) *The Post-Development Reader*. New York: Zed Books, pp. 377–403.

Rodney, W. (1972) *How Europe Underdeveloped Africa*. Dar-es-Salaam: Tanzania Publishing House.

Rosenstein-Rodan, P. (1943) 'Problems of industrialization of South and Eastern Europe', *Economic Journal*, 53 (2): 205–11.

Rostow, W.W. (1960) *The Stages of Economic Growth: A Non-Communist Manifesto*. Cambridge: Cambridge University Press.

Runciman, W.G. (1972) *Relative Deprivation and Social Justice*. Harmondsworth: Penguin.

Sachs, W. (1992). *The Development Dictionary: A Guide to Knowledge and Power*. London: Zed Books.

Seers, D. (1972) 'The meaning of development', in N.T. Uphoff and W.F. Ilchman (eds) *The Political Economy of Development*. Berkeley, CA: University of California Press, pp. 123–9.

Sen, A. (1992) *Inequality Reexamined*. Cambridge, MA: Harvard University Press.

Sen, A. (1999) *Development as Freedom*. New York: Knopf.

Shiva, V. (1989) *Staying Alive: Women, Ecology and Development*. London: Zed Books.

Stewart, F. (1985) *Basic Needs in Developing Countries*. Baltimore, MD: Johns Hopkins University Press.

Stitt, S. and Grant, D. (1993) *Poverty: Rowntree Revisited*. Aldershot: Avebury.

Streeten, P. and Burki, S.J. (1978) 'Basic needs: some issues', *World Development*, 6 (3): 411–21.

Streeten, P. with Burki, S.J., Ul Haq, M., Hicks, N. and Stewart, F. (1981) *First Things First: Meeting Basic Needs in Developing Countries*. New York: Oxford University Press.

Sunkel, O. (1969) 'National development policy and external dependence in Latin America', *Journal of Development Studies*, 6: 23–48.

Townsend, P. (1974) 'Poverty and relative deprivation', in D. Wedderburn (ed.) *Poverty, Inequality and Class Structure*. Cambridge: Cambridge University Press, pp. 57–74.

Townsend, P. (1979) *Poverty in the United Kingdom*. Harmondsworth: Penguin.

United Nations (1951) *Measures for the Economic Development of the Underdeveloped Countries*. New York: UN.

United Nations (1971) 'Social policy and planning in national development', *International Social Development Review*, 3: 4–15.

United Nations (1996) *Report of the World Summit for Social Development: Copenhagen, 6–12 March 1995*. New York: UN.

United Nations (2001) *Report of the World Social Situation*. New York: UN.

United Nations Development Programme (2000) *Human Development Report 2000*. New York: UNDP.

United Nations Development Programme (2001). *Human Development Report 2001.* New York: UNDP.

Wahid, A. (ed.) (1994) *The Grameen Bank: Poverty Relief in Bangladesh.* Boulder, CO: Westview Press.

Wallerstein, I. (1980) *The Capitalist World Economy.* Cambridge: Cambridge University Press.

Waterston, A. (1965) *Development Planning: Lessons from Experience.* Baltimore, MD: Johns Hopkins University Press.

Wilson, W.J. (1987) *The Truly Disadvantaged: The Inner City, The Underclass and Public Policy.* Chicago: University of Chicago Press.

Wilson, W.J. (ed.) (1993) *The Ghetto Underclass: Social Science Perspectives.* Newbury Park, CA: Sage.

World Bank (1990) *World Development Report, 1990: Poverty.* Washington, DC: World Bank.

World Bank (2001) *World Development Report, 2000/2001: Attacking Poverty.* Washington, DC: World Bank.

Yunus, M. (1991) *Grameen Bank: Experiences and Reflections.* Dhaka: Grameen Bank.

3 SOCIAL POLICY AND RURAL DEVELOPMENT: FROM MODERNIZATION TO SUSTAINABLE LIVELIHOODS

Summary

The notion of 'rural development' has undergone a profound transformation over the past four decades. This chapter examines its evolution from signifying just modernization and capitalization of the countryside in the 1960s to a more balanced approach nowadays in which rural development is seen as a multi-sector strategy for simultaneously addressing questions of economic growth, poverty alleviation and livelihood support. After examining the strengths and weaknesses of the modernization paradigm, it considers the rise of anti-poverty policies in the 1970s. The consequences of structural adjustment and rise of the Washington Consensus on Agriculture (WCA) in the 1980s and 1990s are discussed, culminating in the emergence of a new paradigm for rural development which stresses a flexible, broad-based approach responsive to the diverse needs of particular countries and productive groups. Combining economic growth and social investment aims, a multi-institutional and cross-sector approach is envisaged in which the State, civil society, private sector and international agencies each play important roles in promoting rural development. From a social policy perspective, this new approach is epitomized in the growing adoption of the sustainable livelihoods framework (SLF) as a comprehensive analytical device that prioritizes the interests of those rural groups traditionally neglected by mainstream modernization policies. Despite its undoubted limitations, the focus of the SLF on people, its holistic conceptualization of rural development and adoption of a multi-institutional, participatory approach, is providing fresh opportunities for policy-makers and practitioners to seriously address the pressing needs of rural populations.

Rural development for whom?

'Rural development' is a term that has been subject to many interpretations in both academic and practitioner circles. For most of the twentieth century, and especially during the post-war period, it was virtually synonymous with a narrow, 'modernization' view of progress. Urban-based industrialization was seen as the engine of growth, while the basic role of the rural sector was to support this process. Following the logic of industrialization, agricultural production would be commercialized, capitalized and mechanized to maximize efficiency and provide economies of scale. The application of Western science and farm management techniques to boost agricultural production was seen as an essential component in this process of rural transformation. Surplus labour would be displaced from the countryside to the towns and cities to supply the expanding industrial and service sectors. Benefits would, in that infamous hydrological metaphor, automatically 'trickle down' to the poor, conveniently removing the need for major government intervention to redirect development benefits to more needy groups.

Yet this conception of rural development has proved inadequate as a prescription for rural progress in the South. The undisputed persistence of widespread poverty, deprivation and insecurity is ample testimony to its shortcomings. Since the early 1970s, when the modernization paradigm as a universal prescription for economic and social advancement started to come seriously under fire, the definition of what constitutes 'rural development' has evolved and matured significantly. It is now more widely recognized that this Western-based notion of rural advance is insufficient on its own and must be broadened. It cannot be denied that the conventional model has been instrumental in achieving key macro-development goals such as the production of commercial export crops, higher living standards for some groups and the strengthening of nationhood through institution building. However, it has also neglected the interests of the rural majority, which has been (and in many instances continues to be) seen by many policy-makers and planners as marginal to the mainstream development process.

Within the holistic notion of social policy adopted in this volume, rural development is redefined as a process whose central preoccupation is the wellbeing of the entire population in the countryside, focusing in particular on the needs of the poor. From a social policy perspective, this entails a concern not just for providing statutory welfare services such as health care and education. It involves adopting a broader and more comprehensive livelihoods approach that embraces all those production-based and other aspects of people's lives that contribute to their well-being. This framework can serve as an analytical tool for understanding the dynamism and complexity of people's livelihoods and causes of poverty or insecurity. At the same time, it may act as a prescriptive device for pinpointing where interventions can most effectively be made to address livelihood problems. Embedded in this notion, therefore, are two closely related aspects. On the one hand, is the *technical* question of which inputs should be harnessed to provide an appropriate solution for addressing rural problems. On the other hand, is the equally important *political* issue of how to prioritize such actions in order that these technical solutions may be effectively applied and the interests of impacted groups placed high on the development agenda.

The significance of rural development

Before examining the general history of rural development and considering in detail the sustainable livelihoods framework, it is worth explaining the logic and rationale behind the adoption of such an approach to rural development that seeks to benefit a wide range of groups and bring them into the mainstream of national economic and social development. This section will examine several key reasons for the need to promote rural development in the South.

- Rural areas are characterized by persistently high levels of poverty and deprivation in spite of decades of national economic growth.
- The rural sector continues to be a crucial source of employment despite high rates of out-migration and urbanization in the context of a general process of 'de-peasantization'.
- Agricultural production remains a vital contributor to the overall process of economic growth, while small producers themselves are major suppliers of staple food crops.
- The direct participation of rural people in the design and implementation of development interventions that address poverty alleviation and natural resource conservation goals is essential.

A fundamental starting point for policy-makers, planners and practitioners must be to tackle absolute rural poverty. Several decades of modernization strategies with their 'trickle-down' assumptions have done little to alleviate mass poverty. The International Fund for Agricultural Development estimates that three-quarters of the world's 1.2 billion poorest people earning less than one dollar per day live and work in rural areas and that, even by 2020, this figure will remain high at 60 per cent (IFAD, 2001). Although the period 1970–90 saw improvements in rural poverty indices, during the 1990s the trend stalled due to inadequate national development policies as resources were switched to address urban issues, coupled with a massive reduction in the value of agricultural aid.

The proportion of the rural population below the poverty line has increased in many countries, especially in those with bimodal agrarian structures that have a marked polarization in land distribution and wealth and which neglect small producers in mainstream policy-making. Between 1965 and 1988, this figure worsened significantly in many nations including Brazil, Ecuador, Peru, Zambia, Kenya and the Philippines. In these same countries, indices of land-lessness (wage labourers) and quasi-landlessness (tenancy and sharecropping) have remained high or are increasing (Cristodoulou, 1990). Furthermore, the rural poor are increasingly concentrated in low-potential areas with poor agro-ecological potential and, frequently, high levels of conflict. Trade liberalization has offered few tangible benefits to the rural poor except, possibly, in countries where the agricultural sector has been included in labour-intensive, pro-poor economic growth strategies (Killick, 2001). Significantly, in countries with small farmer-friendly rural development policies, such as Thailand and India, the proportion of rural poor has actually decreased, although absolute numbers remain high.

In terms of the provision of basic services such as health care, education, water and sanitation, due to decades of neglect and public under-investment, rural areas fall way behind urban centres in virtually all developing countries. To take health services as an example, Afghanistan has a rural coverage of 17 per cent (urban = 80 per cent), Zaire 17 per cent (urban = 40 per cent) and Myanmar 11 per cent (urban = 100 per cent). Again, it is no coincidence that those countries with strong rural development policies enjoy substantially higher levels of provision; 86 per cent in South Korea (compared with 97 per cent in urban areas) and 100 per cent in Mauritius, for example (Jazairy et al., 1992). Investment in the education sector follows a similar pattern, with very marked, disproportionately low levels of public spending for the farming population in Asia, Africa and Latin America when compared with their urban-based manual and white-collar counterparts (Todaro, 2000). Although adult illiteracy has steadily declined in the South, it is universally higher in the country-side with rates of over 50 per cent still common (IFAD, 2001).

Another major reason for promoting broad-based rural development is that this sector is still a major (although gradually declining) source of employment, despite the general process of 'de-peasantization', falling fertility rates in the countryside and out-migration. The rural sector accounted for 47 per cent of overall employment in developing countries in 1999 compared with 66 per cent in 1970 (Ashley and Maxwell, 2002). This figure is much higher in some regions; the rural sector still accounts on average for almost 60 per cent of the labour force in low- and middle-income countries, rising to around 70 per cent in East Asia and sub-Saharan Africa (World Bank, 1997). The urban population in all developing countries has increased rapidly from 26 per cent in 1975 to an estimated 50 per cent by 2015. Some nations have experienced substantially higher indices, such as Brazil, for example, which will see an increase over the same period from 61 to 86 per cent (UNDP, 1999). Rural–urban migration as a source of urban population growth is also high, ranging from 35 per cent in Argentina to 64 per cent in Nigeria (Todaro, 2000). It is evident that rural populations are adopting more diversified livelihood strategies that involve routinely spending part of the year in urban informal sector activities to supplement their incomes, and deriving up to 80 per cent of total household income from non-farming activities (Ellis, 2000; Start, 2001; Ashley and Maxwell, 2002).

A third, related consideration, which underlines the fundamental importance of adopting a broad-based strategy, is the contribution of rural growth to overall economic development. Generally, there has been a halving of the contribution of the rural sector to the national economy from its average of 60 per cent during the 1960s. However, this fact should not undermine the continuing importance of rural and agricultural investments in promoting economic and social progress in the countryside. Rapid increases in GNP in sub-Saharan Africa and Asia from 1965–88 were underpinned by high rates of growth in agricultural production. Small farmers, often erroneously labelled by modernization-style planners and policy-makers as a brake on development, an archaic remnant of a pre-industrial age, have in fact played a major role in this modernization process. As research has shown, there is a close correlation between the growth of agriculture and the economy as a whole (World Bank, 1982; IFAD, 2001). Agricultural expansion stimulates demand for inputs produced in other sectors of the economy, while rural households constitute a major market for manufactured goods. Agriculture may provide the engine of rural economic growth, especially at the 'early development' stage, while it can also have a major impact on poverty alleviation (Ashley and Maxwell, 2001, 2002).

Furthermore, as the rural majority, small farmers play a particularly important strategic role. They account for up to 95 per cent of staple food crop production (rice, wheat and maize, etc.) in most developing countries and an equal proportion of commercial cash crops (coffee, tea, cocoa and cotton, for example) in many nations (Jazairy et al., 1992). It is true that their position has been undermined by the long-term decline in agricultural commodity prices, while many subsidies for agricultural inputs such as fertilizers have been removed. Furthermore, as Killick (2001) notes, small producers are finding it increasingly difficult to cope with the pressures of international competition and commercialization of production.

There can be no doubt that demographic, environmental and commercial pressures are mounting on the small farm sector. Yet rather than constituting a simple industrial reserve army of labour, doomed to disappear with the passage of time as the so-called 'modern' sector expands, small rural producers constitute an enduring economic linchpin, whose productive human capital contributes directly to GNP, livelihood provision and national food security. Although historically the small farm economy has shrunk, its vitality, persistence and dynamism in the face of growing pressures testifies to its enduring importance in developing countries (Goodman and Redclift, 1982; Shanin, 1988). This fact underlines the need for small rural producers to be universally incorporated into the mainstream development agenda.

In addition to these major contributions to development, the role of rural society in supplying social and political capital must also be recognized. Project and programme experience over the last decade has demonstrated quite unequivocally that one major reason (although by no means the only one) for success or failure depends on the extent to which people's participation is effectively harnessed. Capital in the form of networks of relationships, social structures and a variety of organizational forms is now recognized as a key building block in development initiatives. Rather than being seen as the source of underdevelopment at worst or, at best, as passive beneficiaries, rural groups and communities must now be viewed as active providers of solutions and key inputs based on their knowledge and experience. In virtually the whole gamut of development interventions, the mobilization of social and political capital is as essential as the acquisition of physical, human or financial assets.

This is true throughout most of the development project spectrum, but is particularly critical in those kinds of interventions that require a strong community role in terms of political articulation and governance. This would include, for example, grassroots resistance movements to population displacement caused by infrastructure projects such as hydropower schemes, community-based natural resource management, primary health care schemes and even micro-credit programmes. As will be explored in more detail below, a successful outcome to many development initiatives of this type is heavily dependent on the organization of rural groups and enhancement of their social capital. No other social group can provide this key ingredient except rural inhabitants themselves.

Rural development as modernization

A central question facing all industrializing countries has been the nature of the 'agrarian transition' and the role of agriculture in particular, on the road to development. During the early development phase in particular, rural production must generate a surplus to serve and somehow support or complement urban-based industrialization. In addition, the countryside must help supply labour for nascent industries and generate internal markets for manufactured goods (Byres, 1982). How these goals are achieved will vary considerably according to the political economy of development within nation-states and internationally. Country experiences in this context are not uniform but highly diverse, defying rigid categorization.

However, to polarize the argument for illustrative purposes, three broad models of agrarian transition may be distinguished in which rural development is fashioned in distinctive ways as a component of national development: (1) the Western, capitalist modernization paradigm, (2) the Stalinist model, and (3) the small farmer approach. From a social policy perspective, the key issue is how a model of agrarian transition shapes patterns of rural development and, in turn, how each approach treats the mass of the rural population in terms of productive and social investments. In other words, will the rural population be crudely squeezed to quickly extract a surplus regardless of the economic and social cost in the countryside, or will it be nurtured and supported as a major asset and significant pillar of national growth? The responses to these questions are crucial since they will affect people's livelihoods and well-being in a profound manner.

All three paradigms identified above have significant social policy implications. The modernization paradigm is clearly the dominant policy model and, as discussed below, has characterized mainstream rural development in the capitalist developing world. In the West, according to economic theories such as the Lewis (1954) two-sector model and Rostow's (1960) 'stages-of-growth' analysis, development necessarily involves the induced structural transformation of the economy and transfer of 'surplus' labour from traditional agriculture to urban-based industry. This theoretical stance was also closely paralleled by import substitution industrialization (ISI) ideas advanced by Raul Prebisch and others at the Economic Commission for Latin America (ECLA). The reasoning was that the terms of trade for primary commodity exports would inexorably decline, placing the developing world at a disadvantage, and that the strengthening of domestic industry behind tariff barriers should be emphasized. Both modernization and dependency theory economics thus encouraged neglect of the countryside, especially the small farm sector, while its potentially broader social development role was consistently downplayed.

In its most extreme form, during the 1950s and early 1960s, modern agricultural development was equated with industrialized farming in large-scale production units based on imported technologies that could achieve substantial economies of scale to yield commercial profits. As part of an attempt by the Western powers to promote poverty alleviation through non-revolutionary means, community development programmes were initiated throughout the developing world during the 1950s (Holdcroft and Jones, 1982). Following the principle of life-saving external assistance, originally embodied in the Marshall Plan for war-torn Europe, aid-funded agricultural development programmes were also introduced. Based on the American 'transfer-of-technology' or diffusion model of agricultural research and extension, it was 'assumed that farmers could increase their agricultural productivity by allocating existing resources more efficiently and by adopting agricultural practices and technologies from the industrial countries' (Eicher and Staatz, 1998: 12). By the mid-1960s, however, a somewhat more broad-based view of agricultural development potential had made inroads. Some Western economists were already challenging the view that agriculture contributed little to macro-economic growth (Johnston and Mellor, 1961; Nicholls, 1964).

Furthermore, the poor record of success of the diffusion approach led theorists to question many of its underlying assumptions. Earlier views of small (or 'peasant') producers as a monolithic, universally conservative block opposed to any form of innovation gave way to the notion of the 'progressive farmer'. According to the 'allocative efficiency' hypothesis put forward by Schultz (1964), traditional farmers are 'poor but efficient' users of the meagre resources at their disposal adopting existing technology. Small farmers are, Schultz argued, rational economic beings who would respond readily to economic incentives to maximize profits. This would, however, depend on government provision of new technological packages and investments to strengthen this human capital through appropriate education and training, as well as through the provision of price and fiscal incentives. Thus, the switch from a 'diffusion' to a 'high-payoff input' model provided intellectual legitimacy for the expansion of high-yielding varieties of wheat and rice developed in Mexico and the Philippines respectively during the 1960s (Ruttan, 1998). This Green Revolution has since generated dramatic increases in food production, employment and farmer incomes in many areas, while enhancing national food self-sufficiency (Hayami, 1985).

Yet as an example of broad-based rural development, the Green Revolution has come under widespread criticism for tending to favour landlords and large farmers in ecologically privileged, irrigated valleys while by-passing the needs of the far more numerous land-poor producers in marginal upland, rain-fed areas. Doubts have been cast over the assumed scale-neutrality of the Green

Revolution model, while its negative impacts on the distribution of land and income are noted as being especially marked in bimodal or highly inegalitarian societies, especially in South America, for example (Griffin, 1979; Pearce, 1980; Lipton and Longhurst, 1989). In terms of catering for the needs of a minority of rural producers, therefore, the Green Revolution embraced a narrow view of rural development. Although valuable in promoting other, macro-economic and political development goals, it did in effect largely ignore the needs of the rural majority by conveniently assuming that the wealth thus generated would 'trickle down' to the poorest rural groups.

Fighting rural poverty

By the early 1970s, the modernization model had come under heavy criticism for failing to tackle mass poverty and, in many cases, substantially widening the gap between rich and poor. A more interventionist approach, it was thought, would be needed to generate employment and incomes, while target-ing benefits at needy groups without waiting for these problems to be resolved automatically. Famously, Robert McNamara, as president of the World Bank, suggested in 1972 that the institution should prioritize the poorest 40 per cent of the population in developing countries, highlighting the fact that little had been done to address the problems of subsistence farmers. Bank economists and other academics then put forward the notion that incremental growth should be accompanied by interventions to ensure more equitable distribution to help alleviate poverty (Chenery et al., 1974). This was followed by a series of poverty-focused Bank sector policy papers that marked a veritable 'assault' on world poverty in the fields of rural development, health, basic education, low-cost housing and land reform (Coombs and Ahmed, 1974; World Bank, 1975). During the same intense period of policy re-examination, at the World Employment Conference in 1976, the International Labour Organization called on member-states to adopt a 'basic human needs' approach. This proposed that basic minimum material and non-material needs of the poor could be met under a variety of political regimes even at relatively low levels of income per head (Streeten et al., 1981; Stewart, 1985). While most policy prescriptions were framed within existing socio-economic structures, some analysts argued for a 'stronger' and more distributive approach as the only effective means of satis-fying basic needs and tackling poverty (Wisner, 1988).

This watershed in development theorizing did induce significant changes in policy and strategy that moved in the direction of a more comprehensive rural development approach. It was now more widely accepted that the goals of enhancing crop production, generating markets and tackling poverty could be achieved through public spending on the small farm sector rather than exclu-sively on large, 'modern' plantations, livestock enterprises and capital-intensive farms. The potential for achieving rural economies of scale came to be perceived as grossly exaggerated. Research showed that small farms generated substantially more output and employment per hectare than large land holdings. In fact, large estates are often notoriously unproductive, with vast areas left idle for purely speculative and rent-seeking purposes, as has been clearly shown in areas such as Amazonia (Hall, 1989; Mahar, 1989). Furthermore, even in the early 1970s it was becoming recognized that rural development interventions must be carefully tailored economically and ecologically to fit the resource endowments of particular regions rather than Western-induced, blueprint solutions being indiscriminately applied (Ruttan and Hayami, 1998).

The growth-with-equity philosophy adopted during the 1970s by development organizations has been translated into action on the ground, although with what long-term effect is still a matter of considerable debate. Since then, a substantial proportion of funds has been ploughed into a whole range of basic production-based as well as human needs-type projects and programmes. An attempt at combining these approaches was designed in the shape of integrated rural development programmes (IRDPs). These were synergistic interventions that attempted to complement increases in agricultural production with the provision of basic health, education, sanitation and other key services. However, the potential of an IRDP approach was undermined by a series of problems that regularly surfaced. These included high project costs, poor cross-sector coordination, bureaucratic complexity and lack of beneficiary participation, together with the failure to address fundamental structural barriers such as skewed land ownership. This led to a fall in the popularity of IRDPs during the 1980s as an approach to poverty alleviation (Lele, 1975; World Bank, 1987; Howell, 1990; Tendler, 1993). Be that as it may, however, the *principle* of integration and cross-sector coordination has been incorporated into many smaller-scale development initiatives as a guiding principle, not least of all within the sustainable livelihood framework itself.

There has been a growing commitment on the part of aid organizations towards broader-based rural development. This was reflected in a marked shift in World Bank lending during the 1970s. Beforehand, there had been an almost exclusive emphasis on large-scale infrastructure development, but from 1974–78 poverty-focused agriculture and rural development came to absorb over half of Bank lending (Ayres, 1984). However, the effectiveness of Bank policies in actually reaching the rural poor has been called seriously into question. This has been on the grounds both of the limitations of the institution itself as well as the wider contextual constraints under which it must operate (Payer, 1982; Ayres, 1984; Rich, 1994). At a more general level, one study of bilateral and multilateral overseas development assistance concluded that, 'the amount of aid going to activities which are intended to directly benefit the poor ... is at best around one-fifth' (White, 1996: 97). As Cassen and others (1994) have shown, aid may have a positive if limited impact on poverty but its effectiveness is seriously constrained by external commercial and political pressures as well as by a lack of donor governments' commitment to seriously addressing poverty.

Many criticisms have been levelled at the effectiveness of attempts to ameliorate, through poverty-focused policies, the historically (still) dominant modernization approach to rural development. Many of these negative impacts were, arguably, exacerbated during the structural adjustment era of the 1980s and 1990s. Adjustment was meant to assist small farmers by removing monopolistic State marketing practices and raising farm-gate prices while stimulating export crop production. However, farmers are more often than not denied access to the essential inputs such as land, seeds, fertilizers and extension services required to realize such market potential (Ahmed and Lipton, 1997). Furthermore, incentives for large-scale export crop production have encouraged land concentration as well as environmental damage through deforestation and the intensive use of agro-chemicals (Commander, 1989; Duncan and Howell, 1992; Weeks, 1995; Reed, 1996).

A 'Washington Consensus' on poor country agriculture (WCA) attributes the agriculture of poor regions to under-capitalization, lack of international competitiveness, poor resource endowments, and an unequal distribution of resources as well as institutional failures, the latter including political and organizational shortcomings. Major solutions are sought through the intensification of farm productivity by means of technological improvements. This has always been a major goal of policy-makers, but whereas in the past efforts were focused on specific crops, as in the Green Revolution, the modern approach would be more broad-based. Policy and institutional reform would stimulate a liberalization process based on public–private partnerships to encourage agricultural diversification, decentralization and small farmer participation at all stages from design to evaluation (Maxwell et al., 2001).

Yet although the WCA agenda has many acknowledged virtues, it has come under fire for several reasons (Kydd and Dorward, 2001). These include, firstly, the fact that farm economies at different stages of evolution will require variable prescriptions and not a universal blueprint. Secondly, many rural populations are still heavily dependent on the production of semi-tradable cereals rather than cash crops. Thirdly, small-scale farmers in poor areas may be less and less able to compete on international markets due to increases in transaction costs, falling world food prices and generally greater risks. Thus, despite the rhetoric of poverty alleviation, the WCA is in practice biased towards an intensification perspective that effectively excludes the majority of the rural poor living in vulnerable and marginal circumstances. To help bridge this gap, an alternative (or at least complementary) discourse on agriculture has emerged in parallel based on developing pro-poor, environmentally sound Green Revolution technologies and sustainable agricultural systems for small producers. These developments are linked to a broader, sustainable livelihoods approach that examines the wider potential of rural households and communities in their pursuit of diversified economic activities in farming and non-farming, rural- and urban-based activities.

Frustration with the many limitations of the capital-intensive model of rural development and its failure to adequately address the needs of the rural majority has thus prompted a search for alternative approaches. A broad, post-WCA consensus has emerged amongst international development organizations and aid donors on rural development priorities (Ashley and Maxwell, 2001, 2002; Maxwell et al., 2001). Poverty reduction is put forward as the main, overarching objective. Strategies for achieving this should be based on agricultural growth with heavy involvement of the private sector and government providing key infrastructure and other investments together with policy support (DFID, 1997; EC, 2000; World Bank, 2000).

Small farm agriculture alone cannot be the means for achieving these aims since it is subjected, as already noted, to many limitations and constraints. Boosting the rural non-farm economy (RNFE) is increasingly seen as a crucial strategy for alleviating poverty and strengthening livelihoods. There is also a renewed concern for protecting poor and vulnerable rural groups subjected to variable risks and uncertainty. Government is once again seen as being responsible for guaranteeing food security and protecting livelihoods through a number of production- and consumption-related measures ranging from traditional emergency relief to new multi-institutional forms of social provision. Social protection interventions are particularly important in dealing with the effects of conflict and HIV/AIDS, which has had devastating consequences in many countries, especially sub-Saharan Africa (Devereux, 2001). Cross-cutting themes on this new rural development agenda are sustainable development and beneficiary participation.

There has, thus, been a shift in thinking towards what some see as a 'new development paradigm', aimed at achieving 'participatory and environmentally sustainable growth based on poverty alleviation' (Jazairy et al., 1992: 14). It is a moot point whether, as Shepherd argues, there has been a comprehensive 'paradigm shift in the theory and practice of rural development' (1998: 10). However, it is undeniable that the past decade has seen a concerted effort by academics and development practitioners to identify a set of analytical and prescriptive tools capable of doing justice both to the complexity of rural development problems and to the need for diverse and more appropriate solutions. Such an approach is reflected in the 'sustainable livelihoods framework' (SLF).

Social investment for sustainable rural livelihoods

The sustainable livelihood approach draws on over two decades of work on a range of issues such as poverty, vulnerability, farming systems, participation and sustainable development. Its origins may be traced to the World Commission on Environment and Development, which proposed 'sustainable livelihoods' as an integrating concept, defined as 'adequate stocks and flows of food and cash to meet basic needs' (WCED, 1987: 2). The concept was later extended by Chambers and Conway (1992) to include dimensions such as capabilities, and became the subject of further analysis during discussions surrounding publication of the UK government's *White Paper on International Development* (DFID, 1997).

In technical terms, the SLF is an analytical device for understanding the complex forces that condition people's livelihoods and situations of poverty. Yet it also contains a wider political message by prioritizing the eradication of poverty and the strengthening of livelihoods as a fundamental objective of planned development, through situation-specific interventions tailored to meet the livelihood needs of particular groups. This approach is therefore consistent with the search for an alternative approach to the modernization paradigm of rural development. Thus:

> A livelihood comprises the capabilities, assets (including both material and social resources) and activities required for a means of living. A livelihood is sustainable when it can cope with and recover from stresses and shocks, and maintain or enhance its capabilities and assets both now and in the future, while not undermining the natural resource base. (Scoones, 1998: 5)

The SLF is above all a dynamic schema involving a range of variables in an iterative process (see Figure 3.1). Rather than taking as its point of departure the conventional notion of poverty as measured against income or consumption criteria, a livelihoods framework assumes that people pursue multiple objectives; not just higher incomes but also improved health, access to education, reduced vulnerability and less exposure to risk. This is achieved by drawing upon a range of capital assets: financial, human, physical, natural and social. Conspicuous by its absence in the original framework, however, is the notion of political capital, or people's capacity to mobilize pro-actively in defence of livelihoods. This is by no means synonymous with social capital, which does not necessarily involve politicized behaviour. Subsequent modifications of the SLF have included the political dimension (Baumann and Sinha, 2001). Other attributes such as local or indigenous knowledge could be added to the list of capital assets.

Livelihood strategies may involve the pursuit of a range of rural-based (farming and non-farming) and non-rural activities (Ellis, 2000). Such versatility is particularly critical as growing pressures on traditional farming have driven many small rural producers to migrate to seek off-farm employment as a complementary source of income and livelihood. This phenomenon has significant implications in terms poverty alleviation through development of the rural non-farm economy. A note of caution is in order, however, since the potential for rural diversification is seriously constrained by the availability of financial, human and social capital as well as infrastructure, service and market linkages (Wiggins and Proctor, 2001). Thus, it is essential that planning for the rural non-farm economy takes due account of the comparative advantages and economic potential of rural areas at different stages of evolution (Start, 2001).

Consistent with a post-modern, action-oriented approach to rural development, people are seen as being driven in part by their own individual or group preferences and priorities. Outcomes are not seen as necessarily being predetermined by prevailing structures of power and asset distribution (the pessimistic

Figure 3.1   The original sustainable livelihoods framework

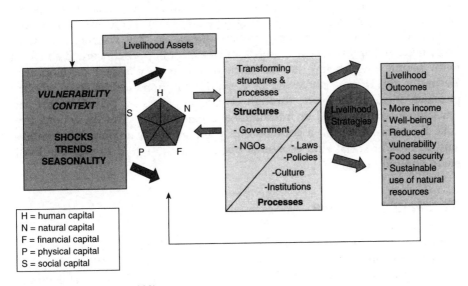

Source: Farrington et al. (1999).

view). There is, SLF proponents argue, scope for progressive change by harnessing forms of local capital and working through institutions to produce specific solutions to given livelihood problems (the optimistic view). Capital assets are resources that support livelihoods in a strictly material sense but they also have wider significance. Social, human, natural and other capitals provide a source of meaning and power that may be mobilized to challenge the status quo and the rules which govern distribution of and control over these resources (Sen, 1997). The radical approach developed by Freire (1972) to grassroots development was always far more about strengthening people's confidence in their own abilities to take action to influence the course of events that affect their daily lives, rather than about 'raising awareness' (*conscientizaçõ* in Portuguese) as such.

Yet rural people's power is influenced and constrained by contextual factors such as vulnerability as well as by encompassing structures and processes. Vulnerability or deprivation 'can be understood through the inter-linked dimensions of physical weakness, isolation, income-poverty, vulnerability and powerlessness' (Chambers, 1997: 7). It may be conditioned by shocks (climatic and political), trends (resource stocks) and seasonal variations in key livelihood matters such as crop prices. In turn, moulding the context within which rural people apply their livelihood assets are those overarching or transforming structures (government and private sector) and processes (laws, policies, cultures and institutions) which help to determine appropriate livelihood strategies and outcomes.

The livelihood approach brings together three core principles: namely, a focus on *people*, a *holistic* approach to analysis and policy prescription, and an emphasis on *macro–micro links* (Farrington et al., 1999). These are entirely consistent with the vision of social policy offered in this volume. Firstly, as explained in Chapter 1, social analysis and social policy are concerned above all with people's well-being as the main objective of planned development. Secondly, this is now perceived as a multi-institutional endeavour, whether pursued through the State, through civil society (NGOs, private sector and grassroots communities) or international organizations. Thirdly, actions may take the form of one or a combination of either social welfare interventions and/or broader social and economic investments designed to promote livelihood strengthening.

People at the centre

A minority of scholars and practitioners has for many years been trying to bring people onto the policy agenda as active participants, prioritizing their needs above macro-economic, modernization goals. Yet it is a sad reflection on the myopia of mainstream development approaches that innovative thinkers have had to bend over backwards in order to overtly 'put people first' (Chambers, 1983, 1997; Cernea, 1985; Burkey, 1993). The desirability and efficacy of actively incorporating impacted people into the process of needs analysis as well as in rural project or programme design, execution and management has over the years been cumulatively underlined in many publications (Oakley and Marsden, 1984; Cernea, 1985; Rondinelli, 1993; Mosse et al., 1998). There is also a substantial literature on field methodologies such as rapid rural appraisal (RRA) and participatory rural appraisal (PRA) developed since the 1980s to facilitate this process (Scoones and Thompson, 1994; Chambers, 1997).

Directly addressing people's needs as a central development objective has been fuelled in part by altruistic and human rights concerns (Maxwell, 1999). However, it has also been driven by pragmatism. As illustrated in Figure 3.1, people contribute various capital assets to the development process. Without romanticizing the issue, it is fair to say that many of these attributes and capacities are to be found only amongst the people themselves. Traditional knowledge of local ecosystems, for example, often lies at the heart of environmental management (Hall, 1997a, 2004). At the same time, well-organized groups are increasingly critical elements in determining process outcomes, especially when they are able to form strategic alliances with other institutional actors and scale-up their impact, for example, through social–environmental movements (Ghai and Vivian, 1992; Freidmann and Rangan, 1993; Blauert and Zadeck, 1998). For example, effective community organization is particularly critical in the governance of common property natural resources in which individual and collective benefits must be carefully negotiated in order to avoid environmental degradation.

Although attractive in principle, however, the challenge of incorporating people's participation into community-based natural resource management and other similar schemes is fraught with practical difficulties (Ostrom, 1990; Hall, 1997a; Agrawal and Gibson, 1999; Leach et al., 1999). Outsiders frequently have unrealistic expectations about the propensity of poor groups to contribute resources and to take part in participatory exercises, especially in the project management phase. Groups may appear to be cohesive communities but may in fact be divided by conflicts that need to be taken into account in project design and execution as well as policy formation (Leach et al., 1997; Cooke and Kothari, 2001). Generations of vertical, clientelistic politics and patronage, for example, can totally undermine attempts to induce collective cooperation. Communities are often expected to contribute time, labour and material resources, yet planners often ignore the need for proper incentive‐structures to be put in place which offer a return without creating long-term dependence. The gender dimension of inequality in the distribution of decision-making powers at household and community levels is often bypassed, even by apparently progressive policy-makers and practitioners (Guijt and Shah, 1998).

Understanding power relations is an integral part of the livelihood approach, and empowerment of the rural poor seen as a way forward. Empowerment is here defined as the ability of groups to actively exercise a decisive influence over the outcomes of development processes in their favour. Yet this potential will remain very limited unless social capital is complemented by *political capital*. Governments will, by their very nature, always tend to manipulate the grassroots according to the official agenda, benevolent or otherwise (Hall, 1986). In this instance, civil society must play the lead role in empowering deprived rural groups to enable them to gain access to a greater share of development benefits. Although entrenched bureaucracies and rural power structures remain formidable barriers to people's empowerment, much has been achieved.

Many cases exist of rural development projects and programmes in which grassroots organizations acting in collaboration with NGOs, progressive State bodies and international donors have achieved a degree of empowerment, sometimes leading to wider policy reform. Brazil's official 'extractive reserves' set up for rubber tappers is a case in point, but there are many others (Hall, 1997a). These include several diverse but related fields such as sustainable agriculture (Farrington and Bebbington, 1993; Bebbington, 1998; Guijt, 1998), resource conservation and development (Ghai and Vivian, 1992; Carney and Farrington, 1998) and forest management (WCFSD, 1999; Wolvekamp, 1999). During the 1990s, NGOs have been particularly successful in 'scaling up' their activities to achieve a wider impact through working with government in service provision as well as in lobbying and advocacy activities (Edwards and Hulme, 1992). However, this by no means constitutes a 'magic bullet', and the NGO sector must face up to major problems of adequately measuring performance and ensuring accountability (Edwards and Hulme, 1995).

A holistic approach

A rural livelihoods approach, 'allows the identification of livelihood-related opportunities and constraints regardless of where these occur'. It suggests that, although the analysis of such problems may be integrated or holistic, 'implementation of these need not be multi-sectoral … [but] … can best be initiated in response to particular opportunities or needs, even within sub-sectors, and then gradually expanded' (Farrington et al., 1999: 2). Thus, in social policy terms, progress may be achieved either through conventional welfare programmes (education, health, housing) or by means of social investments in key, non-welfare sectors such as agriculture or resource conservation. In order to increase the likelihood of efficacy and sustainability, actions should be determined by the requirements of specific circumstances and negotiated directly with beneficiaries, not prescribed in advance. The correct sequencing of events and establishment of the most appropriate institutional arrangements become keys to success.

As part of the process, beneficiary participation is a major variable and has often been successfully incorporated into development initiatives. However, as with so many development tools, the rhetoric of beneficiary (or 'stakeholder') participation has often outweighed the reality. Early optimism surrounding the potential benefits of community participation has been curtailed by the operational difficulties of successfully incorporating socially conflictive and spatially fragmented populations into development projects and programmes. It may be possible to achieve some participation goals such as cost-sharing, enhancing project efficiency and building beneficiary capacity, although this can be problematic. Insensitive research and appraisal can lead to whole dimensions being missed, especially where multiple livelihood strategies are involved, seriously undermining the viability of rural projects and programmes (Ellis, 2000). However, apparent technical success begs the wider question of the extent to which participation is being used as a manipulative instrument to serve planners' interests rather than as a means of strengthening the power and autonomy of beneficiary groups, a far more vexed, political issue (Friedmann, 1992; Dudley, 1993; Cooke and Kothari, 2001).

Another central concept within this holistic approach is the notion that rural development cannot be left to single institutions but must involve multiple actors. Experience shows that to do otherwise is to court disaster. Although roles undoubtedly overlap, each institution brings a unique contribution to this process which, if properly organized, may provide a structure in which the whole is greater than the sum of the parts. The reverse may occur, of course, if the institutional package is badly put together and organizations compete in a negative fashion or unnecessarily duplicate actions (as often occurred, for example, in the case of integrated rural development programmes). In many innovative experiences, previously indifferent or even hostile bodies are gradually learning to collaborate with each other, providing 'good government' to the mutual benefit of all participants (Tendler, 1996; Mosse et al., 1998). This process of forming alliances and influencing policy for promoting sustainable rural development, based around a common language and shared institutional arrangements, has been labelled 'mediation' (Blauert and Zadeck, 1998). The phenomenon of 'synergy' across the chasm that previously separated public and private spheres has come increasingly under scrutiny as a potentially powerful development catalyst (Evans, 1996).

Institutions play distinctive roles that may complement each other in ways that allow the scaling-up of development action. Although the State no longer holds a monopoly over planned development it is still uniquely placed to provide an overarching legal or policy framework to facilitate change. Non-governmental organizations have greater ease of contact with the grassroots, which frequently remain hostile to central government. They may also engage in active lobbying for reforms in project intervention and wider policies, attributes that may in fact be compromised once NGOs are drawn into service-provision *in lieu* of government. Local communities often possess valuable social and human capital as well as knowledge of local ecosystems and natural resources of which governments are totally ignorant, but which can be harnessed for development purposes. International development organizations are frequently instrumental in providing financial support for innovative experiments to which governments are very often reluctant to commit domestic funds. Policy reform in fields as varied as primary health care and sustainable development have been driven by international development organizations in the first instance. In addition, the much-maligned private sector is proving to be a key partner in expanding marketing outlets for rural produce as well as in supplying credit through special arrangements for small producers.

Micro–macro links

To fully understand the constraints upon and opportunities for strengthening livelihoods, it is necessary to comprehend the relationship between the local and the wider situation. Put another way, successful implementation will depend both on policy or project *content* and its *context* (Grindle, 1980). Both internal and external factors must be taken into account. It is all very well to argue that actions may be initially localized and then scaled up, yet unless contextual constraints are not tackled and a favourable policy environment created, there is always a high risk that small projects will remain small projects. The developing world is littered with showpiece schemes that are artificially and indefinitely propped up by external funds because governments are not prepared to allocate domestic resources to make them genuinely viable. This phenomenon has more to do with maintaining the image of donor organizations than with promoting self-sustaining development.

In the medium to long term, therefore, the wider picture has to be tackled. Welfare policy and other forms of social investment have to be seen within these broader circumstances. For example, agricultural extension services are often viewed as the key to enhancing human capital and boosting crop production. Yet if farmers have no secure access to land or to other vital production inputs, they will have little incentive to seek extension advice. Broader policy variables governing access to land, credit, seeds and other services therefore have to be tackled simultaneously. In a similar fashion, Amazonian deforestation can in theory be arrested by agroforestry projects that obviate the need for destructive slash-and-burn practices. However, if governments adopt fiscal policies and macro-economic incentives that stimulate cattle ranching and illegal logging while depriving small farmers of mainstream policy support, these innovative projects will remain 'islands' of progress within an expanding sea of destruction (Hall, 1997b).

A livelihood approach is in many respects the culmination of a strong 'bottom-up' development tradition that places great faith in the ability of grassroots organizations to deal with their problems through direct action. Yet a strong note of caution is necessary. Although such action has been instrumental in challenging the modernization paradigm, there is always a danger that local potential may be exaggerated or romanticized, feeding the optimism of intellectuals rather than the stomachs of the poor. Local-level initiatives are surely of fundamental importance in many respects but there is a limit to what they can achieve on their own. Yet community organizations are increasingly aware of the impact that they can have when partnered by progressive elements within the State machine or influential aid donors. During the 1970s and 1980s, when dictatorships and single-party States were more common, government was automatically seen as the enemy that had to be defeated before rural development could be achieved. David had to slay Goliath. Without doubt, civil society organizations have made a distinctive contribution to development by challenging the inequities and abuses perpetrated by mainstream rural development. Yet although strong conflicts of interest undoubtedly remain, the two parties increasingly seek out common ground for negotiation and compromise, in recognition of the contribution which each can make.

It has become almost conventional wisdom to minimize the role of the State as an engine of progressive change. Yet the power of the State to pro-actively intervene to systematically promote social development, rather than simply react in a minimalist way to grassroots pressure, is an important consideration. The State can be seen as having particularly strong development obligations in countries where civil society is weak and disorganized. Equally, the State may be the only vehicle for promoting development in nations that are geographically large and fragmented and/or enjoy a high level of cultural diversity. Whether at national, regional or local level, the State can be a force for positive rural development that is supportive of people's livelihoods. For example, the strong role of regional government in promoting integrated rural development and primary health care in north-east Brazil has been well documented (Tendler, 1993, 1996). Likewise, the cases of South Korea and Taiwan, as well as those of West Bengal and Kerala in India, all testify to the power of government to promote comprehensive rural development (Crow, 1992).

Only the State has the necessary financial and organizational capacity to undertake major social investments in welfare and other sectors, one of the key factors in the recent achievements of East Asian countries (Watt, 2001). Thus, governments have to be persuaded to correct the imbalances of the past and rectify the significant levels of rural under-investment. Yet due to the conditionalities imposed by structural adjustment and to other global forces, the nature of the State's role has gradually changed. From being sole provider on the basis of institutionalized monopolies, it has become more of a facilitator and source of support for other actors such as non-governmental organizations and private companies (Cook and Kirkpatrick, 1995). The provision of basic infrastructure such as electricity, road building and telecommunications, as well as other services such as agricultural extension and marketing, are increasingly becoming privatized. In Latin America, the State is moving away from direct implementation of certain kinds of development, sub-contracting and supporting private enterprise and civic initiative (Bebbington and Thiele, 1993; Bebbington, 1998). This process has become so far advanced in Bangladesh that it has been labelled a 'franchise state' (Wood, 1997). There is a strong argument for public sector reform to streamline the role of government in contrasting national contexts in order to make the State more efficient and to maximize its economic and social development impact (Turner and Hulme, 1997).

In terms of the livelihoods framework, however, State action cannot be considered universally benevolent and it is often likely to involve priorities based on building nationhood favouring economic elites for purely political purposes. Governments are normally far more concerned about pursuing political and wider strategic goals than in promoting broad-based rural development. Such priorities inevitably go hand in hand with considerable costs in terms of the adverse impacts on people's livelihoods. One obvious example is the extermination of indigenous peoples by colonizing forces, with State connivance (Davis, 1977; Colchester, 1985). Another relates to the large population displacements usually associated with hydropower schemes where, until relatively recently, little provision was made for the comprehensive resettlement of those evicted (Cernea, 1990; Cernea and Guggenheim, 1993; World Bank, 1994; WCD, 2000).

The above notion of building sustainable rural livelihoods as a long-term policy objective should not obscure the fact that insecurity as a major source of poverty may need to be addressed through complementary, short-term measures as part of a comprehensive approach to dealing with risk and vulnerability (Devereux, 2001). It is thus argued that there is still a role in rural development for social protection to ameliorate livelihood shocks. Conventionally, protection has taken the form of income transfers through donor-financed emergency relief and public works programmes following crises induced by natural disasters. Expanding and institutionalizing such redistributive transfer mechanisms to deal with non-emergency situations of poverty and vulnerability is problematic in view of the huge costs, administrative complexity and political ramifications involved. However, new social protection strategies for rural areas are emerging which can reduce risk in the short term and contribute towards livelihood strengthening.

Selective and tailored public interventions to help individuals, households and communities manage risk can, it is argued, provide social protection while providing an avenue out of poverty (Holzmann and Jorgensen, 2000). Measures include maintaining access to basic social services such as education and health, fighting social exclusion, promoting economic activities and providing safety nets through cash and food transfer programmes to vulnerable groups such as women and children in particular. As a form of rural social policy, however, such protection interventions must be seen in perspective as providing just temporary relief, which in all probability have a limited impact on poverty alleviation. Indeed, unless very carefully considered, they may well perpetuate the structural mechanisms that generate deprivation, dependency and suffering in the long term.

Conclusion

This chapter has explored contrasting notions of rural development, and the transition from exclusive dominance of the modernization paradigm towards the complementary adoption by many institutions of a sustainable livelihoods approach. Such a perspective represents a significant advance in terms of systematically addressing the needs of groups whose interests have until now been relatively ignored in the mainstream planning process. It forms a key element within an emerging rural development agenda that prioritizes the production and consumption needs of those vulnerable and marginalized groups traditionally ignored in mainstream policy-making. As a technical tool, the SLF complements and builds upon existing participatory methodologies such as stakeholder analysis. It has already been applied in a number of contrasting situations both to analyse the complex roots of rural poverty and to explore potential solutions. These include, for example, natural resource conflict in Western Orissa, poverty assessments in Pakistan and Zambia, monitoring and evaluation of wildlife enterprises in Kenya, community-based natural resource management and tourism in Namibia (Farrington et al., 1999) and small-scale fisheries (Allison and Ellis, 2001), to name but a few. Furthermore, agencies such as DFID, CARE and UNDP have adapted the original framework to make it more applicable to varied contexts (Carney, 2002).

A livelihoods perspective is thus a useful integrating device that can pinpoint livelihood bottlenecks and specific constraints, especially at the local level. By providing a common analytical framework, it can also facilitate (although not guarantee) much-needed cross-sector and cross-disciplinary collaboration between, for example, natural and social scientists. As noted above, however, there are formidable political obstacles to its widespread use as a development tool for tackling problems experienced by the poor. In addition, there are significant potential operational and procedural problems in applying this methodology. By its very nature, it requires cross-disciplinary collaboration on the part of practitioners, it is extremely time-consuming and therefore relatively expensive when compared with more conventional, top-down data-collection techniques. In addition, many critics would say that the SLF is far too micro-focused and too incremental, ignoring deep-seated structural barriers to change.

Adoption of a livelihoods approach, by definition, falls within a 'process' planning perspective in which project or programme design and implementation take place gradually as livelihood opportunities and constraints become clearer, rather than following the conventional 'blueprint' path with its predetermined objectives and outcomes. Historically, non-governmental organizations have been far more amenable to the use of such iterative methods, which demand sensitivity and trust on the part of funding organizations towards recipients. However, such flexibility has often proved to be incompatible with the rigid budget cycle management procedures of most official donor agencies and their insistence on quantitative change indicators. While some aid bodies have been making an effort to incorporate new methods into their operations, there is room for much greater progress in this area. Whether due to sheer bureaucratic inertia or whether justified on the grounds of 'accountability', aid bodies are still very reluctant to give up their standard demands.

While a livelihoods approach has its technical merits, it can only be truly effective if it has political backing. Strengthening and sustaining livelihoods will in many if not most rural situations entail challenging local power structures and the distribution of resources and capital assets. High-level commitment to promoting redistributive change in favour of the rural population at large is a rarity and the product of very specific historical circumstances. The temptation amongst national authorities is to rely too heavily on short-term, social protectionist interventions rather than to grasp the nettle of more fundamental reforms. As we have seen, it is more likely that grassroots organizations emerge to put pressure on governments for incremental policy reform. Furthermore, aid donors may exercise their own influence and leverage, often in conjunction with community organizations and NGOs, to promote policy dialogue for progressive change towards a livelihoods perspective.

From a social policy perspective, the notion of sustainable rural livelihoods is highly relevant. As both an analytical device and a practical tool, the livelihoods framework highlights the social policy concern with the well-being of people as the central focus of development efforts. This process will involve both micro- and macro-level actions through a whole range of institutional channels. Thus, development may be achieved through conventional social welfare interventions via social services, statutory regulation or the tax system. However, in common with the broader definition of social policy adopted in this volume, the livelihoods approach incorporates economic, social, environmental and other dimensions that directly or indirectly affect people's well-being in both foreseen and unintended ways. Such a framework should be indispensable in the rural development field as an analytical tool and practical guide in the design and implementation of more appropriate social policies. The gradual 'mainstreaming' of a sustainable livelihoods approach within the planning agendas of development organizations around the globe augers well for pro-poor rural development. These notions are equally relevant to the urban context, and the next chapter will therefore examine evolving social policies for addressing poverty and livelihood issues in the burgeoning cities and towns of the South.

Recommended Reading

The following texts offer a critique of conventional rural development policies and practice, and review new initiatives in this field oriented towards an anti-poverty agenda.

- Eicher, C.M. and Staatz, J.M. (eds) (1998) *International Agricultural Development*, 3rd edn Baltimore, MD: Johns Hopkins University Press. A broad collection of landmark articles on the evolution of thinking around agricultural and rural development since the 1960s.
- Shepherd, A. (1998) *Sustainable Rural Development*. Basingstoke and London: Macmillan. A useful critique of mainstream modernization approaches to rural development and a conceptualization of the livelihoods approach.
- Scoones, I. (1998) 'Sustainable rural livelihoods: a framework for analysis', *Working Paper* 72. Brighton: Institute of Development Studies. An outline and discussion of the original basic sustainable livelihoods framework.
- Carney, D. (2002) *Sustainable Livelihoods Approaches: Progress and Possibilities for Change*. London: DFID. This paper traces the evolution of the livelihoods approach and its adaptation to a variety of different situations.
- *Development Policy Review*, 19 (4), December, 2001. This is a special issue on 'Rethinking Rural Development'. A very pertinent, post-Washington Consensus review of rural development policies in the South and the emergence of a new anti-poverty agenda.

References

Agrawal, A. and Gibson, C. (1999) 'Enchantment and disenchantment: the rise of community in natural resource conservation', *World Development*, 27 (4), April.

Ahmed, I. and Lipton, M. (1997) 'Impacts of structural adjustment on sustainable rural livelihoods: a review of the literature', *IDS Working Paper* 62. Brighton: Institute of Development Studies.

Allison, E.H. and Ellis, F. (2001) 'The livelihoods approach and management of small-scale fisheries', *Marine Policy*, 25: 377–88.

Ashley, C. and Maxwell, S. (2001) 'Rethinking rural development', *Development Policy Review*, 19 (4), December: 395–425.

Ashley, C. and Maxwell, S. (2002) 'Rethinking rural development', *ODI Briefing Paper*, March.

Ayres, R. (1984) *Banking on the Poor: The World Bank and World Poverty*. Cambridge, MA: MIT Press.

Baumann, P. and Sinha, S. (2001) 'Linking development with democratic processes in India: political capital and sustainable livelihoods analysis', *Natural Resource Perspectives*, 68, June.

Bebbington, A. (1998) 'NGOs: mediators of sustainability/intermediaries in transition?', in Blauert and Zadeck (eds), op. cit., pp. 55–74.

Bebbington, A. and Thiele, G. (1993) *NGOs and the State in Latin America: Rethinking Roles in Sustainable Agricultural Development*. London: Routledge.

Bernstein, H., Crow, B. and Johnson, H. (eds) (1992) *Rural Livelihoods: Crises and Responses*. Oxford: Oxford University Press/Open University.

Blauert, J. and Zadeck, S. (eds) (1998) *Mediating Sustainability: Growing Policy from the Grassroots*. West Hartford, CT: Kumarian.

Burkey, S. (1993) *People First: A Guide to Self-Reliant, Participatory Rural Development*. London: Zed Books.

Byres, T.J. (1982) 'Agrarian transition and the agrarian question', in Harriss (ed.), op. cit., pp. 82–93.

Carney, D. (2002) *Sustainable Livelihoods Approaches: Progress and Possibilities for Change*. London: DFID.

Carney, D. and Farrington, J. (1998) *Natural Resource Management and Institutional Change*. London: Routledge.

Cassen, R. and Associates (1994) *Does Aid Work?*, 2nd edn. Oxford: Clarendon Press.

Cernea, M. (1985) *Putting People First: Sociological Variables in Rural Development*. Baltimore, MD: Johns Hopkins University Press.

Cernea, M. (1990) *Poverty Risks from Population Displacement in Water Resources Development*. Harvard Institute for International Development, Development Discussion Paper 355, August.

Cernea, M. and Guggenheim, S. (eds) (1993) *Anthropological Approaches to Resettlement: Policy, Practice, Theory*. Boulder, CO: Westview Press.

Chambers, R. (1983) *Rural Development: Putting the Last First*. Harlow: Longman.

Chambers, R. (1997) *Whose Reality Counts?* London: Intermediate Technology Publications.

Chambers, R. and Conway, G. (1992) 'Sustainable rural livelihoods: practical concepts for the 21st century', *IDS Discussion Paper* 296. Brighton: Institute of Development Studies.

Chenery, H., Ahluwalia, M., Bell, C., Duloy, J. and Jolly, R. (1974) *Redistribution with Growth*. Oxford: Oxford University Press.

Colchester, M. (1985) *An End to Laughter: Tribal Peoples and Economic Development*. London: Survival International.

Commander, S. (ed.) (1989) *Structural Adjustment and Agriculture: Theory and Practice in Africa and Latin America*. London: Overseas Development Institute/James Currey.

Cook, P. and Kirkpatrick, C. (eds) (1995) *Privatisation Policy and Performance*. London: Prentice Hall.

Cooke, B. and Kothari, U. (eds) (2001) *Participation, the New Tyranny?* London: Zed Books.

Coombs, P. and Ahmed, M. (1974) *Attacking Rural Poverty: How Non-Formal Education Can Help*. Washington, DC: World Bank.

Crow, B. (1992) 'Rural livelihoods: action from above', in H. Bernstein et al. (eds), *Rural Livelihoods: Crises and Responses*. Oxford: Oxford University Press/Open University, pp. 251–73.

Cristodoulou, D. (1990) *The Unpromised Land: Agrarian Reform and Conflict Worldwide.* London: Zed Books.

Davis, S. (1977) *Victims of the Miracle: Development and the Indians of Brazil.* Cambridge: Cambridge University Press.

Devereux, S. (2001) 'Livelihood insecurity and social protection: a re-emerging issue in rural development', *Development Policy Review*, 19 (4), December: 507–19.

DFID (1997) *Eliminating World Poverty: A Challenge for the 21st Century.* London: Department for International Development.

Dudley, E. (1993) *The Critical Villager: Beyond Community Participation.* London: Routledge.

Duncan, A. and Howell, J. (eds) (1992) *Structural Adjustment and the African Farmer.* London: ODI/James Currey.

EC (2000) 'EC policy and approach to rural development', *mimeo.* Brussels: European Commission, DG Development – Rural Development and Food Security.

Edwards, M. and Hulme, D. (eds) (1992) *Making a Difference: NGOs and Development in a Changing World.* London: Earthscan.

Edwards, M. and Hulme, D. (1995) *Non-Governmental Organizations – Performance and Accountability: Beyond the Magic Bullet.* London: Earthscan.

Eicher, C.K. and Staatz, J.M. (eds) (1985) *Agricultural Development in the Third World.* Baltimore, MD: Johns Hopkins University Press.

Eicher, C.K. and Staatz, J.M. (eds) (1998) *International Agricultural Development*, 3rd edn. Baltimore, MD: Johns Hopkins University Press.

Ellis, F. (2000) *Rural Livelihoods and Diversity in Developing Countries.* Oxford: Oxford University Press.

Evans, P. (1996) 'Government action, social capital and development: reviewing the evidence on synergy', *World Development*, 24 (6), June: 1119–32.

Farrington, J. and Bebbington A. (1993) *Reluctant Partners? Non-Governmental Organizations, the State and Sustainable Agricultural Development.* London: Routledge.

Farrington, J., Carney, D., Ashley, C. and Turton, C. (1999) 'Sustainable livelihoods in practice: early applications of concepts in rural areas', *Natural Resource Perspectives*, 42, June. London: Overseas Development Institute (ODI).

Freire, P. (1972) *Pedagogy of the Oppressed.* Harmondsworth: Penguin.

Friedmann, J. (1992) *Empowerment: The Politics of Alternative Development.* Oxford: Blackwell.

Friedmann, J. and Rangan, H. (eds) (1993) *In Defence of Livelihood: Case Studies on Environmental Action.* West Hartford, CT: Kumarian.

Ghai, D. and Vivian, J. (eds) (1992) *Grassroots Environmental Action: People's Participation in Sustainable Development.* London: Routledge.

Goodman, D. and Redclift, M. (1982) *From Peasant to Proletarian: Capitalist Development and Agrarian Transitions.* Oxford: Blackwell.

Griffin, K. (1979) *The Political Economy of Agrarian Change.* London: Macmillan.

Grindle, M. (1980) *Politics and Policy Implementation in the Third World.* Princeton, NJ: Princeton University Press.

Guijt, I. (1998) 'Assessing the merits of participatory development of sustainable agriculture: experiences from Brazil and Central America', in J. Blauert and S. Zadeck (eds), *Mediating Sustainability: Growing Policy from the Grassroots.* West Hartford CT: Kumarian, pp. 100–28.

Guijt, I. and Shah, M.K. (1998) *The Myth of Community: Gender Issues in Participatory Development.* London: IT Publications.

Hall, A. (1986) 'Community participation and rural development', in J. Midgley, A. Hall, M. Hardiman and D. Narine (eds) *Community Participation, Social Development and the State.* London: Methuen.

Hall, A. (1989) *Developing the Amazon: Social Conflict and Deforestation in Brazil's Carajás Programme*. Manchester: Manchester University Press.

Hall, A. (1997a) *Sustaining Amazonia: Grassroots Action for Productive Conservation*. Manchester: Manchester University Press.

Hall, A. (1997b) 'Peopling the environment: a new agenda for research, policy and action in Brazilian Amazonia', *European Review of Latin American and Caribbean Studies*, 62, June.

Hall, A. (2003) 'Enhancing social capital: productive conservation and traditional knowledge in the Brazilian rainforest', in D. Posey (ed.) *Human Impacts on Amazonia: The Role of Traditional Knowledge in Conservation and Development*. New York: Columbia University Press.

Harriss, J. (ed.) (1982) *Rural Development: Theories of Peasant Economy and Agrarian Change*. London: Hutchinson.

Hayami, Y. (1985) 'Assessment of the Green Revolution', in C.K. Eicher and J.M. Staatz (eds), *Agricultural Development in the Third World*. Baltimore, MD: Johns Hopkins University Press, pp. 389–96.

Holdcroft, L. and Jones, G. (1982) 'The rise and fall of community development in developing countries, 1950–1965: a critical analysis and implications', in G. Jones and M. Rolls (eds), *Progress in Rural Extension and Community Development. Vol. 1: Extension and Relative Advantage in Rural Development*. Chichester: John Wiley. pp. 207–31.

Holzmann, R. and Jorgensen, S. (2000) *Social Risk Management: A New Conceptual Framework for Social Protection and Beyond*. Social Protection Discussion Paper No. 6. Washington, DC: World Bank.

Howell, J. (1990) 'Rural poverty and external aid', *Development Policy Review*, 8 (3), September: 269–86.

Hulme, D. and Edwards, M. (eds) (1997) *Too Close for Comfort? NGOs, Donors and the State*. Basingstoke: Macmillan.

IFAD (2001) *Rural Poverty Report 2001: The Challenge of Ending Rural Poverty*. Oxford: Oxford University Press.

Jazairy, I., Alamgir, M. and Panuccio, T. (1992) *The State of World Rural Poverty*. London: IT Publications/International Fund for Agricultural Development.

Johnston, B. and Mellor, J. (1961) 'The role of agriculture in economic development', *American Economic Review*, 51 (4): 566–93.

Jones, G. and Rolls, M. (eds) (1982) *Progress in Rural Extension and Community Development. Vol. 1: Extension and Relative Advantage in Rural Development*. Chichester: John Wiley.

Killick, T. (2001) 'Globalisation and the rural poor', *Development Policy Review*, 19 (2): 155–80.

Kydd, J. and Dorward, A. (2001) 'The Washington Consensus on poor country agriculture: analysis, prescription and institutional gaps', *Development Policy Review*, 19 (4): 467–78.

Leach, M., Mearns, R. and Scoones, I. (1997) 'Challenges to community-based sustainable development: dynamics, entitlements, institutions', *IDS Bulletin*, 28 (4), October: 4–14.

Leach, M., Mearns, R. and Scoones, I. (1999) 'Environmental entitlements: dynamics and institutions in community-based natural resource management', *World Development*, 27 (2), February: 225–47.

Lele, U. (1975) *The Design of Rural Development: Lessons from Africa*. Baltimore, MD: Johns Hopkins University Press.

Lewis, W.A. (1954) 'Economic development with unlimited supplies of labour', *Manchester School of Economic and Social Studies*, 22 (2): 139–91.

Lipton, M. and Longhurst, R. (1989) *New Seeds, Poor People*. London: Unwin Hyman.

Mahar, D. (1989) *Government Policies and Deforestation in Brazil's Amazon Region.* Washington, DC: World Bank.

Maxwell, S. (1999) 'What can we do with a rights-based approach to development?', *Briefing Paper*, No. 3, September. London: Overseas Development Institute.

Maxwell, S., Urey, I. and Ashley, C. (2001) 'Emerging issues in rural development', January. London: Overseas Development Institute.

Mosse, D. et al. (eds) (1998) *Development as Process.* London: Routledge/ODI.

Nicholls, W.H. (1964) 'The place of agriculture in economic development', in C.K. Eicher and W.W. Lawrence (eds) *Agriculture in Economic Development.* New York: McGraw-Hill, pp. 11–44.

Oakley, P. and Marsden, D. (1984) *Approaches to Participation in Rural Development.* Geneva: ILO.

Ostrom, E. (1990) *Governing the Commons: The Evolution of Institutions for Collective Action.* Cambridge: Cambridge University Press.

Payer, C. (1982) *The World Bank: A Critical Analysis.* New York: Monthly Review Press.

Pearce, A. (1980) *Seeds of Plenty, Seeds of Want.* Oxford: Clarendon Press.

Reed, D. (ed.) (1996) *Structural Adjustment, the Environment and Sustainable Development.* London: Earthscan.

Rich, B. (1994) *Mortgaging the Earth: The World Bank, Environmental Impoverishment and the Crisis of Development.* London: Earthscan.

Rondinelli, D. (1993) *Development Projects as Policy Experiments.* London: Methuen.

Rostow, W.W. (1960) *The Stages of Economic Growth.* Cambridge: Cambridge University Press.

Ruttan, V.W. (1998) 'Models of agricultural development', in C.K. Eicher and J.M. Staatz (eds), *Agricultural Development in the Third World.* Baltimore, MD: Johns Hopkins University Press, pp. 155–62.

Ruttan, V.W. and Hayami, Y. (1998) 'Induced innovation model of agricultural development', in C.K. Eicher and J.M. Staatz (eds), *Agricultural Development in the Third World.* Baltimore, MD: Johns Hopkins University Press, pp. 163–78.

Schultz, T.W. (1964) *Transforming Traditional Agriculture.* New Haven, CT: Yale University Press.

Scoones, I. (1998) 'Sustainable rural livelihoods: a framework for analysis', *Working Paper* 72. Brighton: Institute of Development Studies.

Scoones, I. and Thompson, J. (eds) (1994) *Beyond Farmer First.* London: IT Publications.

Sen, A. (1997) 'Editorial: human capital and human capability', *World Development*, 25 (12), December: 1959–61.

Shanin, T. (1988) *Peasants and Peasant Societies.* Harmondsworth: Penguin.

Shepherd, A. (1998) *Sustainable Rural Development.* Basingstoke: Macmillan.

Start, D. (2001) 'The rise and fall of the non-farm rural economy: poverty impacts and poverty options', *Development Policy Review*, 19 (4): 491–505.

Stewart, F. (1985) *Planning to Meet Basic Human Needs.* London: Macmillan.

Streeten, P., Burki, S., ul Haq, M., Hicks, N. and Stewart, F. (1981) *First Things First: Meeting Basic Human Needs in Developing Countries.* Oxford: Oxford University Press.

Tendler, J. (1993) *New Lessons from Old Projects: The Workings of Rural Development in Northeast Brazil.* Washington, DC: World Bank, Operations Evaluation Department.

Tendler, J. (1996) *Good Government in the Tropics.* Baltimore, MD: Johns Hopkins University Press.

Todaro, M.P. (2000) *Economic Development*, 7th edn. New York: Addison-Wesley.

Turner, M. and Hulme, D. (1997) *Governance, Administration and Development: Making the State Work.* Basingstoke: Macmillan.

UNDP (1999) *Human Development Report 1999*. Oxford: Oxford University Press.

Watt, P. (2001) *Social Investment and Economic Growth: A Strategy to Eradicate Poverty*. Oxford: Oxfam.

WCD (2000) *Dams and Development: A New Framework for Decision-Making*. London: Earthscan.

WCED (1987) *Food 2000: Global Policies for Sustainable Agriculture*. London: Zed Books.

WCFSD (1999) *Our Forests, Our Future*. Report of the World Commission on Forests and Sustainable Development. Cambridge: Cambridge University Press.

Weeks, J. (ed.) (1995) *Structural Adjustment and the Agricultural Sector in Latin America and the Caribbean*, London: Macmillan/Institute of Latin American Studies, University of London.

White, H. (1996) 'How much aid is used for poverty reduction?', *IDS Bulletin*, 27 (1), January: 83–99.

Wiggins, S. and Proctor, S. (2001) 'How special are rural areas? The economic implications of location for rural development', *Development Policy Review*, 19 (4): 427–36.

Wisner, B. (1988) *Power and Need in Africa*. London: Earthscan.

Wolvekamp, P. (ed.) (1999) *Forests for the Future*. London: Zed Books.

Wood, G. (1997) 'States without citizens: the problem of the franchise state', in D. Hulme and M. Edwards (eds), *Too Close for Comfort? NGOs, Donors and the State*. Basingstoke: Macmillan, pp. 79–92.

World Bank (1975) *The Assault on World Poverty*. Baltimore, MD: Johns Hopkins University Press.

World Bank (1982) *World Development Report 1982*. Oxford: Oxford University Press.

World Bank (1987) *World Bank Experience with Rural Development, 1965–87*. Washington, DC: World Bank, Operations Evaluation Department.

World Bank (1994) *Resettlement and Development: The Bankwide Review of Projects Involving Involuntary Resettlement, 1986–93*. Washington, DC: World Bank, Environment Department.

World Bank (1997) *World Development Report 1997: The State in a Changing World*. Oxford: Oxford University Press.

World Bank (2000) *World Development Report, 1999–2000*. Washington, DC: World Bank.

4 SOCIAL POLICY AND URBAN DEVELOPMENT

Jo Beall[1]

Summary

This chapter discusses the challenges of urban development, paying particular attention to the growing problem of urban poverty, and it reviews the social policies that have been formulated to improve urban conditions especially for the poor. The chapter is divided into four sections. The first section introduces the urban context, offering a definition of what constitutes an urban area. It traces the growth of urban poverty, describes its characteristics and lays out the challenges posed by the urbanization of poverty. The following section focuses on the areas of social policy that are historically most commonly associated with urban development, access to shelter and basic services. It explores the relationship between these services and poverty reduction and examines the ways in which this has been delivered over recent decades. Section three is concerned with urban livelihoods – that other key dimension of urban social development, understood here not only as making a living in the city but more broadly as the systems by which urban dwellers support themselves and survive. As such, the livelihoods perspective adopted acknowledges the importance not only of productive processes but also of reproduction (domestic work and child care) and social relations and networks that ensure some form of security. Section four discusses the challenges facing city governments in implementing urban social policy, given their institutional location vis-á-vis other levels of government and other stakeholders acting in and on the urban context. It concludes by examining what lessons can be drawn for social policy aiming to address old and new forms of urban social disadvantage.

Growing urban poverty

Until relatively recently, poverty in developing countries was seen mainly as a rural phenomenon and, as pointed out in Chapter 3, the world's poor are still

---

[1]Development Studies Institute (DESTIN), London School of Economics and Political Science.

predominantly rural dwellers. However, the ranks of the urban poor are growing rapidly and there is increasing need to understand and address urban social disadvantage. While recognizing that there are often strong links between urban and rural poverty and that livelihood strategies often straddle the rural–urban divide, meeting the challenges posed by growing urban poverty has become a priority. Indeed, urban poverty has today risen to the top of the international social policy agenda. However, policies to address urban poverty are often incoherent, not least because they are based on an unclear understanding of the characteristics of urban poverty and the processes that accompany it, such as social exclusion. The institutions of urban governance are often ill-prepared for the enormous and increasing demands being placed upon them. They are badly equipped to generate sufficient employment or to provide or even maintain existing infrastructure necessary for local economic development.

In these circumstances, the commitment to social investment is sorely tested, even though the benefits for urban development and social well-being are widely recognized. There is a greater appreciation today that the challenges of urban poverty are multifaceted and require clear and coherent social policy responses. By addressing urban social disadvantage, the welfare and livelihood opportunities of the urban poor can be enhanced and, at the same time, urban and indeed national social and economic development can be more broadly advanced to improve the welfare of all. Effective forms of policy implementation that involve responsive government and the active participation of the poor are essential if the challenges of urban poverty and deprivation are to be addressed.

The urban context and urban poverty

One of the complexities of tackling social disadvantage in cities is that there is disagreement about the criteria that should be used to distinguish between rural and urban areas. One approach stresses the quantitative dimensions of urbanization and defines urban areas in terms of population size. A second approach stresses the qualitative dimensions of urbanism, for example by examining urban lifestyles and what cities represent to the people who live in them. Both approaches are useful for social policy and should be seen as complementary rather than mutually exclusive. Most commonly, however, numerical or demographic data are used to examine the population size of settlements. If the population of a settlement within a defined administrative boundary exceeds a specified figure, it is classified as urban. Today census officials around the world employ this approach, although it has a number of weaknesses. Firstly, numerical criteria are arbitrary and, because they vary between countries, it is difficult to make accurate international comparisons. Secondly, census classifications of urban boundaries may be misleading if they encompass agricultural land or agricultural communities, or if they exclude newer built-up areas on the periphery that are effectively part of the city.

Urbanization and urban growth

Demographers have attempted to modify their approach to accommodate some of these criticisms. In a seminal and widely respected paper on the subject Davis (1965) argued for demographic criteria to be standardized. He proposed that a figure of at least 20,000 be used to designate an urban place, while 100,000 be used to designate a city. He suggested that the population of the contiguous built-up area be included in this enumeration irrespective of administrative boundaries. Davis also argued for *urbanization* to be defined as both a process and a measure. As a process, urbanization involves a growth in the absolute numbers of people living in urban areas. As a measure, urbanization is the proportion of a national population living in urban centres. Davis' definitions inform the volumes of urban statistics produced by international organizations such as the World Bank and United Nations today. A wealth of data are collected on demographic trends by national governments and international organizations such as the United Nations. A general overview can be obtained by focusing on three key statistics.

The first of these is the urban population, which is the number of people living in urban areas expressed in absolute terms. It can be used to calculate the urbanization level or the degree to which a given population is urbanized. The urbanization level is the proportion of the total population living in urban centres, and is normally expressed as a percentage. An increase in the urbanization level can be a product of rural–urban migration but it usually results from rural settlements growing to a size where they are reclassified as urban, or when boundaries of cities or metropolitan areas are extended to incorporate areas that were previously classified as rural. A third statistic concerns urban growth. This is a growth in the absolute numbers of people living in urban areas. It usually results from natural increase (the excess of births over deaths) within urban areas but can also be the result of migration into urban areas.

Care should be taken when examining urbanization data because the situation is not always as straightforward as it may seem. For instance, *definitions of cities and urban areas* vary from country to country and even from census to census. When the urban population increases dramatically, it is often because the national government's definition of what constitutes an 'urban' area has changed. For example, according to China's State Statistical Bureau, by the end of 1996, urban residents accounted for about 43 per cent of the country's population, when in 1994 only 20 per cent of the population was considered urban. One of the main reasons for this shift was rapid growth in hundreds of Chinese towns reclassified as cities in recent years (World Bank, 1995). In addition, there is the question of where *boundaries* are drawn. For example, the 'core city' of Beijing contained 2.3 million people in 1990. The 'inner city, inner and outer suburban districts and counties' contained 10.8 million (World Bank, 1999: 157). Either of these totals could be stated as the total population of the city of Beijing. However we analyse the data, this illustrates the massive changes that are taking place in patterns of urbanization in the twenty-first century. On a

Table 4.1 Urban population – hundreds of thousands of people residing in urban areas

	1955	1965	1975	1985	1995	2005	2015	2030
			Actual				Forecast	
World	872	1,185	1,543	1,997	2,574	3,227	3,962	5,117
More developed regions	501	625	733	808	877	927	972	1,015
Less developed regions	371	560	809	1,189	1,697	2,301	2,991	4,102
Africa	41	66	104	162	251	379	548	864
Asia	293	426	593	847	1,192	1,595	2,043	2,736
Latin America and Caribbean	86	133	196	271	350	426	499	599

Source: Adapted from UNDP (1998).

Table 4.2 Urbanization – percentage of population residing in urban areas, 1950–2030

	1955	1965	1975	1985	1995	2005	2015	2030
			Actual				Forecast	
World	31.6	35.5	37.8	41.2	45.3	49.7	54.4	61.1
More developed regions	58.0	64.6	69.9	72.5	74.9	77.4	80.0	83.7
Less developed regions	19.6	23.6	26.7	31.9	37.6	43.5	49.3	57.3
Africa	16.4	20.7	25.2	29.6	34.9	40.7	46.4	54.3
Asia	19.0	22.4	24.6	29.2	34.7	40.6	46.6	55.2
Latin America and Caribbean	45.3	53.4	61.2	68.2	73.4	77.1	79.9	83.7

Source: Adapted from UNDP (1998).

global scale, unprecedented urbanization levels are being reached. In 2006, urban dwellers will outnumber their rural counterparts for the first time ever. Table 4.1 shows that the global urban population is set to double from 2.6 billion in 1995 to 5.1 billion in 2030. By that time, three out of five people in the world will be living in cities.

Throughout the first half of the twentieth century, most of the industrialized countries became steadily more urbanized, while the developing countries of the South remained predominantly rural. Table 4.2 shows how, even by 1975, 70 per cent of the population of more developed regions lived in urban areas, whereas the same figure for the developing countries was only 27 per cent. Nevertheless, since 1975 the gap between industrial and developing countries has been narrowing. By 1995, one in three urban dwellers was found in cities of the developing countries compared to one in four in the industrialized North. Projections show that half of the population of developing countries will become urban dwellers in 2015 and it is expected that 57 per cent, a total of 4.1 billion people, will reside in urban areas by 2030.

These figures have prompted fear in some circles but in fact it is unlikely that the urban population will continue growing indefinitely. Projections suggest an urban growth rate of about 0.9 per cent per annum in 2025–30 for developing

Table 4.3 The world's total and urban population shares (%)

		1955	1965	1975	1985	1995	2005	2015	2030
				Actual				Forecast	
More developed	Total	31.3	28.9	25.7	23.0	20.6	18.4	16.7	14.5
regions	Urban	57.5	52.8	47.5	40.5	34.1	28.7	24.5	19.8
Less developed	Total	68.7	71.1	74.3	77.0	79.4	81.6	83.3	85.5
regions	Urban	42.5	47.2	52.5	59.5	65.9	71.3	75.5	80.2

Source: Adapted from UNDP (1998).

countries and about 0.7 per cent for the same period in the developed world. However, global urban growth rates have been declining for most of the second half of the last century and they are expected to continue doing so at the beginning of this century. In developing countries, the urban growth is projected to continue declining between now and 2030.

Many factors have combined to bring about these changes, but one is particularly significant. Table 4.3 shows how the developing countries' share of the world's urban population has risen roughly in line with its total population share. In other words, the South's share of city dwellers has increased mainly because its share of the world's total population has increased; from 68 per cent in 1955 to 79 per cent and rising in 1995. This suggests that natural increase is the single most important factor in urban growth, despite the fact that fertility rates are generally lower in urban rather than rural areas. The influence of rural–urban migration should not, however, be underestimated. Migrants to cities are predominantly young and this inevitably contributes to high rates of natural increase.

Substantial differences exist between the regions of the developing world. In terms of population size, Asia (excluding Japan) was home to 64 per cent of urban dwellers in the less developed regions in 1995. Asia is followed by Latin America and the Caribbean (21 per cent) and Africa (15 per cent). In 1975, 13 per cent of the urban population in the less developed regions was in Africa and 24 per cent in Latin America and the Caribbean. It is expected that the share of Latin America and the Caribbean will decrease at the start of the next century and urbanization in Africa will increase.

Mega-cities

The largest cities in the world have historically been located mainly in industrialized countries. However, as evident from Table 4.4, this is now changing and the number of mega-cities, defined as cities with 10 million or more inhabitants, is increasing rapidly. By 2015, it is expected that 22 of the 26 mega-cities will be located in the developing world. Asia will contain 18 of them, meaning

Table 4.4 The world's largest cities in 1995 and 2015 (population in millions)

1995		2015	
1. Tokyo, Japan	27.0	1. Tokyo, Japan	28.9
2. Mexico City, Mexico	16.6	2. Bombay, India	26.2
3. São Paulo, Brazil	16.5	3. Lagos, Nigeria	24.6
4. New York, USA	16.3	4. São Paulo, Brazil	20.3
5. Bombay, India	15.1	5. Dhaka, Bangladesh	19.5
6. Shanghai, China	13.6	6. Karachi, Pakistan	19.4
7. Los Angeles, USA	12.4	7. Mexico City, Mexico	19.2
8. Calcutta, India	11.9	8. Shanghai, China	18.0
9. Buenos Aires, Argentina	11.8	9. New York, USA	17.6
10. Seoul, Republic of Korea	11.6	10. Calcutta, India	17.3
11. Beijing, China	11.3	11. Delhi, India	16.9
12. Osaka, Japan	10.6	12. Beijing, China	15.6
13. Lagos, Nigeria	10.3	13. Metro Manila, Philippines	14.7
14. Rio de Janeiro, Brazil	10.2	14. Cairo, Egypt	14.4
15. Delhi, India	9.9	15. Los Angeles, USA	14.2

Source: Adapted from UNDP (1998).

that Asia's share of mega-cities is set to increase from 50 per cent in 1995 to 69 per cent in 2015. Of the remaining eight mega-cities, four will still be Latin America, one more city (Cairo) will be African and two will be North American (New York and Los Angeles). However, the rate at which some cities are growing appears to be slowing.

Berry (1976) was the first to observe that some cities in the industrialized world reached a point where they stopped growing or actually began to decrease in size as their populations were moved into suburban areas or smaller cities. He called this process *counter-urbanization* and it occurred during the 1980s in cities such as Birmingham in the United Kingdom and Detroit in the United States. There are reasons to believe that counter-urbanization is also happening in some cities of the South (UNDP, 1998). It is also worth remembering that not all urban dwellers live in large cities. Half of the world's urban population still lives in urban centres with fewer than 500,000 inhabitants, where often the social dynamics and livelihood strategies of the urban poor are different from those extant in mega-cities. Whatever the scale, all the statistics point to an inevitable growth in urban poverty and social disadvantage.

Understanding urban poverty

Quantitative perspectives on urbanization suggest that we live in a rapidly urbanizing world, and demand on jobs, housing and urban services is growing, to the detriment of the urban poor. However, in order to understand the problems that may be associated with rapid urban growth it is also necessary to consider the qualitative dimensions of life in cities. From a social development perspective, this means attempting to understand the dimensions of urban poverty associated with irregular income, squalid living conditions and precarious access to infrastructure and services. An important caveat underpinning the analysis of urban poverty is that it should not be seen in isolation from its wider structural causes in the rural, national and international arenas.

In the 1950s, it was widely believed that urban poverty was a temporary phenomenon that would disappear with the 'take-off' towards modernization (Rostow, 1960). However, it soon became clear that symptoms of poverty such as the informal economy and informal settlements were not disappearing and in many cities they were actually expanding. This led sociologists to focus on 'marginal' city dwellers who were said to be perpetuating a 'culture of poverty' (Lewis, 1966). When Lipton (1977) published his 'urban bias' thesis, arguing that cities consumed a disproportionate share of national investment, this confirmed extant assumptions and ensured that mainstream development efforts were focused firmly in the direction of rural areas for decades to come.

However, changes in the world economy have drastically affected cities of the developing countries over the past quarter of a century. Structural adjustment programmes introduced in many developing countries during the mid-1980s had a particularly negative impact on urban areas. Urban dwellers were more integrated into cash economies so they suffered more from the lifting of subsidies, for example on basic foodstuffs, transport and housing, or from the introduction of user fees such as for education and health services. As policies to downsize the public sector took hold, many urban dwellers were laid off from public sector jobs and swelled the ranks of the new poor, reinforced by constraints on new investment as a result of the shift in emphasis from non-tradables to tradables, which saw the bulk of investment moving to rural areas (Moser, 1992).

At the start of the 1990s, studies of these social impacts of economic reform, combined with evidence of demographic trends towards increased urbanization, served to force urban poverty on to the social development agenda. Both the World Bank and the United Nations Development Programme opened the decade with policy papers signalling their intention to prioritize urban poverty (UNDP, 1991; World Bank, 1990) and at the end of 2002 the World Bank concluded the year with a series of urban-focused conferences designed to signal the increasing importance being placed on the urban context and urban poverty. These policy debates are stressing the importance of inequality and rising levels of social exclusion, often associated with the impact of global economic forces and the barriers faced by the poor as they attempt to access goods and services (Beall, 2002b; Townsend and Gordon, 2002). Furthermore, many poor people live in highly unequal cities so that inequality, together with the accompanying relations underpinning social exclusion has become a critical dimension of urban poverty and urban social policy (Beall et al., 2002a). Poor urban dwellers may be closer to facilities and services than poor people in the countryside, but this does not mean they can necessarily afford or access them. For example, poor women can be denied appointments at clinics, or children from discriminated minorities can be refused entry to schools (Beall, 1995).

Characteristics of urban poverty

Despite its new priority status, it is important to recognize that analysing urban poverty as a separate category does pose problems (Wratten, 1995). As discussed above, the definition of what constitutes an urban area is somewhat arbitrary. Sometimes, inconsistent population thresholds are employed and, at other times, a nebulous notion of urban lifestyle is applied which ignores the great heterogeneity that exists in both rural and urban areas and the evident links between them (Tacoli, 1998). This makes the definition of a city, town or village extremely difficult to grasp. Furthermore, viewing urban poverty as a separate category allows its symptoms to be separated from its causes. Poverty manifests itself in different ways in urban and rural areas, but it is often caused by similar factors such as: external shocks like war or famine; international economic relationships requiring debt repayments or macro-economic austerity; and low social spending by national governments. A dualistic spatial classification risks focusing on the city level and ignoring wider issues relating to the rural, national or international arenas.

Nevertheless, poverty in cities does have particular characteristics which merit special attention. Beall (2000) identifies three: their livelihood systems, their vulnerability in relation to jobs and access to services, and the environmental hazards they negotiate. Urban livelihood systems are very different from those pursued in the countryside. Urban labour markets and the position of the poor within them provide the single most important determinant of poverty in urban areas (Amis, 1995), and the poorest are often found among the unemployed and the casually employed, especially workers within the informal economy (Beall, 2002a). However, urban livelihoods are also more complex than those facing rural dwellers, with urban households employing highly diversified livelihood strategies involving the family members, community structures and wider political arenas as they attempt to obtain goods and services (Beall, 2002a; Rakodi, 2002).

The urban poor experience vulnerability for very different reasons to their rural counterparts. They may pay more for their goods and services and are often more vulnerable to changes in market conditions, price increases and there is a decline in real wages, because they live in an almost entirely monetized economy. The operation of the land market is a particular feature of urban areas that adversely affects the poor, who are squeezed off valuable land and forced into peripheral or marginal locations. Insecurity of tenure is compounded by insecure living conditions brought about by crime and a lack of public safety. The poor are disproportionately affected, not least because they often have an ambiguous relationship with the police. Urban societies can also be very violent and violence is a frequent accompaniment to urban poverty (Beall, 2000; Rakodi, 2002).

Urban dwellers are also distinguished from their rural counterparts through their relationship with the built environment. Poor living conditions, such as appalling overcrowding, contaminated water, poor or absent sanitation, lack of services and the constant threat of floods, landslides or industrial pollution, all mean that the urban poor are exposed to severe environmental health risks. There is a substantial literature on the health and well-being of low-income urban dwellers (Hardoy et al., 1990; Bradley et al., 1991). In their book *Cities of Hunger*, for example, Pryer and Crook (1988) have even argued that the combination of increasing poverty, decaying physical environments, inadequate shelter and declining investment in urban infrastructure and services has meant that health conditions are deteriorating faster in cities of the developing countries than in the surrounding rural areas.

Although the characteristics of urban poverty are clear to discern, the inadequacies of city-level data make its study difficult. Where data exist at the city scale, they are often old, disputed or incompatible with national-level data sets. A key issue is where the poverty line is drawn and whether national poverty lines adequately take into account the higher costs of living in urban areas. That they fail to do so helps explain why official national-level statistics often underestimate the extent of urban poverty (Devas et al., 2001).

Housing and basic services

Access to secure shelter and basic services has traditionally been considered one of the most vital components of urban social policy. Both have also been directly linked to the level of overall national development not only in the sense that higher income countries have better housing conditions and services, but in the sense that development effort must be committed to addressing urban needs. Basic services include water supply and sanitation, urban transport, health and education services. Along with housing, they are closely related to urban poverty reduction. Different approaches to housing and basic service provision in developing countries have been formulated and their respective merits have been widely discussed. These will be considered in more depth in this section.

Relationship to poverty reduction

Housing and basic services are an important determinant of health. Health is one of the most important assets the poor have in their pursuit of sustainable livelihoods. Adequate housing and basic services, along with knowledge about hygienic practices, can help to protect people from the elements, noise and air pollution, insects and rodents, infectious diseases and accidents involving hazardous waste in instances where the home is also a workplace. Basic services also play a vital role in environmental sustainability by preventing the pollution of rivers and aquifers and the destruction of the ozone layer. Secondly, serviced housing is an economic asset. For many people, their home is their most valuable possession. Its value may increase over time and it can be used to generate rental income or as a place to work. Housing can also form an important part of a nation's or a city's fixed capital, with a buoyant housing market helping to fuel economic growth in other areas. Evidence that untreated human waste deters economic investment can be gleaned from the 1991 cholera epidemic, which cost Peru an estimated one billion dollars in lost tourism and exports. Thirdly, and perhaps most importantly, housing and basic services can contribute towards the less tangible aspects of well-being – dignity, privacy, security and more harmonious relations between different household members.

Attempts to evaluate housing conditions in developing countries are hampered by a lack of reliable statistics. Many countries collect no data on housing conditions. Some fail to include large numbers of new dwellings in their estimates because they do not match official criteria defining what constitutes a house. This can create the impression that the problem is one of quantity (the housing deficit) when it actually has as much if not more to do with quality, the living conditions in and around already existing dwellings (UNCHS/Habitat, 1996). There is also the problem of defining what constitutes adequate housing. Many developing countries continue to apply building regulations inherited from former colonial powers and perpetuated by town planners trained in the Western tradition (Devas and Rakodi, 1993). However, uniform standards do not allow for cultural differences and demand-driven approaches. For example, high levels of occupancy and limited private space may be more acceptable in cultures where the extended family is highly valued. Separate and more generous living spaces are sometimes valued highly in Muslim countries, where women may be obliged to spend most of their time at home (Jenkins, 1997). There are further differences between rural and urban areas. Water and sanitation services, for instance, may be less of a priority for rural dwellers if a nearby river provides both with little health risk and no requirement to pay. There are also interconnections between rural and urban areas in relation to housing and services. Migrant workers may be disinclined to invest in a good-quality urban house if they aim to spend the bulk of the year or house the majority of their family in a rural home.

The call to provide a variety of affordable and appropriate housing and services should not be used as an excuse for ignoring the widespread and indisputable inadequacies of housing and basic services in developing countries. Satterthwaite (1997) estimates that in 1990 at least 600 million people in the urban areas alone of Latin America, Africa and Asia lived in housing of such poor quality that it constituted a threat to their health and lives. The urban poor rent or construct shacks made of waste materials on the urban periphery or share rundown tenement flats in city centres. Some, such as the 250,000 pavement dwellers of Bombay, live literally on the street (UNCHS/Habitat, 1996). They and their rural counterparts also lack access to the most basic of services. At present, an estimated 2.6 billion people die each year from diarrhoeal disease caused by water contamination (UNDP, 1995).

There is also the question of highly unequal standards, particularly in urban areas. In Hong Kong, for example, million-dollar apartments nestle alongside the floating homes of boat people. City averages obscure high levels of overcrowding for the poor. In Karachi (Pakistan) the 40 per cent of the population living in informal settlements or *katchi abadis* have between 2 and 3 square metres per person, while those living in adjacent areas have between 23 and 33 square metres per head (UNCHS/Habitat, 1996). The picture is similar regarding basic services. In many cities, a piped water supply and sewerage connection only reach a minority of urban dwellers, invariably those concentrated in middle- or high-income areas. Moreover, investment and subsidies are often concentrated on existing services rather than at extending services to informal settlements (Jarman, 1997). The poor are often left to buy water of a worse quality and at a higher price from private vendors. In the words of Stephens (1996), 'the poor pay more for their cholera'.

Housing policies

In the 1950s and 1960s, the leaders of many newly independent States began to construct large-scale public housing projects. These were often intended to redress the injustices of colonialism and function as a symbol of national pride. Underlying them was a belief that the State should take responsibility for housing its citizens. However, despite their symbolic status, many governments in the developing world drew heavily on European traditions that were simply not sustainable. For example, in attempting to provide housing of a high standard with all services attached, many governments ran out of money after only a small number of units had been constructed. To cover costs, some governments took out loans but these had to be repaid with interest. When the costs were passed on to tenants, most could not afford to pay. Some, such as the notorious 'super blocks' built in Caracas in Venezuela, became slums where tenants sub-let single rooms to whole families and authorities failed miserably to keep up with maintenance. Others were sold, rented or even given to middle-class families, civil servants or those connected to the regime in power.

By the 1970s it was clear that this strategy was failing the urban poor, the vast majority of whom were building their own homes in slums and informal settlements. This led to burgeoning informal land and housing markets, parallel to and unregulated by the formal system. Some governments responded by investing in rural areas to remove the incentive for migration to cities. Many took more drastic measures such as the bulldozing of informal settlements and slums. Neither strategy has managed to resolve the perceived problem. As UNCHS/Habitat (1996: 199) has acknowledged:

> It is a well-known fact that between 30 and 60 per cent of the housing units in most cities in the South are illegal in that either they contravene land ownership laws or they contravene building and planning laws or codes. Many contravene both sets of laws.

The last few decades have witnessed increasing acceptance of the idea that urban populations should be accommodated rather than displaced. Turner

(1972, 1976) was one of the first to suggest a new way of meeting the housing challenge, through self-help housing. This entailed government supporting the efforts of poor people to construct their own homes instead of attempting to produce high-quality, completed housing for all. The ideas of the intermediate technology school complemented those of Turner. This group argued that cheaper, often locally produced materials should replace uniform standards and designs in house building. International donors such as the World Bank embraced the idea of reducing standards and costs in housing as a viable means of ensuring housing for a large number of people.

'Self-help' housing projects have generally taken one of three forms. The first is sites-and-services schemes. These usually require governments to acquire land, mark out plots and connect them to services such as roads, drains, water supplies and electricity. The plots are then sold for people to construct their own homes. The main problem with this approach is that government funds are usually only sufficient to pay for cheap land at the urban periphery. Poor people often work in city centres and cannot afford the time and money needed to commute from the outskirts. Even plots on cheap land are often sold at prices that are beyond the reach of most poor people. This means they end up in the hands of middle-income families who use them for occupation or investment.

The second approach is core housing. This is a variation of sites-and-services and consists of a simple structure built by the authorities on the serviced plot. The purchaser is able to add extensions to the house when time and money allow. This approach is problematic because it adds to the cost of the plot, making it too expensive for many poor people. Planners have also proved reluctant to embrace 'dweller control' wholeheartedly and have continued to enforce rigid regulations regarding the shape and size of extensions added to core houses, which make them undesirable or unaffordable for many poor people. Women-headed households in particular have sometimes lacked the skills, time or finance to construct even the most basic of extensions or houses (Moser and Peake, 1987). In cases where skilled supervisors have been employed, the overall costs have sometimes been higher than in public housing schemes because unskilled workers often require more supervision.

The third approach is upgrading. This entails improving existing slums or informal settlements rather than attempting to relocate all their inhabitants. Improvements normally take the form of water, sewerage or electricity connections, but they have also entailed landscaping and the provision of community centres, medical facilities and schools. Upgrading should ideally be a participatory exercise involving a representative cross-section of the community. Otherwise people may be required to pay for improvements they never requested. However, one difficulty with participatory upgrading projects is that conflicts can arise between different community members. If one or two households are unwilling or unable to pay for the cost or allow their homes to be demolished to make way for the new amenities, the whole project can be prevented from going ahead. A second difficulty concerns urban elites who resist upgrading on the grounds that it legitimates illegal settlements and raises the value of assets owned by people who have broken the law.

At the beginning of the 1990s, the World Bank signalled a move towards what it called an enabling approach to housing the urban poor (World Bank, 1990). This focuses on the whole range of 'inputs' needed to ensure the healthy functioning of housing markets. On the supply side, this can entail the rationalization of legal and regulatory frameworks and measures to increase competition and reduce monopolies in the construction industry. On the demand side, there have been efforts to improve access to private housing finance and settle disputes over tenure or land ownership. Rather than focusing exclusively on the poorest groups, the enabling approach advocates integrated policies that provide a range of housing options for a range of different income groups.

The main problem with the enabling approach is that, in calling for more integration, it risks switching the focus away from poor people and other groups who are often least well served by market-based housing policies. The recent focus on rental housing (Gilbert and Varley, 1990) may offer a partial solution to this problem. Rental housing is particularly important for those who work in low-paid jobs in central city locations and for those who earn an income from casual work that requires them to move on a seasonal basis (UNCHS/Habitat, 1996). Kumar (1996) demonstrates that even low-income landlords often rent out rooms or floor space to even poorer tenants. Renting thus offers the poorest a place to live and the poor a chance to earn a living from one of their most valuable assets.

Basic services

As with housing, the provision of basic services has historically been seen as the responsibility of the State in many developing countries. The main impetus to much water and sanitation development, for example, was the action plan that emerged from the Mar del Plata international conference on water in 1977, that formed the basis for the International Drinking Water Supply and Sanitation Decade, 1981–90. The programmes implemented under the plan were national government-led and aimed at universal coverage by 1990. They contained some elements of community participation, tended to prioritize rural areas and stressed the health benefits of water and sanitation. The debt crisis in the developing countries and the economic slump in the industrial North during the 1980s ensured that the target of universal coverage was never achieved. Structural adjustment programmes added to the imperative for governments to reduce spending and items cut first were the less politically visible ones such as sewerage, capital investment and maintenance. When the decade came to a close, delegates met at New Delhi and proclaimed the more modest target of 'some for all rather than more for some', basic services echoing a basic needs approach to development.

By the early 1990s, the international consensus, driven by the World Bank and UNDP, was that State provision of services was financially unsustainable. The Dublin Conference, the follow-up to Mar del Plata, issued a statement emphasizing that past approaches had failed to recognize that water was an economic good. The UNCED or 'Earth Summit' removed functions from government by emphasizing that planning and implementation should be based on the effective demand of users and that willingness to pay was a 'secondary but vital' desired behaviour within communities. In the late 1990s, the World Bank operationalized these ideas through its Demand-Responsive Approach (DRA). This sees communities as consumers who must be willing to pay tariffs in order to access resources. As with housing, the role of national governments is to provide an 'enabling' environment for new service providers such as private companies and NGOs to operate effectively. The new providers are intended to bring effectiveness and efficiency to the provision of basic services, as well as distancing them from political considerations.

The use of private companies to provide basic services poses a number of problems. Privatized companies are not accountable to the people they serve, unlike governments, especially local government. Indirect accountability is supposed to be ensured by the regulatory role of government but Batley (1996) questions the capacity of many governments in developing countries to carry out this function effectively. The result has often been that privatized utilities focus on more profitable middle- and high-income consumers and pay relatively little attention to the urban poor, who may be left in a worse position than under State-led approaches by the requirement to pay service charges (Beall et al., 2000a; McDonald and Pape, 2002).

Relying on NGOs to provide urban basic services is also problematic. Some successfully promote integrated approaches combining service delivery with hygiene promotion, micro-credit or child care in informal settlements and slums. However, the area-based nature of their interventions poses two major problems. Firstly, there is the question of linking local to city-level services. For example, the NGO Orangi Pilot Project (OPP) in Karachi assists local communities in providing their own sanitation at a fraction of the cost charged by the local authority. Renowned internationally for their success in participatory service provision, the NGO has nonetheless experienced inordinate difficulty in securing the cooperation of the metropolitan authority in connecting neighbourhood-based sanitation to the city's main sewers (Hassan, 1997).

Secondly, there is the question of city-wide inequalities. By focusing exclusively on low-income areas, NGOs preclude the possibility of cross-subsidization at the city level and are forced to recover costs from the poor themselves. Cost recovery in water and sanitation is often justified on the grounds that the poor already pay more for their water from private vendors. This should not be seen as 'willingness to pay' given that water is vital for life (Beall et al., 2002c). The proportion of income poor urban households spend on water is a good indicator of urban poverty and a fairer solution would be to use the charges paid in wealthier areas to subsidize poorer ones. This is being attempted by the post-apartheid metropolitan authority in Johannesburg, which is experimenting with a system of rising block tariffs that includes a life-line tariff that sees the first few kilolitres of water are free, with costs being imposed thereafter (Beall et al., 2000a).

Urban livelihoods

Where urban poverty is on the increase and when the urban poor are asked what they prioritize, they invariably say 'jobs'. However, jobs and especially formal jobs are scarce and urban livelihoods difficult to construct. Chapter 3 of this book examines livelihoods from a rural perspective. This section focuses on livelihoods in the urban context. A livelihoods perspective acknowledges the importance not only of productive processes, but also of reproduction (domestic work and child care), consumption and social relations in ensuring sustainable livelihoods (Beall, 2002a).

The first dimension of urban livelihoods explored here relates to income-generation strategies, principally those involving the informal economy and export-oriented manufacturing. The second dimension relates to strategies that foster informal ties of social security. These include reducing consumption by household members, using social networks, and forming urban social movements. Each strategy is based on social relationships and is located along a continuum, linking households to communities and wider political processes (Beall, 2001). There are also substantial variations in the livelihood systems pursued by different individuals within the same household (Beall and Kanji, 1999).

Earning an income

Changes in the global economy have had a marked impact on job opportunities in urban centres. Structural adjustment and economic recession have hit hard over the past two decades. By the late 1980s, urban per capita incomes had reverted to 1970 levels and in some countries to 1960s levels (World Bank, 1990). These wage reductions, along with retrenchments in the public sector, have swelled the ranks of the informal economy in many cities of the South. In the face of this, it is important to recognize that the urban poor are not a homogeneous mass and their condition does not always remain static. While some are merely coping against all odds, others are able to improve their situation through time. In the context of global economic forces, some have been excluded, while others have been included, as some cities have managed to carve out a niche in the new global economy. For example, several Asian and Latin American cities have become successful Free Trade Zones (FTZs). It is important to note, however, that even when the urban poor are connected into the global economy, it is often under unfavourable terms. There is pressure towards increasing casualization of labour, informalization of contracts within an 'unbundled' production process and heightened pressure to deliver piece-work under conditions of labour insecurity and work informality.

The first well-known attempt to define the informal economy was made by Hart in 1973 when he led an ILO employment mission to Ghana and Kenya. He identified seven features said to characterize it: ease of entry, small scale of operations, use of indigenous resources and adapted technology, labour-intensive work, use of skills acquired outside the formal school system, minimal capital investment and maximum use of family labour. He also drew a clear distinction between the formal and informal sectors. Hart's work was influential in transforming negative images of the informal economy, which had previously been seen as a feudal remnant or a parasite retarding growth in the formal sector. However, his model has been subject to extensive criticism. His seven characteristics paint a highly generalized picture that fails to capture the heterogeneity of the informal economy. His separation of the two economies also fails to recognize the links that exist between them through, for example, various types of sub-contracting arrangements (Bromley and Gerry, 1979).

These criticisms have led to the adoption of a looser definition of the informal economy as characterized simply by a lack of regulation and a high degree of competition. It is also generally recognized that a continuum exists, linking the formal and informal extremes of the economy, with activities, firms or workers that are more or less 'formal' placed somewhere between the two. The informal economy remains, then, something of an umbrella term that encompasses a broad range of unregulated activities including self-employment, casual work and home-based production and is also known as the 'shadow economy', 'black economy', 'hidden economy' and 'real economy' (Allen, 1999).

The informal economy has been labelled a 'women's sector' by some policy-makers because it often contains a high proportion of female workers. This may be a result of restricted formal sector demand for women's labour or lower levels of educational attainment by women. However, it is also important to recognize that many women work in the informal economy because it enables them to combine reproductive and productive responsibilities more easily. For example, they can feed their families at the same time as preparing food for sale. Such diversification plays a key role in countering women's vulnerability. Nevertheless, the vast majority of urban women workers are located at the survivalist end of the informal economy. The survivalist sector works long hours, earns little money and is subject to harassment and even violence from patrons, the police and criminals.

Another key area of urban employment is export-oriented manufacturing in the Export-Processing Zones (EPZs), which constitute a highly visible manifestation of the operations of the new global economy. They are particularly prevalent in East Asia and Latin America but are also a feature of the landscapes of, for example, Mauritius, Sri Lanka and Bangladesh. The majority of EPZ workers are young single women and their wages are generally lower than those of their male equivalents. Nevertheless, regular employment does appear to have empowered some women, increasing their influence in household decision-making (Kabeer, 2000). Unfortunately, this does not negate the impact of poor working conditions for both men and women in many forms of urban manufacturing, including in the EPZs.

Alongside gender is the phenomenon of generation as an important determinant of the ways in which the urban poor generate income. The pensions of elderly people, however small, can provide an invaluable source of guaranteed income in households where younger members have insecure sources of income. Elderly people also enable other household members to engage in income generation outside the home when they take on child care responsibilities (Beall, 2002c). However, urban elders also live lives marked by abuse, neglect and fear of crime and violence (Buchandron et al., 1997). Children play an important role in income generation in poor urban households. In many cities it is the norm for children to engage in paid employment, which can be beneficial for themselves and their families. However, working children can be exposed to particular dangers in urban areas and the problems facing street and working children are critical to urban social policy (Beall, 1997).

Policy support to income-earning

Policy approaches aimed at the working poor can be divided into three main types. First there is the legalist approach. This draws heavily on the work of De Soto (1989), who argues that informal workers are dynamic entrepreneurs but that the growth of their businesses is stymied by excessive government regulation. He found that in Peru it took 289 days to secure legal status from the government for one informal business wanting to formalize. The World Bank promotes a variation of De Soto's ideas by encouraging governments to adopt an 'enabling role' *vis-à-vis* small businesses (World Bank, 1990). Cutting red tape is one element in this. The *Nueva Ley de Industrias* introduced in Peru in 1983 reduced the complexities involved in registering and licensing small businesses, gave them tax breaks and exempted them from certain forms of labour legislation. Other elements can include the provision of credit for small businesses, often through specialized units set up inside retail or development banks, and technical assistance in the form of business skills training.

A contrasting approach to the urban informal economy is the structuralist approach, which emphasizes the causes underlying the poverty and social injustice often experienced by workers in the informal economy and in EPZs. The International Labour Organization (ILO) is the major organization articulating this approach. However, in policy terms it parallels the World Bank by encouraging informal businesses through the provision of credit and training. Nevertheless, rather than promoting deregulation, as does the World Bank, the ILO argues for the progressive application of labour legislation as informal enterprises become formalized. Central to its policy vision is the advancement of 'core labour standards'. The main aim of this approach is to attack the structural causes of poverty such as unequal economic relations between North and South, but it has yet to be translated into concrete policies (Rodgers et al., 1995). However, it has become a controversial focus of debate and has attracted widespread attention. This is because some in the South see core labour standards as trade barriers through the back door and as undermining the means by which many developing countries can be competitive (Kabeer, 2000). An alternative policy approach is the empowerment of informal and EPZ workers through mobilization and here the ILO has had some success in helping mobilize trade unions, for example in the Philippines, Indonesia and Thailand.

The third approach to the informal economy is embodied in the work of many NGOs in urban areas. They have improved upon the legalist approach by building up the capacity of informal sector workers to resolve their own problems. For example, ADOPEM in the Dominican Republic trains urban women in managerial, accounting and banking procedures (Freeman et al., 1997). NGOs have also improved upon the structuralist approach by attempting to reach groups that are often excluded from the trade union movement, such as domestic workers and child workers. However, perhaps the most important feature of the NGO approach is that it has tended to take a more holistic view of the problems faced by the working poor. The Self-Employed Women's Union in India, for example, is exemplary here, being involved in informal banking, informal health insurance, shelters for victims of domestic violence, urban planning and advocacy work around the rights of informal workers (Freeman et al., 1997). The poor do not experience their lives in neat compartments, and integrated approaches such as these lie at the heart of policy informed by a livelihoods perspective. Nevertheless, question marks remain over the extent to which the NGO approach to the working poor has the potential to bring about fundamental transformations in their lives. NGOs tend to operate on a relatively small scale, which limits their capacity to attack the structural causes of urban poverty. If worker exploitation is really to be a thing of the past, concerted efforts will need to be made by national governments and the international community, above and beyond city boundaries.

Social networks, social security and social change

Urban livelihood systems are constituted not only by the productive activities described above. Another key component is the range of activities built around social relationships. These begin inside the household where conflicts and negotiations take place between individual members over how to reduce consumption or increase production in the face of economic hardship. However, households are also linked to one another in the wider community. Women, in particular, forge social networks that are used to produce goods and services at a lower cost than might have been the case on an individual household basis. At times, community-based organizations aim for more radical goals and challenge formal political processes as they negotiate access to city-level goods and services. Each of these three levels of interaction plays a role in forging sustainable urban livelihoods.

Analysis of informal social support as a part of urban livelihoods has to begin at the household and/or family level. Micro-level studies of how urban households have adapted to difficulties associated with structural adjustment suggest that extended family and community support is tenuous when poverty is widespread and severe and under these conditions urban households often have to fall upon their own resources, with weaker or more vulnerable household members bearing the brunt of the belt-tightening process (Chant, 1991; Beall,

1995; Kanji, 1995; Moser, 1996). For example, when real household income falls, women and children enter the labour market for the first time or work longer hours. Under these conditions older women and young girls take on the lion's share of domestic work at the expense of girls' education. Indebtedness increases when expenditure can be reduced no more and it has been suggested that in some contexts an increase in domestic violence may be associated with increases in urban poverty (Gonzalez de la Rocha, 1994).

Urban livelihoods are constituted not only in the spaces inside households, but also in the spaces between them. Livelihood systems often involve people organizing around the allocation of resources at the community level. Studies of this type of social interaction have historically focused on rural areas, with Scott (1976, 1985) and others pointing to the existence of a 'moral economy', in which social risk is ensured against collectively through, for example, landowners and minor officials acting as patrons for the landless and near-landless. The approach has been criticized for exaggerating the extent to which inter-household cooperation exists (Popkin, 1979) and for confusing altruism with what are in fact generalized informal social security arrangements (Platteau, 1991).

However, social networks and reciprocal relationships also exist in urban areas. Recent evidence suggests that intra-familial networks are as critical to informal social security in urban areas as in rural areas, while extra-familial social networks form a vital part of urban livelihood strategies when they function as informal relationships of mutual support between different households (Beall, 2001). Under certain conditions these networks can sometimes take on a more formal character and become community-based organizations (CBOs) mobilizing common resources (Beall, 2001; Mitlin, 2001). Moser's (1998) asset-vulnerability framework presents CBOs as an asset for the poor that is often used productively.

However, informal social networks and community-based organizations are not a panacea for urban poverty and vulnerability. They can be easily eroded, for example, in contexts characterized by urban violence (Moser and Holland, 1997) or severe economic hardship or when CBOs are used instrumentally by powerful community members or for other organizational goals (Beall, 2001). Relations between households also often reproduce the gender inequities that characterize intra-household relations (Tripp, 1994). Moser and Peake (1987) argue that while women are frequently responsible for the day-to-day running of urban community organizations they seldom graduate to positions of political leadership. This can lead to difficulties for policy-makers and planners trying to prioritize service provision in consultative ways. Rodriguez (1994), for example, describes how women in Quito in Ecuador struggled for services such as water, crèches, a primary school and market, only to find that some of their objectives were opposed by their own all-male neighbourhood committee.

Important though informal social networks are at the household and community level, they are rarely able to radically alter the position of the urban poor. For example, opinion is critically divided as to whether the celebrated communal kitchen movement in Lima (Peru) was simply geared towards meeting the immediate needs of providing food for struggling urban neighbourhoods, or constituted a proto-social movement able to bring about more fundamental transformations. Barrig (1996) argued that it was a needs-based movement because kitchens competed with each other for scarce State resources and failed to make strategic connections between their own struggle and those of other kitchens and movements, thereby ensuring that they failed to influence the State in meaningful ways. Lind and Farmelo (1996), on the other hand, distinguished between those kitchens organized in a top-down fashion by the State and more autonomous kitchens whose members participated in political decision-making.

When organizations go beyond the community arena to the *city level*, they have the potential to become what Castells (1983) described as urban social movements, or to contribute to urban citizenship through processes of democratic decentralization (Heller, 2000; Douglass and Friedmann, 1998) and focused State–society partnerships. Here the most celebrated examples are the participatory budgeting processes of Brazilian cities such as Porte Alegre and Recife (Abers, 1998). However, the reality of organization for social change at the urban scale is that it is often promoted and harnessed by informal collective vehicles that do not always operate in the interests of the common or collective good. The degree of organization depends on the extent to which particular categories of people are bound together and the nature of the ties that bind. These might be fairly horizontal ties based on ethnicity, caste and hometown associations among migrants or they may be asymmetrical ties based on clientelism, patronage and debt bondage. Informal networks and sources of social security can provide lifelines to desperate people and relieve the pressure on State and other formal providers of welfare. However, they can also be pernicious, oppressive and sometimes brutal. The implications for the urban policy challenge are well captured in the Cities Alliance *2001 Annual Report,* which is worth quoting at some length:

> Disputes will be resolved not through the courts, but through informal local mechanisms, often arbitrary and sometimes violent. Although they may reside within the administrative boundary of a town or city, their local authority may well be a slumlord or mafia leader, rather than city council staff, who will often no longer attempt to assert their jurisdiction or even enter the slums. As illegal or unrecognized residents, these slum dwellers will have no property rights, nor security of tenure, but will instead make whatever arrangements they can in an informal, unregulated and expensive parallel market. This scenario is not only certain, it is already the reality in urban areas in many developing and transition countries, as weak urban governance meets the impact of growing inequality, corruption and imbalances in resource allocation. Ignoring this policy challenge risks condemning hundreds of millions of people to an urban future of misery, insecurity and environmental degradation on a truly awesome scale. (Cities Alliance, 2001: 3)

Implementation and urban governance

In recent decades, the role of the State has diminished, both in housing and basic service provision and in job creation and economic planning and organization. However, this has not meant a total eclipse of the State and certainly not the local State (World Bank, 1997). On the contrary, in recent years 'decentralization fever' (Tendler, 1995) has placed an increased focus on city government. This section begins by examining the factors behind this and goes on to examine how the roles and responsibilities of city governments have changed in recent years, not least in relation to social policy.

There are three main reasons why city governments are becoming the main focus of efforts to combat poverty in urban areas. These have been touched upon in previous sections. The first reason relates to the failure of centralized State planning to deliver basic services of an adequate standard (Stren, 1991). It is thought that city governments, along with the private sector and NGOs, might offer the possibility of more efficient and sustainable models of service provision (Batley, 1996). The second reason is the re-emergence of the democratic process in many developing countries. This has fuelled urban social movements demanding more say in the governance of the city and has given rise to multi-sectoral approaches involving, in turn, a wide variety of stakeholders. In such contexts, city governments have come to be seen as important vehicles for increasing participation and accountability and the key State partner in urban partnerships. A third reason is the new priority attached to poverty reduction by many national governments and by major international donor agencies. This, together with a dawning realization, prompted largely by demographic trends, that a majority of the world's poor will soon be living in cities, has resulted in increased attention being paid to the contribution of lower tiers of government.

The relationship between city government and poverty reduction

In terms of its competencies and functions, city government is theoretically able to address urban poverty in two key ways. It has a service function in ensuring the provision of basic services for urban populations. It also has a governance function designed to ensure the service function is carried out in accordance with local priorities. This operates through the election of councillors representing all local interests who take decisions that are implemented by officials. However, this is an idealized version of city government. In the first place, there is no guarantee that political parties will represent all local interests, especially disadvantaged groups such as the poor (Grindle and Thomas, 1991). In the second place, in urban contexts as in any other in developing countries, especially:

> a wide variety of factors – from the availability of sufficient resources to the structure of intergovernmental relations, from the commitment of lower level officials to the reporting mechanisms within the bureaucracy, from the political leverage of the opponents of the policy to accidents of timing, luck and seemingly unrelated events – can and do frequently intervene between the statement of policy goals and their actual achievement. (Grindle, 1980: 3)

Governance and government are frequently used interchangeably, suggesting to some groups that these terms mean the same thing. In fact, governance is the product of interactions between government and other institutions. It has been pointed out that the institutional perspective 'seeks to mobilize diverse social institutions including the market, the community and the State to promote people's welfare' (Midgley, 1995: 139). State, society or market institutions in turn can be sub-divided, with the State comprising central, local and (in federal systems) provincial spheres, and advocates of decentralization imply that local government is ideally placed to facilitate this 'participatory mode' on behalf of the State (UNDP, 1991; World Bank, 1990). However, local governance can be complicated too. Even local government can be separated into metropolitan and municipal tiers of local government, embracing elected councillors (the politicians) as well as paid officials (the bureaucrats). Civil society at city level can be complex, involving a wide array of organizations and interests. 'Pork-barrel politics' have for a long time been a feature of urban politics. At city or town council level the relationship between citizens, politicians and officials is closer than with higher tiers of government and the opportunities for malfeasance greater. Some actors involved in urban governance and policy belong to a combination of institutions; for example, public utilities or municipal service corporations involve elements of the State and the market, while officials or politicians might also be members of civil society organizations or ally themselves with particular interest groups. All are defined by the context and constraints within which they operate, including their source of power, authority and legitimacy (Devas et al., 2001).

However, acknowledging that city governance involves a number of institutional actors does not necessarily remove local government's capacity to shape outcomes in favour of the urban poor. First, through its governance function, city government is able to mobilize State and society actors at a number of levels, including higher tiers of government and at the levels of local and community organization. In the past, local government was seen as the vehicle by which society could elect local politicians to make decisions that could be implemented by neutral officials. It is still the case that the poor must have effective political representation. However, current thinking and practice promotes active local citizenship with people themselves participating in decision-making rather than simply electing politicians in one-off exercises to take decisions on their behalf. Despite persistent apathy in many cities, new channels such as development forums can be created for civil society to participate in city government decision-making (Abbott, 1996) and for citizens to have a say in governance and government (Douglass and Friedmann, 1998). 'Embedded' links between city government and civil society have the potential to create a 'State–society synergy' that functions as a catalyst for development (Evans, 1996) and this has been shown to be particularly effective in terms of the delivery and management of urban services (Ostrom, 1996).

City government also has the potential to mobilize the State and the market through its *service function*. Before it was thought that city government alone could provide basic services for all the city's residents. Now it is increasingly acknowledged that city government often has neither the financial nor the institutional capacity to provide for rapidly expanding urban populations (Stren, 1991). The private sector is perhaps more efficient in producing services but is less likely to meet the needs of the poor. The solution is thought to lie in city government abandoning its old role of rowing and attempting instead to steer private-sector production towards more equitable outcomes (Devas, 2001). This has led to the introduction of alternative models of service delivery based on franchising or contracting out certain services; privatizing (selling off) assets and service organizations; and the formation of public utility or municipal service corporations (Batley, 1996).

Strengths and weaknesses of new forms of urban governance

There are a number of clear advantages to this new perspective on urban governance. It manages to combine the strengths of State, society and market and in so doing neutralizes their weaknesses. For instance, private sector efficiency can be combined with an NGO-style focus on social justice. NGO strengths in working closely with communities can be combined with the State's focus on accountability and ability to cross-subsidize from rich to poor. However, a number of potential difficulties have already been identified. In service provision, attempts to achieve real improvements for the poor have been hampered by revenue constraints. City governments have been given unfunded mandates by central governments. They have also faced great difficulties in persuading wealthy urban dwellers to cover the cost of extending services to poorer parts of the city. For example, in Johannesburg attempts to redress inadequacies in water and sanitation services dating from the apartheid era were met by a rates boycott in one of the wealthiest suburbs of the city (Beall et al., 2002a).

In terms of governance, city governments face further formidable obstacles. In opening their doors to the poor they are liable to be greeted by unwelcome guests in the form of highly organized groups representing urban elites or organizations huge in size, representing single interest groups. The power of local government to shape outcomes in favour of the poor is also undermined by the influence of market forces beyond their control. These are manifested in foreign investors threatening relocation and international credit ratings that require constant vigilance. There are also endless internal problems to be tackled such as widespread corruption and inadequate institutional capacity. As the situation stands, one of the most formidable problems facing those attempting to deliver urban social policy is the disjuncture between the huge size of the challenge and the limited capacity of the actors and institutions having to deal with it.

Conclusions

This chapter began by contrasting qualitative with quantitative approaches to defining urban areas. It was emphasized that both are necessary to inform urban social development and in order to understand and be able to respond to the challenges of urban poverty in cities and towns of the South. Succeeding sections combined both approaches. First, urban trends showed that the majority of the world's poor will soon be living in cities, and that many of these cities will have 10 million or more inhabitants. Then, urban poverty was examined and found to have a number of dimensions warranting particular focus and attention. First, successive approaches to housing and basic services were reviewed, including the recent move away from State-led provision. The urban livelihoods approach was detailed in the next section, against a background discussion of how many poor urban dwellers make a living. It was stressed that survival was also made possible through social relationships and networks at household, community and city levels, some of which evolved into organized initiatives or movements under certain conditions. The final section examined the enhanced role being suggested for city-level government in social policy, as the focal point for State, society and market efforts to combat urban poverty.

The social policy dimensions of an urban livelihoods perspective are most important with respect to the shift from a residualist or safety net approach, through a focus on incremental policies towards a more holistic perspective on how to address human development and welfare. In the urban context, the residual model is most evident in the historic neglect of the urban poor in general, based on the assumption that urban dwellers are better off than rural dwellers and that families can take care of stragglers. This in turn has informed understandings of and policies directed at the urban informal sector, which has by and large been left to look after itself. The incremental approach was most evident in housing provision during the early development decades. Today, increasingly, recognized good practice sees local economic development and the provision of housing and urban services in cities and towns, as being undertaken as part of intersectoral approaches designed to bolster the livelihood opportunities of the poor. In the context of decentralization, there is a growing role for local government in the implementation of such strategies, even when sectoral policy remains the responsibility and competency of higher levels of government.

Recommended Reading

- Beall, J., Crankshaw, O. and Parnell, S. (2002) *Uniting a Divided City: Governance and Social Exclusion in Johannesburg*. London: Earthscan. This book provides a rare city case study of the social dimensions of urbanization and the social policy challenges posed by inequality, poverty and social exclusion in urban contexts.
- Ferguson, J. (1999) *Expectations of Modernity: Myths and Meanings of Urban Life in the Zambian Copperbelt*. Berkeley, CA: University of California Press. Grounded in a historical perspective, this excellent urban ethnography highlights the ways in which poor urban dwellers pursue livelihoods and how policy has failed them over the years.

- Gilbert, A. (1992) 'Third World cities: housing, infrastructure and servicing', *Urban Studies*, 29: 435–60. This article provides a useful overview and synopsis of the key policy issues confronting policy-makers and planners in their efforts to service the needs of the growing numbers of urban poor.
- Satterthwaite, D. (1997) 'Urban poverty: reconsidering its scale and nature', *IDS Bulletin*, 28 (2): 9–23. This article reviews the debates and evidence on urbanization and the link with increased urban poverty. It also looks at the characteristics of urban poverty that are often different from the experience of the rural poor.

References

Abbott, J. (1996) *Sharing the City*. London: Earthscan.

Abers, R. (1998) 'Learning democratic practice: distributing government resources through popular participation in Porto Alegre, Brazil', in M. Douglass and J. Friedmann (eds) *Cities for Citizens: Planning and the Rise of Civil Society in a Global Age*. Chichester: John Wiley, pp. 39–65.

Allen, T. (1999) 'From "informal sectors" to "real economies" in Africa', in T. Shanin (ed.) *Expolary Economies*. New York and Moscow: Ford Foundation/Moscow School of Social Science, pp. 412–36.

Amis, P. (1995) 'Making sense of urban poverty', *Environment and Urbanization*, 7 (1), April: 145–58.

Barrig, M. (1996) 'Women, collective kitchens and the crisis of the state in Peru', in J. Friedmann, et al. (eds) *Emergencies: Women's Struggles for Livelihood in Latin America*. Los Angeles, CA: UCLA Latin American Studies Center.

Batley, R. (1996) 'Public–private relations and performance in service provision', *Urban Studies*, 33 (4/5): 723–52.

Beall, J. (1995) 'Social security and social networks among the urban poor in Pakistan', *Habitat International*, 19 (4): 427–45.

Beall, J. (ed.) (1997) *A City for All: Valuing Difference and Working with Diversity*. London: Zed Books.

Beall, J. (2000) 'Life in the cities', in T. Allen and A. Thomas (eds) *Poverty and Development into the 21st Century*. Oxford: Oxford University Press, pp. 425–42.

Beall, J. (2001) 'Valuing social resources or capitalizing on them? Limits to pro-poor urban governance in nine cities of the South', *International Planning Studies*, 6 (4): 357–75.

Beall, J. (2002a) 'Living in the present, investing in the future: household security among the urban poor', in C. Rakodi and T. Lloyd-Jones (eds) *Urban Livelihoods: A People-Centred Approach to Reducing Poverty*. London: Earthscan, pp. 71–95.

Beall, J. (2002b) 'Globalization and social exclusion in cities: framing the debate with lessons from Africa and Asia', *Environment and Urbanization*, 14 (1), April: 41–51.

Beall, J. (2002c) '"A new branch can be strengthened by an old branch": livelihoods and challenges to inter-generational solidarity in South Africa', in P. Townsend and D. Gordon (eds) *World Poverty: New Policies to Defeat an Old Enemy*. Bristol: Policy Press, pp. 325–48.

Beall, J. and Kanji, N. (1999) 'Households, livelihoods and urban poverty', *Urban Governance, Partnership and Poverty Working Paper Three*. Birmingham: University of Birmingham.

Beall, J., Crankshaw, O. and Parnell, S. (2000a) 'Local government, poverty reduction and inequality in Johannesburg', *Environment and Urbanization*, 12 (1), April: 107–22.

Beall, J., Crankshaw, O. and Parnell, S. (2000b) 'Economic growth and the livelihood strategies of the urban poor in Johannesburg', *Journal of Economic and Social Geography*, 91 (4): 379–96.

Beall, J., Crankshaw, O. and Parnell, S. (2002a) 'Urban water supply, sanitation and social policy: lessons from Johannesburg, South Africa', in P. Townsend and D. Gordon (eds) *World Poverty: New Policies to Defeat an Old Enemy*. Bristol: Policy Press, pp. 251–70.

Beall, J., Crankshaw, O. and Parnell, S. (2002b) *Uniting a Divided City. Governance and Social Exclusion in Johannesburg*. London: Earthscan.

Beall, J., Crow, B., Simon, S. and Wilson, G. (2002c) *Sustainability*. Milton Keynes: Open University Press.

Berry, B.J.L. (ed.) (1976) *Urbanization and Counter-Urbanization*. Beverly Hills, CA: Sage.

Bradley, C., Stephens, C., Harpham, T. and Cairncross, S. (1991) *A Review of Environmental Health Impacts in Developing Countries*. Washington, DC: World Bank.

Bromley, R. and Gerry, C. (eds) (1979) *Casual Work and Poverty in Third World Cities*. Chichester: John Wiley.

Bunchandranon, C., Howe, G. and Payumo, A. (1997) 'Ageing as an urban experience', in J. Beall (ed.), *A City for All: Valuing Difference and Working with Diversity*. London: Zed Books, pp. 141–58.

Castells, M. (1983) *The City and Grassroots: A Cross-Cultural Theory of Urban Social Movements*. London: Edward Arnold.

Chant, S. (1991) *Women and Survival in Mexican Cities: Perspectives on Gender, Labour Markets and Low-Income Households*. Manchester: Manchester University Press.

Cities Alliance (2001) *2001 Annual Report: Cities Without Slums*. Washington, DC: Cities Alliance.

Davis, K. (1965) 'The urbanization of the human population', *Scientific American*, 213: 40–53.

De Soto, H. (1989) *The Other Path: The Invisible Revolution in the Third World*. London: I.B. Taurus.

Devas, N. (2001) 'Does city governance matter for the urban poor?', *International Planning Studies*, 6 (4), November: 393–408.

Devas, N. and Rakodi, C. (1993) *Managing Fast Growing Cities: New Approaches to Planning and Management in the Developing World*. Harlow: Longman.

Devas, N., Amis, P., Beall, J., Grant, U., Mitlin, D., Rakodi, C. and Satterthwaite, D. (2001) *Urban Governance and Poverty*. Birmingham: International Development Department, University of Birmingham.

Douglass, M. and Friedmann, J. (eds) (1998) *Cities for Citizens, Planning and the Rise of Civil Society in a Global Age*. Chichester: John Wiley.

Evans, P. (1996) 'Government action, social capital and development: reviewing the evidence on synergy', *World Development*, 24 (6): 1119–32.

Freeman, A., Pickup, F. and Rashid, L. (1997) 'Women's income-generating activities in the informal sector', in J. Beall (ed.), *A City for All: Valuing Difference and Working with Diversity*. London: Zed Books, pp. 50–9.

Gilbert, A. and Varley, A. (1990) 'Renting a home in a Third World city: choice or constraint?', *International Journal of Urban and Regional Research*, 14 (1): 89–108.

Gonzalez de la Rocha, M. (1994) *The Resources of Poverty: Women and Survival in a Mexican City*. Oxford: Blackwell.

Grindle, M. (1980) *Politics and Policy Implementation in the Third World*. Princeton, NJ: Princeton University Press.

Grindle, M. and Thomas, J. (1991) *Public Choices and Policy Change: The Political Economy of Reform in Developing Countries.* Baltimore, MD: Johns Hopkins University Press.

Hardoy, J., Cairncross, S. and Satterthwaite, D. (1990) *The Poor Die Young: Housing and Health in Third World Cities.* London: Earthscan.

Hart, K. (1973) 'Informal income opportunities and urban labour employment in Ghana', in R. Jolly et al. (eds) *Third World Employment.* Harmondsworth: Penguin, pp. 66–70.

Hassan, A. (1997) *Working with Government: The Story of Orangi Pilot Project's Collaboration with State Agencies for Replicating its Low Cost Sanitation Programme.* Karachi: City Press.

Heller, P. (2000) 'Moving the state: the politics of democratic decentralization in Kerela, South Africa and Porto Alegre'. Paper presented at the International Conference on Democratic Decentralization, Thiruvananthapuram, India, 23–27 May.

Jarman, J. (1997) 'Water supply and sanitation', in J. Beall (ed.), *A City for All: Valuing Difference and Working with Diversity.* London: Zed Books, pp. 182–93.

Jenkins, E. (1997) 'Housing, gender and work in Dhaka', in J. Beall (ed.), *A City for All: Valuing Difference and Working with Diversity.* London: Zed Books, pp. 79–87.

Kabeer, N. (2000) *The Power to Choose.* London: Verso.

Kanji, N. (1995) 'Gender, poverty and economic adjustment in Harare, Zimbabwe', *Environment and Urbanization*, 7 (1): 37–56.

Kumar, S. (1996) 'Landlordism in Third World urban low-income settlements: a case for further research', *Urban Studies*, 33 (4–5): 753–82.

Lewis, O. (1966) 'The culture of poverty', *Scientific American*, 215 (October): 19–25.

Lind, A. and Farmelo, M. (1996) 'Gender and urban social movements: women's community responses to restructuring and urban poverty', *UNRISD Discussion Paper 76.* Geneva: United Nations Research Institute for Social Development.

Lipton, M. (1977) *Why Poor People Stay Poor: Urban Bias in World Development.* London: Maurice Temple Smith.

McDonald, D. and Pape, J. (2002) *Cost Recovery and the Crisis of Service Delivery in South Africa.* London: Zed Books.

Midgley, J. (1995) *Social Development: The Development Perspective in Social Welfare.* London: Sage.

Mitlin, D. (2001) 'The formal and informal worlds of state and civil society: what do they offer to the urban poor?', *International Planning Studies*, 6 (4), November: 377–92.

Moser, C. (1992) 'Adjustment from below: low-income women, time and the triple role in Guayaquil, Ecuador', in H. Afshar and C. Dennis (eds) *Women and Adjustment Policies in the Third World.* Basingstoke: Macmillan.

Moser, C. (1996) *Confronting Crisis: A Comparative Study of Household Responses in Four Poor Urban Communities.* Washington, DC: World Bank.

Moser, C. (1998) 'The asset vulnerability framework: reassessing urban poverty reduction strategies', *World Development*, 26 (1): 1–19.

Moser, C. and Holland, J. (1997) *Urban Poverty and Violence in Jamaica.* Washington, DC: World Bank.

Moser, C. and Peake, L. (eds) (1987) *Women, Human Settlements and Housing.* New York Tavistock.

Ostrom, E. (1996) 'Crossing the great divide: coproduction, synergy and development', *World Development*, 24 (6): 1073–87.

Platteau, J.P. (1991) 'Traditional systems of social security and hunger insurance: past achievements and modern challenges', in E. Ahmad, J. Dreze, J. Hills and A. Sen (eds) *Social Security in Developing Countries.* London: Clarendon Press.

Popkin, S.L. (1979) *The Rational Peasant: The Political Economy of Rural Society in Vietnam.* Berkeley, CA: University of California Press.

Pryer, J. and Crook, N. (1988) *Cities of Hunger: Urban Malnutrition in Developing Countries.* Oxford: Oxfam.

Rakodi, C. (2002) 'Introduction', in C. Rakodi and T. Lloyd-Jones (eds) *Urban Livelihoods: A People-Centred Approach to Reducing Poverty.* London: Earthscan, pp. 1–9.

Rodgers, G., Gore, C. and Figueiredo, J. (1995) *Social Exclusion: Rhetoric, Reality, Responses.* Geneva: International Institute for Labour Studies.

Rodriguez, L. (1994) 'Barrio women, between the urban and the feminist movement', *Latin American Perspectives*, Issue 82, 21 (3), Summer: 32–48.

Rostow, W.W. (1960) *The Stages of Economic Growth: A Non-Communist Manifesto.* Cambridge: Cambridge University Press.

Satterthwaite, D. (1997) 'Urban poverty, reconsidering its scale and nature', *IDS Bulletin*, 28 (2): 9–23.

Scott, J. (1976) *The Moral Economy of the Peasant, Rebellion and Subsistence in Southeast Asia.* New Haven, CT: Yale University Press.

Scott, J. (1985) *Weapons of the Weak: Everyday Forms of Peasant Resistance.* New Haven, CT: Yale University Press.

Stephens, C. (1996) 'Healthy cities or unhealthy islands: the health and social implications of urban inequality', *Environment and Urbanization*, 8 (2), October: 9–30.

Stren, R. (1991) 'Old wine in new bottles? An overview of Africa's urban problems and the "urban management" approach to dealing with them', *Environment and Urbanization*, 3 (1): 9–22.

Tacoli, C. (1998) 'Beyond the rural–urban divide', *Environment and Urbanization*, 10 (1): 3–4.

Tendler, J. (1995) *Good Government in the Tropics.* Baltimore, MD: Johns Hopkins University Press.

Townsend, P. and Gordon, D. (eds) (2002) *World Poverty: New Policies to Defeat an Old Enemy.* Bristol: Policy Press.

Tripp, A.M. (1994) 'Rethinking civil society: gender implications in contemporary Tanzania', in J.W. Harbeson et al. (eds) *Civil Society and the State in Africa.* Boulder, CO: Lynne Rienner.

Turner, J. (1972) 'Housing as a verb', in J. Turner and R. Fichter (eds) *Freedom to Build.* London: Macmillan, pp. 1–19.

Turner, J. (1976) *Housing by People: Towards Autonomy in Building Environments.* London: Marion Boyars.

UNCHS/Habitat (1996) *An Urbanizing World: Global Report on Human Settlements 1996.* Oxford: Oxford University Press for UNCHS/Habitat.

UNDP (1991) *Cities, People and Poverty: Urban Development Co-operation for the 1990s*, UNDP Strategy Paper. New York: UNDP.

UNDP (1995) *World Urbanization Prospects*, UNDP Population Division. New York: UNDP.

UNDP (1998) *Human Development Report.* New York: UNDP.

World Bank (1990) *Urban Policy and Economic Development: An Agenda for the 1990s*, World Bank Policy Paper. Washington, DC: World Bank.

World Bank (1997) *World Development Report 1997.* Oxford: Oxford University Press.

Wratten, E. (1995) 'Conceptualizing urban poverty', *Environment and Urbanization*, 7 (1): 11–36.

5 BASIC EDUCATION FOR SOCIAL DEVELOPMENT

Summary

The early optimism that surrounded rapid expansion of formal education as a key to economic development and nation building in developing countries became soured during the 1970s and 1980s. Major problems persist of high non-completion rates, poor quality, continuing illiteracy and gender bias. Education priorities were re-focused in the 1990s on promoting basic education (primary schooling, non-formal and popular education approaches). Policy-makers decided that this would be a more effective way of stimulating economic progress while serving the needs of the poor, strengthening livelihoods, improving social indicators and supporting human rights. Yet translating policy goals into concrete action has proved more elusive. Although some governments have devised new models of education and experimented with decentralization, public spending cutbacks in this sector together with minimal overseas development assistance for basic education continue to undermine its effectiveness. Greater political and financial commitment is needed at both national and international levels, together with a multi-sector approach that integrates education policy into a broad-based, anti-poverty development model.

Education as salvation

No area of development activity has inspired such optimism as that of education. Planners and politicians alike, in both North and South, have consistently drawn attention to the potential of educational investment for actively promoting both national and personal advancement. Education has been universally portrayed as synonymous with progress, lack of education with backwardness. When all else fails, the promise to invest in education is usually guaranteed to win popular support. Political rhetoric aside, however, few serious observers in fact doubt that there is a correlation between levels of educational provision on the one hand and, on the other, development performance. This is so whether development is measured in terms of macro-economic yardsticks such as gross national product (GNP) per capita or in terms of social indicators such as infant mortality rates. Yet the relationship between education and development is far from being as clear-cut as many contend.

It is appealing and convenient for governments to promote the idea that investing in formal education will simultaneously enhance progress of both the nation and its people. However, following the rapid expansion of school enrolments at all levels in developing countries during the post-war period, there has been much disillusionment with the apparent failure of education, especially formal education, to deliver broad-based development. This has led to a re-examination of education priorities and a broader conceptualization of the nature and purpose of educational endeavours. As will be discussed in greater detail below, the exclusive preoccupation with generating human capital through the expansion of formal education, especially at secondary and tertiary levels, as the 'key' to progress, has come under heavy fire. The international aid community has been especially prominent in forcing through this policy shift although, as discussed in Chapter 9 of this volume, funding commitments have not been commensurate with the rhetoric. Many policy-makers now perceive education not just (or even principally) as a precondition for economic growth in the modern sector. It is now also viewed as a life-enhancing series of initiatives in both formal and non-formal education areas that may be used to promote human and social development.

In these terms, education thus constitutes a key element of social policy in two major dimensions. Firstly, investment in formal education is a major vehicle for human resource development. Modern industrial, agricultural and commercial activities all require adequate supplies of properly educated and trained labour. For many, acquiring an education signifies completing primary and secondary school and graduating from university as a passport to a modern sector job. However, large sectors of the population in developing countries remain outside of the largely urban-based government, industrial and commercial sectors. The universal suitability of a Western model of education based on formal schooling and institutionalized occupational training has thus been called into question. Strong arguments have been made in favour of prioritizing basic and non-formal education as being more appropriate to the livelihood needs of large sectors of the population and generating broader social benefits.

A second area of growing concern to education specialists thus relates to the design and implementation of educational policies and strategies which, whether inside or outside of the formal school system, address the immediate livelihood needs of traditional and rural populations. In addition to basic literacy and numeracy, productive and organizational skills in key fields such as agriculture, forestry, health training and environmental management, for example, now all form part of this wider educational agenda. In this view, for example, strengthening social capital and empowering communities to be able to mobilize in defence of their own interests is at least as important as building human capital based on the productive capacities of individuals. This is tantamount to a revolution in mainstream thinking on the role of education as a development tool, and one that is still heavily resisted in some circles.

Education for modernization

In this section we plot the rapid expansion of formal education in developing countries since the 1960s and the perceptions of policy-makers that this sector would stimulate economic growth and nation-building, while satisfying growing social demand for entry into modern sector, waged employment.

Optimism and expansion

The post-war period has seen rapid expansion of the formal education sector in developing countries, much faster than in the industrialized nations over the same period (Coombs, 1985; Todaro, 2000; Watkins, 2000). During the 1960s and 1970s, public spending on education increased more than in any other social sector and it now accounts on average for some 15 per cent of recurrent government expenditure in the South, comparing favourably in this respect with the 12 per cent allocated in the North (UNDP, 1999). However, this figure rises significantly in some cases such as Mexico (23 per cent), Thailand (20 per cent), South Africa (24 per cent) and Uganda (21 per cent). Public expenditure allocated to education in the South overall has risen as a proportion of GNP from 2.9 per cent in 1970 to 4.1 per cent in 1982, although by the late 1990s it had fallen back to 3.8 per cent (Lewin, 1987; UNDP, 2000).

Between 1960 and 1990, total gross enrolments at all three levels in the South rose from 163 million to 440 million, an increase of almost 270 per cent (compared with around 30 per cent for the North), at an average rate of 5 per cent every year. The largest absolute increase was at primary level, which accounted for 78 per cent of all enrolments. Net primary enrolment levels have soared since the 1960s to the present time in all major regions (see Figure 5.1). In Latin America and the Caribbean primary enrolment levels over the past three decades have risen from 60 to 90 per cent, in East Asia from 60 to 95 per cent, in South Asia from 45 to 70 per cent and in sub-Saharan Africa from 25 to almost 60 per cent. Primary school enrolments in the developing world have increased by 11 per cent since 1990 (EFA, 2000). Brazil, as one example, more than doubled its net primary intake between 1970 and 1998 (Brazil, 2000). However, the fastest rate of growth in formal education in developing countries has been experienced at secondary and tertiary levels (12.7 and 14.5 per cent per annum respectively). Between 1965 and 1987, for example, net primary enrolments in low- and middle-income countries increased by 33 per cent overall, compared with 86 per cent for secondary and 166 per cent for tertiary education (World Bank, 1990a).

The driving forces

Several economic, social and political factors have driven this huge expansion. The intellectual basis for investing in formal education as a prerequisite for

Figure 5.1   Net primary enrolment rates (%), 2000

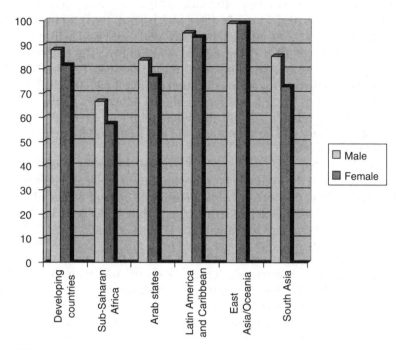

Source: DFID (2000), based on UNESCO figures.

economic growth was laid by human capital theorists such as Schultz (1961), Becker (1964) and Harbison (1973). They argued that acquisition of human skills and knowledge was essential to complement the accumulation of physical and natural capital in the drive towards modernization and that, without this 'missing ingredient', development would remain an elusive goal for poorer countries. Human capital theory generated economic tools such as manpower forecasting and cost–benefit analysis of the private and social rates of return to education. Thus, the planned expansion of formal education, especially at secondary and tertiary levels, would yield carefully calculated supplies of skilled labour so essential for the new expanding, post-independence public sectors as well as for the anticipated industrial 'take-off' to self-sustained growth (Rostow, 1960). Anderson and Bowman (1973) were even more specific, suggesting that such a take-off could only be achieved once countries had passed the 40 per cent 'literacy threshold'.

Sociologists reinforced this unilinear paradigm by underscoring the need for Western-style, 'modern' values, institutions and social structures as preconditions for progress. What better way to propagate such values and institutions than through the school and college system? Formal education was increasingly emphasized by social scientists and policy-makers as a vehicle for encouraging the spread of supposed key Western values of individualism, competition and achievement (Lerner, 1958; Hoselitz, 1960; McClelland, 1964). At the same time, as the Cold War developed, educational provision could also help shore up the developing world against a rising tide of communism. The pattern of international development assistance mirrored these priorities. For example, when the World Bank started to invest in education during the 1960s and early 1970s, over 50 per cent of its lending was for vocational education. At the same time, 43 per cent was allocated to general education, with well over half this amount supporting secondary and tertiary levels and just 6 per cent for primary schooling (Haddad et al., 1990).

The human capital approach gave educational planning a scientific gloss that, however, belied the arguably far more important social and political forces driving expansion in this sector. Public pressure to expand access to schooling increased radically after independence when white-collar jobs became available in the new government bureaucracies. Formal education was soon generally perceived as the quickest escape route from poverty and into the modern world of urban living. Notwithstanding other considerations, such aspirations were highly rational in economic terms. As economists have shown (Blaug, 1970; Todaro, 2000), the private returns to education in developing countries increase markedly, especially at the post-secondary level. From the individual's point of view, therefore, the optimal strategy is to strive for the highest possible paper qualifications in order to maximize income-earning power.

Social demand has also been exacerbated by rapid urbanization in the South, fuelled both by natural increase and by accelerating out-migration from a countryside generally lacking in adequate rural investments (see Chapters 3 and 4 in this volume). United Nations figures show that cities in many African and Latin American countries have been growing at rates of 4–6 per cent a year (Todaro, 2000). Between 1980 and 1999, the urban population as a proportion of the total rose in middle-income countries from 32 to 41 per cent. However, this figure varies considerably from 75 per cent urbanized in Latin Amercia and the Caribbean to 34 per cent in sub-Saharan Africa (World Bank, 2001).

In their turn, governments were only too pleased to respond to public demand by building schools and universities, since this has several attractions. Governments have been anxious to respond to the educational and other demands of the politically far more important urbanized population in developing countries. Notwithstanding any perceived links with economic growth, educational investment was and continues to be a major vote-catcher. Furthermore, in the often large and culturally diverse States stitched together by the colonial powers, schooling serves as a powerful tool for nation-building and the legitimization of political rulers. The imposition of a national curriculum and development ideology together with a *lingua franca* has allowed central governments and political parties to consolidate their power (Murray Thomas, 1983). Clear cases such as Indonesia, Malaysia, Zambia, South Africa and Zimbabwe exist where education has been used as a nation-building mechanism. Chinese education policy in the administration and incorporation of

Tibet provides a good example of such a strategy (Bass, 1998). In fact, there is scarcely a nation that has not at some stage used a formal education system for pursuing overtly political ends.

In addition to producing any direct economic or political pay-off, the promotion of formal education has come increasingly to be perceived by policy-makers as a question of basic children's rights. The right to free primary education is enshrined in the *Universal Declaration of Human Rights* (1948, Article 26). A series of four UNESCO regional conferences from 1960 to 1966 declared the target of achieving universal primary education (UPE) by 1980, and by 1970 in Latin America. The landmark *World Conference on Education for All* held in Jomtien, Thailand, in 1990 called for universal access to education in the fight against poverty. As discussed in greater detail below, Jomtien helped broaden the notion of quality 'basic education' and, at another meeting in 1996, declared the goal of achieving UPE by the year 2015. This was also one of eight Millennium Development Goals declared by the UN in 2000. The follow-up to Jomtien, the *World Education Forum* was held in Dakar, Senegal, in April 2000. The Dakar 'Framework for Action' defined education not just as a fundamental human right but also as 'the key to sustainable development and peace' (UNESCO, 2000). The *Convention on the Rights of the Child* (1990, Articles 28 and 29), ratified by almost all nations, declared the obligation of governments to provide free and compulsory primary education. This emerging, rights-based view was reinforced at the *World Summit for Social Development* (Copenhagen, 1995) and the *Fourth World Conference on Women* (Beijing, 1995).

The reality of education

Despite early optimism regarding the transformative power of education, it soon became apparent that formal schooling was not the panacea for development that many policy-makers and politicians had portrayed. This section will consider some of these major shortcomings.

Poor quality, non-completion and gender bias

As we have seen, expansion of the education system, and of formal schooling in particular, has conventionally been expected to provide simultaneous solutions to major development challenges, including those of economic growth, political unification and poverty eradication. This is quite a tall order, to say the least. Unsurprisingly, achievements have fallen well short of those early expectations. Notable problems with the formal education sector in the South include high non-completion rates, the low quality of instruction, educational qualification inflation, a bias towards universities at the expense of basic education, a persistent gender gap and under-investment due to public spending cuts. These shortcomings have severely undermined the ability of education as a social policy instrument to maximize people's well-being in terms of human resource development. However, as will be discussed below, new initiatives in educational policy and strategy design as a tool for broader social development and livelihood strengthening promise to enhance this potential.

Ministries of Education everywhere make a great play of the fact that net primary school enrolments have expanded steadily over the past decades to reach, if not a state of UPE, then at least significantly high levels. Official net primary enrolments average 86 per cent for all developing countries and often reach over 90 per cent for individual nations (UNDP, 2000). In 1996, based on declarations made at the Jomtien, Copenhagen and Beijing conferences, the Development Assistance Committee (DAC) of the OECD set an International Development Target of achieving UPE by 2015, a goal reiterated at the *World Education Forum* in Dakar in 2000. However, only three regions – East Asia and the Pacific, Latin America and the Caribbean, and Eastern Europe and Central Asia – are expected to achieve this goal by 2015. The challenge of UPE is clearly greatest in South Asia and sub-Saharan Africa, which are projected to achieve levels of 80 and 70 per cent respectively. Sub-Saharan Africa and South/West Asia account for 42 million and 47 million respectively of the developing world's 113 million children who do not attend school at all (EFA, 2000).

Official enrolment figures mask high levels of non-completion. Although Latin America has reached near universal levels of primary school enrolment, on average one-quarter fail to complete. This figure rises to over 40 per cent in South Asia and over one-third in sub-Saharan Africa (Watkins, 2000). For the South as a whole, 75 per cent of primary school entrants reach grade five, falling to 58 per cent for the poorest nations. The differential between cities and countryside is also marked. In India, for example, over 80 per cent of urban children are enrolled but this figure drops to 60 per cent in rural areas (UNICEF, 1999). In the drive to achieve UPE, furthermore, teacher–pupil ratios have reached an average of 70 : 1 in government schools (Hanmer and Naschold, 2000).

In secondary education, the gross enrolment rate for all developing countries is calculated at 54 per cent for males and 45 per cent for females, yet even these figures give an optimistic view. Median dropout rates are put at almost 40 per cent in Africa and 18 per cent in Asia and Latin America (UNICEF, 1999; Todaro, 2000). Transition rates to secondary education in Africa are amongst the lowest in the world, averaging less than 40 per cent, with many countries below 10 per cent, including Niger, Tanzania, Mozambique and Burkina Faso. Illiteracy amongst people of 15 years of age and over in developing countries fell dramatically from 60 per cent in 1960 to 31 per cent in 1995. However, population growth drove up the absolute number of illiterates by 150 million to 870 million over the same period. There is some cause for optimism in the latest figures, which reveal that the number of illiterate adults fell from 895 million in 1990 to 880 million in 1998 and was projected to reach 875 million by 2000 (EFA, 2000; Skilbeck, 2000). The worst affected regions in terms of illiteracy levels are South Asia (50 per cent), sub-Saharan Africa (43 per cent), East Asia (16 per cent) and

Latin America (13 per cent). Adult illiteracy rates can, however, reach much higher levels, as in Swaziland with 90 per cent and Kenya at 77 per cent (Skilbeck, 2000).

While access to education is universally class-biased, the tendency towards a two-tier structure in developing countries has become even more pronounced during the 1990s. According to critics, the public system is becoming a 'ghetto for the underprivileged', increasingly abandoned by those who can afford to place their children in the ever-expanding private education sector which prospers in the wake of an underfunded and mismanaged State system (Jellema, 2000: 29). Another prominent feature of this period of educational expansion has been the persistent gender gap in access (see Figure 5.1). According to one calculation, in 66 out of 108 countries, female enrolment at primary and secondary levels is at least 10 per cent lower than for males (Todaro, 2000). Of those children not enrolled at school (145 million), about two-thirds are girls. In 1995, 79 per cent of males in developing countries were literate, compared with 62 per cent of women, while girls enjoy just over half the number of years of schooling as their male counterparts (UNDP, 1999; UNICEF, 1999). This gap is largest in the poorest countries as well as in the Middle East and North Africa. Female literacy is especially low, for example, in Niger (7 per cent), Burkina Faso (9 per cent), Nepal (14 per cent), Afghanistan (15 per cent), Mozambique (23 per cent), Ethiopia (25 per cent), Bangladesh (26 per cent), Morocco (31 per cent) and India (38 per cent). This may be compared with achievements in Latin America (Brazil 83 per cent, Chile and Cuba 95 per cent and Colombia 91 per cent) and a range of other countries including South Korea (97 per cent), Fiji (89 per cent), Jordan and Mauritius (79 per cent) and Malaysia (78 per cent).

Public spending bias and structural adjustment

During the 1980s, real per capita spending on education in the South dropped dramatically by some 40 per cent in Latin America and by 65 per cent in sub-Saharan Africa (Colclough and Lewin, 1993). Although there is evidence to suggest that many governments are now giving a higher funding priority to primary education than in the past, spending at this level is still grossly inadequate. UNESCO data reveal that in 1998 governments in the South spent on average less than 1.7 per cent of GNP on primary education, with some allocating less than 0.7 per cent (EFA, 2000).

Yet the failure of governments to adequately fund primary education has been matched by disproportionately high levels of spending on the tertiary sector in nearly all developing countries (see Figure 5.2). The substantial private returns to university education in the South, inflated by large government subsidies that reduce the costs to (largely urban, middle-class) students, and despite recent funding cutbacks, have helped to maintain public demand for post-secondary qualifications. In developing countries as a whole, the mere 6 per cent of students pursuing tertiary education absorb around 40 per cent of

Figure 5.2 Ratio of higher versus primary costs per student year

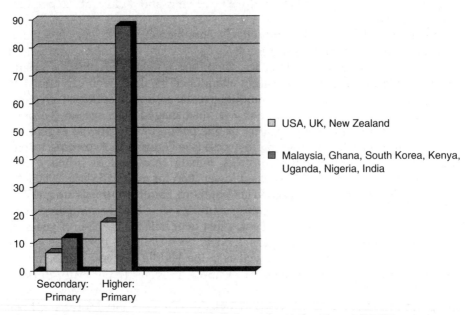

Source: Todaro (2000: 332).

public educational expenditure. A university student costs on average 88 times as much as a primary school pupil to educate, rising to as high as 146 times (Todaro, 1994; UNICEF, 1999). Underlining the degree of university subsidy and inequality of access, it is worth noting that on average in developing countries 66 per cent of government educational spending at university level benefits the wealthiest quintile of the population while just 3 per cent is accrued by the poorest quintile (UNICEF, 1999).

There are many causes of low primary enrolments and completion. The correlation between low school attendance and poverty is universally very close, the cases of sub-Saharan Africa and South Asia being marked. Demographic pressure due to continuing high fertility rates is also a problem in some areas. In view of competing political demands on education budgets, governments cannot provide for the needs of an ever-growing school population, especially during times of financial stringency. Economic recession, climatic and natural disasters, as well as the HIV/AIDS pandemic, have also added pressures on governments and individuals. Increasingly, parents must pay a proportion of their children's education as policy-makers adopt cost-recovery strategies. For many parents, education is becoming a luxury that they simply cannot afford. Direct expenses involved in providing books, uniforms, transport and exam fees can absorb up to 20 per cent of household income. Furthermore, the indirect or opportunity costs of sending their children to school can be prohibitively high in terms of lost productive and domestic labour, especially for girls. Furthermore, cultural and religious practices may lead to the deliberate exclusion of girls.

In addition to the question of non-achievement of targets, unequal access and the public investment bias towards the tertiary sector, another parallel and controversial debate concerns the whole question of whether the model of formal schooling followed in the South is entirely appropriate to the development needs of these countries. Alarm bells had started to ring loudly by the late 1970s and early 1980s, when levels of educated unemployment amongst the youth of developing countries reached huge proportions. As Coombs noted, the mismatch between the numbers of qualified graduates and job opportunities, 'became so severe as to challenge the basic integrity of their education system and the efficacy of the whole educational development strategy' (1985: 194). On the demand side, the blame for this imbalance could also be placed on the failure of less developed economies to grow fast enough to supply adequate numbers of skilled manual and white-collar jobs. Nevertheless, on the supply side, the over-production of young people entering the job market with formal qualifications came to be seen by policy-makers as a problem.

One enduring consequence of the excess of supply over demand for skilled labour has been what Dore (1976) famously labelled the 'diploma disease'. That is, a paper-chase in which the 'price' of a modern-sector job in terms of the required certification is continuously driven upwards as more and more school and university graduates pursue proportionately fewer and fewer jobs. The education system, Dore argued, has been distorted to make the passing of examinations, rather than the acquisition of knowledge, an end in itself, the ultimate aspiration. Ritualistic, rote learning becomes the norm. 'In the process of qualification ... the pupil is concerned not with mastery, but with being certified as having mastered. ... If education is learning to *do* a job, qualification is a matter of learning in order to *get* a job' (Dore, 1976: 8). Consequently, although schooling is clearly indispensable for modern-sector development, in this didactic and qualification-driven form, it is thought by some critical observers to discourage the emergence of personal qualities that are crucial for industry such as initiative and creativity (Dore and Oxenham, 1984).

As we have seen, the 1960s and 1970s was a period of rapid growth in government educational expenditure in developing nations. By the early 1980s, however, this expansion had slowed down considerably. Spending in real terms was levelling off or declining in many countries. Such reductions were well under way, even before the imposition of structural adjustment, due to poor economic performance and falling government fiscal revenues. A study of 37 developing countries over the period 1972–82 showed that, in most cases, government spending on education had already been significantly reduced (Lewin, 1987). However, adjustment during the 1980s certainly exacerbated this problem, leading to a 'culture of cuts' and crisis management in which the education sector became a prime target, affecting both the availability and quality of schooling. In the Philippines, for example, education spending per capita in 1984 was 30 per cent lower than in 1979, and 40 per cent less in Jamaica (Graham-Brown, 1991).

Primary schooling has proved especially vulnerable during this period of austerity. Between 1975 and 1981, for example, the proportion of the education budget allocated to first-level schooling in Africa fell from 40 per cent to 30 per cent, while the reverse applied to the secondary sector (Lewin, 1987). This trend continued under adjustment, with primary education in Latin America and sub-Saharan Africa suffering major setbacks. Enrolment and continuation rates faltered, while budgets for materials and equipment as well as maintenance of school buildings were drastically reduced, in some cases to almost zero. Teachers' salaries, which typically comprise 90 per cent or more of recurrent education expenditure, have also been severely eroded, leading to low morale and the recruitment of a growing army of unqualified instructors. Deteriorating standards of education have made demand more price-elastic. The recent introduction of user charges for education in Tanzania (the only country in Africa to briefly enjoy UPE, during the 1970s), has led to a drop in enrolments, which stood at just 57 per cent in 1997 (Eele et al., 2000; Hanmer and Naschold, 2000).

Education in general, and primary education in particular, has been more vulnerable to spending cuts compared with other social sectors. For governments, educational planning has the advantage of being largely under domestic control (compared with debt-servicing for example) and has a great potential for making savings since it constitutes a major element in social expenditure – typically three times that of health, for example. Furthermore, education benefits have a long lead-time and, in a situation where planning horizons are extremely short-term, cuts can be made without too many immediate adverse repercussions for politicians.

Within this context, first-level schooling has been considered a politically 'soft' target, being primarily rural in most countries and away from the urban centres of power. In many countries during the 1980s, such as Burkina Faso, Mauritania, Senegal, Malaysia, Sri Lanka and Thailand, spending on primary and secondary education was squeezed while subsidized university education for the urban middle classes was expanded (Lewin, 1987). Yet there was no inevitability about these decisions, since some countries such as Zimbabwe and Zambia did make efforts to maintain levels of educational spending during the 1980s as a conscious political choice (Graham-Brown, 1991). Yet, even in these cases, the bias towards secondary and tertiary levels was maintained.

Education for social development

As discussed above, disillusionment has been growing since the 1970s with the general failure of mainstream education policy to effectively address development needs. On one hand, this has been due to the rapid expansion of formal education in response to social and political pressures, especially at secondary and tertiary levels. This has fuelled 'educational inflation', distorted public education spending patterns and led to relative neglect of basic and primary schooling. On the other hand, this process of expansion and the resulting problems have called into question the almost sacred assumption that Western-style schooling is the only serious policy option for achieving economic and social development. An alternative approach, it was increasingly being argued, would be to help correct past biases by diversifying educational investment and altering priorities to better cater for the needs of all children.

The agenda is set

At the dawn of the 1990s, the view that education was merely a tool for providing human capital in the drive towards economic growth had been seriously challenged in several quarters. Yet although alternative models had been suggested, there was no central agenda to guide policy-makers and planners in the reformulation of education policy goals and strategies. This task fell to the Jomtien conference on *Education for All* (1990), which attempted to systematize the disparate ideas that had emerged over the previous two decades and to put education back at the centre of a broader, international development agenda. Together with principles espoused in the *Convention on the Rights of the Child* (1990) and the *World Summit for Children* (1990), the Jomtien 'World Declaration on Education for All' expanded the notion of basic education.

In this new vision, however, education loses none of its transforming potential. It represents the culmination of an evolving notion of education as capable of promoting economic and social development that has emerged, albeit in faltering stages, since the 1970s. Thus, '... education is the single most vital element in combating poverty, empowering women, promoting human rights and democracy, protecting the environment and controlling population growth' (UNICEF, 1999: 13). Furthermore:

> Lack of basic education undermines all other efforts to improve health and nutrition, address the causes and impact of HIV/AIDS, reduce infant, child and maternal mortality, enhance opportunities for more productive livelihoods and promote a civil society committed to democracy, good government and the realization of other fundamental rights. (DFID, 2000: 1)

Within this all-encompassing view, 'Basic education is a proven weapon against poverty, opening up access to knowledge and skills and helping to break down barriers that exclude poor and marginalized people from political and economic life' (Jellema, 2000: 27). In a nutshell, 'Ensuring the right of education is a matter of morality, justice and economic sense' (UNICEF, 1999: 7).

The Jomtien declaration underlines children's right to a quality basic education that will be relevant to their needs. The education priorities set include early childhood care and development, the attainment of UPE, occupational-based training for youth and adults, the reduction of adult illiteracy, and the acquisition of real-life skills, knowledge and values required for promoting sustainable development. Two international development targets emerged out of Jomtien and subsequent meetings; firstly, the target of UPE in all countries by 2015 and, secondly, the elimination of gender disparity in primary and secondary education by 2005. Jomtien helped to galvanize a growing policy consensus amongst international development agencies on the need to broaden educational access and achieve such targets through both primary schooling as well as non-formal skills training. However, whether this consensus will translate into a reordering of education sector investments, especially by national governments using domestic funds, is debatable.

As already indicated, the economic and social benefits of widening and diversifying education policy to tackle pervasive problems such as poverty and gender inequality had been indicated back in the early 1970s. Post-Jomtien, however, the links between educational investment and socio-economic progress were re-emphasized and underlined. Education, it was again argued, is beneficial not just for promoting growth as reflected in macro-economic statistics such as GNP per capita. It also encourages social or human development in terms of addressing poverty, teaching appropriate production and livelihood skills, and has a direct impact on key social variables such as fertility and health status. According to UNICEF (1999: 21), a veritable 'education revolution' has been taking place, '… whose principles are now broadly understood and shared and whose central elements are emerging in varying configurations around the world'. These are summarized by UNICEF (1999) as: (1) learning for life; (2) improving access to, quality and flexibility of basic education; (3) promoting gender sensitivity; (4) recognizing the State as a major partner in multi-institutional arrangements to foster this process; and (5) caring for young children.

'Learning for life' encapsulates the idea that schooling should impart basic literacy and numeracy, more advanced survival skills in the areas of livelihood and production, health and nutrition as well as pyscho-social abilities of co-operation, negotiation, communication and decision-making. This notion is coupled with the idea that multi-dimensional assessment methods should be introduced rather than relying just on numerical ranking based on exam results. The UNESCO–UNICEF 'Monitoring Learning Achievement' (MLA) project, for example, attempts to develop an international framework for this purpose. Embodied in the 'learning for life' concept (itself reminiscent of the earlier notion of 'lifelong learning') are the vocational-type goals hitherto included under the non-formal education label.

Guaranteeing children's right to receive an education of good quality is the most important central theme of this new agenda. It is underpinned by the *Convention on the Rights of the Child* (1990) and is fed by worldwide experiences of improving educational provision through both conventional and other means. The hallmark of the various approaches adopted is flexibility, in which methods are not prescribed in advance but adapted to local conditions and the specific needs of local children. More conventionally, techniques such as double shifting (or 'hot-seating') and use of local construction materials may reduce costs and improve the efficiency of schools.

Although the Jomtien declarations were high profile, there was nothing fundamentally new in this stance. Educational specialists had since the 1970s and even much earlier been advocating the merits of investing in basic and non-formal education. However, governments had been reluctant to spend domestic funds on innovative schemes for the masses and it was left to the international agencies such as UNESCO (with its 'Fundamental Education' programme, for example) to experiment with alternative approaches. By the 1950s, various parts of the developing world had already seen innovative educational experiences associated with community development, integrated rural development, literacy training, technical and vocational training and agricultural extension (Dore and Mars, 1981). Yet these education initiatives of the 1950s and 1960s were conceived almost exclusively in terms of encouraging the growth of human capital, as a form of investment into economic growth and modernization. During this time, at the height of the Cold War, these programmes were underpinned by geo-political concerns over the struggle against Communism and extension of the West's sphere of influence. The 'Alliance for Progress' in Latin America, for example, is a notable case in point.

Schooling and economic development

Strengthening links between schooling and macro-economic development remained the overriding policy priority set by international organizations throughout the 1970s and 1980s. There were two major emphases within this broad agenda. Firstly, the privatization and diversification of vocational education and, secondly, improving the effectiveness of formal schools. The latter was stressed because of the perception that enhancing school quality and efficiency both improved individual performance and had a positive influence on economic development (Fuller, 1986). In particular, primary education was targeted during the 1980s due to its perceived positive impact not just on productivity but also on health, nutrition and other key social indicators of development. Lending by the World Bank for primary schooling rose from less than 5 per cent of its education portfolio during 1970–74 to 28 per cent in 1986–89 (World Bank, 1990b). The concern to maintain school quality became even more pronounced under conditions of austerity imposed by structural adjustment (Fuller and Habte, 1992). However, in spite of the concern with improving school quality, the link between education and development was more directly explored in the vocational education sub-sector.

During the 1980s, about 40 per cent of funding by multilateral agencies for education supported vocational education and training (VET). However, this was heavily biased in favour of skilled workers in established firms through on-the-job training schemes. This policy largely ignored the huge informal sector, which absorbs between 35 and 70 per cent of the urban labour force in developing countries (Todaro, 2000). In order to enhance productivity, critics argued, funding for VET should be differentiated. High- and middle-income countries with relatively well-developed industrial sectors should strengthen their existing VET systems through a more selective approach, developing direct links with fast-growing industrial sectors. Low-income nations, in contrast, should focus more on the informal sector where subsistence and entrepreneurial skills should be taught that could not be imparted through formal schooling or conventional apprenticeship schemes. Programmes to disseminate appropriate technologies, teach management skills and provide low-cost credit for micro-enterprises were now emphasized (Middleton and Demsky, 1989; World Bank, 1991). At the same time, the privatization of vocational training and withdrawal of State funding has been advocated by the World Bank, a policy that has met with some criticism on the grounds that it undermines the need to develop relevant industrial skills (Bennel and Segerstrom, 1998). Going further, however, policy-makers now seek more flexible arrangements for primary schools that facilitate access for groups traditionally excluded by conventional schooling.

Making primary schools more efficient and responsive to local needs has also been a feature of education policy since Jomtien and well beforehand. The well-known 'Escuela Nueva' schools in rural Colombia, for example, employ multi-grade teaching methods, are carefully located for easy access, have curricula and teaching materials relevant to rural areas and are supported by local communities (Schiefelbein, 1992). This model has been extended to other countries such as Guatemala, Brazil and the Philippines. Another example of flexible provision is the Philippines 'Cordilleras Mobile Teaching Project', in which ambulant teachers equipped with educational backpacks take schools to children at special learning centres in mountainous areas. The Bangladesh Rural Advancement Committee (BRAC), which started life as a small project, now has some 34,000 schools teaching basic literacy, numeracy and social awareness, adapting its curriculum and timetable to local needs while retaining access for pupils to the formal school system. As UNICEF (1999) points out, there are many more examples that could be quoted of such flexibility, adaptability and gender sensitivity being put into practice.

The importance of expanding and improving the quality of formal education as a prerequisite for technological change and economic progress, especially in dynamic and fast-growing economies in which labour supplies must be flexible to adapt to changing markets, continues to be underlined by human capital theory. Various studies have shown how, outside of the 'modern' sector also, formal and non-formal education may enhance productivity in the agricultural and urban informal sectors, attacking poverty through increased earnings (Haddad et al., 1990; World Bank, 1990a). Social rates of return to education are very high in low- and middle-income countries, especially at the primary level (World Bank, 1995; Todaro, 2000). In addition, there are other, unmeasured social gains arising from externalities that are not computed by the monetary units employed in conventional cost–benefit analysis. These benefits can, however, be revealed by specific studies.

Popular education and community-based development

Until the early 1990s, the education policy agenda, or at least that set by international organizations, continued to focus on strengthening macro-economic growth and modernization, either through improving the formal school system or through more appropriate vocational education programmes. Social development goals as a part of the education policy agenda remained almost incidental. Although this was to be challenged during the 1990s, opposition to the human capital bias within education dates back at least to the 1970s. Based on the ideas of Karl Marx and Antonio Gramsci, Paulo Freire criticized conventional education as an essentially manipulative instrument that helps to maintain a repressive social order and discourages individual creativity, progress and freedom. According to Freire (1972), formal schooling is organized like a banking system in which officially sanctioned 'knowledge' is deposited into the heads of pupils by teachers so that it can be withdrawn at the appropriate time according to a prescribed formula, serving the interests of power holders. Though not without his critics (see, for example, Berger, 1974, and Blackburn, 2000) Freire's ideas, together with those of 'Liberation Theology' associated with the radical wing of the Catholic Church formed the intellectual foundation of the 'popular education' movement in Latin America (Kane, 2001). This emerged during the 1970s under dictatorial regimes in various countries such as Brazil, Argentina, Chile and Colombia, in which religious and lay workers, as well as an emerging group of increasingly vociferous non-governmental organizations (NGOs), mobilized communities for reformist and sometimes radical development initiatives.

As discussed in Chapter 1 of this volume, in this model education comprises not just formal instruction or skills training. After all, the State-controlled 'community development' movement of the 1970s had promoted this aim during the 1970s (Dore and Mars, 1981). Popular education was rather different, involving a broader, consciousness-raising effort by NGOs in which poor and deprived communities are encouraged to band together to define their own social and economic problems and devise appropriate solutions. Whether the central problem has ever really been a lack of popular 'consciousness' as such, an attitude that some critics such as Berger (1974) consider highly patronizing, or whether inaction is really due to a lack of self-confidence and organizational capacity, is a moot point (Hall, 1986). What cannot be denied, however, is that, by and large, these initiatives sought to encourage local self-determination and to strengthen social capital, often using unconventional methods of group organization and education. Freire's original use of literacy training as a vehicle for change was soon complemented and overtaken by action across a much broader front (Kane, 2001).

Community-based development projects have proliferated in major livelihood-related areas such as agriculture, land acquisition, primary health care and, more recently, natural resource conservation (Harrison, 1983; Taylor and Mackenzie, 1992; Hall, 1993, 1997a, 1997b, 1999, 2003, 2004; Castañeda, 1994; Escobar, 1995; Stoesz et al., 1999; Kane, 2001). Indeed, veritable social movements have grown around key issues such as land reform, involuntary resettlement associated with hydropower schemes, indigenous rights and urban neighbourhood issues (Hall, 1990, 1994, 2000b; Foweraker, 1995). With the demise of dictatorships and strengthening of civil society, as well as dictates from the Vatican, nowadays the Catholic Church plays a far less active role at grassroots level than it used to. However, a plethora of national and overseas NGOs, usually supported by multilateral and bilateral donors, have formed a powerful network for grassroots development and change which remains highly active in its pursuit of educational alternatives for social development. Such networks have been highly effective especially at the international level in areas such as human rights and the environment (Keck and Sikkink, 1998).

By the early 1970s, official aid organizations had also started to question the modernization paradigm and its assumption that poverty would be self-rectifying through a process of 'trickle down'. A landmark 1972 speech by Robert MacNamara, then President of the World Bank, outlined a new anti-poverty focus for the institution that other international donors soon followed. 'Redistribution with Growth' (Chenery et al., 1974) and providing for 'Basic Human Needs' (ILO, 1976; Streeten et al., 1981) underlined the need for appropriate policies designed to cater specifically for the needs of poor and disadvantaged groups that had not automatically benefited from economic modernization. Funding by the World Bank, the major source of development assistance for education, was only slowly adjusted to meet these new development goals. By the late 1980s, a much larger share of its lending for education was allocated to primary schooling, while the virtues of non-formal education for tackling rural poverty had been placed on the policy agenda (Coombs and Ahmed, 1974; World Bank, 1975). However, from 1977–86, only 22 per cent of total Bank lending for education went to support primary schooling and a further 13 per cent to non-formal skills training (Haddad et al., 1990).

Basic education for social development

In terms of social development, primary education is particularly important in improving fertility control and health status. Cross-national studies have long revealed a generally inverse relationship between educational attainment and family size, although this relationship may vary in time and space (World Bank, 1990a). A UNICEF analysis of over 90 countries showed that, of various interventions, education has the greatest impact on health indicators such as infant and under-five mortality, life expectancy at birth and fertility. Enhancing girls' access to primary schooling is especially critical in improving social development indicators, a fact noted in many studies.

A 10 per cent increase in girls' primary enrolment may decrease infant mortality by 4.1 deaths per 1,000, and a comparable rise in girls' secondary education by a further 5.6 deaths per 1,000 (UNICEF, 1999). Bown (1990) analysed over 40 community projects and discovered a strong correlation between female literacy and positive social impacts. These included improved child health care, greater use of oral rehydration therapy (ORT) and immunization, better family spacing and improved child nutrition. In its turn, better nutrition improves the learning capacity of poor children, which is hampered by protein deficiency. The acquisition of literacy and numeracy skills also empowers women and enables them to establish new forms of economic organization and gain access to credit, as well as play a stronger decision-making role within the household and community. Since women carry a disproportionate burden of deprivation and landlessness, improvements due to education may help break the vicious circle of poverty and lack of schooling. It has been argued that investing in women's education is potentially the single most important contribution to fostering human development (Summers, 1994).

Thus, the post-1990 education policy 'revolution' for developing countries involves teaching both academic and survival skills, enhancing access and quality (with a focus on primary schooling) and promoting gender sensitivity. As laudable as these objectives are, however, they amount to nothing unless they can be realized through the implementation of appropriate policies. Thus, at the centre of this strategy, is the need for a strong State that can guarantee children's right to a satisfactory basic education, as underlined in several articles of the *Convention on the Rights of the Child* (1990). The State must supply the political will to undertake reforms, allocate adequate funding and be prepared to enter into partnership with key elements of civil society (World Bank, 1997). However, as Katarina Tomasevski (2003: 2) notes in her damning critique, although education is ostensibly portrayed 'as the cause of and panacea for all the diseases of society', governments everywhere are reluctant to invest adequately in this sector as a basic human right.

Following Jomtien, several countries have placed basic education high on the policy agenda, embarking on nationwide campaigns to boost educational spending and organization. In Brazil, 'Education For All' received strong government backing from the early 1990s, and when President Fernando Henrique Cardoso took office in 1995 a mobilization campaign ('Wake Up, Brazil, It's Time for School!') was launched. Measures included the transfer of federal funds to local schools and municipalities, improvements to national testing and the greater use of media for distance learning (Hall, 2003). From 1991–98, net primary (7–14 years) enrolments rose from 86 to 95 per cent (Brazil, 2000). In the Philippines since 1995, the designation of a 'National School Enrolment Day' forms part of a countrywide effort to boost primary school participation rates. In 1994, Malawi proclaimed universal free primary education and produced a huge increase in enrolments, mobilizing high levels of international support as a result (UNICEF, 1999).

Although the State must retain overall responsibility for educational planning and budgeting, the formation of partnerships with NGOs, communities, religious bodies and commercial enterprises is increasingly common and necessary. Sometimes, this amounts to little more than cost sharing, brought about by the introduction of user fees as a result of economic adjustment and austerity. The *Convention on the Rights of the Child* (1990) states that primary education should be compulsory and available free to all. Yet this is far from being the case and many children are excluded by the direct and indirect costs of schooling. In Cambodia, for example, three-quarters of the cost of public primary education is borne by households, while those in Vietnam pay half. Contradicting the ambitious 'Education For All' agenda, increasing private costs have led to falling enrolments and retention in a number of countries. In other cases, such partnerships may actively involve local communities in running primary schools and in devising local solutions. The IDEAL programme in Bangladesh and the CHILDSCOPE project in Ghana, for example, both work along these lines (UNICEF, 1999).

Decentralization

Decentralization as a means of forming partnerships amongst key players in the process of education management is gaining popularity. In the Brazilian state of Minas Gerais, major decision-making powers over financial, adminis- trative and pedagogical matters, were shifted from the state capital to local school boards, resulting in substantially improved enrolment and retention rates. The EDUCO programme in El Salvador, which targets rural children, places control of local rural preschools and primary schools in the hands of community associations. In Mali, government officials and NGOs collaborate in district-level teams working with communities to set up school management committees (UNICEF, 1999). A related and increasingly popular policy solution for increasing school efficiency is the adoption of demand-side financing tech- niques. In order to eliminate 'waste' in public spending, funds are not allocated centrally but on the basis of educational demand through mechanisms such as vouchers, stipends and capitation grants. Thus, 'money follows students' based on the assumption that parental choice is thus increased (World Bank, 1986, 1995; Patrinos and Araisingam, 1997). However, to be effective decentralization policies must be supported by strong government commitment and strength- ened management capacity at local level involving government, schools and parents. Otherwise, there is a strong danger that such measures may lead to more corruption and lower education quality.

Basic education and social policy

Education can be considered a tool of social policy in two dimensions. Firstly, as a form of human resource development, investment into formal schooling at primary, secondary and tertiary levels is necessary to develop a human capital base of skilled workers for the modern industrial and commercial sectors. How to limit the oversupply of such qualified labour or, alternatively, how to increase the effective demand for it within labour markets, remain perennial problems for educational and economic planners. Secondly, what has been termed 'lifelong' education for social development in a broader sense, involv- ing formal and various non-formal techniques, is necessary to cater for the livelihood and citizenship needs of large, more traditional groups. These include those in the urban informal sector and the rural subsistence economy as well as those groups that tend to be marginalized by conventional education such as indigenous groups and refugees. Here, progress cannot be measured by macro-economic figures but rather by improvements in basic social indicators such as literacy and health status.

Yet it is pertinent to ask whether the post-Jomtien 'revolution' fully faces up to the second of these challenges, that of promoting education as social development. Despite the lofty statements made at Jomtien and Dakar, as well as by national governments, educational planning is still driven overwhelmingly by political forces. UNICEF estimates that it will cost $7 billion a year over 10 years to achieve UPE by 2015. Only a limited proportion is likely to come from international sources. Donor allocations to education have been falling steadily or stagnating since the late 1980s, and presently just 1.3 per cent of annual overseas development assistance is spent on basic education (Bennel and Furlong, 1998; Randel et al., 2000). As Chapter 9 of this volume demonstrates, although the World Bank has made major strides in providing greater support to basic education, the record for other multilateral as well as most bilateral donors is much bleaker. Furthermore, in spite of attempts to improve the efficiency of educational spending and management through initiatives such as decentralization, for example, significant strengthening of basic education would probably require the reallocation of some resources from the highly subsidized tertiary sector. Yet very few developing countries have chosen to reallocate resources to basic education and health sectors. The advent of Poverty Reduction Strategy Papers (PRSPs) as a form of social conditionality for debt relief may induce some re-examination of public spending patterns in this regard (see Chapter 9).

Under conditions of extreme austerity in many developing countries, as mentioned above, the cost burden of primary schooling is increasingly being shifted onto households, with grave implications for school access and retention levels. A review of countries that managed to universalize primary education early in their development process (such as Cuba, Costa Rica, Botswana, Zimbabwe and Mauritius, amongst others) showed that a major common policy was to guarantee equity of educational provision at all levels while maintaining spending on materials for teachers and students (Mehrotra, 1998). Too few governments are politically committed enough to 'Education For All' goals to make the necessary spending allocations to provide universal and free primary schooling. In addition, limited institutional capacity and poor accountability are also likely to undermine the ability of governments to manage the education sector.

Another question must be raised over the emphasis that is currently being placed on formal schooling for children and the apparent neglect of non-formal education for both children and adults. In Latin America and elsewhere, for example, there has been a rich tradition of community-based 'popular education' that has made a major contribution to social development through projects for adult literacy, health, nutrition and many other livelihood activities. It is recognized that NGOs have been instrumental in promoting literacy drives, especially for women and girls, as well as various forms of non-formal education for development (Skilbeck, 2000). Yet many observers believe that governments could build more strongly upon this tradition by forming stronger partnerships with NGOs and civil society to tackle problems of poverty and unemployment, citizenship preparation and governance (La Belle, 2000).

There are indeed signs of a revival of interest in non-formal education and many studies illustrate its value as a social development tool. For example, in Papua New Guinea, a community-based non-formal education movement has enabled hundreds of the country's local languages to be used to teach literacy in pre-school and adult programmes (Siegel, 1997). Non-formal vocational training programmes have been successful in providing employment opportunities for poorly educated urban youths (Leonardos, 1999). In another study, non-formal strategies were seen as offering hope for street children who had been bypassed by conventional schooling (Leonardos, 1995). In the field of environmental management for sustainable development, non-formal education is absolutely crucial for success (Hall, 2004). Indeed, this is a two-way process in which 'educators' may themselves be educated. Local indigenous knowledge often informs outside policy-makers and practitioners on the design and implementation of locale-specific strategies for conservation and development.

Conclusion

As we have seen in the preceding sections, education policy for developing countries has undergone major modifications since the 1960s. Initially, mainstream education was conceived almost exclusively in terms of human capital formation to fuel modern sector economic growth. From the 1970s, this vision was moderated by the discovery that education could contribute in many ways to the development process other than by churning out certificated graduates to become white-collar workers. In addition to supplying such skilled and highly qualified human resources, schooling could address the survival and livelihood needs of all citizens. Through the 1970s and 1980s, both formal and non-formal educational channels as well as more radical, community-based approaches, thus came to be seen as appropriate vehicles for tackling poverty, for improving key social indicators such as fertility, mortality and morbidity and for enhancing citizenship.

In 1990, the Jomtien conference and the *Declaration of the Rights of the Child* underlined the right of children to receive a sound and flexible basic education designed to serve a range of needs for specific groups. At the follow-up 'World Education Forum' held in Dakar, Senegal, a decade later, the *Framework for Action* underlined the need for global commitment to achieving universal, free primary education. Governments were called upon, and some have responded, to make a political commitment to boosting education and, in particular, to invest more heavily into primary schooling, where social returns are high. At the same time, international donors were called upon to increase levels of official assistance to basic education. The Global Campaign for Education, launched in 1999, mobilized international NGO support behind this quest (Watkins, 2000).

This chapter has reviewed the expansion of formal education to serve a diverse development agenda, and considered some of the major problems that persist in terms of low enrolments, high dropout rates, poor quality and financial cutbacks. The rise of basic education policy during the 1990s was examined as a tool for promoting economic and social development through improved primary schooling and non-formal education in particular. Basic education as an instrument of social as well as economic policy has been underlined, although the above-mentioned problems persist, requiring greater official commitment domestically and internationally.

Ultimately, however, education on its own of whatever variety does not hold any magic key to development. Education may indeed be a decisive factor in determining individual income-earning potential. Yet unless educational investments are integrated with the generation of employment opportunities, education will have little direct impact. Education may also be a vital ingredient for improving social indicators such as infant mortality and nutrition levels. However, without parallel interventions to resolve livelihood problems such as access to land and other basic production and social services, schooling itself will be of limited use. In the final analysis, the onus is on governments, civil society and international organizations to construct a policy and political environment in which the potential of education to help fuel a broad development process may eventually be realized.

The next chapter will consider the expansion of health systems in the developing world. Somewhat paralleling the education debate above, it will demonstrate how primary or basic health care has been neglected in favour of more expensive secondary health care policies which tend to benefit wealthier groups, reducing the potential impact of this sector on poverty alleviation and social development.

Recommended Reading

The following sources provide a good overview of the main issues relating to education policy, with special reference to basic education, in developing countries.

- Watkins, K. (2000) *The Oxfam Education Report*. Oxford: Oxfam. This is an up-to-date survey of education policies and development, very highly recommended.
- Kane, L. (2000) *Popular Education and Social Change in Latin America*. London: Latin America Bureau. The best analysis of popular education, its roots and application in various contexts.
- Bennel, P. and Furlong, D. (1998) 'Has Jomtien made any difference? Trends in donor funding for education and basic needs since the late 1980s', *World Development*, 26 (1),

January: 45–59. A concise analysis of indifferent donor performance in terms of financial commitments to achieving the Education For All goals set by the 1990 Jomtien conference.

- Tomasevski, K. (2003) *Education Denied: Costs and Remedies*. London: Zed Books. A hard-hitting critique of government education policy around the globe from a human rights perspective. Katarina Tomasevski argues powerfully that neo-liberalism has distorted education priorities and denied this basic right to millions of children.

References

Anderson, C. and Bowman, M. (1973) 'Human capital and economic modernization in historical perspective', in *Proceedings of the Fourth International Conference of Economic History*. Paris: Mouton.

Bass, C. (1998) *Education in Tibet: Policy and Practice since 1950*. London: Zed Books.

Becker, G. (1964) *Human Capital: A Theoretical and Empirical Analysis, with Special Reference to Education*. Princeton, NJ: Princeton University Press.

Bennel, P. and Furlong, D. (1998) 'Has Jomtien made any difference? Trends in donor funding for education and basic education since the late 1980s', *World Development*, 26 (1): 45–59.

Bennel, P. and Segerstrom, J. (1998) 'Vocational education and training in developing countries: has the World Bank got it right?', *International Journal of Educational Development*, 18 (4): 271–87.

Berger, P. (1974) *Pyramids of Sacrifice*. Harmondsworth: Penguin.

Blackburn, J. (2000) 'Understanding Paulo Freire: reflections on the origins, concepts and possible pitfalls of his educational approach', *Community Development Journal*, 35 (1): 3–15.

Blaug, M. (1970) *An Introduction to the Economics of Education*. Harmondsworth: Penguin.

Bown, L. (1990) *Preparing the Future: Women, Literacy and Development*. London: ActionAid.

Brazil (2000) *EFA 2000, Education For All: Evaluation of the Year 2000*. Brasilia: National Institute for Educational Studies and Research.

Castañeda, C. (1994) *Utopia Unarmed: The Latin American Left after the Cold War*. New York: Vintage.

Chenery, H.B, Ahluwalia, M.S., Bell, C.L.G., Duloy, J.H. and Jolly, R. (1974) *Redistribution with Growth*. Oxford: Oxford University Press.

Colclough, C. and Lewin, K. (1993) *Educating All the Children: Strategies for Primary Schooling in the South*. Oxford: Clarendon Press.

Coombs, P. (1985) *The World Crisis in Education*. Oxford: Oxford University Press.

Coombs, P. and Ahmed, M. (1974) *Attacking Rural Poverty: How Non-Formal Education Can Help*. Baltimore, MD: Johns Hopkins University Press.

DFID (2000) *Education For All: The Challenge of Universal Primary Education*, Consultation Document. London: Department for International Development.

Dore, R. (1976) *The Diploma Disease: Education, Qualification and Development*. London: Allen and Unwin.

Dore, R. and Mars, Z. (eds) (1981) *Community Development: Comparative Case Studies in India, the Republic of Korea, Mexico and Tanzania*. London: Croom Helm.

Dore, R. and Oxenham, J. (1984) 'Educational reform and selection for employment – an overview', in R. Dore and J. Oxenham (eds) *Education Versus Qualifications?* London: Allen and Unwin, pp. 3–40.

EFA (2000) *Education For All: Year 2000 Assessment.* Paris: UNESCO.

Eele, G. Semboja, J., Likwelile, S. and Ackroyd, S. (2000) 'Meeting international poverty targets in Tanzania', *Development Policy Review*, 18 (1), March: 63–83.

Escobar, A. (1995) *Encountering Development: The Making and Unmaking of the Third World.* Princeton, NJ: Princeton University Press.

Foweraker, J. (1995) *Theorizing Social Movements.* London: Pluto Press.

Freire, P. (1972) *Pedagogy of the Oppressed.* New York: Herder and Herder.

Fuller, B. (1986) *Raising School Quality in Developing Countries*, World Bank Discussion Paper 2. Washington, DC: World Bank.

Fuller, B. and Habte, A. (eds) (1992) *Adjusting Educational Policies: Conserving Resources while Raising School Quality*, World Bank Discussion Paper 132. Washington, DC: World Bank.

Graham-Brown, S. (1991) *Education in the Developing World: Conflict and Crisis.* Harlow: Longman.

Haddad, W., Carnoy, M., Rinaldi, R. and Regel, O. (1990) *Education and Development: Evidence for New Priorities.* Washington, DC: World Bank.

Hall, A. (1986) 'Community participation and rural development', in A. Hall, J. Midgley, M. Hardiman and D. Narine, *Community Participation, Social Development and the State.* London: Methuen, pp. 87–104.

Hall, A. (1990) 'Land tenure and land reform in Brazil', in R. Prosterman, M. Temple and T. Hanstad (eds) *Agrarian Reform and Grassroots Development: Ten Case Studies.* Boulder, CO: Lynne Rienner, pp. 205–32.

Hall, A. (1993) 'Non-governmental organizations in Brazil under dictatorship and democracy', in C. Abel and C. Lewis (eds) *Welfare, Equity and Development in Latin America.* London: Macmillan, pp. 421–37.

Hall, A. (1994) 'Grassroots action for resettlement planning', *World Development*, 22 (12), December: 1793–809.

Hall, A. (1997a) *Sustaining Amazonia: Grassroots Action for Productive Conservation.* Manchester: Manchester University Press.

Hall, A. (1997b) 'Peopling the environment: a new agenda for research, policy and action in Brazilian Amazonia', *European Review of Latin American and Caribbean Studies*, 62, June: 9–31.

Hall, A. (1999) 'Social movements, empowerment and productive conservation', in J. Mullen (ed.) *Rural Poverty, Empowerment and Sustainable Livelihood.* Aldershot: Ashgate, pp. 14–34.

Hall, A. (2000a) 'Environment and development in Brazilian Amazonia: from protectionism to productive conservation', in A. Hall (ed.) *Amazonia at the Crossroads: The Challenge of Sustainable Development.* London: Institute of Latin American Studies, University of London, pp. 99–114.

Hall, A. (2000b) 'Privatizing the commons: liberalization, land and livelihoods in Latin America', in W. Baer and J. Love (eds) *Liberalization and its Consequences: A Comparative Perspective on Latin America and Eastern Europe.* Cheltenham: Edward Elgar, pp. 232–58.

Hall, A. (2003) 'Education reform in Brazil under democracy', in M. D'Alva Kinzo (ed.) *Brazil Since 1985: Economy, Policy and Society.* London: Institute of Latin American Studies, University of London, pp. 269–87.

Hall, A. (2004) 'Enhancing social capital: productive conservation and traditional knowledge in the Brazilian rainforest', in D. Posey (ed.) *Human Impacts on Amazonia: The Role of Traditional Knowledge in Conservation and Development.* New York: Columbia University Press.

Hanmer, L. and Naschold, F. (2000) 'Attaining the international development targets: will growth be enough?' *Development Policy Review*, 18 (1), March: 11–36.

Harbison, F. (1973) *Human Resources as the Wealth of Nations*, Oxford: Oxford University Press.

Harrison, P. (1983) *The Third World Tomorrow*. Harmondsworth: Penguin.

Hoselitz, B. (1960) *Sociological Factors in Economic Development*. New York: Free Press.

ILO (1976) *Meeting Basic Needs: Strategies for Eradicating Mass Poverty and Unemployment.* Geneva: International Labour Office.

Jellema, A. (2000) 'Trends in basic education', in R. Randel, T. German and D. Ewing (eds) *The Reality of Aid 2000*. London: Earthscan, pp. 27–36.

Kane, L. (2001) *Popular Education and Social Change in Latin America*. London: Latin America Bureau.

Keck, M. and Sikkink, K. (1998) *Activists Beyond Borders: Advocacy Networks in International Politics*. Ithaca, NY: Cornell University Press.

La Belle, T.J. (2000) 'The changing nature of non-formal education in Latin America', *Comparative Education*, 36 (1): 21–36.

Leonardos, A.C. (1995) *Effective Strategies and Approaches for Reaching Street and Working Children Through Education: Reviewing Recent Developments*. Paris: International Institute for Educational Planning, UNESCO.

Leonardos, A.C. (1999) *Non-Formal Vocational Training Programmes for Disadvantaged Youth and their Insertion into the World of Work: Towards a Framework for Analysis and Evaluation*, IIEP Occasional Papers 83. Paris: International Institute for Educational Planning, UNESCO.

Lerner, D. (1958) *The Passing of Traditional Society*. New York: Free Press.

Lewin, K. (1987) *Education in Austerity: Options for Planners*, Fundamentals of Educational Planning 36. Paris: International Institute for Educational Planning, UNESCO.

McClelland, D. (1964) 'A psychological approach to economic development', *Economic Development and Cultural Change*, 12: 320–4.

Mehrotra, S. (1998) 'Education for all: policy lessons from high-achieving countries', *International Review of Education*, 44 (5/6): 461–84.

Middleton, J. and Demsky, T. (1989) *Vocational Education and Training: A Review of World Bank Investment*, World Bank Discussion Paper 51. Washington, DC: World Bank.

Murray Thomas, R. (ed.) (1983) *Politics and Education: Cases from Eleven Nations*. Oxford: Pergamon.

Patrinos, H. and Araisingam, D.L. (1997) *Decentralization of Education: Demand-Side Financing*. Washington, DC: World Bank.

Randel, J., German, T. and Ewing, D. (2000) *The Reality of Aid 2000*. London: Earthscan.

Rostow, W.W. (1960) *The Stages of Economic Growth: A Non-Communist Manifesto*. Cambridge: Cambridge University Press.

Schiefelbein, E. (1992) *Redefining Basic Education for Latin America: Lessons to be Learned from the Colombian Escuela Nueva*. Paris: International Institute for Educational Planning, UNESCO.

Schultz, T. (1961) 'Investment in human capital', *American Economic Review*, 51, March: 1–17.

Siegel, J. (1997) 'Formal vs. non-formal vernacular education: the education reform in Papua New Guinea', *Journal of Multilingual and Multicultural Development*, 18 (3): 206–22.

Skilbeck, M. (2000) *Education for All – Global Synthesis*. Paris: UNESCO.

Stoesz, D., Guzzetta, C. and Lusk, M. (1999) *International Development*. Boston, MA: Allyn and Bacon.

Streeten, P. et al. (1981) *First Things First: Meeting Basic Human Needs in Developing Countries*. Oxford: Oxford University Press.

Summers, L. (1994) *Investing in All the People: Educating Women in Developing Countries*, EDI Seminar Paper 45, Washington, DC: World Bank.

Taylor, D. and Mackenzie, F. (1992) *Development from Within: Survival in Rural Africa*. London: Routledge.

Todaro, M. (1994) *Economic Development*, 5th edn. London: Longman.

Todaro, M. (2000) *Economic Development*, 7th edn. Reading, MA: Addison-Wesley.

Tomasevski, K. (2003) *Education Denied: Costs and Remedies*. London: Zed Books.

UNDP (1999) *Human Development Report 1999*. Oxford: Oxford University Press.

UNDP (2000) *Human Development Report 2000*. Oxford: Oxford University Press.

UNESCO (2000) '181 governments adopt framework for action at the World Education Forum', *Press Release*, 28 April.

UNICEF (1999) *The State of the World's Children*. Geneva: UNICEF.

Watkins, K. (2000) *The Oxfam Education Report*. Oxford: Oxfam.

World Bank (1975) *The Assault on World Poverty*. Washington, DC: World Bank.

World Bank (1986) *Financing Education in Developing Countries*. Washington, DC: World Bank.

World Bank (1990a) *World Development Report 1990: Poverty*. Washington, DC: World Bank.

World Bank (1990b) *Primary Education: A World Bank Policy Paper*. Washington, DC: World Bank.

World Bank (1991) *Vocational and Technical Education and Training: A World Bank Policy Paper*. Washington, DC: World Bank.

World Bank (1997) *World Development Report, 1997: the State in A Changing World*. Washington, DC: World Bank.

World Bank (2001) *World Development Report 2000/2001: Attacking Poverty*. Washington, DC: World Bank.

6 HEALTH SYSTEMS IN DEVELOPING COUNTRIES

Mrigesh Bhatia and Elias Mossialos[1]

Summary

This chapter highlights key health care issues facing policy-makers in developing countries in the context of a 'dual health burden'. This comprises, firstly, the unfinished agenda of dealing with infectious diseases such as TB and malaria and, secondly, the emerging epidemics of HIV/AIDS and rise of non-communicable diseases in the South. The first section describes the burden of disease in terms of morbidity and mortality to set the context for our analysis. This is followed by an overview of the health care systems in developing countries along with trends in financing and delivery of health care and a closer look at pharmaceutical policies. Finally, we synthesize and analyse the available evidence on health systems developments. In investigating the policy responses to the health problems specific to developing countries, there is reason to believe there have been serious consequences resulting from governments moving away from the primary health care (PHC) agenda set forth in the World Health Organization (WHO) Alma-Ata declaration in 1978[2] and towards health policy reform favouring privatization and the implementation of vertical programmes to tackle specific diseases. In the light of the complexity of the dual health burden facing developing countries, there is a substantial need for coordinated national health policies and a need to focus on PHC and public health policies that have proven effective in controlling the rapid proliferation of infectious disease.

The burden of disease

Developing countries[3] are characterized by relatively high population growth rates, low gross national product (GNP) per capita, low standards of living,

---

[1]Department of Social Policy, London School of Economics and Political Science.
[2]At a joint WHO–UNICEF conference at Alma-Ata (in the former USSR), governments of 134 countries called for acceptance of the WHO goal of Health For All by the year 2000 and proclaimed primary health care as the means to achieving this goal.
[3]For this chapter developing countries are defined as those with a GNP per capita of less than $2,995 e.g. low-income and low middle-income countries as defined by the World Bank, 2001.

Table 6.1   Trends in mortality rate and life expectancy in selected countries, according to level of development (1980–99)

Countries/regions	Life expectancy at birth		Infant mortality rate		Under-five mortality rate	
	1980	1999	1980	1999	1980	1999
Low income	*53*	*59*	*112*	*77*	*177*	*116*
The Gambia	40	53	159	75	216	110
Indonesia	55	66	90	42	125	52
India	54	63	115	71	177	90
Lower middle income	*66*	*69*	*55*	*32*	*84*	*40*
China	67	70	42	30	65	37
Philippines	61	69	52	31	81	41
Thailand	64	69	49	28	58	33
Sri Lanka	68	73	34	15	48	19
Upper middle income	*66*	*69*	*52*	*27*	*67*	*34*
Republic of Korea	67	73	2	8	27	9
Malaysia	67	72	30	8	42	10
Brazil	63	67	70	32	81	40
High income	*74*	*78*	*12*	*6*	*15*	*6*
UK	74	77	12	6	14	6
Japan	76	81	8	4	11	4
Singapore	71	78	12	3	13	4

Source: World Bank (2001).

including poor standards of health, education, housing and sanitation. These countries contain about 75 per cent of the world's population but have only 12 per cent of the world's GNP (World Bank, 2001). Over the last few decades, developing countries have benefited from significant improvements in health status across the globe. Life expectancy has been rising and mortality rates have been on the decline in the developing world (Table 6.1). Three million fewer children under five years now die each year, mainly as a result of immunization against six vaccine-preventable diseases (UNICEF, 2002). Following the successful eradication of smallpox, efforts have been expanded towards controlling a number of infectious diseases such as polio, leprosy, tetanus and guinea worm with the aim of eradicating these diseases in the near future. More than 175 countries are polio-free (UNICEF, 2002) and there were only 537 cases of polio reported worldwide in 2001 (*Lancet*, 2002). Similarly, India, which has the majority of the world's leprosy cases, hopes to eliminate leprosy by 2005[4] (Kumar, 2001). Given the availability of low-cost health care interventions, there is potential to further reduce the avoidable burden of disease in many developing countries.

---

[4]According to the World Bank's appraisal of India's national leprosy elimination project, the prevalence of leprosy has decreased from 24 cases per 10,000 of the population in 1993 to 5 cases per 10,000 in 2000 (Kumar, 2001).

However, in spite of such optimism, policy-makers in developing countries are also concerned about the future. Although overall mortality rates have been on the decline, infant mortality rates and maternal mortality rates are still unacceptably high. Ten million children continue to die from preventable diseases each year and more than 600 million children still live in poverty (UNICEF, 2002). Less than 5 per cent of children in the poorest countries have access to routine immunization services, compared to almost 100 per cent of children in industrialized countries (Brundtland, 2002). Providing access to basic health-care services to the vast majority of poor in the developing world is still every policy-maker's dream. Widespread resurgence of diseases such as tuberculosis (TB) and malaria, which until recently were under control, are an important public health concern. Likewise, the problem of malnutrition, which requires intensive public health initiatives, remains widespread in developing countries and one of the most important risk factors contributing to the global burden of disease (WHO, 2002).

In addition, as a result of demographic and epidemiological transition,[5] there are newer concerns that need to be addressed. More resources are needed to tackle the rising threat of epidemics of non-communicable diseases and chronic conditions like cancer, diabetes, obesity, cardio-vascular diseases, acute respiratory diseases and injuries (Sein and Rafei, 2002). In addition, there is a rapidly ageing population, presenting concerns over the growing health-care needs of the elderly. Finally, the recent HIV/AIDS epidemic is a serious challenge, demanding significant amounts of health resources. More than 4 million children below the age of 15 years have died from AIDS since the beginning of the epidemic. In fact, HIV/AIDS is already threatening and even reversing the modest health gains made by the developing world over the years in terms of reduced mortality rates and increased life expectancies. Further complicating the HIV/AIDS epidemic is the fact that there is a limited coordinated public health system in Africa (where 70 per cent of infected people live) to facilitate analysis of prevention strategies in order to prioritize them in the light of scarce resources. There is little knowledge of the cost-effectiveness evidence based on current prevention strategies, which precludes necessary planning and decision-making within the health system (Walker, 2003). Hence, policy-makers in developing countries are faced with a 'dual health burden'. On the one hand, the 'unfinished agenda' of infectious diseases, malnutrition and complications of childbirth; on the other, emerging epidemics of HIV/AIDS and non-communicable diseases (WHO, 1999).

Differentials in health indicators amongst the regions of the world have always existed and continue to do so in the twenty-first century. On the one hand, developed countries have the best health indicators in terms of life expectancy,

---

[5]Demographic transition is characterized by a shrinking proportion of children, an increase in the median age of the population and rising life expectancy (Basch, 1999). 'Epidemiological transition' results in non-communicable diseases becoming a major cause of morbidity and mortality instead of communicable diseases. 'Health transition' is a broader concept which includes both demographic and epidemiological transition and relates to wider cultural, social and behavioural determinants of health (Cadwell, 1993).

low morbidity and mortality patterns; on the other, developing countries characteristically suffer from low life expectancy and high morbidity and mortality patterns. It can be observed from Table 6.1 that developing countries experience a significantly higher infant and under-five mortality rate, and thus much lower life expectancies than the developed world. For example, the under-five mortality rate is on average about 25 times higher in the least developed countries compared with high-income countries. An infant mortality rate of 100 per 1,000 live births in the least developed countries means that 1 child in every 10 dies before its first birthday, even in the twenty-first century (World Bank, 2001). According to Sen and Bonita (2000), if all countries experienced the under-five child death rates of Japan, there would be only 1 million child deaths each year instead of the current 11 million. Similar variations are also observed in maternal mortality rates and life expectancy at birth between developed and developing nations. According to the latest update on maternal mortality, based on 1995 estimates of the total 514,000 maternal deaths, 98 per cent of these occurred in developing countries (UNFPA, 1999). It is rare for maternal mortality rates to be greater than 10 per 100,000 live births in most developed countries and yet it is common to observe maternal mortality rates greater than 500 per 100,000 live births in some developing countries; as, for example, in the Central African Republic, Chad, Malawi, Nepal, Senegal, Tanzania, Uganda and Zambia (World Bank, 2001).

Similar variations also apply to life expectancy at birth. In fact, life expectancy at birth of around 80 in the most developed countries is double that of the least developed countries (Sen and Bonita, 2000). A female child born in Malawi can expect to live for 40 years, about 44 years less than in Japan. However, if infant and child mortality were eliminated, there would be an increase in the life expectancy of nine years in Africa and eight years in India (World Bank, 1993). This point highlights the importance of directing health policy agendas to tackling the severe problem of under-five mortality, which would result in increased life expectancy.

When one turns to the international poverty line, it is not surprising to observe a significant proportion of the population in many developing countries living on less than $2 a day. Such a situation is unacceptable and hence, in September 2000 at the United Nations Millennium Summit, world leaders agreed to a set of time-bound and measurable goals and targets. The 189 member-states of the United Nations have pledged to meet, by 2015, eight goals (Table 6.2). These goals provide a framework for the entire UN system to work coherently towards and encapsulate the common aim of the world's political leaders to free their 'fellow men, women and children from the abject and dehumanizing conditions of extreme poverty'. The UN Development Group has been established to ensure that these goals remain the primary focus. Some countries are making progress towards the Millennium Development Goals (MDGs), but improvement is uneven and, as is well known, not nearly rapid enough. East Asia and parts of South Asia are doing particularly well, yet progress in Latin America is slow and much of sub-Saharan Africa and Central Asia are hardly advancing at all, or, even worse, regressing.

Table 6.2   Millennium Development Goals (MDGs) by 2015

Goals	Targets
Eradicate extreme poverty and hunger	Halve the proportion of people whose income is less than a dollar a day Halve the proportion of people who suffer from hunger
Achieve universal primary education	Children everywhere complete a full course of primary schooling
Promote gender equality and empower women	Eliminate gender disparity at all levels of education
Reduce child mortality	Reduce U5MR by two-thirds
Improve maternal health	Reduce MMR by three-quarters
Combat HIV/AIDS, malaria and other diseases	Halt and reverse the incidence of HIV/AIDS, malaria and other major diseases
Ensure environmental sustainability	Halve proportion of people without access to safe drinking water Significantly improve the lives of at least 100 million slum dwellers Reverse loss of environmental resources and integrate principles of sustainable development
Develop a global partnership for development	Develop non-discriminatory trading and financial system Address the special needs of the least-developed countries (tariffs and quota-free access) Deal with debt problems of developing countries Provide access to affordable, essential drugs in developing countries and make available new technologies

Source: United Nations (2002).

One contribution of the 1993 *World Development Report* (World Bank, 1993) was to measure the global burden of disease in terms of disability-adjusted life years (DALYs).[6] It takes into account life years lost both as a result of premature death and years lived with disability. DALYs were developed as a refinement of an earlier approach (Ghana Health Assessment Project) to quantify mortality based on the number of useful days of life lost from premature mortality and disability (Lucas, 2002). Serious regional imbalances in the distribution of the burden of disease are observed. For example, the industrialized countries, which account for almost a fifth of the world's population, bore less than 10 per cent of the total burden of disease (Table 6.3).

DALYs are increasingly being used in a number of countries both as a burden of disease measure and in cost-effectiveness league tables for comparing costs per DALY averted by different interventions. In fact, the essential package of basic health services promoted by the 1993 *WDR* is based on costs per DALY

---

[6]To understand the technical basis for DALYs and its calculations readers can refer to Murray (1994) and Fox-Rushby and Hanson (2001).

Table 6.3 Mortality and burden of disease in the world by income (1998)

Burden of disease	High-income countries, DALYs (000)	(%)	Low- and middle-income countries, DALYs (000)	(%)
Infectious disease	4,482	4.25	404,597	35.09
Maternal conditions	398	0.38	31,852	2.76
NCD	87,732	83.27	507,631	44.00
Injuries	12,739	12.09	208,934	18.10
Total	105,351	100.00	1,153,014	100.00

Source: WHO (1999).

Table 6.4 Public health packages in low-income countries

Package/interventions	Cost per DALY (US$, 1990)
Essential clinical services	
Short course of chemotherapy for TB	3–5
Management of the sick child	30–50
Prenatal and delivery care	30–50
Family planning	20–30
Treatment of STDs	1–3
Limited care[1]	200–350
Packages	*Per capita*
Public health package[2]	4.2
Essential clinical services package	7.8
Total public health and clinical services	12.0

[1]Limited care includes assessment, advice, alleviation of pain, treatment of infection and minor trauma.
[2]Includes EPI, plus school health, health education, monitoring and surveillance, vector control, prevention of AIDS, tobacco and alcohol control programmes.
Source: World Bank (1993).

averted and is about $12 in low-income countries. The public health and clinical services package includes integrated management of childhood illness, immunization, family planning, an AIDS prevention programme, treatment of sexually transmitted diseases (STDs) and TB, and a school health programme (World Bank, 1993). All these interventions are highly cost-effective (for example, each costs less than $50 per DALY averted in low-income countries; see Table 6.4). However, the DALY methodology has been criticized by a number of researchers (Anand and Hanson, 1997; Paalman et al., 1998; Williams, 1999; Powles and Day, 2002) who question their use as a decision-making tool for allocating resources. Criticisms refer to the fact that the data on which DALYs are based are weak in developing countries. Additional concerns include the use of age and disability weights, deriving weights based on 'expert' judgement rather than population preferences and calculating years of life lost using 'ideal' life rather than expectancies.

Although the burden of diseases in developing countries is shifting to non-communicable diseases, it must be emphasized that communicable diseases, maternal and perinatal conditions and malnutrition remain a major concern in these countries. For example, in sub-Saharan Africa, two out of every three years of healthy life lost were due to these conditions (Murray and Lopez, 2002). Nonetheless, such global/regional-level data include high- as well as low-income populations, and hence the aggregate burden of disease may inadequately represent the problems of the poor. Instead of undertaking regional analysis, Gwatkin and Guillot (1999) extended the work of Murray and Lopez by estimating the burden of disease among the world's poorest and richest population groups.[7] Their analysis confirms the fact that non-communicable diseases and injuries are less important to the global poor and that high priority should be given to programmes aimed at tackling communicable diseases to improve the health of the poor and to lessen the poor–rich health difference. Thus, the situation in developing countries is complicated by the differential rates of the epidemiological transition for rich and poor sub-populations, where the rich are afflicted by 'Western diseases' while the poor struggle with mainly preventable communicable diseases.

Developing countries are an extremely diverse and heterogeneous group, with significant variations in terms of life expectancy and mortality patterns, and considerable differences in the capacity of their health care systems. For example, compared to the South-East Asian regional average, Sri Lanka, a country with a low per capita income of $820 has one of the most impressive health indicators in the region. Current life expectancy is 73 years, infant mortality is around 15 per 1,000 live births and the maternal mortality rate is 30 per 100,000 live births. In fact, Sri Lanka experiences similar health indicators to the developed world. Like Sri Lanka, Kerala in India is another commonly cited example of good health at low cost. In addition, Kerala is also used to demonstrate the variation in health status among states in India. Although the infant mortality rate for India as a whole is 74 per 1,000 live births, it is less than 20 in Kerala (World Bank, 2001). This is in spite of the fact that Kerala is one of the lowest-income states in India. Examples such as Kerala state and Sri Lanka raise important issues about the determinants of health and factors contributing to good health at low cost.

Cross-national comparisons yield an inverse relationship between income and health whereby poorer countries, as measured by GDP per capita, generally suffer from higher rates of mortality than wealthier countries (World Bank, 1993). Thus, there is an observed linear relationship (although with diminishing returns) between income and life expectancy, such that a slight increase in income at the lowest levels results in a greater proportional increase in life expectancy. However, with higher income levels this observed increase diminishes (World Bank, 1993). One would speculate that economic development should lead to improved health (whether for impoverished sub-populations or

---

[7]Communicable diseases cause 59 per cent of deaths and 64 per cent of DALYs loss among the 20 per cent of the global population living in countries with the lowest per capita incomes, compared with 34 per cent of deaths and 44 per cent of DALYs loss among the entire global population (Gwatkin and Guillot, 1999).

Table 6.5 Factors contributing to improved health status in China, Costa Rica, Kerala state and Sri Lanka

Policy factors	Suggested indicators
Historic commitment to health as a social goal	Legislation Government expenditures Establishment of hospitals and health centres Missionary influences
Social welfare orientation	Preventive health measures Food subsidies Educational programmes Land reform
Participatory orientation	Universal franchise Extent of decentralization NGO and community involvement
Equity orientation	Health, education and nutritional status of women and minorities Urban/rural coverage
Intersectoral policies for health: linkages between social and economic development	Sustained improvement in health statistics Incentives and mechanisms to ensure linkages Training programmes

Source: Rosenfield (1985).

countries). However, the most significant evidence, contradicting the causal relationship between income and health, is found in four countries (China, Costa Rica, Cuba and Sri Lanka) and the Indian state of Kerala. The major factors, common to these countries, which contributed to their significant improvements in health at low cost, are discussed by Rosenfield (1985) and are presented in Table 6.5. The governments of these countries have endorsed effective health-promoting public policies such as preventive health measures (hygiene and sanitation[8]), universal immunization, food subsidies, educational programmes and land reforms (Cadwell, 1985). Therefore, there is significant evidence that underlines the importance of health prevention and improved public health services in improving health in resource-poor countries.

Given the huge disparity both among and within states in India, Gwatkin et al. (2000) performed an analysis based on poorest and richest quintiles. Significant variation was observed for various socio-economic, health and population

---

[8]The importance of water supply and sanitation hardware in reducing mortality remains arguable. Feacham et al. (1992) contend that provision and use of water supply and sanitation hardware may have played a substantial role in the mortality reductions achieved in Costa Rica, sanitation may have been important in Sri Lanka, but in China, the Indian state of Kerala and Cuba the role of water supply and sanitation was minor.

indicators between the richest and poorest quintiles. For example, the infant mortality rate was 44 per 1,000 live births in the richest quintile whereas it was 109 in the poorest quintile. Such analysis not only highlights a wide gap between the rich and the poor but also draws attention to the limitations of reporting aggregate/average measures. Thus, variations both between countries and within countries remind us of two facts. Firstly, health gains have not been distributed equally (Sen and Bonita, 2000). Secondly, developing countries are a very diverse group and caution is advised in making generalized conclusions when discussing their health-care systems.

Developing countries are entering the twenty-first century with a very high burden of disease despite the availability of basic low-cost preventive and curative measures to avoid premature deaths and disabilities. In addition, rapid unregulated urbanization is resulting in further pressures to develop the necessary infrastructure to provide basic services and facilities. The majority of the urban population lives in slums in absolute poverty due to the recent unprecedented expansion of urban centres in developing countries, in particular of 'urban settlements' which are both illegal and unplanned (Wangombe, 1995). These 'squatter settlements' are characterized by extreme poverty, inaccessible health and social services, and degraded and unclean environments lacking drainage, water supply and waste disposal. The proliferation of these settlements has resulted in severe health problems such as malaria in conjunction with frequent outbreaks of epidemics of largely vaccine-preventable diseases and diseases of malnutrition (Wangombe, 1995). According to Islam and Tahir (2002), urbanization in developing countries is a consequence of rural poverty and deprivation. However, unlike the developed world where urbanization coincided with industrialization and economic growth in urban settings, poverty in many cities in developing countries remains widespread. Thus, there is a lack of sufficient resources to cope with rapid urbanization, which presents a serious need for improved planning and financing of urban health services emphasizing public health services and primary health care (PHC).

This analysis of the health burden faced by developing countries reveals that effective preventive actions through organized public health policies and primary health care could address these major health problems (Holland and Gilderdale, 1977) as there is strong evidence that PHC has and can bring about marked gains in health (Hall and Taylor, 2003). Furthermore, PHC has been shown to be successful in significantly improving the population's health, especially in rural areas, in several countries in the 1970s, including China, India, Guatemala and Venezuela; as Newell (1975) stated, 'primary health care works'. Likewise, successful PHC strategies have been reported in many of the 150 countries that have incorporated these policies into their health systems (Zakus and Cortinois, 2002). However, the current focus of health systems in developing countries, which is addressed in the following section, is not on these initiatives. Moreover, they may not be appropriate for dealing with the dual burden of diseases in the face of significant resource constraints.

Table 6.6   Health-care system inputs in selected countries according to level of development (1990–98)

Countries/regions	Health expenditure per capita (US$)	Physicians per 1,000 people	Nurses/midwives per 1,000 people[1]	Hospital beds per 1,000 people
Low income	*21*	*0.5*		*1.3*
The Gambia	13	–	–	0.6
Indonesia	8	0.2	0.7	0.7
India	20	0.4	0.5	0.8
Lower middle income	*62*	*1.9*		*3.5*
China	33	2.0	0.9	2.9
Philippines	33	0.1	0.4	1.1
Thailand	112	0.4	1.0	2.0
Sri Lanka	26	0.2	1.1	2.7
Upper middle income	*318*	*1.6*		*3.3*
Republic of Korea	349	1.3	2.3	5.1
Malaysia	81	0.5	1.6	2.0
Brazil	309	1.3	–	3.1
High income	*2,702*	*2.8*		*7.2*
UK	1,686	1.7		4.2
Japan	2,284	1.9		16.5
Singapore	841	1.4		3.6

[1]Nurses/midwives data from WHO/SERO and Table B–15 (p. 55) Annex B of the report.
Source: World Bank (2001).

Health systems

Basch (1999) views health-care systems as an organized arrangement to provide promotive, preventive, curative and rehabilitative services to its population using resources allocated for that purpose. Health systems in developing countries vary in size, organization, and level of development and capability to perform effectively and efficiently. While those countries that are least developed struggle to provide basic health care to their populations, there are others whose health systems are highly developed. Table 6.6 provides the health systems resources in terms of personnel and hospital beds by level of development in selected countries. It is obvious that there is significant variation in health system inputs between developed and developing countries but also among developing countries themselves. This variation is due partly to differing cultural values, economic capabilities, domestic political pressures and demands of world events (Basch, 1999). However, in spite of this variation, most health-care systems in low-income countries have to deal with similar issues in terms of generating additional revenue, correcting resource allocation imbalances, improving the efficiency of the health-care system, ensuring coverage to the poor population for basic health services and ensuring good-quality services. The following sections briefly present the historical and current trends in financing and provision of health-care systems in developing countries.

Historical background and the role of international organizations and agencies

Most of the developing countries under colonial rule had health systems that were hospital-based, providing high-technology services to urban elites. Many of these countries in the post-colonial period attempted to rectify this situation by pursuing equity objectives in terms of providing health care to all. It was understood that the State would play a fundamental role in the financing and delivery of health care (Sen and Koivusalo, 1998). Hence, a number of countries expanded their health infrastructures. The efforts of the State towards providing universal access were further reinforced by the WHO Alma Ata declaration of 1978. This declaration emphasized primary health care as the means for providing comprehensive, universal and equitable health services. There were nine basic components of PHC: health education, food supply, proper nutrition, safe water and basic sanitation, maternal and child health care, immunization, prevention of endemic diseases, treatment of common diseases and injuries, and provision of essential drugs (WHO, 1981). Thus, there was meant to be a shift away from larger hospitals and towards community-based delivery of health services. During the time of this ideological change in health planning and provision, however, resources in most developing countries continued to be directed largely towards urban-based hospitals at the expense of prevention and promotion (Sein and Rafei, 2002).

Likewise, there was much hesitation on the part of politicians in developed countries to accept PHC, particularly the crucial role of communities in the delivery of health services (Hall and Taylor, 2003). This external pressure, coupled with resource constraints, led to a shift towards 'Selective Primary Health Care', focusing specifically on reducing child mortality through PHC interventions, as it was believed that PHC was too idealistic and unattainable regarding total population coverage (Warren, 1988). This shift contravened the original goals of PHC of community participation as essential to meet the population's health needs, and advocated once again the vertical programmes (specific to tackling diseases contributing to child mortality) rather than 'horizontal', comprehensive health care (Unger and Killingsworth, 1986).

Along with this shift in the political agenda, there were other practical and operational constraints on undertaking PHC and achieving 'health for all' (Sein and Rafei, 2002). With the establishment of the necessary health infrastructure in many countries in Asia including rural areas (for example, India and Pakistan), in theory, everyone had access to primary health care. However, in practice many of these services were not available due to inadequate resources (lack of drugs, non-availability of doctors and health staff) and insufficient training. In some of these countries almost 80 per cent of the clinical budget is consumed by salaries. This leaves little for drugs, maintenance and other operating costs. Training of health workers at the community level is a crucial ingredient for the success of primary health care and general health development (Morgan and Deutschmann, 2003). However, insufficient training and equipment in conjunction with inadequate funding prevented the service quality envisaged at the conception of PHC, and these factors were later cited by the World Bank as reasons for its failure (Hall and Taylor, 2003). In addition, the importance of community participation in improving PHC may not have been realized in many developing countries, where, especially in rural communities, notions of community involvement are not associated with self-reliance but interdependence (Rifkin, 1996; Zakus and Cortinois, 2002). Thus, differing views by the originators and applicators of these important concepts made the successful implementation of PHC less likely.

Moreover, the historically dominant role of the WHO[9] in health policy planning has shifted towards the World Bank in recent times as the leading force at the international level. According to Buse and Gwin (1998), the World Bank is the leading financier of health-sector activities in developing countries and a major voice in shaping national and international policy debates. At the national level a more pluralistic[10] policy environment has emerged (Frenk, 1995) with power spread among many interest groups competing for influence over policy (Walt and Gilson, 1994). This is reflected within a number of countries by their move away from an epidemiologically focused planning process to one where economics is more central. The 1980s saw the World Bank strongly advocating the role of privatization in health-sector reform, with little mention of primary health care. It argued that an expanded role for markets and the private sector increases both allocative and technical efficiency in the financing and provision of services (World Bank, 1987). Indeed, some Bank officials believed that public hospitals and health centres should be handed over or sold to the private sector or, alternatively, profit-making management companies should be brought in to run them. Such a system would then be supported by differentially applied user charges.

However, this view was revised in the late 1980s as it became apparent that economic theory was not able to give a clear-cut answer to the appropriate mix between public and private sectors and that this should be decided on a case-by-case basis (Bennett, 1991). Therefore, the World Bank changed tack and now has a less polarized viewpoint, emphasizing that the provision of health services cannot simply be handed over to the private sector due to the substantial imperfections in the health market. It argued that a private market could operate efficiently only if it works in the environment of a well-functioning

---

[9]The WHO, which once provided leadership in international health issues, faces serious resource constraints (Vaughan et al., 1996). It has been increasingly criticized for its ineffective role both at national and international levels (Vaughan et al. 1996; Buse and Gwin, 1998; Walt, 1998; Horton, 2002) and internally, for its complex bureaucracy and outdated organizational structure (Peabody, 1995).

[10]Health policy was previously dominated by the WHO and ministries of health. However, many other professionals are now also involved, such as social scientists, trade lawyers, other ministries, NGOs, foreign aid donors, UN organizations, regional and multilateral banks, private companies and industry associations, consultancy firms, charitable foundations, research institutions and criminal organizations (Lee et al., 2002).

market system that provides price signals that accurately reflect the social and financial costs of production (World Bank, 1989). Given that this is not necessarily the case in health systems, the Bank recognized that a different approach is needed.

The 1990s heralded a new period of policy debate, calling for more generic health-sector reforms than the primary health-care policy that dominated the 1980s, encouraged by publication of the 1993 *World Development Report*. This recognized the need to set clear priorities for those governments with limited resources and hence answers to such questions were devised. Countries began to assess both the effectiveness of particular interventions together with their cost (Green, 1999). Indeed the Bank's initial privatization model of health-sector reform was adopted by many of the donor agencies, therefore strongly influencing the policies of countries receiving foreign aid.

Over recent decades the network and volume of world trade has grown considerably and, in response to this, the GATT evolved in 1995 into the World Trade Organization (WTO). Unlike the Bank and WHO, the WTO has regulatory powers and therefore its impact on health is potentially more significant than that of other organizations. The aim of the agency is to reduce trade barriers to goods and services and to mediate trade disputes between countries. The presumption of the WTO system is that greater freedom of trade will improve human welfare through economic growth. More specifically, with respect to health services, Drager (1999) notes that increased trade could increase competition, introduce technology and management expertise and possibly increase export earnings. However, it may also exacerbate current inequalities in access to health services and encourage the migration of skilled health professionals from areas in which there is already a shortage. The key is to ensure that health-related issues are recognized in the trading system and therefore it may well be prudent to encourage the involvement of other agencies such as the World Health Organization. They could provide essential guidance for those health professionals in the early stages of their involvement in the health trading system.

One critique of the current health-sector reform models is their tendency to be prescriptive in content. The result is a tendency to disguise or confuse the link between reforms and inequality. In order to move health care in a more equitable direction, policy-makers need to draw on effective theory of health-care systems and inequality interactions. However, the majority of the health policy and management literature of the 1980s and 1990s displays this prescriptive nature, indicated by three main characteristics (Mackintosh, 2001).

- A technocratic focus: structural changes and technical goals are desirable rather than political objectives.
- Structural proposals are a combination of market mechanisms with decentralization of public management and regulation of health care.
- Reforms are given an equity objective.

Mackintosh (2001) cites the 1993 *WDR* as displaying a characteristic mix of technocratic prescriptive and equity themes, putting forward health-sector reform in low-income countries simply as an application of reform undertaken in rich countries. Examples drawn from East and Southern Africa support this argument, where health-sector reform seems to be driven largely by donor models rather than reform proposals originating from within the local health-care system (Mogedal and Steen, 1995). Reforms were strongly supported by donor governments and the World Bank and sought to privatize secondary and tertiary care, since this was perceived to primarily serve the middle classes, while making primary care more responsive via the decentralization of accountability and a mix of user fees.

Despite being presented in policy documents as having an equalizing influence, these reforms are widely viewed as having had a deliberately non-egalitarian impact. This is because charges legitimize exclusion and unequal access, and fees always affect the poor most severely. As the aim of these reforms is to separate health-care systems for the less well off from those more fortunate, inequality becomes more entrenched. Lastly, the conception of the weak role of the public sector in health care inherent to these reforms is a worrisome factor. With 'increased commercialization' and segmentation within health-care systems, the pressure on government agencies to play less of a role in provision and delivery is likely to increase.

In recent years, major international organizations like the World Bank, WHO, UNICEF and the UNDP are collaborating on major public health initiatives like the 'roll back malaria' campaign, TB initiative, global alliance for vaccines and immunization (GAVI), along with other private organizations (global public–private partnerships, GPPP). For example, partners for GAVI include the World Bank, WHO, UNICEF and the Bill and Melinda Gates Foundation. In addition, there are several government agencies and development departments such as the Canadian and Swedish International Development Agencies (CIDA and SIDA respectively), the UK Department for International Development (DfID) and the US Agency for International Development (USAID), all with their own strategies. In order to be more effective and efficient and have a greater impact, it is necessary to have a more coordinated approach towards such initiatives. Yet, it is unlikely that these organizations are coordinating their activities, and problems arise in measuring the impact of these actions on population health.

The WHO recently established the Commission on Macroeconomics and Health, focusing on economic development and productivity, in an attempt to increase its influence upon developing countries' policies (WHO, 2001). Major criticisms of this Commission have been voiced, primarily regarding what is perceived by many as an inappropriate shift away from the social determinants of disease and the previous goals of PHC, and encouraging a vertical approach to eradicating disease rather than developing integrated health systems (Waitzkin, 2003). Critics argue that such 'vertical' international initiatives concentrate on specific disease conditions and not the development of an overall effective health system. Reid and Pearse (2003) describe these initiatives as 'antithetical to health systems response' and likely to result in weakening of the health systems. Concerns have also been expressed over the global public–private partnerships schemes, involving in particular the trans-national pharmaceutical companies (Buse and Walt, 2000a, 2000b; Buse and Waxman, 2001).

Table 6.7   Components of health-sector reform programmes in developing countries

Improving the performance of the civil service	Reduction in staff numbers; improved salary packages and performance incentives; better personnel and financial management systems
Decentralization	Decentralizing responsibilities for management and revenue generation to lower levels of government (e.g., the district) and to health facilities (e.g., hospitals)
Improving the functioning of ministries of health	Developing their strategic and policy role in monitoring performance and setting priorities; reducing their role in direct management of services
Broadening the choices for health financing	Introducing user fees, community financing schemes, social health insurance
Introducing managed competition	Separating purchasers from providers; encouraging competition between providers
Working with the private sector	Improving laws and regulations to promote expansion and improved performance; introducing systems for contracting with, subsidizing or franchising the private sector

Source: Cassels (1995).

Financing and delivering health care

There has been a growing emphasis on the market forces model for service delivery in the 1980s and 1990s which originated in the industrialized countries but subsequently went on to influence governments in resource-poor countries, partly through international donors. Although this change has not been without considerable support, the effects of such a change have compromised the equity and access goals of the PHC emphasis of the 1970s. The main components of health-sector reform programmes in less-developed countries have been usefully categorized by Cassels (1995) and are summarized in Table 6.7. Each of the points identified by Cassels as a key to health-sector reform will be dealt with in turn, firstly looking at how the performance of the civil service and ministries of health can be improved. The next section examines ways of broadening the choices of health financing. The issues of decentralization, managed provision and the private sector are discussed in the final section.

Improving the performance of the civil service and ministries of health

The late 1980s and early 1990s were characterized by a reduction in the role of government in developing countries' economies. In line with this trend, whilst governments may have a smaller role to play in the direct provision of services, their role in policy development, coordination and regulation is increased. Therefore, attention must be focused on ensuring that governments are capable of performing these key roles (Bennett and Mills, 1998). However, international organizations such as the World Bank are doubtful of developing countries' capacity to perform these roles. The Africa Management in the 1990s World Bank research programme distinguished between two types of capacity and, in turn, approaches to improving them. The first is technical capacity, often associated with the supply of skills. The transfer of new technology, methods and systems equated with training education and technical assistance which complements local supply is essential to development (Dia, 1996). It is this area of capacity that traditionally has been the primary focus of development programmes.

In parallel with technical capacity is institutional capacity, namely the ability of a country to make use of available technical capacity and resources. Countries in Africa are often unable to make use of their resources effectively because of deficiencies in this area; they lack the institutional base with the required legitimacy, accountability, stability, enforceability and incentives. As a result, political and economic achievements are often overturned because they are never fully adopted by the broader civil society, which would make them sustainable (Dia, 1996). Effective government performance is central to the creation of market-oriented, secure and productive economies and democratic political systems in developing countries (Grindle and Hilderbrand, 1995). Therefore, capacity-building to improve public-sector performance is vital. Governments are contracting out a range of services from acute clinical care to non-clinical care, such as cleaning. Each different type of contract is likely to require different combinations of capacities, and therefore a certain degree of flexibility is also important. Thus, it is impossible to give a clear-cut solution to capacity-building for contracting out generally. However, an outline strategy has been suggested by Bennett and Mills (1998) and is described below.

The first step requires a strengthening of the basic administrative system in government departments; for example, filing to ensure relevant documentation can be easily accessed. Related information systems need to be improved to allow contractors' performance to be monitored so that future decisions are made on the basis of evidence. The role of individual organization members involved in a task as well as their inter-communication is often unclear, yet both are key to a well-run project. When negotiating contracts it is important that the organization receiving the service has direct influence over the contract throughout the process to ensure that their needs are met. It is also important for governments to make available clear guidelines to orient the contracting process as well as to draw upon the experience acquired in other sectors and from other countries. Measures against corruption also form an important part of any such contract. Finally, working with central ministries to remove rigid bureaucratic rules that threaten the effectiveness of contracting out would improve overall outcomes.

Grindle and Hilderbrand (1995) note that many capacity-building schemes in the past have often focused on areas including training activities, organizational performance and administrative procedures. However, these are not the most effective means of improving performance. They identify the key drivers of effective public-sector performance to be a strong organizational culture, good management practices and effective communication networks; not rules, regulations, procedures and pay scales. They also looked at the motivational forces behind individual performance and found that they were most affected by opportunities for meaningful work, shared professional norms, teamwork and promotion based on performance rather than training in specific skills.

The main problem with capacity-building and institutional performance (specifically in African countries in this instance) is explained by Dia (1996) as lying in the connection between formal and informal institutions. Formal institutions were frequently inherited from the colonial era and as a result often do not reflect actual societal behaviour and incentives; hence they may easily suffer from a crisis of legitimacy and enforcement. However, informal organizations must also strive to remain up-to-date with fast-moving global developments in technology and management strategies. Therefore, convergence between adapted, formal institutions and renovated, informal indigenous institutions must be encouraged. In the short term, another key factor limiting contracting-out services will be the level of private-sector development. This problem applies especially to those services requiring the greatest investment and expertise such as clinical services (Mills, 1998).

Trends in financing health care

Globally, the health market is a major industry. In 1995, total global spending on health was 9.1 per cent of the world's GDP (Peabody et al., 1999). However, there is significant variation in health expenditures across regions. For example, 88 per cent of total global health expenditures were spent by the OECD countries, which constitute just 15 per cent of the world's population. In contrast Asia as a whole, home to 60 per cent of the world's population, accounts for only 3.4 per cent of global expenditure on health (Peabody et al., 1999). Similar discrepancies are observed within many developing countries, where hospital-based, high-tech medical care consumes the majority of the health budget. In developing countries, between 70 and 80 per cent of total expenditure on health is spent on curative services, with the remainder allocated to preventive and community services (World Bank, 1987). However, 70 per cent of the population resides in rural areas and suffers from conditions that could be prevented and treated using low-cost interventions, for which very few resources are earmarked. Therefore, there is a serious imbalance in the allocation of scarce health resources, favouring curative and hospital services at the expense of effective public and primary health services, which could alleviate the majority of health problems. Despite this misallocation, health care financing remains a crucial element in the organization of a health system.

Taxation and social insurance are health-funding methods that are publicly financed, whereas private financing is provided mainly through voluntary insurance and out-of-pocket payments (Appleby, 1992; Mossialos and

Figure 6.1 **Public versus private expenditure in country groups by level of development in the 1990s**

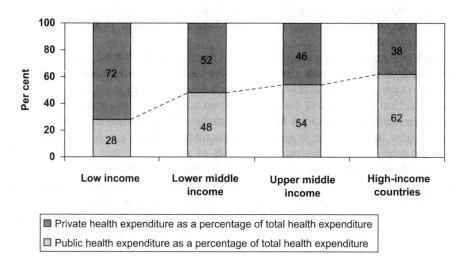

Source: World Bank (2001).

Thomson, 2002).[11] In terms of financing health care, there are several differences between developed and developing countries. Firstly, in the 1990s average public expenditure on health as a percentage of GDP was much higher in developed countries at 6.2 per cent compared with the South at 1 per cent (World Bank, 2001). Secondly, unlike in the industrialized world where there is a single major funding source such as general taxation in the UK or social insurance in Germany, many developing countries rely on multiple sources of financing. Finally, private contributions from out-of-pocket payments constitute a major funding source in many developing countries (see Figure 6.1). There is ample evidence to suggest that financing health care through either taxation or social insurance payments is more progressive, since these systems pool risks and avoid placing a direct burden on individuals who are in need of health care. Out-of-pocket payments at source are regressive and result in a catastrophic burden on the poor and unhealthy. For example, one estimate found that a quarter of Indians who were not poor when hospitalized became so because of the expenses incurred (Peters et al., 1999).

Nevertheless, reliance on out-of-pocket payments directly to government health-care facilities and private health-care providers including traditional healers is a major source of funding in most low-income countries in Asia and

---

[11]The advantages and disadvantages of these different funding methods are beyond the scope of this chapter, and readers are referred to Mossialos et al. (2002).

Africa.[12] Resource constraints and rapid technological advances on the one hand, coupled with higher public expectations for health care on the other, along with the demographic and epidemiological transition, is exerting unprecedented pressure on the limited health system resources of low-income countries.

Such pressures, along with the overall fiscal reforms introduced under the IMF and/or World Bank direction, have led many governments in low-income countries to raise revenue through alternative means. Given the weak tax collection systems and the absence of an adequate workforce in the formal sector to contribute to social insurance, more and more developing countries are introducing user fees to generate revenue for health care. As the most convenient method for charging user fees is at source, it is not surprising that most of the health-financing reforms in low-income countries have attempted to increase revenue from user charges (for example, sub-Saharan Africa and Asia). Surveys in African countries have shown that most of them have introduced some form of fee system for government health-care facilities (Gilson et al., 1995; Gilson, 1997; Sepehri and Chernomas, 2001). This trend has reached unprecedented levels, to the extent that it is now the single largest source of health financing in some countries. For example, private out-of-pocket payments account for 80 per cent of total health expenditure in India (World Bank, 2001).

Besides generating revenue, the proponents of user charges argue that they improve efficiency and equity (World Bank, 1993; Shaw and Giffin, 1995). However, user charges may be a poor tool for generating revenue given the high costs of implementing exemption mechanisms and developing accounting and fee-collection systems. Sepehri and Chernomas (2001) suggest that the evidence regarding the revenue-raising potential of user charges is mixed and well below initial expectations. It is claimed that user charges improve efficiency by reducing unnecessary demand, but it is also uncertain to what extent the reduction in demand also affects services that are actually needed. Evidence from a number of developing countries suggests that where user fees have been introduced or increased, service utilization has decreased (Gilson, 1997; Gilson et al., 2000; Sepehri and Chernomas, 2001).

Wilkinson et al. (2001) present an interesting case study of rural South Africa, where all user fees in primary health-care clinics were abolished by 1997, resulting in increased utilization of curative services. As regards quality, studies have shown that if the revenue is retained at the facility and is ploughed back into the system the service generally improves. User fees, in the absence of insurance options, place an impossible financial burden on households in low-income countries (Arhin-Tenkorang, 2000). In terms of equity, there is evidence to suggest that user charges are regressive as they discriminate against the poor by reducing demand from low-income groups more than for high-income

---

[12]Gilson (1997) observed that more than two-thirds of all African countries charge user fees for government health services.

groups. Although exemption mechanisms have been suggested to compensate for adverse effects on the poor, evidence suggests that successful implementation of exemption mechanisms has been extremely difficult (Gilson et al., 2000). The failure of the user fee policy and its negative impact on the poor in part has been attributed to poor design, planning and implementation.

It is clear that governments in developing countries are not in a position to provide even basic health services packages ($12–22 per capita for low- and middle-income countries) as advocated by the World Bank (1993). A recent summary description of health financing in WHO member-States by Musgrove et al. (2002) confirmed that in many poor countries total health spending is very low, even to the cost of a package containing only a short list of highly justified interventions. Hence, it is clear that government spending on health care is currently inadequate. In addition, there is also a case for increased spending since evidence suggests that out-of-pocket payments decline with increased government spending (Musgrove et al., 2002).

Because of severe limitations on government resources, it is likely that developing countries will only provide a basic preventive and curative package to the majority of the population. Given privatization trends and the increasing proportion of the population able and willing to pay, it is expected that private insurance will grow in some developing countries. India, which has recently opened up its health insurance market to the private sector, would make an interesting study in terms of investigating increased coverage by private insurance over time. However, it is likely that the role of private insurance would be very selective in most developing countries and that it would be utilized mainly by high-income earners.

The challenge facing governments in developing countries is to replace regressive out-of-pocket payments as a method of funding health care with a pre-payment mechanism with risk-pooling characteristics. This substitution would result in a financing principle based on the ability to pay and not just ability to benefit. Achieving greater fairness in financing is feasible through risk pooling; that is, those who are healthy subsidize those who are sick and those who are rich subsidize those who are poor (WHO, 2000a). Thus, it appears that financing reforms in many developing countries is likely to focus on introducing and strengthening local decentralized health insurance schemes with the aim of substituting out-of-pocket payments. However, it is unrealistic for many developing countries to expect near total coverage from introducing social insurance schemes like that observed in most OECD nations, given that the percentage of people under formal employment is quite low in many developing countries (Charmes, 2000). So is the capacity required to generate, pool and allocate resources, design and monitor schemes and provide human resources and infrastructure. Hence, social insurance schemes will probably have gaps in coverage and such pressures would increase with rising costs over time. None the less, because of weak taxation systems in many countries, a social insurance system may generate resources to cover more people.

Abel-Smith and Rawal (1994) showed from a survey of larger employers outside the government sector in Tanzania (where only 3 per cent of the population was employed in the formal sector) that they were spending on average 11 per cent of their payroll on employees' health care. This demonstrated their lack of satisfaction with government health services. Nevertheless, those who could readily be covered by insurance were making considerable use of the more expensive government hospital services. Abel-Smith and Rawal (1994) recommended that a compulsory health insurance scheme be introduced for the formal employment sector, covering a wider range of health services at low cost. The scheme would also have the desirable economic effect of lowering employers' labour costs while making it possible to improve the standards of government health services.

However, given the concerns over capacity to initiate health insurance schemes at national level, another option being experimented with are 'micro-insurance units' (MIU), local community-based insurance schemes that operate at the grassroots level and are voluntary, contributory and risk-pooling endeavours (Davies and Carrin, 2001; Dror, 2002). By their very nature, such schemes experience problems of moral hazard[13] and adverse selection[14] that could be minimized. Such initiatives are being tested in the Philippines and Uganda. Over time, such micro-schemes could be merged to form ever-larger risk pools and may eventually lead to the emergence of single regional or national risk pools (Davies and Carrin, 2001). Some of the more advanced developing countries in Asia and specific regions with more developed health-care systems are aspiring towards universal coverage by expanding existing insurance schemes or introducing new schemes (Nitayarumphong and Mills, 1999; Barnighausen and Sauerborn, 2002).

None the less, there are some unique difficulties facing such micro-insurance schemes. These include small group size, the target populations' low and irregular income, higher exposure to the impact of local catastrophe and added risks from poor information on risk probability (Dror, 2002). All of these determinants lie outside the control of small communities, which cannot be expected to deal with these problems on their own. Moens (1990) stressed the need to recognize both the importance of community participation as well as the limitations of financial management capacity at the grassroots level in organizing such risk-coverage arrangements. Without maintaining the strong sense of community in line with financial advances the success of the schemes will be jeopardized due to the key role played by social capital. Dror (2002) points to the financial sustainability of these schemes as a major concern and suggests 're-insurance' as a way to pool risks that a single MIU may find difficult to bear, as in cases of epidemics. This type of re-insurance facility does not yet exist but

---

[13]The possibility of consumers or providers exploiting a benefit system unduly to the detriment or disadvantage of other consumers, providers or the financing community as a whole, without having to bear the financial consequences or their behaviour in part or in full (EOHCS, 2002).

[14]A situation where individuals are able to purchase insurance at rates which are below actuarially fair rates, because information known to them is not available to insurers (asymmetric information) (Witter and Ensor, 1997).

a project to assess its potential has been developed and is being financed by an award from the World Bank's Development Marketplace 2000 and the International Labour Office (Dror, 2002).

However, re-insurance is not a complete answer to all the potential problems of micro-insurance schemes. Re-insurance cannot increase productivity or be a source of funding (Dror, 2002). Furthermore, Brenzel and Newbrander (2002) rightly point out that re-insurance, whilst protecting schemes against catastrophic loss, may result in the premiums being unaffordable. Therefore, alternatives should also be considered such as government subsidies, something that Busse (2002) believes would be necessary in order to ensure adequate population coverage.

Trends in the provision of health care

Overall, the role of the State within the social sector in low-income countries is changing, and the health sector is no exception. Until a decade ago the State, supported by welfare ideology, was a major player in the financing and provision of health care. However, the ability of the State to finance and deliver efficient and equitable health care has been questioned and the pressures of introducing reforms, which limit the role of the State, have been proposed (World Bank, 1993). According to Bossert (1998), ministries of health in middle- and low-income countries have a reputation for being among the most bureaucratic and least effectively managed institutions in the public sector.

In recent years, under the influence of new public management (NPM) and pro-market ideologies, the role of the State has been further redefined as a 'facilitator' and 'enabler', limited to getting the work done rather than directly providing health care (Kaul, 1997). NPM aims to improve the efficiency of public services by introducing various market mechanisms. Such arguments have resulted in policies that emphasize structural changes to the organization and delivery of health services in terms of decentralization and encouraging private-sector involvement through contracting out. There are considerable arguments in favour of privatization, predominantly related to government inefficiencies. However, it is important to consider the effect of shifting away from centralized health provision upon the quality and effectiveness of public health campaigns, which are so critical in developing countries.

Decentralization

Over the years, decentralization has been acknowledged as an instrument capable of improving public services in both the developed and developing world. In recent years, a number of countries have experimented with various types and forms of decentralization initiatives with the aim of improving their health systems (for example, the Philippines, Indonesia, Kenya and Tanzania). Rondinelli (1981) defines decentralization as the transfer of authority for planning, management and decision-making from national levels to sub-national levels. Mills (1994) discusses the four main forms of decentralization. 'Deconcentration' involves the transfer of administrative responsibilities from central to locally based offices of the MOH. 'Devolution' shifts authority and responsibility from central ministries of health to sub-national levels of government such as local government, local authorities or municipalities. 'Delegation' involves transferring managerial responsibility for defined functions to organizations outside the central government structure, which are only indirectly controlled by central government (semi-autonomous organizations). Finally, 'privatization' is the transfer of government functions to voluntary or private organizations.

The strength of the approach proposed by Mills (1994) is the ease with which it classifies institutional arrangements and identifies organizations that are to receive and lose authority and responsibility. However, its weakness is that it does not specify guidance for analysing tasks and functions that are being transferred from one organization to another. Bossert (1998) proposes the principal–agent approach developed by economists as a framework for the analysis of decentralization reforms. In this approach the centre (for example, central government) is viewed as the principal with the objective of equity, efficiency and financial soundness, and the local authorities as the agents who are given the resources to implement general policies to achieve these objectives.

Decentralization thus involves changing power relationships and the distribution of tasks amongst levels of government. Countries considering decentralization reforms need to address the following questions: decentralize to what level, to whom and for what tasks (Mills, 1994)? The success and failure of the decentralized system depends on how these issues are effectively addressed in a given context. The transfer of authority and responsibility increases as we move from deconcentration to privatization. However, even under privatization, legislative, policy-making and regulatory powers are retained by the central authorities (Gilson et al., 1994). Furthermore, the forms of decentralization are not mutually exclusive but could overlap in real life.

Many different forms of decentralization initiatives have been tried in the Panchayati Raj State in India where public services including health were decentralized. In the Philippines, all hospital and public health services were removed from central financial and managerial control and devolved to local government (Newbrander, 1999). This process of devolution can also be seen, to a varying degree, in Papua New Guinea, Thailand and Indonesia, while other countries have delegated certain responsibilities to various national and regional agencies. For example, Gambia, Zambia and Ghana have all established autonomous hospital boards giving hospitals greater independence (McPake, 1996). By involving local communities in the decision-making process and making the services more accountable, it was expected that decentralization would improve the efficiency of service provision and also make service providers more responsive.

However, the evidence to date on the success of decentralization is limited and mixed. Insufficient financial and human resources at lower-level facilities, poor lower-level institutional capacity both administrative and managerial, and negative political and cultural influences at the central (for example, resistance to relinquishing power) and local levels (corruption, local power groups) have led to ineffective decentralization in many countries including Tanzania (Gilson et al., 1994), Philippines, Sri Lanka, Indonesia and Senegal. Another concern in the short run is the need to reorganize and downsize administrative units, which can be highly disruptive and result in inefficient service provision (Lieberman, 2002). In addition, decentralization could give rise to inequalities when it is used as an instrument to raise revenue. Frustrated with resource constraints and management problems, some countries are reverting to a policy of 'recentralization'.[15]

Contracting out of health services

To help overcome some of the inherent inefficiencies in public-sector provision, a number of low-income countries are adopting contractual arrangements with the private sector to deliver both clinical and non-clinical services. Such arrangements in theory are expected to improve efficiency in service delivery as a result of introducing competition while retaining significant control over the whole process. Although contracting out clinical services is less frequently observed than for non-clinical services, case studies[16] of contracting out of both these services in developing countries of Asia and Africa have been reported (Broomberg et al., 1997, for South Africa; Bhatia and Mills, 1997, for Bombay; Beracochea, 1997, for Papua New Guinea; and Tangcharoensathien and Nitayarumphong, 1997, for Thailand). The evidence regarding the benefits of contracting out is mixed. For example, it was observed in the contracting out of non-clinical services in Bombay that private contractors are consistently cheaper but they provide a lower quality of service compared with direct provision by public hospitals (Bhatia and Mills, 1997). For contracting out to be successful, there has to be a degree of contestability (competition on cost and efficiency) in health services, and governments should have the capacity to negotiate, implement and monitor contracts. Bennett and Mills (1998) suggest that in countries which lack basic government administrative capacities, it may be better for the government to provide the public services directly instead of contracting out.

Private-sector expansion

Several reasons have been advanced to explain the rise of the rapidly expanding private sector. One argument posits growing privatization as a deliberate

---

[15]For example, Papua New Guinea has recentralized control of all its hospitals following frequent problems with provincial governments over hospital budgets (Newbrander, 1999).

[16]These country case studies on contracting out are reported in Bennett et al. (1997).

health reform strategy to reduce the role of the State (Zwi and Mills, 1995). Others see it as a response to dissatisfaction with public-sector provision in general and its low perceived quality in particular. Lastly, increased public involvement can be seen as a response to increased consumer affluence (Kumaranayake, 1998). Although the scope and nature of the private sector varies from country to country, as a general trend it is expanding rapidly in most countries. Its role can no longer be ignored, even in those countries where, traditionally, governments have been the major players in financing and delivering health care. Some governments in recent years have liberalized private-sector involvement (for example, Tanzania, Malawi and India), recently opening up their health insurance markets to the private sector.

Input indicators such as health expenditure in the private sector, percentage of health facilities and hospital beds owned, and percentage of the workforce, mainly doctors and nurses working in the private sector, are commonly used as evidence of growing private-sector involvement. For example, in the early 1990s more than half of all hospitals in India were private, while 50 per cent of all physicians in Pakistan worked full time in private practice (Roemer, 1993). In many low-income countries, the majority of treatment for common illnesses, such as acute respiratory diseases as well as diseases of public health importance such as malaria, TB and STDs, are treated by the private sector (Hanson and Berman, 1998; Uplekar et al., 1998; Brugha and Zwi, 1999). There is also growing evidence that it is not only the rich who use privately provided services. The poor also use them, spending a far greater proportion of their income on health care when compared with the rich (Gwatkin and Guillot, 1999).

Proponents of the private sector argue that it improves efficiency and quality while promoting equity (World Bank, 1993). Efficiency gains are likely as a result of property rights, better resource use and an increase in competition. However, given the lack of choice among health care providers in most low-income countries, the degree of real competition that exists in the health sector of these countries is questionable (Bennett et al., 1997). The efficiency of private health service provision is questionable with regard to the critical public health programmes, since private service delivery is essentially curative rather than preventive. With the increased responsibilities of private practitioners, there are potential negative implications for controlling infectious diseases such as TB. Newell stresses the importance of a national strategy for controlling TB that exists, but is eroding, in most developing countries. Private treatment of those infected with TB is generally of poor quality with low cure rates, thus potentially increasing the number of chronic transmitters by eight times (Newell, 2002). In addition, surveying maternal and neonatal health services in 49 developing countries, Bulatao and Ross (2002) found only a 56 per cent likelihood that a typical service was adequate. Furthermore, services were equally weak for public- and private-sector activity.

In addition, it would appear that the private sector promotes efficiency at the cost of distributional justice. It can be argued that, in theory at least, by opening up health-care markets to private providers where no public provision existed previously, the private sector may provide essential health care to a poor population which otherwise would have no access. In addition, middle- and high-income groups would also be expected to utilize the private sector, hence releasing public resources that could be directed to serve the needs of the poor and disadvantaged. However, there is little evidence to suggest that the private sector would open up markets for rural disadvantaged populations in areas where neither government nor NGO health care exists. Moreover, it is commonly observed that the private sector prefers to provide services in urban communities where public services already exist. Similarly, there is no evidence that resources are released and that governments have been successful in targeting these resources at the poor. On the contrary, in many developing countries the private sector is an important source of care for poor households (McPake, 1997; Frenk, 2000) who spend a higher proportion of income out-of-pocket for health-related services (Frenk, 1995, 2000).

In terms of access to public or private health services, the poor are at a disadvantage compared with high-income groups. Not only do they have less access to tertiary-level public health-sector facilities but they also tend to use low-quality private services (Smith et al., 2001). Evidence from various studies suggests that the private sector attempts to reduce the input costs of service delivery, thus affecting the quality of services. Moreover, private suppliers also tend to over-provide and raise prices, resulting in the supply of inappropriate services (Yesudian, 1993; Bennett et al., 1994). Private-sector provision can also be inefficient and lead to cost-escalation (Kumaranayake, 1998). Amin (2002) examined private hospital provision in Bangladesh and found that most hospitals lacked essential medical equipment and employed unregistered nurses. Overall hospital quality was poor while doctors and nurses pursued illicit practices to generate income.

Hence, health-sector regulation needs to be developed not only to check the growth and role of the private sector but also to ensure that appropriate services of good quality are provided (Kumaranayake, 1998; Soderlund and Tangcharoensathien, 2000). Various instruments for regulating the health sector have been proposed (Table 6.8) since many developing countries do have basic regulatory legislation (Kumaranayake, 1998). However, given the weak capacity of low-income countries to design, implement, monitor and enforce regulations, the degree to which such mechanisms are likely to be effective is a concern raised by various researchers (Kumaranayake, 1998; Hongoro and Kumaranayake, 2000). Kumaranayake (1998) recommends that low-income countries use legislation to set out minimum standards of health service provision, and beyond this consider non-regulatory interventions including incentive mechanisms as an alternative.

Given the limitations of the government health sector in many developing countries, increasing involvement of the private sector is likely. However, the aim should be to ensure that the public and private sectors work in partnership, exploiting each other's strengths for mutual benefit. This could result in the development of a more effective and efficient health system, which could also be more equitable. The challenge is to achieve the right balance between the public and private sectors and to ensure that adequate regulatory mechanisms are in place to encourage the private sector to provide good-quality services at

Table 6.8   Instruments for health-sector regulation

Variable	Instrument
Prices	Negotiation of salary scales
	Fixing of private-sector charges such as prices for laboratories
Quantities/distribution	Licensing of medical practitioners and facilities
	Bonuses designed to attract providers to rural areas
	Restrictions on capital accumulation
	Capitation schemes to reduce incentive to over-treat
Quality	Monitoring by professional organizations
	Complaints/malpractice procedures
	Control of medical school curricula
	Training

Source: Kumaranayake (1998) and Kumaranayake et al. (2000).

an affordable price. Making citizens aware of their health rights can also go some way to promoting evidence-based medical practice and making providers more accountable.

Pharmaceutical policies

According to Brudon (1997) and Govindaraj et al. (1997) often 20–50 per cent of recurrent government health-sector budget is used to procure medicines and medical supplies. Over one-third of the world's population still lacks access to essential drugs (ED). In the poorest parts of Africa and Asia, the picture is even worse, with over half of the population lacking access to even the most basic essential drugs (WHO, 2000b). The provision of essential drugs and the development of national medicines policies are recognized as crucial elements in health system progress in developing countries. The World Health Organization Medicines Strategy 2000–2003 framework for action in essential drugs and medicines policy (WHO, 2000b) outlines a strategy for developing countries to implement comprehensive programmes in these areas. The success of the framework is to be seen as the initiative timeline closes. Even if the framework is able to meet its outcome measurements, there are other important factors that have not yet been addressed, such as the industry's de-focusing from neglected diseases (ND), which should be re-incorporated into future policies.

The World Health Organization has for over 25 years been the major promoter and supporter of essential drugs and national drug policy concepts. Despite this effort, essential drugs have remained unavailable, unaffordable, unsafe or improperly used in many areas of the world. The 2000–2003 WHO medicines framework outlines four objectives related to ED provision and medicines policy, each divided into several components and expected outcomes. The guiding objectives are as follows (WHO, 2000b).

- *Policy*: ensure the commitment of all stakeholders to national drug policies, coordinated implementation and to monitoring policy impact.
- *Access*: ensure equitable availability and affordability of essential drugs, with an emphasis on diseases of poverty.
- *Quality and safety*: ensure the quality, safety and efficacy of all medicines by strengthening and putting into practice regulatory and quality assurance standards.
- *Rational use*: ensure therapeutically sound and cost-effective use of drugs by health professionals and consumers.

Reported initiatives to date have been able to adequately assess the framework's impact (Ratanawijitrasin et al., 2001). In Bhutan, for example, an initiative to put in place measures outlined by the WHO framework was considered to have been successful. Specifically, improvements in drug availability, affordability and quality control were achieved. However, a similar programme introduced in the Yemen Arab Republic was reported as having been of limited success. This may be for several reasons, including a lack of proper monitoring or even inadequate design of assessment studies. With some exceptions, developing countries' experience in improving the use of medicines with regard to national policies, regulatory interventions and promotion of rational drug use has largely failed to draw concrete evidence on the effectiveness of initiatives (Ratanawijitrasin et al., 2001). A limitation of the policy evaluation studies has been identified as largely relating to the methodology employed. Specifically, the use of post-intervention design, the inability to isolate a specific policy measure for investigation and the heavy reliance on qualitative, descriptive and sometimes subjective assessments may raise doubts over the validity of results.

A correlation between interventions directed at consumers and health care expenditure (Homedes and Ugalde, 2001) suggests another area of WHO focus: that of improving coordination among all actors in the medication cycle as well as with industry, governments, private foundations and international organizations. Large-scale coordination often requires a shift in outside groups' current approach and directives. The World Bank, which has a history of making loans for working with pharmaceutical areas (PA), provides a 'mild' example.

An assessment of 77 World Bank staff appraisal reports showed that 95 per cent of Bank lending for PA is related to hardware areas (such as drug procurement, civil works and computer systems for drug registration) with only 5 per cent allocated to software (such as national drug policy development, rational use of drugs, ED programmes). Although hardware areas are important in developing countries, the WHO framework can be read to advocate a shift towards the development of software areas (Falkenberg and Tomson, 2000). The World Bank may be in a position to bridge the gap through dedication of hardware procurement as a way of strengthening national drug policies and essential drug programmes. However, this 'bridging' requires both additional funds from the Bank as well as specialized technical support, which the Bank has yet to commit.

The obstacles of proper study design and large-scale coordination are addressed by the WHO framework, as are other potential impediments. For example, a strong emphasis has been placed on the monitoring of activity to ensure effective implementation as well as on the development of ED and medicines policies that are closely integrated with national health care systems. The framework also targets the updating of ED lists and treatment guidelines with new available medicines. From the procurement side, the framework advocates efficient management, cost-effective production and good drug donation programmes. This sometimes conflicts with the business objectives of the pharmaceuticals industry (Henry and Lexchin, 2002). The industry's concern with the cost of drug development, competition from the generics industry, internal market competition and the cost of fortifying patent rights has made it increasingly concerned with maintaining profits. For developing countries, which rely on industry donations and price controls, this is a worrying trend. External pressure by groups such as the WHO and strong philanthropic missions of some companies may, to some extent, forestall these effects.

However, there is a trend within the industry that the WHO framework has not so far adequately addressed. The focus of private industry research has shifted to diseases of developed world interest, and not on those of the developing world. A review of public and private research initiatives into these appropriately termed neglected diseases (ND) confirms that this trend is already a reality (Henry and Lexchin, 2002). For NDs with a known vaccine such as TB problems of drug resistance and limited efficacy give little benefit to populations of developing countries. For other NDs, such as dengue and Chagas, there is no pre-existing specific treatment. Meeting the need for effective vaccines has been left to public or public–private initiatives that fall outside of traditionally defined industry. Since they lack global coordination, these research efforts may face some limitations in potential impact (Mrazek and Mossialos, 2003). The WHO needs to address this issue and its associated difficulties.

Conclusions and policy implications

The global pattern of disease shows marked variation between different world regions and, as a consequence, creates different challenges for individual governments. The Millennium Development Goals have helped focus attention on the continuing problems faced by developing countries (United Nations, 2002). On a national basis, however, the persistent problem is one of limited resources available to tackle these and many other challenges. Health-care systems in developing countries are very heterogeneous, yet the inputs to them are lower than in the West. Achieving these goals via health-sector reform was a priority of the 1990s. The main challenges of this period were classed by Cassels (1995) into five key areas: namely, improving the performance of the civil service and the functioning of the ministries of health, broadening the choices for health financing, introducing managed competition and working with the private sector. Capacity-building, primarily institutional capacity, is the critical aspect for improving the organizational performance of government bodies and employees. In particular, the major problem experienced by the least-developed countries is their inability to make use of available resources efficiently due to their lack of such institutional capacity. This must be addressed in order to ensure that any long-lasting rewards are derived from political and economic achievements.

The characteristic out-of-pocket payments in developing countries burdens the population and raises many issues, not least those of equity and efficiency. Current reform policies are looking at more progressive means of funding. None the less, user fees are becoming more widespread, the supporters of which argue that they improve equity and efficiency as well as generating revenue. However, others are less positive, alleging that user fees decrease access to services and that the revenue generated is frequently not used as was intended. Private health insurance is becoming more frequent, although clearly a lack of funds within the general population will make this a limited alternative in most developing countries. A more suitable option, yet based on similar principles, may well be the social insurance schemes that help to achieve greater fairness in financing by risk pooling. It is also argued that voluntary, community-based schemes may minimize the problems of adverse selection, although there are potential disadvantages due to the types of population involved and their limited management capabilities. Re-insurance of such schemes has been proposed as one possible solution to the weaknesses of micro-insurance units, although this is itself not free from problems.

The trends in health care provision have shifted in recent decades, reducing the role of the State to facilitate the provision of health care rather than provide it directly. This has promoted policies of decentralization and privatization. The extent to which power relationships change during decentralization and how this process is managed will determine its success. Many different initiatives have been tried but the evidence on their success is mixed. They will need to be monitored over the coming years before any firm conclusions can be drawn. The increasing role of the private sector should, in theory, improve efficiency and access. However, there is currently no evidence to suggest that the poor have benefited from the expansion of this sector. In addition, the quality of care provided by the private sector in some instances has been questioned. Appropriate regulation in this area is essential. Pharmaceutical policy has not yet made available many essential drugs to those in need. In addition, a more global perspective to drug research and development to tackle neglected diseases would help maximize the potential benefits to world health.

The World Bank, WHO and WTO are all key players in the international health arena with roles that are shifting in relative importance. It is vital that some cohesion is established and maintained between them to meet the needs of developing countries efficiently and effectively. However, different ideological and policy approaches may prevent effective collaboration. There has been considerable discussion of health reform, in addition to many concrete changes in the organization of health systems over the past few decades. The more recent economic ideology has influenced reforms focusing on decentralized government and increased use of the private sector in health service provision.

However, these changes offer little provision for ensuring equity and for tackling the health burdens of developing countries such as widespread infectious diseases that require national, coordinated programmes.

As this chapter has demonstrated, there has been a gradual but clear move away from an integrated, cross-sector and preventive health policy aimed at addressing the needs of the poor. Health-care services are nowadays more likely to be accessed by a select few with the ability to pay. In terms of evolving social policy paradigms as discussed in Chapter 1 of this volume, the decline of a primary health-care approach and the switch to a more market-based orientation could signal a move back towards residualism in the health sector. Yet despite the shift away from PHC as the prime health strategy for developing countries, it is probably the most effective, equitable option for bringing these countries through the epidemiological transition. Thus, international organizations and governments of developing countries need to focus on PHC and public health policies in order to maintain the central, coordinated delivery of widespread preventive and primary health services that will best meet the complex needs of populations in these countries within a holistic conception of social provision.

Recommended Reading

- Bennett, S., McPake, B. and Mills, A. (eds) (1997) *Private Health Providers in Developing Countries: Serving the Public Interest?* London: Zed Books. The results of a coordinated research programme on the private health sector, including case studies from Asia, Africa and Latin America.
- Mills, A. (ed.) (2000) *Reforming Health Sectors.* London: Kegan Paul. Countries across the world are attempting to change how health systems are financed, organized and managed. This book sheds light on health-sector reform ideologies, strategies and experiences.
- *World Health Report 2000.* Geneva: WHO. This report contributed towards developing a framework to assess health systems performance and generated much debate over the ranking and methodology employed.

References

Abel-Smith, B. and Rawal, P. (1994) 'Employers' willingness to pay: the case for compulsory health insurance in Tanzania', *Health Policy Planning*, 9 (4): 409–18.
Amin, M.A. (2002) *An Analysis of Private Hospitals Markets in Bangladesh.* PhD Thesis, London School of Hygiene and Tropical Medicine, University of London.
Anand, S. and Hanson, K. (1997) 'Disability-adjusted life years: a critical review', *Journal of Health Economics*, 16 (6): 685–702.
Appleby, J. (1992) *Financing Health Care in the 1990s*, State of Health Series. Buckingham: Open University Press.

Arhin-Tenkorang, D. (2000) *Mobilizing Resources for Health: The Case for User Fees Revisited*, CMH Working Paper Series, Paper No. WG3:6. Geneva: Commission on Macroeconomics and Health, WHO.

Barnighausen, T. and Sauerbourn, R. (2002) 'One hundred and eighteen years of the German health insurance system: are there any lessons for middle- and low-income countries?', *Social Science and Medicine*, 54: 1559–87.

Basch, P. (1999) *Textbook of International Health*, 2nd edn. New York: Oxford University Press.

Bennett, S. (1991) *The Mystique of Markets: Public and Private Health Care in Developing Countries*, Health Economics and Financing Programme, Health Policy Unit, PHP Dept. Publication No. 4, London School of Hygiene and Tropical Medicine, University of London.

Bennett, S. and Mills, A. (1998) 'Government capacity to contract: health sector experience and lessons', *Public Administration and Development*, 18: 307–26.

Bennett, S., Dakpallah, G.P., Gilson, L., Nittayaramphong, S., Zurita, B. and Zwi, A. (1994) 'Carrot and stick: state mechanisms to influence private provider behaviour', *Health Policy and Planning*, 9 (1): 1–13.

Bennett, S., McPake, B. and Mills, A. (eds) (1997) *Private Health Providers in Developing Countries: Serving the Public Interest?* London: Zed Books.

Beracochea, E. (1997) 'Contracting out of non-clinical services: the experience of Papua New Guinea', in S. Bennett et al. (eds), *Private Health Providers in Developing Countries: Serving the Public Interest?* London: Zed Books, pp. 264–75.

Bhatia, M. and Mills, A. (1997) 'Contracting out of dietary services by public hospitals in Bombay', in S. Bennett et al. (eds), *Private Health Providers in Developing Countries: Serving the Public Interest?* London: Zed Books, pp. 250–63.

Bossert, T. (1998) 'Analyzing the decentralization of health systems in developing countries: decision space, innovation and performance', *Social Science and Medicine*, 47 (10): 1513–27.

Brenzel, L. and Newbrander, W. (2002) 'Linking ability and willingness to contribute to microinsurance', in D. Dror and A. Preker (eds) *Social Reinsurance: A New Approach to Sustainable Community Health Financing*. Geneva: International Labour Office.

Broomberg, J., Masobe, P. and Mills, A. (1997) 'To purchase or to provide? The relative efficiency of contracting out versus direct public provision of hospital services in South Africa', in S. Bennett et al. (eds), *Private Health Providers in Developing Countries: Serving the Public Interest?* London: Zed Books, pp. 214–36.

Brudon, P. (1997) *Comparative Analysis of National Drug Policies in 12 Countries*, WHO/DAP/97.6, Action Programme on Essential Drugs. Geneva: World Health Organization.

Brugha, R. and Zwi, A (1999) 'Sexually transmitted disease control in developing countries: the challenge of involving the private sector', *Sexually Transmitted Infections*, 75: 283–5.

Brundtland, G. (2002) 'World Health Organization: state of the world's vaccines and immunizations', *JAMA*, 20: 288.

Bulatao, R. and Ross, J. (2002) 'Rating maternal and neonatal health services in developing countries', *Bulletin of the World Health Organization*, 80 (10): 721–7.

Buse, K. and Gwin, C. (1998) 'The World Bank and global cooperation in health: the case of Bangladesh', *Lancet*, 351: 665–9.

Buse, K. and Walt, G. (2000a) 'Global public–private partnerships: Part I – a new development in health?', *Bulletin of the World Health Organization*, 78 (4): 549–61.

Buse, K. and Walt, G. (2000b) 'Global public–private partnerships: part II – what are the health issues for global governance?', *Bulletin of the World Health Organization*, 78 (5): 699–709.

Buse, K. and Waxman, A. (2001) 'Public–private health partnerships: a strategy for WHO', *Bulletin of the World Health Organization*, 79 (8): 748–54.

Busse, R. (2002) 'The role of subsidies in micro-insurance: closing the "recovery gap"', in D. Dror and A. Preker (eds) *Social Reinsurance: A New Approach to Sustainable Community Health Financing*. Geneva: International Labour Office.

Cadwell, J.C. (1985) 'Routes to low mortality in poor countries', *Population and Development Review*, 2: 171–220.

Cadwell, J.C. (1993) 'Health transition: the cultural, social and behavioural determinants of health in the Third World', *Social Science and Medicine*, 36 (2): 125–35.

Cassels, A. (1995) 'Health sector reform: key issues in less developed countries', *Journal of International Development*, 7 (3): 329–47.

Charmes, J. (2000) 'Informal sector, poverty, and gender: a review of empirical evidence', Paper commissioned for World Development Report 2000/2001. Washington, DC: World Bank.

Davies, P. and Carrin, G. (2001) 'Risk-pooling – necessary but not sufficient?', *Bulletin of the World Health Organization*, 79 (7): 587.

Dia, M. (1996) 'Introduction: unbundling capacity building', in *Africa's Management in the 1990s and Beyond: Reconciling Indigenous and Transplanted Institutions*. Washington, DC: World Bank.

Drager, N. (1999) 'Making trade work for public health', *British Medical Journal*, 319: 1214.

Dror, D. (2002) 'Health insurance and reinsurance at the community level', in D. Dror and A. Preker (eds) *Social Reinsurance: A New Approach to Sustainable Community Health Financing*. Geneva: International Labour Office.

European Observatory on Health Care Systems (EOHCS) (2002) *Glossary*. Copenhagen: EOHCS.

Falkenberg, T. and Tomson, G. (2000) 'The World Bank and pharmaceuticals', *Health Policy and Planning*, 15 (1): 52–8.

Feacham, R.G.A., Kjellstrom, T., Murray, C., Over, M. and Phillips, M. (1992) *The Health of Adults in the Developing World*. Oxford: Oxford University Press.

Fox-Rushby, J. and Hanson, K. (2001) 'Calculating and presenting disability adjusted life ears (DALYs) in cost-effectiveness analysis', *Health Policy Planning*, 16 (3): 326–31.

Frenk, J. (1995) 'Comprehensive policy analysis for health system reform', *Health Policy*, 32 (1): 255–77.

Frenk, J. (2000) 'Changing the role of the state', in A. Mills (ed.) *Reforming Health Sectors*. London: Kegan Paul, pp. 54–80.

Gilson, L. (1997) 'The lessons of user fee experience in Africa', *Health Policy and Planning*, 12 (4): 273–85.

Gilson, L., Kalyalya, D., Kuchler, F., Lake, S., Orange, H. and Ouendo, M. (2000) 'The equity impacts of community financing activities in three African countries', *International Journal of Health Planning and Management*, 15: 291–317.

Gilson, L., Kilima, P. and Tanner, M. (1994) 'Local government decentralization and the health sector in Tanzania', *Public Administration and Development*, 14: 451–77.

Gilson, L., Russell, S. and Buse, K. (1995) 'The political economy of user fees with targeting: developing equitable health financing policy', *Journal of International Development*, 7 (3): 369–401.

Govindaraj, R., Chellaraj, G. and Murray, C.J. (1997) 'Health expenditures in Latin America and the Caribbean', *Social Science and Medicine*, 44 (2): 157–69.

Green, A. (1999) *An Introduction to Health Planning in Developing Countries*, 2nd edn. Oxford: Oxford University Press.

Grindle, M. and Hilderbrand, M. (1995) 'Building sustainable capacity in the public sector: what can be done?', *Public Administration and Development*, 15: 441–63.

Gwatkin, D. and Guillot, M. (1999) *The Burden of Disease among the Global Poor: Current Situation, Future Trends and Implications*, Global Forum for Health Research and Human Development Network. Washington, DC: World Bank.

Gwatkin, D.R., Rustein, S., Johnson, K., Pande, R.P. and Wagstaff, A. (2000) *Socio-Economic Differences in Health, Nutrition and Population in India*, HNP/Poverty Thematic Group of The World Bank. Washington, DC: World Bank.

Hall, J. and Taylor, R. (2003) 'Health for all beyond 2000: the demise of the Alma-Ata Declaration and primary health care in developing countries', *Medical Journal of Australia*, 178 (1): 17–20.

Hanson, K. and Berman, P. (1998) 'Private health care providers in developing countries: a preliminary analysis of levels and composition', *Health Policy and Planning*, 13 (3): 195–211.

Henry, D. and Lexchin, J. (2002) 'The pharmaceutical industry as a medicines provider', *Lancet*, 360: 1590–5.

Holland, W.W. and Gilderdale, S. (eds) (1977) *Epidemiology and Public Health*. London: Henry Kimpton.

Homedes, N. and Ugalde, A. (2001) 'Improving the use of pharmaceuticals through patient and community level interventions', *Social Science and Medicine*, 52: 99–134.

Hongoro, C. and Kumaranayake, L. (2000) 'Do they work? Regulating for-profit providers in Zimbabwe', *Health Policy and Planning*, 15 (4): 368–77.

Horton, S. (2002) 'WHO: the casualties and compromises of renewal', *Lancet*, 359: 1605–11.

Islam, A. and Tahir, Z.M. (2002) 'Health sector reform in South Asia: new challenges and constraints', *Health Policy*, 60: 151–69.

Kaul, M. (1997) 'The new public administration: management innovations in government', *Public Administration and Development*, 17 (1): 13–26.

Kumar, S. (2001) 'India hopes for elimination of leprosy by 2005', *Lancet*, 357: 1106.

Kumaranayake, L. (1998) 'Economic aspects of health sector regulation: strategic choices for low- and middle-income countries', PHP Departmental Publication No. 29. School of Hygiene and Tropical Medicine, University of London.

Kumaranayake, L., Lake, S., Mujinja, P., Hongoro, C. and Mpembenf, R. (2000) 'How do countries regulate the health sector? Evidence from Tanzania and Zimbabwe', *Health Policy and Planning*, 15 (4): 357–67.

Lancet (2002) 'News in brief – global instability threatens polio eradication', *Lancet*, 359: 1414.

Lee, K., Buse, K. and Fustukian, S. (2002) *Health Policy in a Globalising World*. Cambridge: Cambridge University Press.

Lieberman, S.S. (2002) *Decentralization and Health in the Philippines and Indonesia: An Interim Report*, East Asia Human Development. Washington DC: World Bank.

Lucas, A.O. (2002) 'Health policies in developing countries', *Oxford Textbook of Public Health*. Oxford: Oxford University Press, pp. 281–95.

Mackintosh, M. (2001) 'Do health care systems contribute to inequalities?', in D. Leon and G. Walt (eds) *Poverty Inequality and Health: an International Perspective*. New York: Oxford University Press, pp. 175–93.

McPake, B. (1996) 'Public autonomous hospitals in sub-Saharan Africa: trends and issues', *Health Policy*, 35 (2): 155–77.

McPake, B. (1997) 'The role of the private sector in health service provision', in Bennett et al. (eds), op. cit., pp. 21–39.

Mills, A. (1994) 'Decentralization and accountability in the health sector from an international perspective: what are the choices?', *Public Administration and Development*, 14: 281–92.

Mills, A. (1998) 'To contract or not to contract? Issues for low- and middle-income countries', *Health Policy and Planning*, 13 (1): 32–40.

Moens, F. (1990) 'Design, implementation and evaluation of a community financing scheme for hospital care in developing countries: a prepaid health plan in the Bwamanda Health Zone, Zaire', *Social Science and Medicine*, 20 (12): 1319–27.

Mogedal, S. and Steen, S.H. (1995) 'Health sector reform and organizational issues at the local level: lessons from selected African countries', *Journal of International Development*, 7 (3): 349–67.

Morgan, C. and Deutschmann, P. (2003) 'An evolving model for training and education in resource-poor settings: teaching health workers to fish', *Medical Journal of Australia*, 178: 21–5.

Mossialos, E. and Thomson, S. (2002) 'Voluntary health insurance in the European Union: a critical assessment', *International Journal of Health Services*, 32 (1): 19–88.

Mossialos, E., Dixon, A., Figueras, J. and Kutzin, J. (2002) *Funding Health Care: Options for Europe*. Buckingham: Open University Press.

Mrazek, M.F. and Mossialos, E. (2003) 'Stimulating pharmaceutical research and development for neglected diseases', *Health Policy*, 64 (1): 75–88.

Murray, C. (1994) 'Quantifying the burden of disease: the technical basis for disability adjusted life years', *Bulletin of the World Health Organization*, 72 (3): 429–45.

Murray, C. and Lopez, A. (2002) 'Assessing health needs: the global burden of disease study', in R. Detels, J. McEwen, R. Beaglehole and H. Tanaka (eds) *Oxford Textbook of Public Health*. Oxford: Oxford University Press.

Musgrove, P., Zeramdini, R. and Carrin, G. (2002) 'Basic patterns in national health expenditure', *Bulletin of the World Health Organization*, 80 (2): 134–46.

Newbrander, W. (1999) 'The impact of decentralization on hospitals', in R.L. Kolehmainen-Aitken (ed.) *Myths and Realities about the Decentralization of Health Systems*. Boston, MA: Management Sciences for Health.

Newell, J. (2002) 'The implications for TB control of the growth in numbers of private practitioners in developing countries', *Bulletin of the World Health Organization*, 80 (10): 836–7.

Newell, K. (1975) *Health by the People*. Geneva: World Health Organization.

Nitayarumphong, S. and Mills, A. (1999) *Achieving Universal Coverage of Health Care: Experiences from Middle and Upper Income Countries*. Bangkok: Office of Health Care Reform, Ministry of Public Health, Thailand.

Paalman, M., Bekedam, H., Hawken, L. and Nyheim, D. (1998) 'A critical review of priority setting in the health sector: the methodology of the 1993 World Development Report', *Health Policy and Planning*, 13 (1): 13–31.

Peabody, J.W. (1995) 'An organizational analysis of the World Health Organization: narrowing the gap between promise and performance', *Social Science and Medicine*, 40 (6): 731–42.

Peabody, J.W., Rahman, M.O., Gertler, P.J., Mann, J., Farley, D.O., Luck, J., Robalino, D. and Carter, G.M. (1999) *Policy and Health: Implications for Development in Asia*. Cambridge: Cambridge University Press.

Peters, D.H., Kandola, K., Elmendorf, A.E. and Chellaraj, G. (1999) *Health Expenditures, Services, and Outcomes in Africa: Basic Data and Cross-National Comparisons, 1990–1996*, Health, Nutrition, and Population Publication Series. Washington, DC: World Bank.

Powles, J. and Day, N. (2002) 'Interpreting the global burden of disease', *Lancet*, 360: 1342–3.

Ratanawijitrasin, S., Soumerai, S.B. and Weerasuriya, K. (2001) 'Do national medicinal drug policies and essential drug programs improve drug use? A review of experiences in developing countries', *Social Science and Medicine*, 53: 831–44.

Reid, M. and Pearse, E. (2003) 'Whither the World Health Organization?', *Medical Journal of Australia*, 178: 9–12.

Rifkin, S. (1996) 'Paradigms lost: toward a new understanding of community participation in health programmes', *Acta Tropica*, 61: 79–92.

Roemer, M. (1993) *National Health Systems of the World*. Oxford: Oxford University Press.

Rondinelli, D. (1981) 'Government decentralization in comparative theory and practice in developing countries', *International Review of Administrative Sciences*, 47 (2): 133–45.

Rosenfield, P.L. (1985) 'The contribution of social and political factors to good health', in S. Halstead, J. Walsh and K. Warren (eds) *Good Health at Low Cost*. New York: Rockefeller Foundation.

Sein, T. and Rafei, U. (2002) 'The history and development of public health in developing countries', in R. Detels, J. McEwen, R. Beaglehole and H. Tanaka (eds) *Oxford Textbook of Public Health*. Oxford: Oxford University Press, pp. 39–61.

Sen, K. and Bonita, R. (2000) 'Global health status: two steps forward, one step back', *Lancet*, 356: 577–82.

Sen, K. and Koivusalo, M. (1998) 'Health-care reforms and developing countries – a critical overview', *International Journal of Health Planning and Management*, 13: 199–215.

Sepehri, A. and Chernomas, R. (2001) 'Are user charges efficiency and equity enhancing? A critical review of economic literature with particular reference to experience from developing countries', *Journal of International Development*, 13: 183–209.

Shaw, P. and Giffin, C. (1995) *Financing Health Care in Sub-Saharan Africa through User Fees and Insurance*. Washington, DC: World Bank.

Smith, E., Brugha, R. and Zwi, A. (2001) *Working with Private Sector Providers for Better Health Care: An Introductory Guide*. London: Options Consultancy Services Ltd and London School of Hygiene and Tropical Medicine.

Soderlund, N. and Tangcharoensathien, V. (2000) 'Health sector regulation – understanding the range of responses from government', *Health Policy and Planning*, 15 (4): 347–8.

Unger, J. and Killingsworth, J. (1986) 'Selective primary health care: a critical review of methods and results', *Social Science and Medicine*, 22: 1001–13.

UNICEF (2002) *The State of the World's Children: Leadership*. New York: UNICEF.

United Nations (2002) *Millennium Development Goals*. New York: United Nations (http://www.un.org/millenniumgoals).

United Nations Population Fund (UNFPA) (1999) *Maternal Mortality Update: A Report on UNFPA Support to Reduce Maternal Mortality*. New York: United Nations (http://www.unfpa.org/tdp/mmupdate/hilites.htm).

Uplekar, M., Juvekar, S., Morankar, S., Rangan, S. and Nunn, P. (1998) 'After health sector reform, whither lung health?', *International Journal of Tuberculosis and Lung Disease*, 2 (4): 324–9.

Vaughan, P., Mogedal, S., Kruse, S., Lee, K., Walt, G. and Wilde, K. (1996) 'Financing the World Health Organization: global importance of extra budgetary funds', *Health Policy*, 35: 229–45.

Waitzkin, H. (2003) 'Report of the WHO Commission on Macroeconomics and Health: a summary and critique', *Lancet*, 361: 523–6.

Walker, D. (2003) 'Cost and cost-effectiveness of HIV/AIDS prevention strategies in developing countries: is there an evidence base?', *Health Policy and Planning*, 18 (1): 4–17.

Walt, G. (1998) 'Globalisation of international health', *Lancet*, 351: 434–7.

Walt, G. and Gilson, L. (1994) 'Reforming the health sector in developing countries: the central role of policy analysis', *Health Policy and Planning*, 9 (45): 353–70.

Wangombe, J. (1995) 'Public health crisis of cities in developing countries', *Social Science and Medicine*, 41 (6): 857–62.

Warren, K. (1988) 'The evolution of selective primary health care', *Social Science and Medicine*, 26: 891–8.

WHO (1981) *World Health Organization Global Strategy for Health For All by the Year 2000*. Geneva: World Health Organization.

WHO (1999) *Making a Difference: The World Health Report*. Geneva: World Health Organization.

WHO (2000a) 'Health systems: improving performance', *The World Health Report*. Geneva: World Health Organization.

WHO (2000b) *WHO Medicines Strategy 2000–2003: Framework for Action in Essential Drugs and Medicines Policy*. Geneva: World Health Organization (http://www.who.int/medicines/strategy/strategy.pdf).

WHO (2001) *Macroeconomics and Health: Investing in Health for Economic Development*, Commission on Macroeconomics and Health. Geneva: World Health Organization.

WHO (2002) *Reducing Risks, Promoting Health Life: The World Health Report*. Geneva: World Health Organization.

Wilkinson, D., Gouws, E., Sach, M. and Karim, S.A. (2001) 'Effect of removing user fees on attendance for curative and preventive primary health care services in rural South Africa', *Bulletin of the World Health Organization*, 79 (7): 665–71.

Williams, A. (1999) 'Calculating the global burden of disease: time for a strategic reappraisal?', *Health Economics*, 8 (1): 1–8.

Witter, S. and Ensor, T. (1997) *An Intro to Health Economics for Eastern Europe and the Former Soviet Union*. Chichester: John Wiley.

World Bank (1987) *Financing Health Services in Developing Countries: An Agenda for Reform*. Washington, DC: World Bank.

World Bank (1989) *Developing the Private Sector: A Challenge for the World Bank Group*. Washington, DC: World Bank.

World Bank (1993) *Investing in Health: World Development Report*. New York: Oxford University Press.

World Bank (2001) *World Development Report*. Oxford: Oxford University Press.

Yesudian, C.A.K. (1993) 'Behaviour of the private health sector in the health market of Bombay', *Health Policy and Planning*, 9: 72–80.

Zakus, D. and Cortinois, A. (2002) 'Primary health care and community participation: origins, implementation, and the future', in B. Fried and L. Gaydos (eds) *World Health Systems: Challenges and Perspectives*. Chicago: Health Administration Press, pp. 39–54.

Zwi, A. and Mills, A. (1995) 'Health policy in less developed countries: past trends and future directions', *Journal of International Development*, 7 (3): 299–328.

7 SOCIAL WORK AND THE HUMAN SERVICES

Summary

This chapter examines social work and the human services in the context of development and shows how the social work profession and human services programmes are attempting to enhance their relevance to the development needs of the countries of the South. The chapter has three sections. The first section offers a definition of the terms 'social work' and 'the human services' and provides a historical account of their evolution both in the industrial and the developing countries. It shows that the human services and professional social work were exported to the developing countries during colonial times. The next section focuses on the challenges facing social work and the human services. These challenges include the appropriateness of social work and the human services to development, the problem of coverage and the issue of costs. The imposition of structural adjustment programmes in many developing countries since the 1980s has exacerbated the problems facing social work and the human services. Although social funds have been created to address the problem of social need in many indebted countries, the problem has not been solved. The final section shows, however, that social workers and those responsible for the human services have sought to enhance their relevance to development. It reveals that social work and the human services are taking new directions through promoting a more participatory, developmental approach to social welfare. Reference will also be made to the adoption of a pluralistic approach which relies less on government and recognizes the contribution of non-formal welfare institutions, the non-profit sector and private enterprise in promoting people's welfare.

Background

Social work and the human services are closely interrelated. Social workers have historically been involved in the administration and provision of human services programmes and, in turn, the human services have provided social workers with an organizational context within which they can implement their profession's unique practice methodology. Indeed, social work emerged out of the activities of voluntary human service organizations in the late nineteenth century when attempts were made to improve the way these organizations assessed applications for charitable assistance. The link between social work and the human services became even stronger during the middle decades of the twentieth century when government social provisions expanded rapidly in many parts of the world. It was generally accepted at this time that professionally qualified personnel were needed to staff and manage the government's human services or 'social welfare services' as they were then known.

The expansion of government human service programmes in the industrial countries was emulated in the developing countries of the South. Despite fiscal constraints, many governments of the newly independent developing countries also expanded their education, health and human service provisions that had been introduced by missionaries or colonial administrations. They created new ministries (or departments) of social welfare that were responsible for providing services to those with particularly pressing social needs. These agencies focused on the most conspicuous urban problems such as juvenile delinquency, begging, prostitution, alcohol addiction, mental illness and child neglect and abuse. Residential institutions were built, social assistance was introduced and social workers were employed to counsel those in need. In some parts of the developing world, such as Latin America, these services have an older history but in most of the Anglophone territories, social welfare programmes were only introduced after World War II.

Initially, social workers from Europe and North America were employed to staff and manage the human services but, in time, locals were sent to the metropolitan countries to be trained. Subsequently, with the aid of international development agencies and some metropolitan governments, local schools of social work were created. Their number increased rapidly in Africa, Asia and Central and South America during the 1950s and 1960s. Although social work education had previously been introduced in countries such as Chile, India and South Africa, the profession's post-war expansion was particularly pronounced resulting in the creation by the 1980s of a worldwide profession with its own, unique approach to dealing with social needs and solving human problems.

Social work and the human services were initially concerned with the most conspicuous forms of neglect in the cities of the newly independent countries, but it had gradually been recognized that an urban-based, remedial approach did little to improve the welfare of the population as a whole. The needs of the majority of the population who lived in rural areas were seriously neglected. It has also been recognized that the use of residential care, psychological counselling and similar approaches that were imported from the West were inappropriate to the needs of the developing countries. Faced with this challenge, some social workers and social administrators have sought to formulate an alternative developmental or 'social development' approach that has wider scope, focuses on poverty and deprivation and seeks to promote progressive social change. This approach has resulted in the identification of new interventions that many believe are more appropriate to the demands of development. Their efforts have been supported by the United Nations and other international agencies. The need for a broader approach to social welfare that would contribute positively to development has been the theme of numerous meetings sponsored by the United Nations and its affiliated agencies since 1968 when the first Conference of Ministers Responsible for Social Welfare was held in New York. It has been reiterated many times and most recently at the World Summit on Social Development, held in Copenhagen in 1995.

Efforts to promote a developmental approach in social work and social welfare are continuing and progress has been made in re-orientating the human services and professional social work to enhance their relevance to development. However, the problems of inappropriate interventions, of excessive emphasis on remedial welfare and the urban bias of human service programmes have not been entirely resolved. Equally serious is the problem of scarce resources for human service programmes not only in the developing countries but in many industrial countries as well. However, retrenchments in government budgets in many developing countries in recent decades have had a particularly adverse impact on the human services. With fiscal austerity, structural adjustment and the creation of social funds, the original mission of social work and human services has been challenged, and there is an urgent need to reinvigorate their role in the development context.

Social work and the human services

The term 'human services' has been used in preference to the older term 'social welfare services' since the late 1970s when President Jimmy Carter of the United States reorganized and renamed the federal government's Department of Health, Education and Welfare as the Department of Health and Human Services. This was done partly because of the confusion which had arisen over the way the term 'social welfare' was being used. Although the term was widely employed to denote remedial public and voluntary social programmes, such as social assistance, residential care and social work services, many felt that it had a broader meaning, and that it should be used to connote a more general condition of social well-being. Others believed that the term 'social welfare' should be used to refer to a broader range of social programmes including health, social security and education. Yet others argued that it should not be used to describe the provision of services to passive recipients, but should instead connote the sum total of efforts of individuals, families, communities and governments to promote social well-being.

Although the term 'human services' is widely used today, other terms have also been coined and, in some cases, the term 'social welfare' is still employed. The term 'social services' is often used as a synonym for 'human services', particularly in the United States. In Britain, on the other hand, the term 'social services' refers to the whole spectrum of government social programmes including health, housing and social security; the term 'personal social services' is used for services directed at neglected or abused children, the disabled and other needy groups. However, it is not widely used elsewhere. Hardiman and Midgley (1989) suggested that 'social work and welfare services' might be an appropriate designation because of the close association between social work and the human services but this proposal has not been adopted. In many countries of the South, the term 'social development' has been coined to designate social welfare agencies so that it is now not unusual to find that the Ministry of Social Welfare is now known as the Ministry of Social Development or that some combination of the terms social welfare, social services and social development is employed.

These different usages reflect different opinions about the use of the term 'social welfare' and they, in turn, reflect wider beliefs about the proper role of government in social welfare. Different points of view about the role of the State in social welfare as well as the scope of government social human service programmes were discussed in the first chapter of this book and they will not be repeated here. Nevertheless, attention should be drawn to the way the human services were originally intended to fulfil a minimalist, residual approach that focused on the most conspicuously needy groups of people who, it was believed, could not provide for themselves. Advocates of this approach believe that government should only provide welfare services when the family, local community and religious or secular charities cannot assist. This belief has been challenged, and efforts are being made to transcend the residual role of the human services by promoting developmental forms of engagement. But before discussing these issues in more depth, it may be helpful to provide a historical overview of the evolution of the human services and their historic association with social work.

Evolution of the human services

Since ancient times, the promotion and maintenance of 'well-being' has been viewed as a matter for individuals and their families. For centuries, labour power has been the primary means by which people met their basic needs. Although women had a disproportionate responsibility for nurturing and providing care, children and elderly family members were also expected to contribute, through labour, to their own well-being and that of their immediate family. However, for reasons of illness, infirmity or other forms of incapacity, some individuals were not able to make an active contribution and, in these cases, the immediate family was expected to provide for its needy members. This expectation was institutionalized in the traditional culture. Indeed, family responsibility for the care of young children, the infirm, elderly and others has been a cultural requirement in most societies. Wider kin and clan support networks, as well as those of the local community, were also utilized to supplement the family's historic welfare function.

The non-formal or 'traditional' welfare system, as it is also known, has attempted to meet social needs and address the social problems individuals and their families encounter for most of human history. But it has not always functioned effectively. During times of famine or war or other calamities, whole communities and even societies were plunged into destitution and suffering. Even in normal times, poor and oppressed communities with limited access to land or other resources were often unable to meet their own basic needs. In addition, many ordinary families lived on the margins of subsistence and often the death or incapacity of adults would result in destitution. In many cases, the extended family and local community was unable to support those in need.

Although it was previously believed that non-formal welfare institutions would weaken as societies experienced modernization (Clifford, 1966; Cockburn, 1980), it is now recognized that traditional social welfare institutions continue to provide assistance and income support to millions of people around the world. Studies of how traditional welfare institutions function have become much more common in recent times (Bossert, 1988; Chih-Ming, 1988; von Benda-Beckmann et al., 1988; von Benda-Beckmann and von Benda-Beckmann, 1994; de Bruijn, 1994; Midgley, 1994b; Leliveld, 1995; Weiss, 2002). These studies have shown that a great variety of non-formal social security institutions provide income protection to people in agrarian communities, in the urban informal sector and among migrants in many parts of the world.

A good example of the way the non-formal sector functions is Leliveld's (1995) study of social security in Swaziland, a small Southern African nation. Here, government social welfare programmes cover a very small proportion of the population and most people rely on the non-formal system to meet their needs. The social welfare functions of Swazi culture are, of course, very old and provided social protection long before the government established its modern statutory social security scheme. The question of how non-formal welfare institutions can be purposefully integrated with modern-day government programmes will be discussed in more detail later in this chapter. It will be shown that the traditional welfare system can play a significant role in promoting social welfare, and that its role needs to be articulated with that of the governmental and non-profit or voluntary sector.

Formal welfare institutions have also been utilized by needy people either to supplement non-formal sources of assistance or, in some cases, to replace them. This was usually the case when families were faced with destitution and could not provide for their members. Formal welfare institutions, inspired by religious philanthropy, found expression in the pious benevolence of private individuals, and in the efforts of monastic orders and lay organizations. Responsibility for the care of the sick, destitute, disabled and abandoned has historically been discharged in religions such as Christianity and Buddhism by the monastic orders and, over the years, an elaborate system of care evolved. Human services programmes provided by the religious orders still continue today.

Lay organizations inspired by the virtues of Christian charity, such as the *confraternerias* of Latin America, have also contributed to the alleviation of social need. These lay activities gradually gave rise to the emergence and subsequent expansion of secular charity. Many secular charities providing services for many different groups of needy people evolved in Europe and North

America during the nineteenth century. Although most were inspired by religious ideals, they were not administered directly by the churches or other religious organizations. Today, secular philanthropy is well established, and a great variety of organizations concerned with diverse welfare activities, ranging from service provision to political advocacy, now operate in many different parts of the world.

While religious philanthropy has historically dominated the formal welfare system, secular rulers also provided for those in need by enacting statutes dealing with welfare issues and sometimes by creating services for the needy. One of the oldest examples of the use of legislation to promote the welfare of needy and vulnerable people is the Code of King Hamurabi of Babylon (Chambliss, 1954). This body of legislation contains provisions relating to the care and protection of orphans, widows and other needy people. Similarly, Mesa-Lago (1978) reports that the Inca rulers of South America required local communities to cultivate crops on a communal plot of land to feed widows, orphans and other needy people. Local officials were required to maintain a register of needy people and to ensure that their needs were met. Another example comes from the early Islamic period when the Caliph Omar created the first public treasury or *beit-al-mal* into which charitable funds were paid to support those in need. Similar treasuries were established in other Islamic cities at this time (Hasan, 1965; Weiss, 2002).

Of course, a clear distinction between secular and religious law was not drawn until modern times. In some religions such as Islam, the practice of *zakat*, or the poor tax as it is sometimes known, was and still is a religious duty of all citizens. All Muslims are expected to assess and pay their contribution in ways directed by religious teaching and conscience (Weiss, 2002). In Christianity, where charitable giving was also intended to be a matter of personal conscience, secular law often ensured compliance with religious teaching. It was reported by de Schweinitz (1943) that the practice of tithing in medieval Europe was not only encouraged through religious exhortation and peer pressure, but was enforced by legal sanctions. In England, this practice evolved into a comprehensive set of statutory provisions known as the Poor Laws. Although the Poor Laws sought to control vagrancy and begging, they also required the local authorities to impose a tax to assist the elderly and infirm who had no means of support. The Elizabethan version of the Poor Laws, which was enacted in 1601, is regarded by many experts as laying the foundations on which modern-day human services were established. As will be shown in Chapter 8, some experts also perceive it as the beginning of modern, statutory social security.

The Elizabethan Poor Law was the culmination of a series of earlier English statutes intended to control labour mobility and curb vagrancy. Although these statutes imposed harsh penalties on those who left their localities in search of higher wages, they were not very effective. The Elizabethan statute sought to consolidate these provisions and to provide some relief to the 'deserving poor', as they were known. The deserving poor were indigent, unable to work and had no relatives who could support them. Local parishes were required to impose a tax to fund poor relief and to appoint an official, known as the overseer of the poor, to administer the system. Similar provisions were introduced in several Protestant Northern European cities but unlike the Elizabethan system these were not imposed by national governments. In the Catholic regions of Europe, religious charity continued to function as the primary means of helping those in need.

The Elizabethan Poor Law was of great historical significance because it institutionalized the idea of government social welfare responsibility. Initially, this responsibility was limited to needy people who could not care for themselves or who had no-one to care for them. Workhouses were established to accommodate destitute able-bodied people, and almshouses and other specialized residential institutions were subsequently built to house orphans, the destitute elderly and disabled. Although conditions in the workhouses were appalling and attracted condemnation from social reformers, many needy people received cash assistance and continued to live in their own homes. Despite its limited coverage and punitive approach, the Poor Law offered a modicum of support and facilitated the subsequent extension of public welfare provision (de Schweinitz, 1943; Bruce, 1961). By the end of the nineteenth century, when Europe was experiencing rapid industrialization and urbanization, the problems of delinquency, child neglect, prostitution, alcohol abuse, destitution, abandonment and other social problems became widespread. Although religious and secular charities responded as best they could, these problems remained endemic and were widely attributed to the family disintegration and social disorganization that, it was believed, accompanied industrialization. Many social reformers contended that these problems could only be adequately addressed through government intervention. Some reformers, such as the Fabians in Britain, argued that efforts to deal with the most conspicuous problems of urban neglect through government social welfare programmes would fail unless these efforts were accompanied by massive State intervention designed to create employment, reform working conditions in the factories, and to provide adequate housing, health care and income security (Bruce, 1961). In time, this point of view prevailed and, as was noted earlier, by the middle decades of the twentieth century, government social programmes in Europe and other industrial nations had expanded exponentially.

Government social programmes also expanded in the developing countries at this time. When many of these countries secured independence from European colonial rule in the 1950s and 1960s, the health, education and other social programmes introduced during the colonial era were enhanced, and many countries created new departments of social welfare to extend the limited range of human services established by the missionaries and colonial authorities (Hardiman and Midgley, 1989). However, programmes of this kind had emerged earlier in Latin America. For example, Mesa-Lago (1978) reports that many wealthy Spanish colonists founded charitable institutions or *beneficencias* which were then managed by the Church and religious orders. The first of these was established by Hernan Cortez for orphan girls in Mexico City in 1521. One of the oldest welfare institutions in the Philippines was the Hospital of San Lazaro, which was built in 1578 shortly after the Spanish conquest. The Hospital catered for people suffering from Hansen's disease or leprosy (Landa Jocano, 1980). Similar programmes emerged in other colonial territories and, although they were often managed by the Church, Mesa-Lago (1978) points out that their costs were frequently subsidized by the colonial administrations.

The colonial authorities, and the British in particular, also built and maintained their own governmental residential facilities. The British colonial authorities in India established several reform schools for young offenders in the late nine-teenth century that were directly managed by the government. The English Poor Law was also introduced into some, but not all, of the English colonies. Several of the continental North American colonies adopted the Poor Law and, in 1682, Jamaica was one of the first colonies outside North America to implement its provisions. However, these catered only for European settlers (Cumper, 1972). Although the Poor Law was not widely replicated, modern social welfare programmes introduced into many other territories during the twentieth century reflected Poor Law principles (Midgley, 1984).

Generally, these early welfare efforts emerged locally without any direction from the metropolitan authorities. While they were sometimes managed directly by the local colonial administration, it has already been shown that missionaries and voluntary organizations were usually responsible for these programmes. Often their activities were subsidized by the colonial authorities. These services were concentrated in the urban areas and the social needs of the rural majority were given little attention. This was not only a reflection of colonial attitudes but of the haphazard way the human services evolved.

However, by the mid-twentieth century, efforts were made to standardize and centralize the human service provisions. The British colonial authorities played a leading role by actively expanding government involvement in the human services and creating centralized human service administrations. This process was initiated in 1940 when, as Mair (1944) reveals, the British Colonial Office in London appointed a committee in 1940 to review services in the colonial territories for young offenders and other needy groups. The Committee's recommendations resulted not only in the expansion of government human services but in a more coherent approach which involved the creation of centralized departments of social welfare, the introduction or expansion of residential provisions and the introduction of social work. Later, in the 1950s and 1960s, as the international agencies became involved in social welfare policy and planning, a more widely shared conception of the need for government social welfare services, and of the best way of providing these services, emerged. The United Nations played a particularly important role in promoting the expansion of the human services in the South. As will be shown later in this chapter, it also made a significant contribution to identifying ways in which these programmes can be linked more effectively to national development efforts.

Although it was widely assumed at the time that government would be the primary provider of human services, and that most social workers would be employed in public agencies, governments were not the only source of assistance to those in need. In addition to the family and non-formal welfare institutions, voluntary organizations of a great variety were also engaged in promoting people's welfare. These had proliferated in the North in the mid-nineteenth century and, as will be shown later in this chapter, professional social work emerged out of the efforts of the charities in Europe and North America to rationalize poor relief. Despite the expansion of government involvement in social welfare, and a pervasive statist approach, the voluntary sector has continued to grow. Indeed, after the 1980s, when government social programmes came under sustained attack from politicians and political parties on the political right, the non-profit sector has grown significantly in the North (Salamon, 1995). Much of this growth has, in fact, come from the allocation of public resources to voluntary agencies and the more frequent use of these agencies as contractors to provide services on government's behalf. The voluntary sector has also expanded rapidly in the developing countries and, as was shown in Chapter 1 of this book, many different types of non-government organizations now use quite different approaches to promote people's well-being. As a result of weakening government, and the more frequent use of international aid as well as social funds in the South, these organizations today play a critical role in providing human services (Hulme and Edwards, 1997).

The development of social work

Unlike the human services, social work is a recent innovation. It evolved in the late nineteenth century through the efforts of educated women, primarily in Europe and North America, to create a new profession that would permit them to make positive use of their education by providing assistance to needy people. Since the more established professions of law, medicine and engineering were dominated by men who opposed the admission of women, educated women responded by establishing professions of their own. Like nursing, teaching and librarianship, social work evolved to give expression to the ambitions and the altruism of these women. Their formative efforts have today resulted in a global profession committed to applying their knowledge and skills to enhancing people's welfare.

Initially, most social workers were employed in non-profit organizations. Indeed, social work evolved out of the efforts of the charities to ensure that only those in genuine need were given assistance and that they were helped to become self-sufficient. The Charity Organization Society, which was established in London in the 1860s, pioneered the use of volunteer social workers to undertake a careful investigation of the needs of applicants for poor relief and to help them resolve the problems which impeded their social functioning. By the beginning of the twentieth century, these volunteers were being given a formal training and, as more of the charities began to employ trained volunteers, charity work became professionalized (Lubove, 1965). This innovation attracted widespread international attention, with the result that opportunities for the professional education of social workers proliferated in Europe, Britain and the United States in the early decades of the twentieth century. Initially, social work education was provided at independent, proprietary educational institutions but in time many of these schools affiliated with the universities. This was the case in Britain and particularly the United States where social work training is now well established in the country's universities. Although affiliation with the universities greatly facilitated social work's quest for professionalism, social work education in some developing countries is still offered at non-university training schools.

By the 1930s, social work had also become established in the South. Kendall (2000) reports that the first professional school of social work in the developing world was established in 1925 in Santiago, Chile, as a result of collaboration between Dr Rene Sand, the Secretary General of the Red Cross and Dr Alejandro del Rio, a Chilean physician who subsequently became a senior social welfare official in his country. In Africa, the first social work programme was established as a two-year diploma at the University of Cape Town in 1924. The first social work school in Asia was created in the 1920s at Yenchin University in Beijing, China, with assistance from American foundations. Like the other social work programmes established before World War II, it ceased to function after the Chinese Communist Party came to power. India's first social work programme was established in 1936 when the wealthy Indian industrialist, Sir Dorabji Tata, financed the creation of the Tata Institute of Social Science in Bombay. The Institute still operates today and is widely regarded as India's premier school of social work.

Although many schools of social work were established under private auspices, colonial administrations also encouraged the introduction of social work education, particularly in the 1950s and 1960s. For example, the colonial government of Hong Kong supported the creation of a social work programme at the University of Hong Kong in 1950 that, in 1967, became an independent academic department. Similarly, in Ghana (which was previously known as the Gold Coast), the colonial government began to educate social workers at its own training school in 1950. Ghana had, in fact, been one of the first African countries to establish a separate government department of social welfare and the need for professional training was soon recognized. In 1956, the government entered into an agreement with the University of Ghana to create a social work unit within the Department of Sociology where a more academically grounded education could be provided.

Many other schools of social work were established in the developing countries after independence from European colonial rule. In many cases, these schools were created with the assistance of international development agencies such as the United Nations Children's Fund (UNICEF) or the aid programmes of the governments of the industrial countries. For example, during the 1960s and 1970s, the United States government provided technical assistance to several countries seeking to establish professional social work education. As a result of these efforts, social work is now well established in the developing world. Schools of social work exist in many developing countries today and social workers are employed in many government and non-profit organizations. They also work in the international development agencies. Their activities have been promoted by numerous national professional associations with the support of the International Federation of Social Workers, based in Switzerland. In addition, social work education is represented at the international level by the International Association of Schools of Social Work which was founded in 1928 (Healy, 1995). By the mid-1990s, as Garber (1997) reported, professional social work education was offered at more than 1,600 schools of social work in more than 100 countries.

Social work has a unique methodology that stresses the importance of professional knowledge and skills in determining the causes of needs and problems, identifying the best way of addressing them and implementing solutions. It relies on professionally trained personnel who have the knowledge and skills to work with needy people and help them solve their problems. Generally, this involves a process of intensive individual counselling in which psychological issues are given more emphasis than material concerns. While social workers are not indifferent to material deprivation, many believe that their primary purpose is to treat the emotional and social factors that are associated with material need, and which, they believe, inhibit effective social functioning. However, while a commitment to remedial intervention dominates social work practice, the profession has also developed other forms of intervention which include group and community social work that are less concerned with treatment than with providing services and helping people to improve their social conditions. As will be shown later, these alternative approaches are particularly relevant to the development context.

Although remedial practice has long dominated social work, the remedial emphasis has been controversial ever since the profession's early days. In the early twentieth century, there were sharp differences of opinion among the profession's founders about social work's proper scope and mission. Although most of the social work educators who taught at the first schools of social work in Europe and North America believed in an individualized approach in which a professional worker sought to treat the social problems of their clients through giving sympathetic advice and support, others believed that social work should engage in community organizing to mobilize local people to improve their social conditions. Others argued for an activist approach by which social work would engage in lobbying and political action to bring about social change. Yet others believed that social needs and problems could only be addressed through massive government intervention and that this required the election of progressive political parties that would enact reformist legislation and introduce comprehensive social programmes. These programmes, they believed, would provide an appropriate context in which social workers could practice effectively.

The issue of social work's proper role and scope has been extensively debated by the profession but it has not been resolved and social workers are today engaged in very different forms of practice. Despite the predominance of remedial social work, social workers are also employed as policy-makers, administrators, group workers, community organizers, lobbyists and activists. While some social workers regard the lack of a standardized practice methodology to be a major disadvantage, others regard it as a strength. They claim that these different practice approaches comprise a repertoire of interventions which social workers can apply in different situations and even simultaneously within specific practice settings to respond to different problems, needs and opportunities. This multi-faceted approach to social work practice is an essential ingredient of the profession's still evolving developmental perspective which, its advocates hope, will become more widely adopted in social work practice and the human services.

Challenges to social work and the human services

By the 1970s, social work and the human services were well established in the South. Most of these countries had created central government ministries or departments of social welfare which delivered services and established national policies for social welfare. By this time, social work had also been introduced in many countries. Opportunities for professional social work education had also proliferated and, as more social workers were trained, the human services were increasingly administered by professionally qualified staff. Although the non-profit sector was small, under the guidance of social workers, it was poised to expand. These developments were supported by the international organizations and aid donors which provided technical assistance and opportunities to share technical knowledge and experiences. By the 1970s, it could be claimed that the expansion of the human services and the growth of social work in the developing world had been a major achievement.

However, despite these achievements and the optimism that characterized the expansion of the human services, social work and the human services were facing severe challenges. At the time, few social workers and social administrators recognized that the excessive emphasis on remedial intervention, urban bias and the neglect of economic development were impeding the effectiveness of human services programmes; indeed, most were oblivious to these difficulties. Many also failed to appreciate the extent to which social welfare had failed to contribute to national development. While many nationalist leaders believed that programmes to enhance social welfare were desirable, they were also mindful of the overriding need for economic development. The failure of many social workers and human service administrators to address this issue as well as other challenges had a negative impact on the human services. On the other hand, some were aware of these problems and some were prompted to identify new forms of social work and human service intervention that would be suited to development and the needs and circumstances of the developing countries. The United Nations actively supported these efforts and, in time, a new and distinctive 'developmental' approach to social welfare emerged. However, it was some time before most social administrators and social workers recognized the seriousness of the challenges they faced. A failure to address these challenges impeded the effectiveness of the human services.

Appropriateness, coverage and costs

The allocation of public resources to the human services in many developing countries in the 1950s and 1960s did not mean that these services reached the population as a whole. Indeed, as was noted earlier, social welfare services were introduced by the colonial authorities to deal with the most conspicuous urban social problems such as juvenile delinquency, destitution, begging, child abuse and neglect. By attempting to treat these problems through casework, residential services and limited social assistance programmes, the wider problems of poverty and deprivation were neglected. The fact that the rural population lived in appalling conditions of poverty was hardly recognized, and the prevalence of ill-health, malnutrition and illiteracy among rural people did not, at first, attract much attention. Because the social problems associated with rural poverty were disguised, while the problems of urban deviance, squalor and deprivation were more overt, it was believed that urban problems should be given priority.

However, it was not only a matter of recognizing the extent of social need in the rural areas. At the time, many social workers and social administrators subscribed to the then popular view that economic development would of itself create employment opportunities in the modern sector of the economy and, as the rural poor were drawn into regular jobs, their incomes would rise and the problem of poverty would be resolved. They claimed that it was not the role of social work and the human services to address the wider problem of poverty but instead to treat the most pressing and visible social problems. Indeed, some social work scholars such as Clifford (1966) believed that social work was urgently needed in the developing world to deal with problems of psychological maladjustment and family dislocation caused by modernization. This belief conformed to the residual approach to social welfare that had emerged in the industrial countries in the nineteenth century. Although the residual approach no longer had widespread appeal in these countries, it provided a rationale for social work and the human services.

The cultural appropriateness of social work and human service programmes was another problem. Social work in developing countries had emulated European, and particularly North American theories and practice methods; by the late 1960s, some social workers from the South began to question the usefulness of these approaches. For example, Almanzor (1967), a leading Filipina social work educator, questioned the belief that social work concepts and theories were universal and she argued that many of the principles governing social work practice in the West did not apply to the developing world. Nagpaul (1972), an Indian social worker, fulminated against the uncritical importation of culturally inappropriate social work theories and practice methods from the West and, in a comprehensive critique, Midgley (1981) alleged that social work in the developing world was the product of 'professional imperialism'. Midgley complained that the uncritical replication of Western social work theories and practice approaches in many developing countries had limited the profession's relevance and effectiveness.

Like social work, the human services were also largely inappropriate to the realities and needs of many developing countries. As was suggested earlier, human service programmes relied extensively on residential care, counselling by professional social workers and the payment of social assistance benefits. The idea that these approaches should be the primary mechanisms for human service delivery ignored the fact that indigenous forms of care operated throughout the developing world and that these approaches were incompatible with traditional forms of provision. The creation of orphanages and old-age homes may have housed needy children and elderly people but they were hardly compatible with the obligations in the traditional culture for families and kin to care for their members, including those who were beyond the immediate nuclear family. They were also incompatible with the emphasis placed in the traditional culture on community networks and systems of support. Similarly, as Almanzor (1967) showed, casework counselling by professional social workers was not likely to be effective because traditional cultural values would not permit individuals to share intimate information with an unknown professional worker or to admit that they and their families had emotional and behavioural problems. To do so would dishonour the family.

Inappropriateness was also revealed in the fact that the human service approaches were expensive and, as was noted earlier, limited in the numbers they could serve. Residential services were very costly and could cater for only a small proportion of those in need. While some disabled and elderly people and needy orphans may have been accommodated in residential facilities, most received no assistance at all. Similarly, casework counselling, even if it were appropriate, could not hope to solve the serious social problems facing the developing countries simply because there were not enough caseworkers to deal with these problems. Although some social workers argued that social problems are experienced individually and can only be solved individually, it was obvious that the extent of need was too great to be adequately met by caseworkers.

The problem of using high-cost approaches in the human services was compounded by the comparatively small budgets allocated to the human services. While most independence governments supported the expansion of social work and the human services, resources were scarce and there were many competing demands from other agencies. Generally, industrial and infrastructure investments as well as military and security needs received priority over social service allocations but even within the social sectors, more resources were allocated to education and health than social welfare. These problems had a negative impact on social workers employed in the public sector. Trained as caseworkers but lacking adequate resources and support services, they were unable to respond effectively to the needs of their clients. Residential institutions were crowded and unable to cope, caseworkers were inundated with clients, and social assistance budgets could not meet the needs of even a fraction of those seeking help.

In addition, most social welfare departments enjoyed low status. As Livingstone (1969) reported, their senior officials were often unable to explain their activities to politicians in ways that made sense or demonstrated that they were making a significant contribution to the overriding need for development. Consequently, funding allocations remained low or even declined. For these and other reasons, many social workers in the government human services became demoralized and despondent. A study of social workers in government service in Ghana at the end of the 1970s (Midgley, 1981) revealed that most of these social workers felt undervalued and were dissatisfied with poor promotion prospects, inadequate resources and low status. More than one-half had sought employment elsewhere. Unfortunately, these problems were exacerbated in the 1980s as many countries were faced with serious indebtedness and structural adjustment.

Structural adjustment, social funds and the non-profit sector

Following the international debt crisis of the 1980s, many developing countries sought international assistance to meet their fiscal and debt requirements, and many turned to international lending organizations such as the International Monetary Fund and the World Bank for aid. As is well known, the provision of aid has been dependent on the imposition of conditionalities by these organizations. These conditionality requirements demand that austerity measures be imposed, that the pubic sector be scaled back, that tariffs and taxation be reduced and that trade and other economic regulations be liberalized. Government human service ministries and departments have been targeted for major budgetary cuts, and their operations have been seriously curtailed. Although their budgets were hardly sizeable, they symbolically represent the welfarism that neo-liberals in the international lending agencies deplore. Although other social services such as health and education have also been subjected to sizeable cuts, the human services have suffered disproportionately.

Despite the claim that structural adjustment would rapidly solve the debt problems which plagued countries in the 1980s, many remain heavily indebted and fiscal crises continue to characterize the global economy today. In addition, efforts to promote a vigorous capitalist ethos in the developing world have not produced the desired result. Although there are significant variations between countries and regions, it is widely accepted that the incidence of poverty has risen and that inequalities have become much more marked. In some parts of the South, and particularly in Africa, health, literacy and other social conditions have deteriorated. Despite the significant gains that had been made in raising standards of living in many countries in the 1950s and 1960s, poverty and deprivation are again widespread. It should be pointed out that these conclusions are disputed by many neo-liberal economists and, indeed, by IMF staff themselves, who insist that the situation is not as bad as has been claimed (Gupta et al., 2000).

As the international community has become aware of the resurgence of poverty and deprivation, pressures have been placed on the International Monetary Fund and the World Bank to address the problem. The response, primarily from the World Bank, has been to establish what are known as social funds. Social funds were originally created under World Bank auspices in countries subjected to stringent structural adjustment programmes, and they were intended to alleviate the high rates of unemployment and deprivation caused by public expenditure reductions. One of the first social funds was established in Bolivia in 1987. Known as the *Fondo Social de Emergencia* (Emergency Social Fund) it provided temporary relief to public-sector workers who were laid off as a result of the structural adjustment policies imposed on the country. Although financed directly by the World Bank, it should be noted that the costs of this programme must eventually be repaid by the Bolivian government through normal lending arrangements. Since the creation of the Bolivian fund, social funds have been created in many more countries (Fumo et al., 2000).

By creating social funds, governments are able to secure quick access to credit for poverty reduction and other development purposes. The funds are usually independent of government agencies. They do not normally implement projects themselves but instead provide resources to non-profit and community groups. Originally intended to create short-term employment in public works programmes, they have expanded their activities, and today many are more concerned with infrastructure development than the alleviation of poverty. Indeed, in many countries, they now provide resources for the construction of roads, water supplies, clinics and other facilities. In heavily indebted countries, they are the major source of funding for social projects, but in others they complement mainstream government programmes (Fumo et al., 2000).

There are major variations in the ways social funds operate in different countries but they are characterized by their autonomy and independence from mainline government agencies. Under the influence of neo-liberal ideology, government agencies are regarded as rigid, inefficient and wasteful. Since the funds usually operate independently of government, it is claimed that they are free of cumbersome regulations and bureaucratic management procedures. Futhermore, they are believed to be particularly flexible, innovative and responsive to community needs. Because they provide substantial resources for non-governmental organizations, they are understandably popular in development circles today. But, despite the positive image they enjoy, few systematic evaluations of their impact have been undertaken and it is not self-evident that they are as effective as their proponents claim (Fumo et al., 2000). Indeed, even staff at the IMF concede that the new safety net programmes introduced in countries under structural adjustment have faced difficulties and that the results have been uneven (Gupta et al., 2000). As has been noted already, they have had a negative effect on government human service programmes, especially in low-income countries. On the other hand, some governments are so satisfied with their performance that they now fund their activities directly.

This is the case in higher-income Latin American nations where social funds are substantially financed by national governments with only a small proportion of their revenues coming from donors such as the World Bank.

While it may seem ironic that social funds now provide resources to respond to the social problems that were actually caused by structural adjustment programmes, the situation is exacerbated by the fact that resources allocated to these funds and the programmes they sponsor are not integrated with government human service agencies. In most countries, social funds are tightly controlled by international lenders and often new agencies have been created specifically to disburse these funds, bypassing established government human service agencies and their professional social work staff. As can be imagined, this has demoralized the staff and, together with budgetary reductions, human service provisions have deteriorated. It is particularly unfortunate that efforts to promote a developmental approach in social work and the human services have been impeded by these events.

While structural adjustment and the creation of social funds have contributed to the expansion of the non-profit sector in the developing countries, they are not the only reason for the growth of voluntary activity. Indeed, traditional voluntary associations predated the introduction of religious and secular philanthropy during colonial times, and after independence many more formally constituted voluntary organizations emerged. International non-governmental organizations played an important role in supporting the creation of local voluntary organizations concerned with development activities, and in time donor governments began to fund their operations directly. This was partly because international donors became increasingly frustrated with government human service agencies, which they felt were not functioning effectively and, to make matters worse, wastage and even the misappropriation of funds had become a problem in some parts of the world. As they realized that government human service organizations were unable to deliver effective services, international donors increasingly turned to the non-profit sector, and began to fund local voluntary organizations to implement a range of human service programmes. After social funds were established, non-profit organizations became the preferred vehicle by which international aid would be disbursed.

However, the use of voluntary organizations to provide social services in the South has not been an unrivalled success. Despite the claim that the voluntary sector is able to avoid the bureaucratization and rigidity of government, and that it is more innovative and responsive to local needs, there is a great deal of evidence to show that bureaucratization and unresponsiveness are not the sole prerogative of government (Edwards and Hulme, 1992). Voluntary agencies can be inefficient, sectarian and exclusive in their approach and they can also be wasteful of resources. The problem of duplication and poor service coordination has been documented for many years. Another problem is that contracting with international donors has weakened their entrepreneurial edge. Instead of being innovative and responsive, many have become dependent on international aid and now serve the interests of international donors rather than the poor. This has led to a great deal of frustration, and in some cases their role as autonomous, vibrant agencies for development has been undermined (Hulme and Edwards, 1997). Similar problems have been encountered in the North where voluntary organizations are also heavily dependent on government for funds. Many are also finding that their ability to function autonomously and to be innovative and responsive is being impeded by the demands of contracting (Harris and Rochester, 2001).

On the other hand, few would deny that they can be innovative, comparatively inexpensive, democratic and in tune with grassroots sentiment. The issue is not that the voluntary sector is by definition more effective than government, or vice versa. A host of institutional, organizational, funding, leadership and other issues are involved in determining efficiency and the attainment of goals in both public and private organizations. It is for this reason that some believe that greater efforts need to be made to address organization and managerial issues, and that the harmonization of public and private effort within a wider commitment to promote social development is needed (Midgley, 1995).

The challenge of development

It was noted earlier that many nationalist independence leaders supported the expansion of the social services, especially those who had lived and had been educated in the metropolitan countries and were associated with political parties that campaigned for the introduction of comprehensive social welfare programmes in the middle decades of the twentieth century. Many were impressed with the rapid expansion of health, education, housing, social security and human service provisions in Europe after World War II, and while few believed that their own countries could or should become 'welfare states', most accepted the need for increased public expenditures on the social services. They confirmed the trend towards greater government involvement in social welfare which had begun during the waning years of European imperialism and, in many cases, the independence governments authorized the expansion of the colonial social services. This was compatible with international trends. Many international agencies, including the United Nations, the International Labour Organization (ILO), the World Health Organization (WHO) and the United Nations Children's Fund (UNICEF), actively promoted the spread of social services in the South (Healy, 1995).

This trend was also compatible with the belief that the newly independent developing countries would experience rapid economic development through industrialization and economic modernization. As wage employment opportunities in the modern sector of the economy increased, the proportion of the population engaged in subsistence agriculture would decrease; the incidence of poverty would be reduced as the incomes of many more poor families increased. However, industrialization would be accompanied by urbanization, dislocation and the weakening of traditional cultural obligations and networks. For this reason, as some writers (Clifford, 1966; Cockburn, 1980) explained, governments needed to create new social programmes that could supplement and eventually replace traditional welfare institutions. The introduction of modern social services was not, therefore, regarded as an ideological decision but a necessity engendered by changing social and economic conditions.

Although these ideas supported the belief that government involvement in social welfare was compatible with economic development, the issue of how the social services would be funded raised difficult challenges. In the prevailing climate of statism, it was generally assumed that sustained economic development would generate sufficient tax revenues to meet government obligations and, in addition, that international aid programmes as well as commercial borrowing would support government expenditures on a variety of initiatives. However, many economists were cautious, urging political leaders to defer consumption expenditures so that available resources could, as far as possible, be directed towards infrastructure and industrial investments. In this way, modern productive enterprises would expand and generate the revenues government needed to fund its programmes. In addition, they pointed out that as new employment opportunities were created, incomes would rise and the need for government social services would decrease.

This view gained support during the 1950s and 1960s but the pressures on governments to increase social service allocations increased. Most families wanted access to modern health services and they called on governments to expand educational opportunities for their children. In addition, many governments were under pressure to allocate more resources to non-social service programmes. Military allocations increased rapidly in many parts of the world and investments in large projects such as hydroelectric dams and mass irrigation projects were given preference. As borrowing to fund these investments increased, social service allocations were increasingly constrained. Increasingly, ministers and civil servants responsible for the social services were required to justify their budgetary requests in terms of their economic impact. While those in education and health made plausible arguments that allocations in these fields were necessary for economic development, many of those responsible for the human services were unable to offer justifications of this kind. Accordingly, economic planners gave little priority to social welfare programmes which, they believed, made little, if any, contribution to national development.

These developments created new pressures on social work and the human services to provide a rationale for their programmes that would demonstrate their relevance to national development efforts. It has already been pointed out that most social administrators and social workers were ignorant of these issues or unresponsive to the challenge. But the issue was not entirely neglected and, as Midgley (1994a, 1995, 1996a) has shown, the rudiments of a developmental approach were already being formulated in the late 1940s by social workers in West Africa, who expanded the scope of human services to address rural social needs, not through casework but through literacy training and eventually a variety of programmes which subsequently became known as community development. Later, as already observed above, the term 'social development' was introduced to connote efforts by social work and human services staff to promote progressive social change (Midgley, 1994a, 1995).

However, it took many years before these ideas became widely known and were widely implemented. This is surprising because both the British government and the United Nations have actively promoted the social development approach since the 1950s. The British encouraged the adoption of social development throughout the Commonwealth and, subsequently, the United Nations expended a great deal of effort to spread this approach. In 1968, the organization hosted an important international meeting in New York of government ministers responsible for social welfare where the issue of developmental social welfare was discussed (United Nations, 1969). Although developmental forms of social welfare were introduced in some parts of the South, such as the Philippines and India, social development remains an ideal rather than practical reality in many countries. The fact that the term 'social development' is now widely used in social work and the human services, does not mean that social development has been universally adopted.

One reason for this state of affairs is the retrenchment of human services programmes in many developing countries. As was noted earlier, indebtedness and the imposition of structural adjustment programmes have severely curtailed government human services. But this is also due to the perpetuation of a traditionalist approach to social welfare which continues to emphasize the provision of remedial services within the context of a residual approach that limits government involvement to providing services to the most conspicuously needy groups. Another factor is a lack of clarity about what a developmentalist approach should involve (Midgley, 1996b).

The issue of developmental social welfare has also been raised in social work circles. As was indicated earlier, social work has historically been preoccupied with remedial practice not only in the industrial nations but in the developing countries of the South, and indeed some social workers believe that it is not the profession's role to engage in activities that promote economic development. This position has been criticized by other social workers such as Khinduka (1971), a respected social work educator from India, who criticized social work's lack of commitment to development, pointing out that its emphasis on social treatment was inappropriate in societies marked by mass poverty, deprivation and inequality. He urged the adoption of new forms of practice that would promote economic and social development. However, 20 years later Indian writers such as Bose (1992) were still complaining about the lack of a developmental perspective in social work practice in the country.

Since then, numerous scholars have sought to identify and promote developmental forms of social work practice (Hollister, 1977; Paiva, 1977, 1982; Omer, 1979; Jones and Pandey, 1981; Meinert and Kohn, 1987; Billups, 1994; Lowe, 1995; Midgley, 1996a, 1996b, 1997). Many other organizations concerned with social development have also made a major contribution to the formulation and adoption of a developmental approach. The Inter-University Consortium for International Social Development has effectively promoted social development ideas in the academic world, and through its conferences, workshops and journal, these ideas are now being more widely disseminated. The United Nations has also redoubled its efforts to promote social development not only in the South but also around the world. Although the United Nations had promoted the spread of social development and the adoption of community development in the 1950s, the ascendancy of neo-liberalism in the 1980s, undermined these efforts. The 1995 World Summit was an attempt to reassert the importance of social development (United Nations, 1996). Although the Summit has not resulted in the adoption of policies and programmes that have resolved the serious problems of poverty and deprivation, social development is back on the agenda. It has also been more widely adopted in social work and human services programmes.

New directions in social work and the human services

As has been shown in this chapter, government human services expanded rapidly in the newly independent countries in the years after World War II. Although missionaries and voluntary organizations were also involved in the field, the non-profit sector was small and human services expansion was largely controlled and directed by government. It was generally accepted that the State would be responsible for social welfare. It was also intended that professionally qualified social workers would be recruited on a large scale to provide services, manage programmes and guide the development of the non-profit sector. In this way, they would ensure that the welfare of the population was enhanced.

Despite the prevailing climate of optimism that characterized these developments, it has been shown that the human services faced numerous challenges. They provided limited and temporary assistance to the most needy groups of people in urban areas and, instead of promoting the well-being of the population as a whole, they were primarily concerned with alleviating the most conspicuous urban social problems. The use of inappropriate and costly interventions was also a major problem. Social work was primarily engaged in remedial practice and perpetuated a residual approach to social welfare that was unsuited to the needs and circumstances of the developing countries. As social work and the human services failed to demonstrate their relevance to development, many governments further reduced their already small budgetary allocations and, as staff became increasingly frustrated, the quality of service declined further.

Resource scarcity, ineffectiveness and poor quality of service in many countries prompted some international donors to turn to the non-profit sector to provide social services. With indebtedness and the imposition of structural adjustment programmes in many parts of the South, government human service programmes have been further retrenched. However, the growing engagement of the non-profit sector has not solved the problems facing the public sector. Despite claims that the non-profit sector is by definition more efficient, innovative and responsive, many of the challenges facing government human service programmes also affect the non-profit sector. The claim that the non-profit sector will effectively cope with human need has not been realized. Nevertheless, just as the prevalence of statist ideology in the mid-twentieth century legitimated and supported government responsibility for social welfare, so the influence of a neo-liberal market ideology now justifies non-profit engagement, the creation of social funds and the increasing use of the market to solve societal problems.

The need for new approaches that are less propelled by ideology and are pragmatic and responsive to human need is obvious. There is also an urgent need in the human services field to systematically evaluate interventions and test claims about their effectiveness. While evaluation techniques are now well developed, it is surprising how little high-quality human services evaluation research is actually undertaken. The need to evaluate interventions and identify effective social programmes that work is particularly important because of the persistence of poverty in the developing countries. Effective interventions are also needed to respond to the spread of AIDS, which has been responsible for the deaths of many millions of people, the break-up of families and the large numbers of orphaned and abandoned children in many countries. The human services have also been faced with unprecedented demands arising from wars and civil conflict and the displacement of large numbers of civilians who now live as refugees, dispossessed of their homes and livelihoods.

It is in this context that efforts are being redoubled to reinvigorate social work and the human services and to enhance their capacity to respond to these and other problems. The problems of urban bias and inappropriateness, and the need for cost-effective interventions, are now much more widely recognized. It is also recognized that the statist assumptions which legitimated the expansion of government human services programmes in the 1950s and 1960s needs to be reformulated to accommodate a pluralistic approach which incorporates and harmonizes State, traditional, community and market responses to human need. Indeed, a significant shift in emphasis from a State-centred human service approach to a more pluralistic system has already taken place. Future policy formulation will need to institutionalize this pluralism. However, this also requires that neo-liberal pressures to totally abolish State intervention and marketize the social services in social welfare be resisted.

Also relevant is the role of the indigenous or non-formal welfare system, which, as was noted earlier, has long been neglected by social workers and social administrators. The prediction that the traditional welfare system would weaken under the pressures of industrialization and modernization has not been fulfilled and continues to meet the needs of many individuals and families in both the developing and industrial countries. Much more needs to be done to investigate the non-formal sector, assess its strengths and deficiencies and identify ways of incorporating traditional welfare institutions with modern statutory provision. The academic literature on this topic is now quite extensive. In fact, some of the first studies of the operation of the non-formal system go back decades when scholars such as Gilbert (1976) reported on communal grain storage in West Africa and Little (1965) examined the role of grassroots organizations in low-income communities in African cities. Since then, many more case studies, which show that traditional welfare institutions have great potential to complement statutory provisions, have been published. However, they also show that the tendency to assume that traditional institutions can cope with the pressing social problems facing poor people in the South today is shortsighted. De Bruijn's (1994) account of how traditional family and community responses in the drought-ridden Sahelian region of Africa simply cannot cope with the problems of falling agricultural incomes, and an increase in malnutrition and ill-health is salutary. However, despite a great deal of discussion in the literature, few practical examples of the successful integration of formal and non-formal interventions have been provided. This is equally true in the field of social security.

Nevertheless, attempts have been made in some countries to link the traditional welfare sector to modern human service programmes. One example is *zakat*, which several Islamic governments have incorporated into their formal statutory human services system. Midgley (1994b) reports that in 1962 the government of Saudi Arabia mandated that a half of the *zakat* contribution be paid to support the country's public social assistance programme while the remaining half could be allocated as the donor saw fit. It seems that several other Islamic governments have introduced similar provisions. Perhaps the most important is Pakistan which, during the administration of General Zia ul-Haq, enacted legislation that permits the government's State Bank to deduct *zakat* payments from private bank accounts and allocate the funds to a Federal Zakat Fund. The Fund, in turn, distributes these funds to a variety of organizations including 39,000 local *zakat* committees that provide assistance to needy people. Although it is thought that more than a million needy people are assisted, Weiss (2002) notes that there is an extreme reluctance among the general population to pay *zakat* in this way. Yet in other Islamic countries, governments have created independent organizations to which *zakat* payments are made on a voluntary basis. Organizations of this kind function well in the Gulf States and in Malaysia where each of the State governments has an Islamic Council responsible for the distribution of these donations (Weiss, 2002).

Another example of the integration of traditional and contemporary statutory welfare provisions comes from the State of Sabah in Malaysia which has abolished the relatives' responsibility requirement of its social assistance programme (Amin, 1980). Although most social assistance programmes do not pay benefits if claimants have relatives who can provide support, this requirement has been abrogated and social assistance is now issued to reward relatives who agree to care for needy kin. However, the policy does not apply to the children of elderly claimants, who are expected to care for their parents. Singapore and China have enacted statutes that impose criminal penalties on those who fail to carry out these obligations. Another proposal is to use government resources to support non-formal social security cooperatives such as rotating credit associations and funeral societies that exist in many poor urban communities in the South. By registering these associations, providing training and technical assistance as well as credit, their social security activities could be strengthened

(Midgley, 1994b). Although current pressures for the retrenchment and privatization of government human services programmes impede the implementation of policy innovations of this kind, they could enhance relevance and coverage.

Greater efforts to implement a developmental approach in social work and the human services have also been made. As was noted earlier, the basic elements of a developmental approach were identified by social workers in West Africa in the 1940s and these were implemented in the form of community interventions that not only sought to meet local social needs but, at the same time, attempted to promote local economic development. These efforts were promoted by the British government in the developing countries of the Commonwealth and they were subsequently popularized by the United Nations and other international organizations (Midgley, 1994a). Although many social administrators and workers remained indifferent, social development ideas are now more widely accepted and much progress has been made in identifying and implementing new forms of developmental social welfare.

This has resulted in the widespread adoption of what Midgley (1996b, 1997, 1999) describes as 'productivist' forms of social work and social welfare. He has shown that in a number of developing countries, traditional remedial child welfare approaches have been augmented by community-based preventive services that not only invest in the human capital of children but enhance social capital as local communities mobilize to create day-care centres and engage in other activities that will promote child and family well-being. In other countries, micro-credit and micro-enterprise programmes have been introduced to facilitate the engagement of poor people in the productive economy and peer lending initiatives that encourage cooperative endeavour are commonplace. Community development activities concerned with local infrastructure investments and local agricultural, trade and industrial enterprises have also proliferated. These programmes have the twin objectives of generating income and enhancing social capital. In addition, community asset development has been supported. While these activities are not a panacea for the pressing social problems facing many poor communities, they are more appropriate than the conventional social service approaches that were previously imported from the North. They also complement national development effort and enhance the relevance of social work and the human services to national development.

These initiatives have been accompanied by a modification of conventional social service strategies. The emphasis on residential care has been replaced by a greater recognition of the role of community care and the utilization of traditional cultural family obligations to provide for needy relatives and kin. Social work educational programmes have become more cognizant of the inappropriateness of Western theory and practice methods and many schools of social work have modified their programmes to introduce curriculum content that recognizes local culture, stresses the unique needs and circumstances of their societies, and promotes the adoption of indigenous practice approaches (Midgley, 2001).

However, while much progress has been made, much more needs to be done. Inappropriate and high-cost forms of provision are still widely used, and more experimentation with developmental interventions are needed. Nor can it be claimed that the social work profession has fully embraced new ideas. While an awareness of the need to confront the pressing problems of poverty, deprivation and injustice has indeed been heightened, the profession is still divided and uncertain about its proper role and mission in the context of development (Midgley, 2001). In addition, resource constraints, managerial inefficiencies, low status and a lack of imaginative and innovative policy-making continue to characterize human service programmes in many parts of the world. Also, as was suggested previously, ways of integrating non-formal and modern human service provisions need to be identified and implemented.

Perhaps the most challenging and interesting development has been the attempt to integrate remedial, preventive and developmental functions in social work and the human services within a holistic, community-based model. This approach makes extensive use of group and community social work approaches, but it does not reject the need for remedial interventions, recognizing that there will always be people with special needs that require these interventions. Although efforts to formulate this approach are still ongoing, both the human services and social work practice have benefited from these ideas. They offer the prospect of redirecting the human services and, in some developing countries, have already done so. They also offer new directions for social work and social welfare in the industrial nations.

Recommended Reading

These books examine various issues in the field of social work and human services in developing countries.

- Midgley, J. (1981) *Professional Imperialism: Social Work in the Third World*. London: Heinemann. In one of the first books to address the challenges facing social work in the developing countries, the author contends that professional social work is a Western invention that was exported to the developing countries where it has failed to accommodate the cultural realities and social and economic needs of these countries. The book urges the adoption of a pragmatic approach that indigenizes social work but, at the same time, recognizes the value of mutual international exchanges.
- Hokenstad, M.C., Khinduka, S.K. and Midgley, J. (eds) (1992) *Profiles in International Social Work*. Washington, DC: NASW Press. Hokenstad, M.C. and Midgley, J. (eds) (1997) *Issues in International Social Work*. Washington, DC: NASW Press. These two books are intended to increase awareness among social workers in the United States of the way their professional colleagues operate in other countries and to inform them of the challenges that social workers face in the international arena.
- Healy, L.M. (2001) *International Social Work: Professional Action in an Interdependent World*. Oxford: Oxford University Press. This wide-ranging book examines many

aspects of professional social work in an international context. It provides an informative and helpful introduction to the way social work and the human services function in many different parts of the world.

- Gray, M. (ed.) (1998) *Developmental Social Work in South Africa*. Cape Town: David Philip. Ngoh Tiong, T. and Methta, K.K. (eds) (2002) *Extending Frontiers: Social Issues and Social Work in Singapore*. Singapore: Eastern Universities Press. These two books are representative of a growing literature about social work in African and Asian countries. They show how professional social workers play a vital role in the human services today. Both books also examine the ways in which social workers are playing an active role in promoting a social development approach.
- Specht, H. and Courtney, M. (1994) *Unfaithful Angels: How Social Work has Abandoned its Mission*. New York: Free Press. This polemical book claims that social workers in the United States have abandoned the profession's formative commitment to work with poor people and that they now function as therapists who cater to the middle class and their petty anxieties. Although the book is concerned with social work practice in the United States, its message has relevance to other countries where social workers need to engage more extensively in community and other forms of social work practice that focus specifically on poor people and their needs.

References

Almanzor, A. (1967) 'The profession of social work in the Philippines', in Council on Social Work Education, *An Intercultural Exploration: Universals and Differentials in Social Work Values, Functions and Practice*. New York: Council on Social Work Education, pp. 123–37.

Amin, N.M. (1980) 'Social security protection for the rural population: approaches in Malaysia', *International Social Security Review*, 33: 165–75.

Billups, J. (1994) 'The social development model as an organizing framework for social work practice', in R.G. Meinert, J.T. Pardeck and W.P. Sullivan (eds) *Issues in Social Work: A Critical Analysis*. Westport, CT: Auburn House, pp. 21–38.

Bose, A.B. (1992) 'Social work in India: development roles for a helping profession', in M.C. Hokenstad, S.K. Khinduka and J. Midgley (eds) *Profiles in International Social Work*. Washington, DC: NASW Press, pp. 71–84.

Bossert, A. (1988) 'Formal and informal social security', in F. von Benda-Beckmann, K. von Benda-Beckmann, E. Casino, F. Hirtz, G.R. Woodman and H.F. Zacher (eds) *Between Kinship and the State: Social Security and Law in Developing Countries*. Dordrecht: Foris Publications, pp. 211–28.

Bruce, B.T. (1961) *The Coming of the Welfare State*. London: Batsford.

Chambliss, R. (1954) *Social Thought from Hammurabi to Comte*. New York: Holt, Reinhart and Winston.

Chih-Ming, C. (1988) 'Changing relations between traditional and State social security in Taiwan', in F. von Benda-Beckmann, K. von Benda-Beckmann, E. Casino, F. Hirtz, G.R. Woodman and H.F. Zacher (eds) *Between Kinship and the State: Social Security and Law in Developing Countries*. Dordrecht: Foris Publications, pp. 109–24.

Clifford, W. (1966) *A Primer of Social Casework in Africa*. Nairobi: Oxford University Press.

Cockburn, C. (1980) 'The role of social security in development', *International Social Security Review*, 33: 337–58.

Cumper, G. (1972) *Survey of Social Legislation in Jamaica*. Mona: Institute for Social and Economic Research, University of the West Indies.

de Bruijn, M. (1994) 'The Sahelian crisis and the poor: the role of Islam in social security among Fulbe Pastoralists, Central Mali', *Focaal*, 22/23: 47–64.

de Schweinitz, K. (1943) *England's Road to Social Security*. Philadelphia, PA: University of Pennsylvania Press.

Edwards, M. and Hulme, D. (1992) *Making a Difference: NGOs and Development in a Changing World*. London: Earthscan.

Fumo, C., de Haan, A., Holland, J. and Kanji, N. (2000) *Social Funds: Effective Instruments to Support Local Action for Poverty Reduction?* London: Department for International Development.

Garber, R. (1997) 'Social work education in international context: current trends and future directions', in M.C. Hokenstad and J. Midgley (eds) *Issues in International Social Work*. Washington, DC: NASW Press, pp. 159–71.

Gilbert, N. (1976) 'Alternative forms of social protection for developing countries', *Social Security Review*, 50 (4): 363–87.

Gupta, S., Clements, B., McDonald, C. and Schiller, C. (2000) 'The IMF and the poor', in R. Halvorson-Quevedo and H. Schneider (eds) *Waging the War on Global Poverty: Strategies and Case Studies*. Paris: OECD, pp. 89–111.

Hardiman, M. and Midgley, J. (1989) *The Social Dimensions of Development: Social Policy and Planning in the Third World*, revd edn. Aldershot: Gower.

Harris, M. and Rochester, C. (eds) (2001) *Voluntary Organizations and Social Policy in Britain: Perspectives on Change and Choice*. New York: Palgrave.

Hasan, N. (1965) *Social Security in the Framework of Economic Development*. Aligarh: Aligarh Muslim University Press.

Healy, L.M. (1995) 'International social welfare: organizations and activities', in R. Edwards et al. (eds) *Encyclopedia of Social Work*, 19th edn. Washington, DC: NASW Press, pp. 1499–510.

Hollister, C.D. (1977) 'Social work skills for social development', *Social Development Issues*, 1 (1): 9–16.

Hulme, D. and Edwards, M. (1997) *NGOs, States and Donors: Too Close for Comfort?* London: Macmillan.

Jones, J. and Pandey, R. (eds) (1981) *Social Development: Conceptual, Methodological and Policy Issues*. New York: St Martin's Press.

Kendall, K. (2000) *Social Work Education: Its Origins in Europe*. Alexandria, VA: Council on Social Work Education.

Khinduka, S.K. (1971) 'Social work in the Third World', *Social Service Review*, 45 (2): 62–73.

Landa Jocano, F. (1980) *Social Work in the Philippines: A Historical Overview*. Manila: New Day Publishers.

Leliveld, A. (1995) *Social Security in Developing Countries: Operations and Dynamics of Social Security Mechanisms in Rural Swaziland*. Amsterdam: Thesis Publishers.

Little, K. (1965) *West African Urbanization: A Study of Voluntary Associations in Social Change*. Cambridge: Cambridge University Press.

Livingstone, A. (1969) *Social Policy in Developing Countries*. London: Routledge and Kegan Paul.

Lowe, G.R. (1995) 'Social development', in R. Edwards et al. (eds) *Encyclopedia of Social Work*, 19th edn. Washington, DC: National Association of Social Workers, pp. 2168–72.

Lubove, R. (1965) *The Professional Altruist: The Emergence of Social Work as a Career*. Cambridge, MA: Harvard University Press.

Mair, L. (1944) *Welfare in the British Colonies*. London: Royal Institute of International Affairs.

Meinert, R.G. and Kohn, E. (1987) 'Towards operationalization of social development concepts', *Social Development Issues*, 10 (3): 4–18.

Mesa-Lago, C. (1978) *Social Security in Latin America*. Pittsburgh, PA: University of Pittsburgh Press.

Midgley, J. (1981) *Professional Imperialism: Social Work in the Third World*. London: Heinemann.

Midgley, J. (1984) 'Social assistance: an alternative form of social protection in developing countries', *International Social Security Review*, 84: 247–64.

Midgley, J. (1994a) 'Defining social development: historical trends and conceptual formulations', *Social Development Issues*, 16 (3): 3–19.

Midgley, J. (1994b) 'Social security policy in developing countries: integrating State and traditional systems', *Focaal*, 22/23 (1): 219–30.

Midgley. J. (1995) *Social Development: The Developmental Perspective in Social Welfare*. Thousand Oaks, CA: Sage.

Midgley, J. (1996a) 'Involving social work in economic development', *International Social Work*, 39 (1): 13–25.

Midgley, J. (1996b) 'Social work and social development: challenge to the profession', *Journal of Applied Social Science*, 21 (1): 7–14.

Midgley, J. (1997) 'Social work and international social development: promoting a developmental perspective in the profession', in M.C. Hokenstad and J. Midgley (eds) *Issues in International Social Work*. Washington, DC: NASW Press, pp. 11–26.

Midgley, J. (1999) 'Growth, redistribution and welfare: towards social investment', *Social Service Review*, 77 (1): 3–21.

Midgley, J. (2001) 'Issues in international social work: resolving critical debates in the profession', *Journal of Social Work*, 1 (1): 21–35.

Nagpaul, H. (1972) 'The diffusion of American social work education to India', *International Social Work*, 15 (1): 13–17.

Omer, S. (1979) 'Social development', *International Social Work*, 22 (3): 11–26.

Paiva, F.J.X. (1977) 'A conception of social development', *Social Service Review*, 51 (2): 327–36.

Paiva, F.J.X. (1982) 'The dynamics of social development and social work', in D.S. Sanders (ed.) *The Developmental Perspective in Social Work*. Manoa: University of Hawaii Press, pp. 1–11.

Salamon, L. (1995) *Partners in Public Service: Government–Nonprofit Relations in the Modern Welfare State*. Baltimore, MD: Johns Hopkins University Press.

United Nations (1969) *Proceedings of the International Conference of Ministers Responsible for Social Welfare*. New York: United Nations.

United Nations (1996) *Report of the World Summit for Social Development*, Copenhagen, 6–12 March 1995. New York: United Nations.

von Benda-Beckmann, F. and von Benda-Beckmann, K. (1994) 'Coping with insecurity', *Focaal*, 22/23: 7–31.

von, Benda-Beckmann, F. von, Benda-Beckmann, K. Bryde, B.O. and Hirtz, F. (1988) 'Introduction: between kinship and the State', in F. von Benda-Beckmann, K. von Benda-Beckmann, E. Casino, F. Hirtz, G.R. Woodman and H.F. Zacher (eds) *Between Kinship and the State: Social Security and Law in Developing Countries*. Dordrecht: Foris Publications, pp. 7–20.

Weiss, H. (2002) 'Zakat and the question of social welfare', in H. Weiss (ed.) *Social Welfare in Muslim Societies in Africa*. Stockholm: Nordiska Afrikainstitutet, pp. 7–38.

8 SOCIAL SECURITY POLICIES AND PROGRAMMES

Summary

This chapter discusses the role of social security in development and addresses a number of important issues being debated in the field today. It is divided into five sections. The first section provides a definition of social security, paying attention to different types of social security schemes. The second section traces the historical evolution of social security. It shows that, although social security has roots in the institutionalized obligations to assist those in need that are found in many cultures, modern-day social security programmes first emerged in Europe and were subsequently established in many developing countries through the efforts of international agencies such as the International Labour Organization. The next section examines the current features of social security, paying attention to trends in coverage and the impact of social security programmes on poverty. The fourth section of the chapter discusses a number of key issues in social security, pointing out that social security today faces a number of challenges. These include administrative and fiscal challenges, the need to address social security's contribution to development, and the issue of coverage and inequality. The final section examines the question of privatization, showing that pressures to privatize social security and particularly public pension programmes are becoming more intense. Drawing on the experiences of several countries, the prospects that privatized social security programmes can contribute to poverty eradication are explored. The chapter concludes with a plea for more appropriate forms of social security that enhance development effort and provide social protection for the population as a whole.

Background

Social security is a key component of social policy. This is particularly true in the industrial countries, where social security programmes consume a large proportion of the government's budget. In these countries, social security programmes usually cover the whole population, providing a comprehensive range of income maintenance and support benefits such as retirement pensions, child benefits and unemployment insurance. Many developing countries have also introduced statutory social security programmes of one kind or another but, compared to the industrial nations, social security in these countries is not as extensive or comprehensive. Nevertheless, social security is quite well developed in some parts of the South such as Latin America. Indeed, countries such as Chile, Argentina and Uruguay established social security programmes in the early decades of the twentieth century, well before social security was introduced in the United States.

During the latter half of the twentieth century, social security programmes were also created in many other developing countries. Like the other social services, social security expanded at the time that many developing countries secured independence from European imperial rule. It was believed that these countries would undergo rapid industrialization and that employment in the industrial sector would increase. Accordingly, it was thought that social security would be needed to protect workers from the contingencies of modern life. However, while most developing countries today have some form of statutory social security, this does not mean that the majority of the population is protected by these programmes. Unlike the industrial countries, where most people are covered by social security, many hundreds of millions of people in the developing countries have no social security protection at all. This is because social security still caters primarily to those in regular wage employment, or to those living in urban areas. Generally, those who work in agriculture or in the so-called urban informal sector are excluded.

The limited coverage of social security programmes in developing countries is a major issue in social policy today. The issue of how these programmes can be modified so that they cover a larger proportion of the population is currently receiving attention. A related issue is how social security can function more effectively to contribute to poverty eradication. Although it was previously assumed that social security would reduce the incidence of poverty, the lack of coverage as well as the way social security programmes currently function, limits their effectiveness in combating poverty.

Another question is how social security programmes can contribute more directly to promoting economic development. While social security in the industrial countries is not intended to promote economic development, but rather to maintain income and provide support to those in need, some writers believe that social security in the South should contribute positively to development. Also relevant is the issue of inequality. Social security programmes in many developing countries currently favour some groups in society such as civil servants and urban industrial workers. Some commentators think this is unfair, and believe that social security should instead concentrate resources on the poorest groups. Another problem is that social security programmes have conventionally been targeted at male industrial workers and women have been disadvantaged.

These issues have injected a strong ideological flavour into debates about social security. Perhaps the most ideological of all is the question of social security's privatization. Today, the previously uncontentious belief that governments should provide social security for all citizens has been challenged by thinkers on the political right, and social security has become an ideological arena in which disagreements about the role of government in social welfare are now frequently vented. Many experts now believe that social security should be privatized, and in some parts of the world, such as Latin America, government social security programmes have indeed been replaced by commercial provisions. These issues will be examined in more depth in this chapter, which will show that social security forms an integral part of wider debates about social policy and development.

The definition of social security

As in other social policy fields, it is very difficult to provide a precise definition of social security. The term is used loosely and means different things in different countries. For example, in the United States, the term refers exclusively to the federal government's old-age retirement and disability insurance programme. It is not used to connote the country's unemployment insurance or social assistance schemes. Unlike other countries, social assistance in the United States is known as 'welfare'. On the other hand, in Britain social security is defined more broadly to refer to all income support and maintenance programmes, including old-age retirement insurance, social assistance for low-income families and universal child allowances. The term is also used in this way in many other countries. However, in Latin America, social security also refers to insurance-funded medical care and, in some cases, the provision of social and recreational services to the members of social security schemes.

The problem of definition is compounded by the argument that the term social security should not refer only to government programmes but that it should include the many different ways people seek to protect their livelihoods (Burgess and Stern, 1991; von Benda-Beckmann and von Benda-Beckmann, 1994). In many developing countries, non-statutory forms of income protection play a very important role. In these countries, many millions of people rely exclusively on traditional supports when faced with economic difficulties. Although these non-formal supports are very important in understanding social security, their inclusion broadens the meaning of the term considerably and makes it difficult to summarize the field. For this reason, the term will be used primarily in this chapter to connote government programmes that provide cash payments, known as income benefits, to defined groups of people. Although social security has been used to provide a variety of social services, the term will be used primarily to focus on income maintenance and support programmes. However, non-formal social security institutions will also be discussed, and the issue of how formal, statutory and non-formal traditional systems can be integrated with the modern, statutory system, will be raised.

The close association between social security and income is revealed by terms such as 'income protection' and 'income security' that are often used as synonyms for social security. Generally, income benefits provided through social security may be classed as either *income support* or *income maintenance*. Income support refers to cash payments made by the government to enhance the incomes of groups of people such as low-paid workers or families with children. The universal child benefits or family allowances provided by many European governments are a good example of income support programmes. Schemes of this kind have also been established in Francophone African countries. Another example comes from Hong Kong, where the government pays small, regular benefits to all elderly people irrespective of their economic status, believing that all elderly people should be given additional help.

Income maintenance refers to cash payments made by the government to groups of people whose incomes have been interrupted or terminated because of what are known as *contingencies*. Contingencies include the death of the family breadwinner, an accident or illness, unemployment, retirement or disability. By providing a cash benefit, social security programmes seek to prevent affected workers and their families from becoming destitute. Income maintenance benefits are usually higher than those paid in the form of income support, but they are usually insufficient to ensure that the recipient can maintain an adequate standard of living. For this reason, income maintenance benefits must often be supplemented by other income sources.

Although income maintenance programmes are designed primarily for people who have regular jobs and steady earnings, they may also cover those who are self-employed. In the industrial countries, self-employed people are usually protected by social security even though protection may be restricted to certain contingencies. In the developing countries, income maintenance programmes are generally restricted to those in regular wage employment while those who work in agriculture and the informal sector are usually excluded.

Income maintenance benefits may be paid temporarily to assist those facing short-term financial difficulties or they may be paid on a long-term basis. This is the case with elderly people who have retired or disabled people who are unable to work. Income maintenance benefits may also be paid to people who have never been able to work such as those who were born with a mental or physical disability.

Although many different definitions of social security have been formulated over the years, the definition offered by the International Labour Organization (ILO, 1984) is perhaps the most comprehensive and widely used. Based on various international conventions, the ILO defines social security as: '... the protection which society provides for its members through a series of public measures against the economic and social distress that otherwise would be caused by the stoppage or substantial reduction of earnings resulting from sickness, maternity, employment injury, invalidity and death.' (1984: 3). While this definition does not cover all the contingencies and services provided through social security around the world, its emphasis on income protection, statutory basis and governmental responsibility captures the essence of the term.

Types of social security

Income support and income maintenance are provided through five different types of social security programmes. These are social insurance, social assistance, provident funds, employer mandates and social allowances. Although these different approaches are administered and funded in different ways, they may be used to meet the same type of income need. For example, the income needs of elderly people have been addressed through all five approaches. Many European governments use social insurance to protect the elderly, but in India, the government uses the social assistance approach for this purpose. As indicated earlier, the government of Hong Kong uses the social allowance approach and, until recently, the government of China used the employer mandate approach to require its State-owned enterprises to provide pensions to retired workers. Provident funds are used to provide retirement benefits in many developing countries.

Social insurance is funded from special payroll taxes known as contributions that are levied on workers and their employers. Often, governments supplement these contributions. The revenues raised by social insurance contributions are pooled and may be placed in a trust fund administered by a special government agency. The accumulated revenues are invested and the income is used to pay benefits. However, in most industrial countries, trust funds have not been maintained and revenues are immediately transferred to pay benefits. In this case, the social security programme is described as a pay-as-you-go system. In the former case, it is known as a funded system. To qualify for social insurance benefits, claimants (or their dependants) must have paid contributions for a specified period of time. They must also meet the specific qualifying condition for receiving benefits such as those that apply in the case of illness, accident, invalidity and retirement.

In the industrial nations, social insurance is widely used to provide old-age retirement, sickness, invalidity, unemployment and survivors' benefits. Most people are covered by social insurance in these countries. As noted earlier, coverage is still very limited in the developing countries of the South. This is partly because a relatively small proportion of the population is in regular wage employment and, for this reason, resources to fund social insurance on a larger scale are inadequate. However, because some political leaders and policy-makers reject the need for government involvement in income protection, political factors are also relevant. In those developing countries that do have social insurance programmes, benefits are usually paid to meet the contingencies of old-age retirement, sickness and employment injury. Unemployment is not usually covered by these programmes. Social insurance benefits are usually paid in cash although, in many countries, particularly in Latin America, the insurance method is also used to provide medical and other services.

Provident funds are similar to social insurance. They are financed by the regular contributions of workers but, unlike social insurance, contributions are not pooled and used to pay benefits to other workers. Each employer has a personal designated account into which contributions are paid. The accumulated amount may be matched by contributions from employers. The total amount accumulated in the account is then invested. When a covered contingency arises, benefits may be withdrawn and used to meet the contingency. Provident funds are primarily used to pay old-age retirement pensions but contingencies such as disability are also covered. In some countries such as Singapore, a portion of the accumulated fund may be withdrawn to purchase a home or educate children (Sherraden, 1997). As will be shown later in this chapter, countries that have privatized their social insurance programmes have introduced a variant of the provident fund to provide retirement income protection. However, unlike provident funds, these new privatized provisions are managed by commercial firms rather than government agencies.

Social assistance is funded from general government revenues and is directed at people in designated categories of need whose incomes fall below a defined minimum. Usually, those who are designated as qualifying for social assistance include poor women with children who have been widowed or deserted and who have no means of support. Indigent elderly people and poor people with disabilities are also protected by these schemes. Social assistance payments are made to those who fall within these designated categories and pass an income or 'means test' as it is known. The means test determines whether claimants have assets or alternative sources of income, and whether they qualify for benefits. Historically, social assistance has been denied to the able-bodied and particularly to able-bodied men, but in some countries social assistance may be provided to both men and women who are unable to find employment. Benefits are usually paid in cash but often food rations, travel vouchers, blankets, housing subsidies, prosthetics and other provisions are also given.

Employer mandates are designed to meet specified contingencies through legal mandates which the government imposes on employers. These programmes are, therefore, funded by employers. Although employer mandates provide protection against various contingencies, the most common contingency covered by these programmes is employment injury. The term 'workmen's compensation' is often used to refer to employer mandate programmes that compensate employees for injuries sustained at work. However, mandates requiring employers to pay sickness benefits and provide paid maternity leave are also common. In some countries, employers are required to provide old-age retirement and disability benefits as well.

Because many employers default on meeting their obligations, the employer mandate approach is not regarded as a very effective form of social security. Many social security experts believe that social insurance is a preferable method of providing income protection and they often recommend that employer mandates be replaced with social insurance. However, in some countries, a hybrid employer mandate has emerged by which governments require employers to insure themselves with a private carrier which then meets the claims of workers. In some countries, employers are required to insure themselves with a government agency which meets these claims. Although this approach is similar to social insurance, the costs of the programme are met by employers and not by payroll taxes imposed on workers.

Social allowances are also known as 'demogrant' or universal schemes. This is because they cover specified demographic groups such as children or the elderly irrespective of their incomes or assets. They are funded directly out of government revenues and are paid to those who fall within the designated category.

Social allowances are based on the principle that those who have special income needs arising from old age or large family size should be assisted. Advocates of child allowances believe that families with children have greater demands on their resources than families with no children. For this reason, they should receive an income benefit to help meet their additional needs. Many European countries provide child benefits or family allowances, as these programmes are also known, to all families with children irrespective of their incomes.

The evolution of social security

Although accounts of the history of social security often begin with the creation of the first social insurance programmes by Chancellor Otto von Bismarck in Germany in the late nineteenth century (Rimlinger, 1971; Handel, 1982), social security is, in fact, very old. Early forms of social security can be traced back to hunter-gatherer societies where cultural obligations to care for needy relatives and members of the community were well established. These obligations are still embedded in most cultures, particularly in rural communities. Even in the industrial countries, where individualism, population mobility and other factors have undermined familial obligations, non-formal social supports are still widely used. However, it is generally believed that non-formal supports are not as strong or effective in the industrial countries as they are in the South where traditional cultures continue to exert a strong influence.

Many examples of the role of traditional culture in providing assistance to needy people can be given. These non-formal or traditional welfare institutions were discussed in Chapter 7 of this book and, as was pointed out, there is much more interest in how these institutions function and how they can be linked to modern, statutory services. This issue is being examined by both human services and social security policy-makers. It is now more widely recognized that, despite the pressures of modernization, non-formal systems continue to function in many parts of the world, providing assistance and support to millions of people. Many academic researchers and social security experts recognize the need for more innovative policy thinking about how these institutions can be strengthened and integrated with the modern, statutory welfare system.

Although the beginnings of modern-day social security are often traced to Germany in the late nineteenth century, some historians go back to the reign of Queen Elizabeth I of England who, in 1601, consolidated a number of statutes dealing with beggars and vagrants (de Schweinitz, 1943). They also dealt with poor relief. The Elizabethan statute was known as the Poor Law and, as was shown in Chapter 7, it created a nationwide system of poor relief and labour mobility control which was operated by the local parishes and funded by a special tax known as the 'poor rate'. Local administrative responsibility for the programme was assigned to each parish. The parish appointed an official known as the overseer of the poor who collected the 'poor rate' or tax that was used to fund the system and paid benefits to needy people. He was also responsible for punishing beggars and expelling vagrants. Despite its punitive provisions, the Poor Law laid the foundations for modern-day social assistance programmes not only in Europe but in the overseas territories which were colonized by the English.

The Poor Law was replicated in some of England's North American and Caribbean colonies in the seventeenth century, but it only applied to European settlers and excluded indigenous people. For example, it was noted in Chapter 7 that the Jamaican Poor Law of 1682 catered only to needy English settlers who had become destitute (Midgley, 1984a). Much later, local versions of the Poor Law were enacted in some British colonies such as Cyprus, Mauritius and Hong Kong. The colonial government of Mauritius enacted a Poor Law Ordinance in 1902 to provide temporary relief to deserted wives, widows and to those who became ill or disabled. It also permitted the payment of old-age pensions to the indigent elderly who had no relatives who could support them. Although the colonial government of Mauritius became alarmed at the large numbers of people on poor relief and attempted to curtail the programme, social assistance continued to play a major role in the evolution of social policy in the country. After independence, the programme was augmented by a social assistance child benefit programme designed to alleviate poverty among low-income families (Titmuss et al., 1961). Social assistance was also introduced by some of the states of India to establish an income support programme for the indigent elderly. The first of these programmes was created in Uttar Pradesh in 1957 (Hallen, 1967).

Other types of statutory social security were also introduced into the developing countries during the colonial era, and it is not surprising that they often replicated practices in the metropolitan nations. For example, in the 1950s, social insurance was introduced in many of the African countries ruled by France, and many of these were based directly on metropolitan French legislation (Mouton, 1975). Previously, the Beveridge Report, which facilitated the expansion of social insurance in Britain, had inspired the introduction of social insurance in a number of British colonies (Midgley, 1984b). On the other hand, British colonial officials also encouraged the creation of provident funds, particularly in territories with a small urban, industrial sector (Dixon, 1982, 1993).

Another example of the diffusion of social security to the South is workmen's compensation. Based on the employer mandate approach, workmen's compensation programmes were created in many colonies where industries were emerging. In India, the first workmen's compensation scheme was created in 1923 following agitation by the nascent Indian labour movement (Hallen, 1967). This scheme was based on the original English workmen's compensation statute of 1897. Subsequently, the International Labour Organization (ILO) began to pressure its member-states to adopt its Workmen's Compensation (Accidents) Convention of 1925. The Convention governed workmen's compensation legislation in both the metropolitan countries and the colonies. The ILO has played a major role in promoting the diffusion of social security around the world. Established in Geneva in 1919 at the same time as the League of Nations, the ILO initially focused its efforts on the industrial nations, but after World War II, it actively promoted the adoption of social security in the newly independent developing countries. Although the ILO originally promoted the introduction of employer mandate schemes such as workmen's compensation, the organization subsequently favoured the introduction of social insurance and, in the years following the end of World War II, its staff travelled to many developing countries helping governments to introduce social insurance schemes. Their efforts were most successful in countries where urban industries were already established and where wage employment was expanding. Another organization, the International Social Security Association (ISSA) has also played an important role in promoting social insurance around the world.

Although social insurance was adopted in some developing countries, many poorer developing countries did not introduce insurance-funded programmes. There were exceptions even among some of the higher-income countries, such as Singapore, which preferred to retain its provident fund which had previously been introduced by British colonial officials. While many Anglophone African countries also retained their provident funds, English-speaking Caribbean nations tended to adopt social insurance. Another exception was Communist China, where the employer mandate approach was used instead of social insurance. Here, the government required its State-owned enterprises to provide retirement, employment injury and other benefits to their workers (Dixon, 1981). However, with the closure or privatization of the State-owned enterprises fewer workers are now covered by these schemes and the government is in the process of replacing the employer mandate programme with a combination of social insurance and provident fund savings accounts (Lee, 2000; Chow and Xu, 2001). In Hong Kong, the government chose not to introduce a retirement social insurance programme and instead it created a universal old-age retirement programme which paid a small universal benefit to all elderly people irrespective of their incomes or assets (Tang, 1997).

Several South American countries had already introduced social insurance before the ILO began to promote social insurance in the 1950s and 1960s. As was noted in the introduction to this chapter, southern cone Latin American countries such as Argentina, Chile and Uruguay were early pioneers of social security. However, their approach differed significantly from the ILO model. Instead of having one centralized government agency to administer social insurance for all workers, these countries had separate multiple schemes catering for different occupational groups. Multiple social insurance schemes were established in South American countries, where modern wage employment expanded and where occupational groups were able to organize. Mesa-Lago (1978) has documented the role of different occupational groups which exerted influence on governments to pass legislation that would establish social insurance programmes and protect their interests. Social insurance was first introduced to cover the most influential groups of workers while lower-paid and less influential workers were covered much later. However, by the 1970s, many of these schemes had experienced fiscal and administrative difficulties. These problems provided a convenient reason for governments, such as General Pinochet's military regime in Chile, to privatize the system.

As noted earlier, General Pinochet's government privatized Chile's social security system in 1981. This decision was warmly applauded by those on the political right and by free market economists who believe that privatization will create a highly efficient form of income protection and provide greater choice for those who belong to social security schemes. They also believe that a privatized system will promote economic development. These ideas have been actively promoted by the World Bank (1994), which is critical of government-funded social security programmes. Although privatization has been most enthusiastically pursued in Latin America, where countries such as Argentina, Mexico and Peru have followed Chile's example, the World Bank continues its efforts to promote privatization. These efforts are in direct conflict with the ILO and the International Social Security Association (ISSA) that continues to advocate for the use of government social insurance programmes. The issue of social security privatization will be discussed in more depth at the end of this chapter.

Current features of social security

In a very comprehensive study of contemporary social security trends, Dixon (1999) reported that statutory social security programmes of one kind or another had been established in 172 of the world's 221 countries and territories by the mid-1990s. Although no information could be found for 49 countries and territories, this does not mean that they do not have any social security schemes. Indeed, Dixon reports that information has only recently become available for some very small territories. On the other hand, it is known that some large countries do not have any form of social security protection. These countries are all situated in the South, and most of them are very poor. They include Bhutan, Eritrea, Laos, Mozambique and Angola. Dixon also notes that in some countries that have been devastated by civil conflict, social security programmes have either collapsed or have otherwise been severely retrenched. Examples include Afghanistan, Rwanda and Sierra Leone.

Despite the disruption of social security in some parts of the world, the number of countries with social security has remained relatively stable over the last two decades. There has, in fact, only been a relatively small increase in the numbers of countries with social security since the mid-1980s. Most of this increase has been the result of the break-up of larger national entities such as the Soviet Union and the Trust Territory of the Pacific. Similarly, the number of social security systems negatively affected by political and civil disruption has remained small. Because the majority of the world's nation-states now have some form of statutory social security, it seems that social security has become globally institutionalized.

On the other hand, there are continued pressures to privatize social security programmes. There are also great differences in the types of programmes in operation in different nations, the resources allocated to social security, the proportion of the population protected and the effectiveness of social security. The fact that formal social security arrangements still cater for only a small proportion of the population in many developing countries should be taken into account when the global spread and undoubted achievements of social security are considered.

Dixon (1999) shows that *social insurance* is the dominant and preferred approach to social security today. Only 24 countries that have some form of social security do not have social insurance programmes. The most important of these are Australia and Hong Kong. Both countries have historically relied on social assistance as their primary funding approach. Social insurance dominates in Europe, Latin America and North Africa and the Middle East. However, it is not widely used in sub-Saharan Africa, South Asia or the Pacific. The trend towards privatization in Latin America has resulted in the replacement of social insurance schemes with commercially managed individual accounts.

Social assistance is widely used in many countries of the North as a safety net, providing supplemental protection to those who experience financial difficulties and are not adequately protected by social insurance or whose social insurance benefits are too low to maintain them above the poverty line. Social assistance was also introduced to serve a safety net function in many countries of the South where it catered for destitute people, largely in urban areas. However, because of fiscal and economic difficulties, and the imposition of structural adjustment programmes, many countries in Africa, Asia and Central and South America have severely restricted their social assistance schemes and, in some cases, they have ceased to operate.

Although *employer mandate* programmes are criticized by many social security experts, Dixon reports that they remain popular and are still widely used to protect workers against employment injury, sickness and maternity. After social insurance, the employer mandate is the second most prevalent form of social security. As noted earlier, the most significant recent change in the use of the employer mandate approach has occurred in China where the closure or privatization of the State-owned enterprises has resulted in fewer workers being covered by these schemes. A hybrid social insurance and provident fund approach is being introduced in some of the country's provinces.

Social allowances are not common and are to be found primarily in Europe, and particularly in the Scandinavian welfare states. However, they are very rare in the developing countries of the South. A major exception is Hong Kong which, as was shown previously in this chapter, provides a small social allowance benefit for the elderly (Tang, 1997). Dixon reports that Cyprus and Albania have had social allowance programmes to provide universal child benefits since 1985.

Provident funds were established in many British territories during the colonial period and they continue to function in some Anglophone nations, particularly in Africa. However, a number of them have been converted into social insurance schemes. Examples of countries that have placed provident funds with social insurance include Nigeria, Ghana and Gambia. On the other hand, some countries such as Malaysia and Singapore have opted to retain the provident fund approach. Indeed, the Singapore Central Provident Fund is well established and popular (Sherraden, 1997). Although the creation of commercially managed retirement accounts in Chile and other Latin American countries suggests that the provident fund approach is being expanded in the developing world, it should be remembered that provident funds have historically been managed by government agencies rather than commercial firms. Nevertheless, these privatized retirement funds are in other respects very similar to provident funds.

Current studies of social security such as Dixon's have focused largely on formal, statutory programmes but, as noted earlier, hundreds of millions of people around the world make use of non-formal social welfare institutions to meet their needs. However, as was shown in Chapter 7, there are few examples of how governments have purposefully integrated formal statutory provisions with non-formal, traditional welfare institutions. This observation also applies to social security. In most countries, the traditional social security sector exists independently of the modern, statutory sector. Yet, it is obvious that policy innovations are needed to link the two together in a more coherent way. To realize this goal, more research into how the non-formal system operates and how it affects the lives of ordinary people will be needed. Research is also needed to facilitate the development of policies that can harmonize formal and non-formal provisions. It was noted previously that the integration of the informal and the modern, statutory sector is being discussed by academics and policy-makers concerned with social security and, indeed, social work and the human services today (Midgley, 1994; von Benda-Beckmann and von Benda-Beckmann, 1994; Weiss, 2002).

Trends in social security coverage

The expansion of social security programmes in the developing countries of the South since the middle decades of the last century has unfortunately not been matched by a similar rate of coverage expansion. While many more countries today have some form of social security protection, the proportion of the population covered remains small when compared to the industrial nations. Social insurance, employer mandates and provident funds cater to those in regular wage employment in the modern economy, limiting participation to those who are in regular work and whose contribution record qualifies them for long-term benefits. Although the numbers in regular wage employment in the developing countries today are much greater than before, social security protection remains limited to a relatively small proportion of the population.

Accurate data are not widely available but estimates show that the highest rates of coverage by social insurance programmes are to be found in Latin America where the economically most developed countries of the region's southern cone had achieved coverage rates as high as 79 per cent by the end of the 1980s (Mesa-Lago, 1992). These rates refer to the proportion of the economically active population who are protected by social insurance schemes. However, these rates are exceptional. Other Latin American countries such as Bolivia, Colombia, Ecuador, Guatemala, Nicaragua and Peru had coverage rates of less than 33 per cent, while in the Dominican Republic, El Salvador, Honduras and Paraguay, coverage rates were less than 15 per cent. On the other hand, some small Latin American countries such as Costa Rica have achieved a rate of 68 per cent. Costa Rica is one of a handful of countries that have actively sought to extend coverage to its citizens.

Coverage rates in Africa and Asia are very low. Examining trends in the largest economies in Asia, Mesa-Lago (1992) found that only 8 per cent of the labour force was covered by government social insurance programmes in India, while the comparable figures for Thailand and Indonesia were 10 per cent and 12 per cent respectively. An earlier study undertaken by Thompson (1979) showed similar rates and this suggests that coverage has not expanded significantly since the time his research was published. In Africa, many of the poorer nations had rates as low as 1 per cent. In the economically more developed northern African states, such as Egypt and Tunisia, coverage was still below 25 per cent (Gruat, 1990). A study by Goswami (2002) found that India's three major provident funds, which provide retirement pensions for people in regular wage employment, only covered about 35 million people or 9.5 per cent of the labour force. The vast majority of peasant farmers and landless labourers as well as urban informal sector workers have no social security protection. On the other hand, as will be shown later in this chapter, efforts are being made to extend coverage to these workers through crop insurance and special programmes targeted at workers in the informal sector (Jain, 1999).

It has already been pointed out that the social assistance schemes which were established in many countries of the South are often no longer funded and, where they are, they cater primarily for the urban destitute who know about these schemes and are within the proximity of government offices that can respond to their needs. These programmes continue to operate mostly in higher-income countries in Asia, Latin America and the Middle East but, even here, their coverage is skewed towards urban dwellers. In India, where social assistance pensions have been provided by State governments to the destitute elderly since the 1950s, only between 5 and 10 per cent of the elderly population are covered and benefits are very small (Goswami, 2002). As will be shown, the lack of coverage and inequities in access have unfortunate implications for social security's ability to address the problem of poverty.

Issues in social security

As was suggested in the introduction to this chapter, social security raises many challenging issues, and today the field is a lively and controversial one. However, in the years after World War II, when social security programmes expanded rapidly in different parts of the world, the field was not controversial. Of course, some politicians and economists always opposed the idea that governments should provide income support and maintenance but, in the 1950s and 1960s, their views exerted little influence. It was generally accepted that social security was a desirable characteristic of modern society and a key responsibility of government. The acceptance of social security was shaped by the then prevalent belief that governments should intervene in economic and social affairs to promote the well-being of their citizens. After the suffering experienced by many families during the Great Depression, most people at the time rejected the argument that government should not become involved in social welfare, and that the family, religious organizations and charities should instead be responsible for helping those in need.

As noted earlier in this chapter, the expansion of social security was also encouraged in the developing countries in the years following World War II. Assisted by the ILO and other international agencies, the governments of many developing countries introduced social insurance schemes for workers in industrial enterprises, and in many cases employer mandates and social assistance provisions were expanded. Although it was recognized that resources were too limited to create comprehensive social security programmes similar to those established in the Western 'welfare states', many nationalist independence leaders and their political parties believed that the introduction of social security was compatible with their attempts to industrialize their economies. Many wanted their countries to become modern, advanced States and to introduce the same social programmes that had been established in the industrial nations.

The idea that social security is an integral component of the quest for modernity was supported by some social security experts. They argued that the introduction of social security was necessitated by the process of industrial modernization. Writers such as Cockburn (1980) pointed out that industrialization weakens traditional institutions such as the extended family, which had previously cared for those in need. While the extended family was well equipped to provide for its needy members in pre-industrial societies, this was no longer possible in societies experiencing industrialization. As societies industrialize, workers leave their traditional communities in search of jobs in the modern wage sector. Labour mobility results in the dispersal of family members, the replacement of the extended with the nuclear family, and of the decline in cultural obligations to care for needy kin. As traditional familial supports become less effective, governments are compelled to introduce social security to cater for those who cannot work, or for those whose incomes are interrupted or terminated because of unemployment, sickness, workplace accidents and retirement. Modern social security schemes, Cockburn suggested, are an appropriate response to the problems created by industrialization.

Although it is now generally accepted that industrialization has not had the effect Cockburn and other writers predicted, their ideas reinforced the view that the expansion of social security was necessitated by changing economic and social realities and not by ideological beliefs. Although this confirmed the non-controversial nature of social security, by the 1970s social security policy had become the subject of controversial debates in both academic and political circles. Some economists claimed that social security programmes were not, in fact, compatible with economic modernization but that they had harmed economic development. There was growing evidence of administrative ineffi- ciency, wastage and even corruption in social security programmes. Some social security writers pointed out that social security schemes in many devel- oping countries had not only failed to contribute to poverty eradication but had exacerbated inequalities between those who were covered by these programmes and those who were excluded from social security protection.

These arguments fuelled the growing antipathy towards government involvement in economic and social affairs by thinkers on the political Right, who argued that State intervention had impeded economic and social progress. By the 1980s, when right-wing political leaders such as Mrs Thatcher, President Reagan and General Pinochet had assumed office, the firm foundations on which social security had been based were severely shaken. All three political leaders introduced policies that not only undermined government responsibil- ity for social security in their own countries but had wider and more long- lasting effects. The ideological consensus which previously characterized think- ing about social security has now collapsed and calls for the privatization of social security have become much more common.

Before discussing these developments, those issues that have made social security policy so controversial should be examined. As suggested earlier, these issues relate to the administrative and fiscal challenges facing social security; the question of social security's impact on economic development; and the problem of coverage and inequity in social security. All of these have implica- tions for the all-important question of how social security can contribute to the eradication of poverty and the promotion of social development.

Administrative and fiscal challenges

Although social security programmes expanded rapidly in many developing countries during the 1950s and 1960s, adequate attention was not always given to the difficult management challenges facing those responsible for the adminis- tration of these schemes. Social insurance requires the creation of a system that registers participating firms and their workers, ensures that contributions are properly collected and banked, and that procedures for assessing claims and paying benefits promptly are introduced. Other forms of social security such as employer mandates also require efficient administrative procedures such as ensur- ing compliance among participating firms and arbitrating between employers and claimants. Similarly, the determination of eligibility for social assistance is often cumbersome and time consuming. These and other challenges have to be met to ensure that social security programmes operate efficiently.

There were fiscal challenges as well. The cost of social assistance was high and fiscal constraints often precluded their expansion on a significant scale.

As will be shown, growing debt and structural adjustment programmes exacerbated these pressures. However, the situation with social insurance was different. Because the members of social insurance schemes in many developing countries were young and healthy, many national social insurance agencies received more in contributions than they paid out in benefits and, consequently, they accumulated substantial surpluses. In order to protect the interests of workers, these resources had to be invested conservatively and usually this meant that government bonds were used for this purpose. However, many governments regarded social security surpluses as an easy form of revenue, and placing these revenues in government bonds made them vulnerable to expropriation.

Although international agencies such as the ILO and the International Social Security Association provided technical assistance to social security administrators, administrative and fiscal difficulties posed an ongoing challenge. Some countries coped better with these challenges than others. For example, in Latin America, administrative inefficiencies and fiscal problems appeared to be particularly serious. As was noted earlier, several Latin American countries had established multiple social insurance schemes catering for different occupational groups. Unfortunately, these schemes were often badly managed. Various studies showed that the processing of claims was slow and bureaucratic, and that the rules governing the payment of benefits were so cumbersome and complex that many claimants had to use attorneys to negotiate on their behalf (Wolfe, 1968; Mesa-Lago, 1992). Social security administrators were often appointed to their jobs through political patronage, and corruption was common. Political motives also influenced decisions to increase benefit levels. Unions representing groups of workers participating in a particular social insurance fund often negotiated benefit increases with political parties as a condition for electoral support, and in many cases the costs of these increases were not met by increased contribution rates. Consequently, the costs of administering social insurance programmes in many Latin American countries were high in comparison with other countries, and often social insurance funds overspent their budgets, requiring government subsidies to meet their obligations. To make matters worse, social insurance revenues were often poorly invested, resulting in severe losses. Again, governments were compelled to rescue the defaulting schemes. By the 1980s, these fiscal problems had become so severe that it seemed that many funds would become bankrupt (Mesa-Lago, 1989). In addition, public confidence in social security was undermined and many members of social insurance schemes were very dissatisfied with the situation.

Although the serious administrative and fiscal problems experienced by many social insurance funds in Latin America in the 1960s and 1970s were not encountered everywhere, poor training, political patronage, resource constraints and other problems became more widespread. Social assistance programmes were particularly severely affected as many governments in the South became indebted and were compelled to turn to the International Monetary Fund and the World Bank for assistance. As was shown in Chapter 7, the imposition of structural adjustment programmes as a condition for credit resulted in severe cuts in the public sector, and human services agencies were particularly affected. Indeed, social assistance programmes in many developing countries simply ceased to function. Budgetary reductions also affected social insurance agencies that were compelled to reduce their staffing levels. As fewer staff sought to deal as best they could with benefit claims and other administrative matters, the quality of service deteriorated and public discontent increased.

Fiscal difficulties and the decline in administrative efficiency was cited by many critics of social security as a reason why these programmes should be privatized. By transferring responsibility for social protection to commercial providers, these problems would, they argued, be solved. The fact that members of Chile's social insurance schemes were very unhappy with the system was effectively exploited by the Pinochet government as it sought to garner public support for privatization (Mesa-Lago, 1994).

Social security and economic development

Criticisms of the fiscal difficulties encountered by Latin American social security schemes were echoed by the argument that social security expenditures were impeding economic growth. This argument was initially directed at social security in the industrial nations where social security expenditures are very sizeable. Critics claimed that these expenditures reduce savings and thus limit the availability of capital needed for investment and economic development. This argument has been most vigorously articulated by Feldstein (1974, 1977), a professor of economics at Harvard University who served as the chairman of President Reagan's Council of Economic Advisors. Professor Feldstein has used very sophisticated econometric models to support his arguments. Although the Reagan administration attempted to retrench social security, these efforts were not successful, and social security continues to be the largest component of the American welfare system today. The fact that social security consumes huge resources does not appear to have impeded the country's economic development. Indeed, despite social security's fiscal impact, there was no shortage of capital for investment to support the country's extraordinary economic boom in the late 1990s.

However, opponents of social security continue to claim that social security harms economic development (Feldstein, 1998) and some have even argued that economic performance in the United States in the 1990s would have been even better if social security had been abolished (Payne, 1998). Many economists also argue that social security is an expensive luxury that countries today simply cannot afford. With an ageing population and persistent high rates of unemployment in many parts of the North, governments cannot continue to tax the working population to maintain so many dependants on income benefits (World Bank, 1994; Peterson, 1999). In many industrial countries, almost a fifth of the population is now retired and receiving benefits. Another large proportion of the population in these countries are children who do not contribute to economic development. Consequently, they argue, a relatively small proportion of productive workers must support a large number of unproductive people. Since this situation cannot continue, ways must be found to reduce the fiscal burden placed on the working population. One way of reducing this burden is to abolish social security, and to require people to save for their retirement and meet their own needs (Ferrara and Tanner, 1998; Blahous, 2000).

Although the developing countries do not have a large proportion of 'unproductive' old people, critics claim that it is only a matter of time before they encounter the same problem. For this reason, they argue, governments should create mandatory retirement savings schemes that can replace social insurance. Governments that are contemplating the introduction of social insurance schemes should be discouraged from doing so. This point of view has been actively promoted by officials at the World Bank (1994) who believe that commercially managed savings accounts such as those introduced in Chile and other Latin American countries are far preferable to social insurance. Of course, the argument that government social security programmes divert capital for investment to unproductive consumption purposes is also used to support the case for privatization (Singh, 1996; Borzutzky, 2001).

Another argument is that social security has a negative effect on economic development because it reduces work incentives. By providing generous income benefits through social security programmes, governments inadvertently reduce the motivation to work hard and, in this way, undermine the very basis of economic development (Murray, 1984). A related argument is that the payroll taxes imposed on employers to fund social insurance distort labour markets and have a negative effect on employment creation. This argument is particularly relevant to the North. Faced with high payroll taxes, employers in the industrial countries seek to reduce the numbers of workers they employ by using labour-saving technologies; otherwise, they relocate to countries in the South where labour is cheap. The result is high unemployment and economic stagnation. The high rates of unemployment recorded in many European nations in the 1990s are often attributed to the high payroll taxes needed to fund social insurance benefits. It has also been argued that high social security expenditures harm economic development by fuelling inflation. Because payroll taxes reduce disposable income, workers demand higher wages with the result that inflation increases, damaging the economy.

These arguments have been refuted by numerous studies that have found little evidence to support the view that social security has a negative impact on economic development (Koskela and Viren, 1983; Atkinson, 1995; Singh, 1996; Gramlich, 1997). Nevertheless, efforts to refute claims about the deleterious impact of social security on economic development have not been very successful, and it is today widely believed that social security and other government social programmes are a major cause of high unemployment and sluggish economic growth in the North and particularly in Europe where levels of unemployment have remained high for most of the 1990s. Although erroneous, this belief supports the case for privatization.

Social security and inequality

It has been noted already that social security coverage in many developing countries currently favours some groups in society rather than all citizens. Social security programmes such as social insurance and employer mandates cater primarily for urban industrial workers, while those working in the agrarian and urban informal sectors of the economy are excluded from protection. Social allowance schemes do provide universal coverage but programmes of this kind are to be found in very few developing countries. In the few countries that still maintain social assistance schemes, urban dwellers have far greater access than rural inhabitants to benefits. For example, in a study of access to social assistance in Zimbabwe, Kaseke (1993) found that only a small proportion of people living in two poor rural areas in the east of the country knew about the government's social assistance scheme and that very few applied for or received benefits. Only 255 needy people out of a population of nearly 150,000 were receiving social security benefits. Of these, only 36 were in receipt of old-age retirement pensions even though many more elderly people in this impoverished region undoubtedly qualified for assistance. Kaseke found that access to social insurance was similarly inequitable.

Initially, it was believed that industrialization would create wage employment on a large scale and that social security coverage would soon be extended to a much larger proportion of the population. In time, as the developing countries experienced economic transformation, the vast majority of the population would be covered and, as in the industrial nations, universal protection would be achieved. However, the optimism which characterized development thinking in the 1950s and 1960s has waned and it has been recognized that economic modernization and prosperity for the bulk of the population is not an inevitable or even likely process, as was previously believed. Consequently, the hope that industrialization would create wage employment and automatically extend social security coverage has not been realized.

The fact that social security has not provided equitable access to the people of the developing countries has been investigated in several studies. Writers such as Paukert (1968) and Midgley (1984b) stressed the way the exclusion of the majority of the population from social security protection amplified the inequalities that characterized many developing countries. Because social security in these countries is often subsidized by government revenues, there is an inequitable transfer of resources through the tax system from the excluded majority to the minority who benefit from social security and particularly from social insurance schemes. These writers also point out that this minority, which is comprised of civil servants, military officers, white-collar employees and industrial workers, is already privileged by having secure and relatively well-paid jobs. Instead of reducing poverty and inequalities, social security programmes heighten income inequalities in the South.

Although recommendations for addressing the problem have been proposed, only some of them have been implemented. Most significant is the abolition of government subsidies to social insurance schemes. In many countries, these schemes are now funded only by employer and employee contributions. However, much more needs to be done to remedy the inegalitarian distributive flows that still characterize social security in many countries. This requires the introduction of imaginative policy innovations that can extend coverage to the excluded majority (van Ginneken, 1999). Innovative proposals of this kind include the expansion of crop insurance programmes to low-income peasant farmers (Amin, 1980; Mallet, 1980; United Nations, 1981), and extension of social security coverage to informal-sector workers and others who do not belong to these schemes (Midgley, 1984b, 1993; Getubig, 1992; Jain, 1999). Jain (1999) reports, for example, that India's major provident fund now permits informal-sector workers to contribute and a substantial number have joined. Social assistance could also be used more widely to inject resources into the household incomes of very poor families (Midgley, 1984c). Several Indian states have extended social assistance to cover disadvantaged groups (Jain, 1999) and, in Mauritius, the government has for many years used social assistance to pay child benefits to poor families in an effort to supplement their incomes (Titmuss et al., 1961; Midgley, 1984c).

In addition, coverage could be extended by linking non-formal welfare systems with modern-day provisions. As was noted earlier, the issue of how the non-formal welfare system can be integrated with statutory provisions has now been widely discussed in the literature and in Chapter 7, which provides some examples of how this could be achieved. These include the linking of *zakat* to statutory social assistance schemes in Islamic societies, the abrogation of relatives' responsibility to care for needy relatives and the use of social assistance to pay benefits that will actually motivate them to fulfil this task. The prospect of using public resources to support non-formal social security cooperatives, such as rotating credit societies and similar associations, was also mentioned. Again, as Jain (1999) reports, India has made some progress in this regard and, together with non-governmental organizations, the government has created group insurance programmes for a variety of informal-sector workers and other low-income groups. Although there are formidable obstacles to implementing innovations of this kind, the harmonization of the traditional and modern statutory systems could expand coverage and bring social security protection to many people who are currently excluded.

Social security programmes in many industrial and developing countries also have a negative impact on gender equality (Abramowitz, 1988; Sainsbury, 1994). This is partly because social security, and social insurance in particular, has catered primarily for male urban workers who, it was assumed, would be responsible for the welfare of their wives and families. It was believed that most women would marry and that relatively few would engage in full-time employment; consequently, their income protection needs would be met through their husband's membership of social security programmes. It is now obvious that these assumptions were incorrect. Although the proportion of women in full-time employment has increased significantly, especially in the industrial nations, the 'male breadwinner' model still dominates social security thinking in many countries and women are often discriminated against. Discrimination against women workers may take the form of lower benefit levels, the designation of women as the dependants of males, and by a failure to accommodate the way women leave employment to bear and raise children. By leaving employment for periods of time to have children and care for them, their contribution record inevitably suffers. Similarly, social insurance in many countries fails to recognize same-sex domestic relationships and these programmes often discriminate against gay and lesbian couples in stable domestic relationships.

Unlike social insurance, social assistance programmes are often designed to help women with children who have no husbands or other relatives who can support them. However, as was noted previously, these programmes no longer function in many developing countries, and in many of the industrial nations of the North, governments have now introduced work and other requirements as a condition for receiving benefits (Lodemal and Trickey, 2001; Peck, 2001). In some countries such as the United States, social assistance for women has historically been concerned with issues of social control rather than with providing aid to the needy (Abramovitz, 1988), and recently it has been significantly modified to make it more difficult for poor women to receive benefits (Handler and Hasenfeld, 1997; Hansen and Morris, 1999). Today, critics of so-called 'welfare reform' in the United States claim that the new programme exploits popular stereotypes about the allegedly immoral and irresponsible behaviour of women receiving social assistance and particularly of women of colour. Instead of helping them, it punishes and stigmatizes them (Mink, 1998).

Social security, privatization, poverty and development

The problems facing social security today are often cited as sound reasons for abolishing government programmes and replacing them with private provisions. Critics argue that these problems would disappear if income protection ceased to be the responsibility of the State, and if individuals and their families were required to use the market to meet their own needs. They argue that the administrative and fiscal problems facing social security could be more efficiently addressed by private insurance and by pension firms that have far more management and investment experience than the State. Also, by investing the contributions of workers in equity markets, governments would not be able to raid surpluses and workers would receive far higher rates of return. It is also claimed that social security privatization will address the economic problems caused by conventional government schemes. Private retirement accounts will provide a rich source of funds for commercial and industrial investment and thus stimulate economic development. Furthermore, by having control over investment decisions, workers will learn to appreciate the virtues of thrift, hard work and saving. Finally, critics contend that privatization will abolish income pooling and, for this reason, the perverse distributive flows that characterize conventional schemes and create inequalities will be ended.

These ideas had considerable appeal in political circles in the 1970s and 1980s. This was a time when many governments experienced economic difficulties that were widely attributed to excessive interventionism and public spending. Administrative difficulties, which plagued social security in some countries, particularly in Latin America, also undermined support for these programmes. However, while public confidence in social security was shaken, proposals for privatization were politically unpopular in both Britain and the United States and despite efforts by both Mrs Thatcher and President Reagan to undermine government social security programmes by creating opportunities for people to purchase private pensions or open retirement savings accounts, social security remained intact. Instead, as was noted earlier, it was in Chile that the first privatization of social security was undertaken. The privatization created a system of individual social security accounts, managed by commercial firms. Contribution rates, which are levied only on workers, are high and, like provident funds, are accumulated over the worker's lifetime and paid out at the time of retirement. Individuals are permitted to move their accounts among the different management firms to maximize their returns. Although this is intended to stimulate competition, there has been a monopolistic consolidation in the industry with fewer providers now offering services. In addition, high service charges are imposed, and it is generally agreed that administrative costs are far higher than in government-managed social insurance schemes.

The Chilean privatization was introduced with the explicit purpose of promoting economic development, addressing administrative and fiscal problems and fostering greater individual responsibility (Borzutzky, 1991, 2002). It was predicted that the new system would also generate far higher rates of return than those provided by the old social security system. Although the privatized system did indeed produce quite high rates of return during the 1980s, returns had fallen significantly by the 1990s (Williamson and Pampel, 1993; Borzutzky, 2002). In a recent analysis of trends in several Latin American countries that have introduced privatized retirement accounts, Mesa-Lago (2001) confirmed this finding noting that, between 1995 and 2000, rates of return in many countries had fallen and, in some cases, negative rates of return were recorded. Argentina is the most poignant example. Although rates of return were initially quite high, they fell dramatically in the late 1990s and, with the country's fiscal crisis of 2002, the savings of many ordinary people have been wiped out.

Despite claims that a privatized social security system would result in higher savings and thus promote economic development, there is little evidence to show that privatization has in fact made a major contribution to economic development (Borzutzky, 2001). Mesa-Lago (2001) reports that two econometric studies of the Chilean system found that the national savings rate had not increased and that the overall impact of privatization on economic development had, in fact, been negative. One problem is the high transition costs of privatization and the fiscal burden of government minimum pension guarantees. This raises the issue of the ability of poor people to save for their own retirement.

Although it is claimed that a privatized retirement system creates strong incentives for workers to contribute, several studies have found that many workers avoid paying contributions. Many small firms do not enforce the requirement that workers pay into their savings funds, with the result that their lifetime contributions are low. Of course, many workers avoid paying contributions because their incomes are low and contribution rates are high. Another problem is that many low-income workers are not able to save a sufficient amount over their lifetime to meet their retirement income needs (Gillion and Bonilla, 1992; Mesa-Lago, 1994, 2001; Borzutzky, 2002). Although benefits for low-income workers had previously been subsidized by higher-paid workers in the insurance funds, there is no income pooling and thus any redistributive mechanism to subsidize the benefits paid to lower earners. Instead, many retired workers have been compelled to apply for social assistance benefits to supplement their incomes. Women have been particularly negatively affected (Borzutzky, 2002).

The privatization of Chile's social security system has been emulated by several other Latin American countries but it appears that privatization in these countries has faced a number of serious problems. The claim that the administrative and other challenges facing conventional social security programmes would disappear with privatization has not, in fact, materialized (Queisser, 1995; Mesa-Lago, 2001). It is also doubtful that claims about the positive economic benefits of privatization have been realized. While it was argued that privatization would ensure that social security's allegedly negative impact on economic development would be eliminated, and that high growth and prosperity would follow, there is little evidence that the privatization of social security in Latin American countries has, in fact, been accompanied by high rates of economic growth and widespread prosperity.

Nevertheless, many economists and politicians on the political right have continued to urge that social security should be privatized, and they continue to believe that a privatized social security system will bring many positive benefits. However, the failure of the Latin American experience to demonstrate that privatization will, in fact, bring positive social and economic benefits and significantly improve people's welfare has somewhat dampened enthusiasm for further privatization. Despite strong lobbying from the commercial insurance industry in the United States, the Clinton administration maintained a strong commitment to the social security system, and, in Europe, government social security programmes continue to cover most workers even though many governments have introduced fiscal incentives that encourage people to take out private pensions or otherwise save for their retirement. Many Asian countries have also retained their conventional social security systems and some, such as China, are seeking to identify ways in which social security can support economic development. Many Chinese social security experts are impressed with the way the government of Singapore has used its provident fund to generate investment capital for housing and development projects and there is much debate in China today about following Singapore's example (White, 1998).

These developments offer an alternative policy approach to the privatization strategy being pursued in Latin America. On the other hand, Hong Kong recently introduced a new privatized provident fund system and, in the United States, President Bush has expressed strong support for privatization. The president has been heavily lobbied by the commercial pensions and insurance industry and it is likely that the country's social security system will be partially privatized. Many commentators now recognize that privatization has less to do with enhancing the efficiency of social security or with protecting workers than with making profits. Lobbying for privatization by the commercial pension and insurance industry in the United States suggests that the industry recognizes that huge profits are likely to accompany the introduction of a government-mandated commercial retirement system (Baker and Weisbrot, 1999). Clearly, the struggle over social security continues.

Although social security debates today are ideologically laden and focus on issues of privatization, the question of how social security can address the pressing needs of people in the developing nations of the South remains a major challenge. Despite significant economic growth, many developing countries have not experienced the rapid transition to industrialization that had been predicted, and social security coverage remains limited. The idea that rapid industrialization would create mass employment and that social security coverage would be universal now seems far-fetched.

Indeed, economic conditions in many developing countries today have diminished the prospect of social security making a major contribution to poverty alleviation. The impact of global debt and structural adjustment has caused great hardship in many parts of the South. In many poor countries, the situation is still acute. The rising incidence of poverty has been exacerbated by the retrenchment of social assistance programmes that had previously provided a limited safety net for the urban poor. With the retrenchment of social assistance, social security's contribution to poverty alleviation has been even further reduced (Midgley, 1993). By the 1990s, social security seemed to be quite irrelevant to the needs of the developing world.

On the other hand, the idea that privatizing social security and minimizing government involvement in social welfare will alleviate poverty is equally far fetched. Yet this is precisely what the proponents of privatization believe. They claim that a privatized system will stimulate economic growth, creating employment opportunities and generating prosperity for all. They also argue that by encouraging the middle class to use the private market to meet their income protection needs, greater resources will be made available for governments to use to assist those who cannot afford private income protection. By allowing commercial insurers to protect the majority of the population, demands on government will be reduced, permitting them to focus scarce resources more directly on the poor through social assistance programmes.

Future challenges

There is little evidence to show that greater privatization has, in fact, fostered enhanced social programmes for the poor. Despite a high degree of social service privatization in the United States, the government has also curtailed social assistance, and today many poor people are being denied help. It appears that the withdrawal of middle-class people from public programmes results in the deterioration of these services. If the middle class does not participate and benefit from social programmes, they will support proposals for tax cuts and the retrenchment of these provisions. This finding has major implications for social security policy in the South. While social security coverage remains low, the idea that commercial insurers should protect those in wage employment while governments cater for the poor should be resisted. Instead, social security policy-makers should formulate new and imaginative strategies that will provide universal coverage, address inequities and ensure that the population as a whole is protected, doing so in ways that promote economic development.

There are formidable challenges to attaining these objectives. As has been noted earlier, one challenge concerns the question of how social security coverage can be extended to the excluded majority. Another concerns the issue of how social security programmes can contribute positively to economic development. Although these challenges have not been met, tentative steps have already been taken to address the issues of coverage and development. Some scholars have argued that it is possible to extend coverage to the excluded majority through the policy innovations mentioned earlier in this chapter and, in this way, to confront the problem of poverty directly. These proposals range from the introduction of crop insurance to small farmers and supporting indigenous social security practices. It is also possible, at the same time, to modify conventional social security programmes so that they enhance economic participation, increase both production and productivity and thus ensure that social security contributes to economic growth. The potential of a social development or social investment approach to make a significant contribution to enhancing social security's contribution to economic development and, at the same time, improving people's welfare has already been explored (Midgley, 2001) but much more needs to be done to formalize these policy proposals and to test their viability. Nevertheless, these efforts are gradually providing the basis for a new vision of social security in the context of development.

Recommended Reading

The following books discuss major issues in the field of social security in developing countries.

- Midgley, J. (1984) *Social Security, Inequality and the Third World*. Chichester: John Wiley. This was one of the first books to be written about social security in the developing countries. It examines the relationship between social security and inequality, arguing that existing social security policies and programmes exacerbate inequality in the developing world. Various proposals for rectifying this situation and extending social security coverage to the impoverished majority are proposed.

- Ahmad, E., Dreze, J., Hills, J. and Sen, A. (eds) (1991) *Social Security in Developing Countries*. Oxford: Clarendon Press. This edited collection of papers on social security in developing countries ranges over a number of topics related to social security and development. Case studies of social security programmes in different parts of the world are also provided.
- Dixon, J. (1999) *Social Security in Global Perspective*. Westport, CT: Praeger. This comprehensive account of social security in the modern world is an extremely useful reference work. It examines the features of different types of social security programmes around the world and ranks countries in terms of the extensiveness of their social security provisions.
- Cruz-Saco, M.A. and Mesa-Lago, C. (1998) *Do Options Exist? The Reform of Pension and Health Care Systems in Latin America*. Pittsburgh, PA: University of Pittsburgh Press. This book discusses the privatization of social security in Latin American countries since the 1980s and concludes that the so-called social security reforms introduced in many Latin American countries have not been a great success. Despite making needed fiscal and administrative changes, the claim that social security privatization would effectively meet people's social needs has not been realized.
- von Benda-Beckmann, F., von Benda-Beckmann, K., Casino, E., Hirtz, F., Woodman, G.R. and Zacher, H.F. (eds) (1988) *Between Kinship and the State: Social Security and Law in Developing Countries*. Dordrecht: Foris Publications. Van Ginneken, W. (ed.) (1999) *Social Security for the Excluded Majority: Case Studies of Developing Countries*. Geneva: International Labour Organization. The first volume is an edited collection that examines the traditional or 'non-formal' social security sector in developing countries and discusses its potential and shortcomings. The second book provides a number of case studies that discuss ways in which formal and traditional social security systems can be linked so that the excluded majority can be afforded protection.

References

Abramovitz, M. (1988) *Regulating the Lives of Women: Social Welfare Policy from Colonial Times to the Present*. Boston, MA: South End Press.

Amin, N.M. (1980) 'Social security protection for the rural population: approaches in Malaysia', *International Social Security Review*, 33 (3): 165–75.

Atkinson, A.B. (1995) 'Is the welfare state necessarily an obstacle to economic growth?', *European Economic Review*, 39: 46–96.

Baker, D. and Weisbrot, M. (1999) *Social Security: The Phony Crisis*. Chicago, IL: University of Chicago Press.

Blahous, C.P. (2000) *Reforming Social Security for Ourselves and Our Prosperity*. Westport, CT: Praeger.

Borzutzky, S. (1991) 'The Chicago Boys, social security and welfare in Chile', in H. Glennerster and J. Midgley (eds) *The Radical Right and the Welfare State: An International Assessment*. Lanham, MD: Rowman and Littlefield, pp. 79–99.

Borzutzky, S. (2001) 'Chile: has social security privatization fostered economic development?', *International Journal of Social Welfare*, 10 (4): 294–9.

Borzutzky, S. (2002) *Vital Connections: Politics, Social Security and Inequality in Chile*. Notre Dame, IN: Notre Dame University Press.

Burgess, R. and Stern, N. (1991) 'Social security in developing countries: what, why, who, and how?', in E. Ahmad, J. Dreze, J. Hills and A. Sen (eds) *Social Security in Developing Countries*. Oxford, Clarendon Press, pp. 41–80.

Chow, N. and Xu, Y. (2001) *Socialist Welfare in a Market Economy: Social Security Reforms in Guangzhou, China*. Burlington, VT: Ashgate.

Cockburn, C. (1980) 'The role of social security in development', *International Social Security Review*, 33: 337–58.

de Schweinitz, K. (1943) *England's Road to Social Security*. Philadelphia, PA: University of Pennsylvania Press.

Dixon, J. (1981) *The Chinese Welfare System, 1949–1979*. New York: Praeger.

Dixon, J. (1982) 'Provident funds in the Third World: a cross-national review', *Public Administration and Development*, 2 (4): 325–44.

Dixon, J. (1993) 'National provident funds: the challenge of harmonizing their social security, social and economic objectives', *Policy Studies Review*, 12 (1–2): 1197–209.

Dixon, J. (1999) *Social Security in Global Perspective*. Westport, CT: Praeger.

Feldstein, M.B. (1974) 'Social security, induced retirement and aggregate capital accumulation', *Journal of Political Economy*, 83 (4): 447–75.

Feldstein, M.B. (1977) 'Social security', in M.J. Boskin (ed.) *The Crisis in Social Security: Problems and Prospects*. San Francisco, CA: Institute for Contemporary Studies, pp. 17–30.

Feldstein, M.B. (ed.) (1998) *Privatizing Social Security*. Chicago, IL: University of Chicago Press.

Ferrara, P. and Tanner, M. (1998) *A New Deal for Social Security*. Washington, DC: Cato Institute.

Getubig, I.P. (1992) 'Non-conventional forms of social security protection for the poor in Asia', in I.P. Getubig and S. Schmidt (eds) *Rethinking Social Security: Reaching Out to the Poor*. Kuala Lumpur: Asian and Pacific Development Centre, pp. 106–35.

Gillion, C. and Bonilla, A. (1992) 'An analysis of a national private pension scheme: the case of Chile', *International Labour Review*, 131 (2): 171–95.

Goswami, R. (2002) 'Old age protection in India', *International Social Security Review*, 55 (2): 95–121.

Gramlich, E.M. (1997) 'How does social security affect the economy?', in E.R. Kingson and J.H. Schultz (eds) *Social Security in the 21st Century*. New York: Oxford University Press, pp. 147–55.

Gruat, J.V. (1990) 'Social security schemes in Africa: current trends and problems', *International Labour Review*, 129 (4): 405–21.

Hallen, G.C. (1967) *Social Security in India*. Meerut: Rastogi Publishers.

Handel, G. (1982) *Social Welfare in Western Society*. New York: Random House.

Handler, J.F. and Hasenfeld, Y. (1997) *We the Poor People: Work, Poverty and Welfare*. New Haven, CT: Yale University Press.

Hansen, C.J.E. and Morris, R. (eds) (1999) *Welfare Reform 1996–2000: Is there a Safety Net?* Westport, CT: Auburn House.

International Labour Organization (1984) *Introduction to Social Security*. Geneva: International Labour Organization.

Jain, S. (1999) 'Basic social security in India', in W.E. van Ginneken (ed.) *Social Security for the Excluded Majority: Case Studies of Developing Countries*. Geneva: International Labour Organization, pp. 37–68.

Kaseke, E. (1993) 'Rural social security needs: a case study of Mudzi and Mutoko communal districts in Zimbabwe', Doctoral dissertation, University of Zimbabwe, Harare. Cited in J. Midgley and E. Kaseke (1997) 'Challenges to social security in developing countries: coverage and poverty in Zimbabwe', in J. Midgley and M.B. Tracy (eds) *Challenges to Social Security: An International Exploration*. Westport, CT: Auburn House, pp. 103–22.

Koskela, E. and Viren, M. (1983) 'Social security and household savings in an international cross section', *American Economic Review*, 73 (1): 212–17.

Lee, M.K. (2000) *Chinese Occupational Welfare in Market Transition*. London: Macmillan.

Lodemal, I. and Trickey, H. (2001) *An Offer You Can't Refuse: Workfare in International Perspective*. Bristol: Policy Press.

Mallet, A. (1980) 'Social protection of the rural population', *International Social Security Review*, 33 (3–4): 359–93.

Mesa-Lago, C. (1978) *Social Security in Latin America*. Pittsburgh, PA: University of Pittsburgh Press.

Mesa-Lago, C. (1989) *Ascent to Bankruptcy: Financing Social Security in Latin America*. Pittsburgh, PA: University of Pittsburgh Press.

Mesa-Lago, C. (1992) 'Comparative analysis of Asia and Latin American social security systems', in I.P. Getubig and S. Schmidt (eds) *Rethinking Social Security: Reaching Out to the Poor*. Kuala Lumpur: Asian and Pacific Development Centre, pp. 64–105.

Mesa-Lago, C. (1994) *Changing Social Security in Latin America and the Caribbean: Towards Alleviating the Costs of Economic Reform*. Boulder, CO: Lynne Rienner.

Mesa-Lago, C. (2001) 'Structural reform of social security pensions in Latin America: models, characteristics, results and conclusions', *International Social Security Review*, 54 (4): 67–92.

Midgley, J. (1984a) 'Poor Law principles and social assistance in the Third World', *International Social Work*, 27 (1): 19–29.

Midgley, J. (1984b) *Social Security, Inequality and the Third World*. Chichester: John Wiley.

Midgley, J. (1984c) 'Social assistance: an alternative form of social protection in developing countries', *International Social Security Review*, 84: 247–64.

Midgley, J. (1993) 'Social security and Third World poverty: the challenge to policy makers', *Policy Studies Review*, 12 (1–2): 133–43.

Midgley, J. (1994) 'Social security policy in developing countries: integrating State and traditional systems', *Focaal*, 22/23 (1): 219–30.

Midgley, J. (2001) 'Social security and economic uncertainty: towards a developmental rationale', *Asian Pacific Journal of Social Work*, 11 (1): 6–21.

Mink, G. (1998) *Welfare's End*. Ithaca, NY: Cornell University Press.

Mouton, P. (1975) *Social Security in Africa: Trends, Problems and Prospects*. Geneva: International Labour Office.

Murray, C. (1984) *Losing Ground: American Social Policy 1950–1980*. New York: Basic Books.

Paukert, F. (1968) 'Social security and income distribution: a comparative study', *International Labour Review*, 98 (5): 425–50.

Payne, J.L. (1998) *Overcoming Welfare: Expecting More from the Poor and from Ourselves*. New York: Basic Books.

Peck, J. (2001) *Workfare States*. New York: Guilford Press.

Peterson, P. (1999) *Gray Dawn: How the Coming Age Wave will Transform America and the World*. New York: Times Books.

Queisser, M. (1995) 'Chile and beyond: the second generation pension reforms in Latin America', *International Social Security Review*, 48 (1): 23–40.

Rimlinger, G. (1971) *Welfare Policy and Industrialization in Europe, America and Russia*. New York: John Wiley.

Sainsbury, D. (ed.) (1994) *Gendering Welfare States*. Thousand Oaks, CA: Sage.

Sherraden, M. (1997) 'Provident funds and social protection: the case of Singapore', in J. Midgley and M. Sherraden (eds) *Alternatives to Social Security: An International Inquiry*. Westport, CT: Auburn House, pp. 33–60.

Singh, A. (1996) 'Pension reform, the stock market, capital formation and economic growth: a critical commentary on the World Bank's proposals', *International Social Security Review*, 49 (1): 21–44.

Tang, K.L. (1997) 'Noncontributory pensions in Hong Kong: an alternative to social security', in J. Midgley and M. Sherraden (eds) *Alternatives to Social Security: An International Inquiry*. Westport, CT: Auburn House, pp. 61–75.

Thompson, K. (1979) 'Trends and problems of social security in developing countries in Asia', in *The Role of Trade Unions in Social Security: Report of a Regional Seminar*. Bangkok: International Labour Organization, pp. 109–44.

Titmuss, R.M., Abel-Smith, B. and Lynes, T. (1961) *Social Policies and Population Growth in Mauritius*. London: Methuen.

United Nations (1981) *Crop Insurance for Developing Countries*. New York: United Nations.

van Ginneken, W.E. (ed.) (1999) *Social Security for the Excluded Majority: Case Studies of Developing Countries*. Geneva: International Labour Organization.

von Benda-Beckmann, F. and von Benda-Beckmann, K. (1994) 'Coping with insecurity', *Focaal*, 22/23: 7–31.

Weiss, H. (2002) 'Zakat and the question of social welfare', in H. Weiss (ed.) *Social Welfare in Muslim Societies in Africa*. Stockholm: Nordiska Afrikainstitutet, pp. 7–38.

White, G. (1998) 'Social security reforms in China: towards an East Asian model', in R. Goodman, G. White and H. Kwon (eds) *The East Asian Welfare Model: Welfare Orientalism and the State*. New York: Routledge, pp. 175–97.

Williamson, J.B. and Pampel, F.C. (1993) *Old Age Security in Comparative Perspective*. New York: Oxford University Press.

Wolfe, M. (1968) 'Social security and development: the Latin American experience', in E.M. Kassalow (ed.) *The Role of Social Security in Economic Development*. Washington, DC: Department of Health, Education and Welfare, pp. 155–85.

World Bank (1994) *Averting the Old Age Crisis: Policies to Protect the Old and Promote Growth*. Washington, DC: World Bank.

9 INTERNATIONAL DEVELOPMENT COOPERATION AND SOCIAL POLICY

Summary

The chapter opens with a discussion of the definition of 'foreign aid', its historical origins in the post-war period, its volume and distribution in terms of assistance provided by bilateral, multilateral and non-governmental institutions. After examining contrasting ideological views of the impacts of aid on development, specific areas of social policy are considered in which aid has been influential. First, the design and implementation of social safety nets or social funds is examined, which have enjoyed some success in targeting the poor to provide short-term relief from the adverse impacts of structural adjustment. However, a number of limitations and criticisms are noted. The move towards 'social conditionality' is discussed, in which debt relief is tied to the adoption of more systematic and participatory anti-poverty policies through risk management and the preparation of Poverty Reduction Strategy Papers (PRSPs). A second arena of influence has been in social welfare spending and policy leverage, notably education, health and humanitarian assistance. Basic education still accounts for only 1 per cent of aid spending, despite the exhortations made at Jomtien (1990) and Dakar (2000). However, aid organizations have exerted influence to persuade national governments to prioritize education. Finally, in the context of globalization, international aid bodies have probably strengthened their ability to influence domestic social policies, although national governments usually retain control over such policies. Progress in this field will depend on greater aid budgetary allocations being made for social sectors and the strengthened capacity of recipient governments to effectively spend these additional resources.

Aiding development

Technical and financial assistance from the industrialized countries of the 'North' to the developing world or 'South' has become well established since the end of World War II. The term 'international development cooperation' has been deliberately chosen in this volume as a broad label to include all kinds of development-related aid. 'Foreign aid' comprises grants and concessional loans (about two-thirds of total official donor support). International development cooperation is a much broader category that includes non-concessional loans at market rates (making up one-third of official development assistance) in addition to private flows from voluntary agencies. According to the Development Assistance Committee (DAC) of the OECD, in order to be categorized as 'foreign aid' international assistance must have a grant element of at least 25 per cent and have economic development and welfare as its main aims.

The degree of concessionality granted by donors is measured against interest rates on the open market, with 'soft' loans and grants counting as foreign aid. Transfers with little or no concessionality, such as most World Bank (non-IDA) lending for example, are not officially foreign aid although their purpose is similar. No grants, soft loans or credits for military purposes are considered foreign aid, while food aid and technical cooperation (including the services of social planners) do fall into this category. Technical and financial support from the private voluntary sector through a burgeoning range of international non-governmental organizations has also become increasingly important. Although not falling within the DAC's definition of 'official development assistance' (ODA), such NGO support is included in the present discussion. This is because a significant amount of official aid is now channelled through NGOs as implementing institutions and this may have a disproportionately high influence on social development and social policy matters.

The origin of large-scale external economic assistance is normally traced to the Marshall Plan (the 'Economic Recovery Program') launched by the US government following the passing of the US Foreign Aid Act in 1948. From 1948–52, the US granted $13.5 billion ($88 billion in today's terms) to help reconstruct war-ravaged Europe, accounting for some 10 per cent of recipients' GNP (Sogge, 2002). Many observers have pointed out, however, that unlike much foreign assistance today, the Marshall Plan was recipient-friendly and underpinned by Keynesian public investment policies. Economic assistance to developing countries started with the Colombo Plan of 1951, a Commonwealth initiative (later joined by the US and Japan) to assist countries in Asia and the Pacific. From 1950–81 a total of over $65 billion was provided in aid (Arnold, 1985).

Overseas development assistance (ODA) has grown steadily since the 1950s, peaking in the early 1990s and remaining fairly constant since then, but with a more recent tendency to decline (see Table 9.1). At constant 1999 figures, ODA peaked at $63.7 billion in 1992, year of the Earth Summit. It then gradually fell to $56.4 billion in 1999 and $53.1 billion in 2000, a drop of 1.6 per cent in real terms (OECD, 2002). Although some countries such as Japan saw their aid budgets fall significantly over this period (by $1.8 billion in this case), others enjoyed real increases. According to OECD (2002) figures in Table 9.1, the UK's aid budget grew by 35.6 per cent in real terms during the 1990s, as did those of some other countries. These include Belgium (21.7 per cent), Greece (28.7 per cent), the Netherlands (10.0 per cent), Sweden (22.3 per cent), Germany (16.5 per cent) and the US (8.9 per cent). The critique that donors have been 'never richer, never meaner' is thus not entirely justified (German and Randel, 2002: 145).

Table 9.1 Net ODA from DAC countries to developing countries and multilateral organizations ($ million)

	1984–85 average	1989–90 average[1]	1996	1997	1998	1999	2000
Australia	763	987	1,074	1,061	960	982	987
Austria	215	338	557	527	456	527	423
Belgium	443	796	913	764	883	760	820
Canada	1,628	2,395	1,795	2,045	1,707	1,706	1,744
Denmark	444	1,054	1,772	1,637	1,704	1,733	1,664
Finland	194	776	408	379	396	416	371
France	3,080	6,483	7,451	6,307	5,742	5,639	4,105
Germany	2,862	5,634	7,601	5,857	5,581	5,515	5,030
Greece	..	..	184	173	179	194	226
Ireland	37	53	179	187	199	245	235
Italy	1,115	3,504	2,416	1,266	2,278	1,806	1,376
Japan	4,058	9,017	9,439	9,358	10,640	15,323	13,508
Luxembourg	8	22	82	95	112	119	127
Netherlands	1,202	2,316	3,246	2,947	3,042	3,134	3,135
New Zealand	54	91	122	154	130	134	113
Norway	557	1,061	1,311	1,306	1,321	1,370	1,264
Portugal	9	126	218	250	259	276	271
Spain	152	753	1,251	1,234	1,376	1,363	1,195
Sweden	791	1,903	1,999	1,731	1,573	1,630	1,799
Switzerland	294	654	1,026	911	898	984	890
United Kingdom	1,480	2,612	3,199	3,433	3,864	3,426	4,501
United States	9,057	9,536	9,377	6,878	8,786	914	9,955
TOTAL DAC	28,443	49,345	55,622	48,497	52,084	56,428	53,737
Of which:							
EU Members	12,032	26,371	31,476	26,785	27,641	26,784	25,277

[1]Including debt forgiveness of non-ODA claims in 1990, except for total DAC.
Source: OECD (2002).

Two-thirds of ODA is bilateral (government-to-government). As Table 9.1 shows, Japan was the largest donor in 2000 ($13.5 billion), followed by the US (almost $10 billion), Germany ($5 billion), the UK ($4.5 billion) and France ($4.1 billion). One-quarter of all bilateral assistance ($14.5 billion in 2000) is channelled through multilateral bodies rather than directly to individual countries. However, only five countries (Denmark, the Netherlands, Sweden, Norway and Luxembourg) meet the target established by the UN in 1970 that ODA should comprise at least 0.7 per cent of donors' national income. Most European nations allocate around 0.3 per cent and the average stands at 0.22 per cent. At the bottom of the scale, the US gives just 0.1 per cent and Italy 0.15 per cent. Overall, aid as a share of donor government spending has on average fallen significantly from 0.82 per cent in 1990 to 0.58 per cent in 2000 (German and Randel, 2002; OECD, 2002).

In discussions of foreign aid, the importance of non-governmental organizations (NGOs) in terms both of the volume of financial support given and their impact on policy often tends to be under-estimated. Until the late 1980s, this amount was significant but remained constant at $6.4 billion or around 12 per cent of total Western aid (Clark, 1991: 47). By 1998, NGOs were channelling over $10 billion to developing countries, half derived from their own fund-raising activities and half from bilateral agencies (World Bank, 2001: 200). This was the equivalent of two-thirds of all official multilateral lending at the time and surpassed even the volume of assistance disbursed by the World Bank. This figure is now likely to be even higher as direct grants by NGOs have increased from $5.6 billion in 1998 to an estimated $6.9 billion in 2000 (OECD, 2002). By re-allocating official funds channelled indirectly via NGOs, total annual transfers through international private voluntary organizations could at present therefore amount to around $14 billion, the equivalent to perhaps one-third of all remaining official aid transferred directly.

An examination of aid distribution quickly reveals that, despite the rhetoric of international poverty reduction, donors' motivations are multi-dimensional and underpinned only in part by a desire to address the needs of the world's poorest. Commercial, historical and geo-political factors help to account for the fact that the share of aid going to low-income countries dropped from 61 per cent in the 1980s to 56 per cent during the 1990s (World Bank, 2002). The world's 43 'least developed countries' (LDCs), as classified by the UNDP, where the bulk of the world's poor is concentrated, received 24 per cent of official aid in 1988 but this had fallen to 21 per cent a decade later. Over the same period, per capita spending on aid for the poorest countries dropped from $33 to $20. Aid to wealthier countries also fell over this period but far less sharply (UNDP, 2000; German and Randel, 2002). Significant proportions of bilateral aid are conditional upon the recipient's purchase of donor country goods and services ('tied aid'). For the UK, this figure is a modest 14 per cent, but for France it rises to 35 per cent, for Italy 55 per cent, 69 per cent in the case of Canada and no less than 72 per cent for the USA (Randel et al., 2000).

The overriding influence of global and regional geo-political interests on the part of the largest bilateral donors also compromises commitment to poverty alleviation (OECD, 2002). In the case of Japan, the world's largest donor, 60 per cent of its aid goes to countries in South-East Asia with which it has strong trading and political ties, especially to Indonesia, China and Thailand. The US provided substantial aid to South Korea and Taiwan during the 1950s and 1960s, while in 1999–2000 almost one-third of US bilateral aid went to three countries where it has strong strategic interests, namely Russia, Israel and Egypt. Almost half of French aid is allocated to former colonies, notably French Polynesia and New Caledonia, while one-fifth of UK bilateral aid is destined for former colonies in Africa and the Indian sub-continent.

Countries which vote with donors in the UN tend to receive more aid, while foreign assistance is sometimes tied to arms purchases. Western donors spend on average 10 times as much on armaments as on overseas aid. This ratio varies from 8 : 1 in the case of the UK to 33 : 1 for the USA. Some analysts have attributed the gradual decline in aid during the 1990s to the end of the Cold War. Sharp, if temporary, increases in aid flows for economic and humanitarian purposes have occurred following major conflicts such as the Gulf War, Kosovo and East Timor. The global 'war on terrorism' following the tragic events of 11 September 2001 is also resulting in increased aid to Afghanistan, with $5 billion being pledged in January 2002 (World Bank, 2002).

Aid channelled through multilateral institutions is generally regarded as being less directly influenced by donor commercial or strategic interests and driven more closely by development priorities. In recent years, the share of multilateral aid channelled through the UN has been in gradual decline, while that directed through the World Bank and IMF as well as the regional development banks and the EC have increased (see Table 9.2). Critics allege that the decline in quota-based voting rights (based on financial contributions) enjoyed by developing country members in these institutions has made it more difficult for them to influence policy in the direction of poverty alleviation. On the Executive Board of the World Bank, for example, 24 industrialized countries control 71 per cent of the vote, while 158 developing and transitional nations control 29 per cent (German and Randel, 2002).

Aid for social development

With this background in mind, it is pertinent to examine how foreign assistance has influenced the process of economic and social development. This is a notoriously difficult, perhaps impossible, question to answer emphatically. However, for our purposes, three distinct dimensions of the relationship between ODA and development may be distinguished. (1) Macro-analyses regarding the contribution of foreign assistance to the general process of development. (2) Aid allocations to specific social sectors and programmes that have a direct impact on the satisfaction of basic needs such as health, education and housing as well as humanitarian assistance. (3) The use of ODA to promote direct investment and policy change in broader poverty reduction and livelihood strengthening areas such as employment generation and sustainable development. While judgement in the first of these three areas is to some extent a matter of ideological perspective, examination of the second and third should permit conclusions to be reached on how ODA has furthered the goals of social policy in contrasting if often complementary arenas. As discussed in Chapter 1, these relate to social policy as (a) social welfare provider, (b) builder of social safety nets and (c) as part of a holistic and integrated, multi-sector approach to poverty alleviation and development.

The first broad area of debate concerns perceptions on how foreign assistance fits within the political economy of development. That is, does ODA in general have a constructive or a perverse impact upon development? Or is it simply insignificant and of little consequence for developing countries either one way or the other? The theory and practice of aid as an effective development tool

Table 9.2 Gross ODA disbursements by multilateral organizations[1] ($ million, at current prices and exchange rates)

	1984–85 average	1989–90 average	1996	1997	1998	1999	2000
Concessional flows							
International Financial Institutions	163						
AfDF	363	565	626	641	624	516	360
AsDF	18	1,052	1,238	1,157	1,149	1,114	1,135
Caribbean Dev. Bank	–	39	16	23	25	33	36
EBRD	2,647	–	18	17	23	11	5
IDA	572	3,815	6,312	5,902	5,742	6,135	5,479
IDB	235	373	679	574	610	512	442
IFAD	–	230	239	199	232	231	250
IMF[2]	–	960	1,029	–	693	1,007	667
Nordic Dev. Fund	3,981	–	71	47	45	38	39
Total IFIs		6,036	9,113	8,490	8,381	8,518	7,671
United Nations[3]	615						
UNDP	123	944	555	670	604	508	390
UNFPA	407	168	215	216	214	185	133
UNHCR	261	478	281	261	236	253	493
UNICEF	189	543	677	514	484	564	576
UNRWA	256	279	237	264	298	286	301
UNTA	729	237	243	434	282	428	454
WFP	323	847	371	279	270	354	357
Other UN	2,906	716	512	70	134	161	568
Total UN	1,294	4,211	3,091	2,707	2,521	2,741	3,272
EC	–	2,539	5,495	5,394	5,396	5,238	4,763
Global Environment Facility	–	–	–	72	76	66	86
Montreal Protocol Fund	240	–	–	42	152	44	56
Arab Funds	8,439	323	95	98	133	227	215
Total concessional		14,107	18,910	16,874	17,421	17,912	16,804
Non-concessional flows							
International Financial Institutions	235						
African Dev. Bank	661	1,123	1,008	926	635	723	506
Asian Dev. Bank	13	1,518	2,563	5,304	5,623	3,710	2,884
Caribbean Dev. Bank	–	25	26	36	61	77	65
EBRD	8,263	–	395	338	428	366	439
IBRD	373	12,050	10,665	13,624	14,899	13,256	11,831
IFC	1,770	1,410	1,740	1,410	1,724	1,596	1,276
IDB	–	2,161	3,696	4,933	6,051	7,934	6,662
IFAD	11,316	–	22	33	–	40	33
Total IFIs	207	18,287	20,115	26,604	29,421	27,703	23,696
EC	78	429	509	1,010	1,029	855	608
Arab Funds	11,601	66	–	–	–	–	–
Total non-concessional		18,782	20,624	27,614	30,450	28,559	24,304

[1] To countries and territories on Part I of the DAC List of Aid Recipients.
[2] IMF Trust Fund, SAF and PRGF.
[3] The data for UN agencies have been reviewed to include only regular budget expenditures. This has led to revisions of UNDP data since 1990. For WFP and UNHCR revisions have only been possible from 1996 onwards, while for UNICEF the data are revised from 1997. Since 2000, UNHCR operates an Annual Programme Budget which includes country operations, global operations and administrative costs under a unified budget.

Source: OECD (2002).

has for many years come under attack at all points on the ideological spectrum, critiques on the right and left often converging in their vitriol. Thus, it is alleged that aid does not contribute significantly to boosting economic growth or national income (Bauer, 1981; Payer, 1991), while it does little to relieve poverty or food insecurity (Lappé et al., 1980; Adams and Solomon, 1985). Furthermore, aid supports dictatorial and repressive regimes with little concern for authentic development (Hayter, 1971; Bauer, 1981; Hayter and Watson, 1985; Sogge, 2002), encouraging corruption and the expansion of costly, self-serving aid bureaucracies (Hancock, 1991).

Other assessments are more measured, concluding that although there are serious problems with how aid policy is formulated and implemented, if properly used aid can be a positive development tool. It may indeed contribute to boosting national economic performance (Mosley, 1987; Cassen, 1994) and has the capacity to alleviate poverty and promote sustainable development if projects are adequately designed and executed (Madeley, 1991; Riddell, 1987). This is particularly so in the case of countries that are heavily aid dependent and in which external funding has a larger impact than normal. For example, in Uganda, Tanzania and Ghana aid accounts for some 50 per cent or more of government spending, facilitating investment in key social areas such as primary education and health.

While it may be difficult to identify the precise contribution of ODA to furthering human progress, in terms of the proportion of aid allocated to key areas, certain trends are at odds with the goal of promoting social development. For a start, the world's poorest nations are not the largest recipients of ODA by any means. According to World Bank (2002) figures, as already mentioned, the share of aid going to low-income countries dropped from 61 per cent in the 1980s to 56 per cent during the 1990s. Although the bulk of the world's poorest is concentrated in sub-Saharan Africa and South Asia, these regions presently receive just 42 per cent of foreign assistance (German and Randel, 2002). The 32 countries classed as 'least developed' by the UNDP receive less than one-third of the ODA given to low- and medium-income nations (UNDP, 2000). Assistance to the most heavily indebted poor countries (HIPC) fell from 30 per cent of the total aid budget in 1990 to 28 per cent in 2000. However, special measures such as the HIPC Initiative on debt relief initiated in 1996, and the Enhanced HIPC Initiative of 1999, have made strides in easing the debt burden accumulated by over 30 of the poorest countries. There is a growing awareness amongst some aid donors of the need both to increase aid levels and to target assistance more effectively at the poorest countries. This is considered essential if significant progress is to be achieved in terms of meeting the Millennium Development Goals, which optimistically include the halving of world poverty and giving every child primary education by 2015 (DFID, 2002).

In terms of social-sector spending, the record of ODA has been mixed. Following independence, welfare programmes in developing countries tended to follow an incremental approach in which services were gradually expanded in response to urban-based political demands and justified on the grounds of human capital formation for economic growth, with aid being used to support such policies (Hardiman and Midgley, 1982). As discussed in Chapter 1, since the 1970s there has been a greater focus on poverty alleviation and rights-based approaches in which the needs of the less privileged sectors of society are directly targeted on the grounds of promoting social development and social justice. Foreign assistance is frequently portrayed as vital in attaining the Millennium Development Goals, especially in strongly aid-dependent countries for which external support accounts for a high proportion of central government spending in vital areas such as basic education, health and humanitarian assistance.

Yet despite the lofty rhetoric adopted by the aid donor community in its policy statements, assistance to social welfare sectors remains at low levels. Basic education (defined as formal primary schooling as well as non-formal education, early childhood education, literacy and numeracy programmes) is a case in point. It has been lauded in the development literature as a priority investment area for the purposes of both boosting economic growth and promoting social development (Colclough and Lewin, 1993). At the 1990 Jomtien (Thailand) Conference on *Education for All*, Southern governments and aid donors committed themselves to placing a higher priority on basic education in their spending plans. This was against a backdrop of declining aid to the education sector, about 5 per cent of which was allocated to basic education, during the 1980s. It was calculated that, to meet the primary Education For All (EFA) target by 2000, an extra $2.5 billion of donor assistance per annum would be required (Colclough and Lewin, 1993). This was over three times total bilateral and multilateral spending for this sector at the time.

The 1990s saw a mixed response from Southern governments and international donors to the challenge mounted at Jomtien (Bennell and Furlong, 1998). During this period, the World Bank (1995) played a lead role, emphasizing in its policy statements the importance of primary education in promoting development. Total Bank funding (IBRD and IDA) for education almost doubled in absolute terms from $964 million in 1989 (equivalent to 4.5 per cent of total Bank lending) to $1.7 billion in 1994 (10.4 per cent of Bank lending). Over this period, the proportion of Bank lending for basic education rose from one-third to almost two-thirds of education spending but regional distribution was uneven. In South Asia, some 80 per cent of this Bank funding was for basic education, compared with almost 60 per cent in Latin America and less than 50 per cent in sub-Saharan Africa (SSA). The largest beneficiary of increased Bank lending to the education sector has been Latin America and the Caribbean (LAC), where the institution has had a substantial impact on education policy (discussed below).

Closer examination of Bank policy reveals some anomalies, however. Bennell and Furlong (1998) note how in the case of sub-Saharan Africa, despite the rhetoric of needing to expand basic education in a region with the world's lowest primary enrolment levels, Bank funding for this purpose during the 1990s fell considerably. All Bank transactions with SSA are from the soft-loan International Development Association (IDA), giving the organization greater control over how these resources are applied. While IDA funds for education declined during the 1990s, however, loans for public-sector reform and private-sector development have increased substantially, reflecting, '...the relative priorities attached to these activities by the Bank' (Bennell and Furlong, 1998: 50).

There has been a varied reaction from UN agencies and multilateral regional development banks to the lead set by the World Bank on prioritizing basic education. UNICEF (1999) has made a clear commitment and devotes two-thirds of its education budget to basic education while the proportion for UNESCO is about half. The policy influence of the three regional development banks was constrained during the 1990s by the fact that together they averaged just one-third of the education spending of the World Bank. The Inter-American Development Bank (IDB) saw its spending in this sector increase during 1990–96 from $108 million to $175 million per annum (62 per cent). The Asian Development Bank increased education spending from $206 million to $362 million per annum (a 76 per cent increase, amounting to 6.6 per cent of its total budget). In the case of the African Development Bank, education funding fell dramatically from $237 million in 1991 to just $8.6 million in 1996 (or 1.2 per cent of its budget).

While there has been a broad if uneven commitment amongst multilateral agencies since Jomtien to attaching a higher priority to basic education, the record of bilateral donors can only be classed as highly mixed. There was an overall increase in bilateral funding for basic education from $350 million (6 per cent of bilateral education aid) in 1990 to $1.1 billion (19 per cent) in 1995, but two-thirds of this increase was accounted for by just three countries (Germany, Japan and the UK). The proportion of total bilateral aid allocated to education stood at around 10 per cent in 1990 and remains at or below this level.

Basic education still accounts for a mere 1 per cent of total bilateral aid overall but this broad figure masks significant donor differences. During the 1990s, a few bilateral donors significantly increased their funding commitments to basic education (notably Germany, Finland, the Netherlands, Switzerland and the UK) and spend up to 5 per cent of their aid budget on this sector. Some donors that had in the 1980s led the way in basic education funding such as Belgium, Sweden, Norway and Denmark, reduced their support in the 1990s. Bennell and Furlong concluded that, '...among the majority of bilateral donors the actual response to the "challenge of Jomtien" has been either negative or fairly minimal' (1998: 55). According to Randel et al., 'donors are currently giving only a quarter of what would be needed, under the terms of the 20 : 20 Initiative, to reach the 2015 UPE target' (2000: 31).

Yet although foreign assistance to education, and basic education in particular, may have remained at relatively low levels, the influence of aid organizations on domestic education policy is arguably much greater than the above figures suggest. Undoubtedly, the Jomtien conference of 1990 and its sequel in Dakar, Senegal, ten years later, have given basic education a higher profile and encouraged some aid organizations at least to match the rhetoric with extra funds. The Dakar 'Framework for Action' defined education as not just a fundamental human right but also as 'the key to sustainable development and peace' (UNESCO, 2000). In the wake of Jomtien, which was sponsored by UNESCO, UNICEF and UNDP, it was concluded that, in spite of persistently inadequate levels of funding, the notion of *Education For All*, '... had definitely gained wider currency worldwide and inspired numerous resolutions and policy statements, as well as legislation and educational planning' (Bennell and Furlong, 1998: 58).

In terms of donor agency policy impacts more specifically, King (1991: ix) argues that '... agency analysis over the past 20 years has increasingly domi-nated the discourse and debate on education in the poorer countries.' Further-more, '... the analytical work of the agencies, and particularly of the largest donor, the World Bank, has been disproportionately influential in comparison with their financial contribution to total educational expenditures'. In some cases, it seems clear that aid agency policy during the 1990s did help persuade recipient governments to afford higher priority to basic education. Brazil, for example, came under much criticism due to its poor education performance during the 1980s and early 1990s (Birdsall and Sabot, 1996). Partly as a result of World Bank and Inter-American Development Bank influence, a major educa-tion reform was introduced in 1996 to decentralize primary education manage-ment to municipal level and introduce demand-side funding mechanisms to stimulate enrolments. From 1993–94, the World Bank granted loans to Brazil for primary-sector reform totalling well over $400 million.

However, it is a moot point whether improvements in education quality have accompanied the increase in the net primary school enrolment rate witnessed during the 1990s in Brazil, now standing officially at 97 per cent (see Chapter 5 in this volume and Hall, 2004). These multilateral inflows ($300 million in 1998) represent a small proportion of Brazil's total education spending but they are concentrated in the policy arena; namely, technical studies, curriculum design, training and evaluation. Thus, Haddad can justifiably claim that in Brazil, '...the multilateral banks exercise a considerable influence on the formulation of education policy' (2000: 187). In other cases, however, such as those of Guatemala and Peru (Avila, 2000; Palacios, 2000), the international agencies seem to have made far less of an impact in overcoming barriers to educational expansion and improvement despite a notable increase in lending to that sector in Latin America generally.

The Brazilian case illustrates an effort by leading bilateral and multilateral donors to go beyond the traditional approach of funding free-standing, donor-managed projects or as DFID (1998: 38) expressed it, 'islands of excellence in a sea of under-provision'. The alternative 'sector-wide approach' (SWAP) repre-sents an attempt by donors to secure wide-ranging education reforms and to influence sector policy through capacity building and streamlining of proce-dures. The World Bank has led the way in promoting a sector-wide approach in foreign assistance to education, while amongst bilateral donors, Denmark, Sweden and the DFID are prominent. Such 'policy-based lending' involves agencies engaging in 'dialogue' with government at all levels as well as civil society to help in policy design and, rather more problematically, its implementation. Typically, funded initiatives under a sector-wide approach might include bringing budgetary cycles into line with partner governments, harmonizing and relaxing reporting requirements, reducing dependence on expatriate personnel while increasing the training of local officials and decentralizing certain decision-making powers to resident delegations (Randel et al., 2000).

If the record on aid allocations for basic education shows some progress but still leaves much to be desired, this is no less true for other social sectors. At the time of the World Summit on Social Development in 1995 bilateral donors were contributing some $6 billion a year towards basic education, primary and reproductive health and sanitation, or about 11 per cent of total ODA. It was calculated that an extra $40 billion per annum would be needed to ensure universal access, including $10 billion in overseas assistance (Randel et al., 2000). Figures for 1999–2000 (OECD, 2002) show that bilateral commitments for education, health and population stood at 15 per cent of the aid budget, or around $8.5 billion. This suggests a gradual move in the right direction but clearly there is no room for complacency.

Another increasingly important aid-supported international social policy arena concerns the use of humanitarian assistance. In 1990, such aid accounted for 3.5 per cent ($2.1 billion) of ODA, tripling to 10.2 per cent ($5.8 billion) by 2000. About 20 per cent of this includes the cost incurred by OECD members of supporting refugees in donor countries (ODI, 2002). On the face of it, this represents a timely response to critical human needs arising from numerous conflict-related crises. Yet critical analysts have drawn attention to the growing politicization of humanitarian aid which threatens to undermine its traditional impartiality and neutrality (Macrea and Leader, 2000; Macrae, 2001). 'Western governments are now applying the humanitarian label to legitimize military interventions, and in doing so are associating humanitarian action with a wider political agenda' (ODI, 2002: 4).

There is clear evidence to support this affirmation (Macrae, 2001; ODI, 2002). Firstly, consistent with the wider aid picture, assistance provided does not necessarily correspond to need. From 1996–99, the top five recipients of humanitarian aid were Bosnia, Serbia and Montenegro, the former Yugoslavia, Israel and Iraq, which together received $2.7 billion. This is twice the amount allocated to the next five recipients, namely, Rwanda, Sudan, Afghanistan, Angola and Indonesia. Secondly, humanitarian aid is becoming increasingly 'bilateralized' as the proportion of aid to governments and NGOs increases along with earmarked contributions to multilateral organizations and non-traditional service providers. Bilateral relief funds are growing much faster than multilateral or untied resources, accounting for 50 per cent in 1990 and 62 per cent in 1998 (DI, 2000). The implication is that 'bilateralization' signifies the growing use of humanitarian aid for political purposes rather than to directly address victims' needs in a transparent fashion. Another operational complication for relief agencies is that, increasingly, humanitarian aid staff work together with, and under the watchful gaze of, development, military and political personnel. Although necessary for diplomatic and security purposes, these arrangements may compromise the independence of field personnel.

Debt and structural adjustment

Another major area in which social policies have been significantly influenced by overseas development assistance relates to the debt crisis and the challenge of addressing the adverse impacts of structural adjustment. The international debt crisis that emerged after 1982 drove a series of IMF- and World Bank-induced macro-economic reforms (based on monetary stability, fiscal balance and export promotion) in over 100 countries during that decade. Premised on the view that the debt crisis was essentially a short-term cash flow problem that would disappear following such reforms, the wider social context was ignored until the late 1980s. Pioneering studies of the social impacts of adjustment revealed widespread problems of reduced per capita GDP and GNP, growing unemployment, reduced real incomes as well as severe cuts in social budgets in vital areas such as health and education which have severely undermined human capital formation and provoked much suffering (Cornia et al., 1987; Ghai, 1991; Whaites, 2001). Understandably, worsening poverty and deprivation affect particular groups such as the landless, temporary wage labourers, women and children. Subjected to a wave of international criticism, the World Bank and IMF initiated a new phase of 'adjustment with a human face' (after the UNICEF report by Cornia et al., 1987). Social safety net programming marked the first step in a process of positive social conditionality that would help ameliorate the negative impacts of economic reform by tying future donor assistance to anti-poverty strategies. In the perhaps prophetic words of the 1990 *World Development Report*, it had been suggested that 'External assistance should be more tightly linked to an assessment of the efforts that would-be recipients are making to reduce poverty' (World Bank, 1990: 4).

A major tool for constructing such safety nets has been the 'social fund', a term that refers to a large variety of poverty alleviation mechanisms designed to target resources quickly and efficiently at poor communities considered to be most deserving. Social funds exist in over 50 countries, principally in Latin America, sub-Saharan Africa, Eastern Europe and Central Asia. They involve current and planned expenditure of some $9 billion through the World Bank and co-funding arrangements with other multilateral and bilateral donors (Fumo et al., 2000). The first was Bolivia's Emergency Social Fund (ESF) in 1987, followed by the Programme to Mitigate the Social Costs of Adjustment (PAMSCAD) in Ghana and the Programme to Alleviate Poverty and Social Costs of Adjustment (PAPSCA) in Uganda. Whether denominated 'emergency social funds', 'social action funds' or 'social investment funds', they are usually (but not always) administered through intermediary bodies relatively independently of government, involving close collaboration with NGOs and other civil society entities in their design and, in particular, implementation at community level. This point is critical since NGOs are key intermediaries in a participatory planning process (supposedly) enabling social funds to be 'demand-led', and thus reflect the felt needs of targeted groups rather than the whims of central policy-makers and politicians, or indeed aid donors themselves.

Social funds embrace many standard measures intended to benefit the poor, ranging from infrastructure improvements, job creation, community projects, social service provision (such as health and education) and decentralization of management. Within a 'set menu' of eligible projects and dependent almost entirely on foreign funding, social funds are in charge of financing and supervising the implementation of small projects, while establishing set procedures and targeting criteria. Crucially, they should respond to demand from local groups, which in practice may range from community associations, NGOs, local government or even representatives of regional and national government. Although social funds are classed as public-sector institutions, they normally have special semi-autonomous status, designed to bypass conventional bureaucracies and red tape, facilitating speedy project implementation and enjoying advantages such as exemption from official regulations on procurement and disbursement. In the same vein, they often experiment with new models such as community contracting arrangements. Furthermore, social fund staff are usually employed on special performance-based contracts and higher salaries than conventional civil servants.

In summary, social funds 'are intended to take quick, effective and targeted actions to reach poor and vulnerable groups ... to stimulate participatory development initiatives by providing small-scale financing to local NGOs, community groups, small firms and entrepreneurs' (Fumo et al., 2000: 9). Funds have been widely praised by some observers as an effective tool for achieving these aims (Subbarao et al., 1997; Bigio, 1998), while others have been far more critical of their effectiveness in reaching the poorest and in promoting longer-term, more sustainable development. Major criticisms of social funds may be grouped into four major categories. These are (a) their limited ability in practice to reach the poorest groups in most need; (b) the extent to which social fund anti-poverty policies are mainstreamed into national policy; (c) the related question of fungibility; and (d) the issue of long-term financial sustainability.

The main criticism of social funds is that they are driven by effective demand rather than need. Thus, one major review concluded that 'social funds are far from universally successful in reaching the poorest regions or poorest groups' (Fumo et al., 2000: 25). In other words, the most politically influential and well-connected bodies, whether community-based, NGO or government, are able to command access to funding rather than the poorest and most disadvantaged, the socially marginalized. Landless farmers, urban squatters, tribal groups, lower castes and women usually lack the means of articulating their needs and getting them onto the policy agenda.

Social funds have adopted geographically based targeting methodologies through the use of poverty mapping and the construction of local poverty indices, as in the case of Bolivia (FIS), Peru (FONCODES), Chile (FOSIS) and Egypt (ESFD). Other means include sector projects in health and education using selective eligibility criteria or the use of self-targeting in public works programmes aimed at only the most desperate prepared to stand in line for a minimum wage or basket of food. Such relief funds could be considered a form of residual welfare, a last resort for those who have no other means of survival. While often necessary in disaster emergency situations, they run the risk of perpetuating a vision of poverty as a social pathology. Furthermore, there is the strong risk that social funds may be used for political purposes to avoid dealing with the more fundamental causes of poverty and vulnerability.

The 'voices of the poor' are indeed 'crying out for change' (Narayan et al., 2000) but in the absence of a strong grassroots movement backed up by government and NGO support these voices are rarely heard. Social funds therefore face the challenge of strengthening local capacity to assist weaker and more marginalized groups to be able to organize more effectively and challenge the dominance of elites such as politicians and businessmen, who frequently manage to sequester social fund benefits for their own advantage. In the case of particularly vulnerable groups that have no political influence, however, it is unlikely that the provision of safety nets can be left to a demand-driven approach. Pro-active, supply-side interventions based on an external diagnosis of needs and a carefully targeted strategy may be more appropriate in such cases. Yet this would require a strong political commitment on the part of government, NGOs and donors alike to allocate the resources necessary and to build in the accountability required.

The other criticisms of social funds relating to mainstreaming, fungibility and financial viability are also serious. There is concern that new social fund structures work in parallel with conventional government structures for as long as the money flows but that they are not integrated into nor do they influence the direction of sector programmes. Lessons learned from the implementation of social funds rarely seem to be more widely adopted in government policy. This is particularly so in view of the apparent fungibility of social funds; namely, that ministries often reduce national budgetary allocations to areas targeted and divert these resources to other uses, producing no net funding gains to addressing the problems in question. This phenomenon was noted, for example, in the cases of Egypt and Honduras but is undoubtedly far more widespread Such an apparent lack of political commitment might well undermine the longer-term financial sustainability of social programmes as outside funding is withdrawn. Interestingly, however, those social funds with the lowest rates of external funding, including Chile, Guatemala and Colombia, are deemed to have been amongst the most successful in terms of innovation (Fumo et al., 2000).

The machinery of overseas development assistance has since the late 1980s supported the expansion of social funds as a social policy mechanism for dealing with the short-term economic and social costs of structural adjustment. As already mentioned, this approach has arguably been residual in nature, based on the 'safety net' concept of devising emergency measures to catch those who might otherwise fall into chronic poverty. Despite their relative success in compensating some victims of austerity, however, social funds have been criticized for bypassing the politically weaker and more needy sectors of society. There has thus been a growing desire on the part of donors to move away from purely remedial responses to crisis situations towards social risk management strategies to be applied in social funds and other social protection mechanisms. Developed by the World Bank, social risk management 'goes beyond public provision of risk management instruments and draws attention to informal and market-based arrangements, and their effectiveness and impact on development and growth'. (Holzman and Jorgensen, 2000: 4). Social risk management thus requires focusing on qualitative outcomes as well as quantitative outputs, undertaking a broader diagnosis of poverty and vulnerability while placing more emphasis on technical support, skills training, micro-finance and long-term capacity-building. In addition, more attention would be paid to local participation and empowerment, decentralization of management responsibilities and the enhancement of social capital to achieve the above aims. Such a broader and more integrated approach is designed to build upon people's assets and is far more consistent with the sustainable livelihood framework as a more holistic approach to social policy design and implementation.

Although social risk management is a new and relatively untested approach to designing social funds, it does imply a move towards comprehensive poverty analysis as part of a longer-term development perspective. Use of diverse and sophisticated research tools, such as more qualitative and participatory poverty assessments, may help to reduce social exclusion from social fund projects. This move is taking place within a wider initiative to tackle 'human poverty' in its broader sense rather than just income poverty, an issue discussed in Chapter 2 of this volume. Initiated by UNDP (1990) in its notion of the Human Development Index, the World Bank's Comprehensive Development Framework (CDF), launched in 1999, seeks to prioritize meeting the needs of the poor. The CDF stresses the importance of non-economic development objectives such as nutrition, health and education status (Narayan et al., 2000; World Bank, 2000). Arguably, therefore, external assistance is seen by some major donors as increasingly conditional not simply upon achieving economic growth but also upon governments adopting 'pro-poor' policy reform measures (Pender, 2001). This approach forms part of an evolving discourse on social protection that has moved from residualism to favour:

> policies and programmes which help households to reduce unnecessary exposure to risk … help the poor to develop and maintain their human capital, to escape from exploitative social relations … and to take calculated investment and production risks which can be expected to have a net positive effect on growth, equality and poverty reduction. (Conway and Norton, 2002: 534)

Thus, a 'trampoline' effect is to be achieved which enables the poor to 'bounce back' via strategies of risk reduction, risk mitigation and coping. The new vision is also differentiated from its older, residual cousin by virtue of the fact that social protection is increasingly justified (mainly by donors rather than by recipient governments, it should be added) as a political right or end in itself rather than as simply an economic instrument.

The major tool for implementing such 'social conditionality' in the South is the Poverty Reduction Strategy Paper (PRSP), launched in September 1999. Debt relief under the Enhanced Heavily Indebted Poor Country Initiative (HIPC II) through IMF adjustment lending and World Bank concessional credits are made conditional upon the preparation of interim and full PRSPs, outlining plans for attaining anti-poverty objectives. PRSPs have replaced Policy Framework Papers as guidelines for national policy-making. By 2002, 10 PRSPs had been approved (for Mauritania, Burkina Faso, Uganda, Tanzania, Niger, Nicaragua, Mozambique, Honduras, Bolivia and Albania), with a further 60 in the pipeline. PRSP preparation and execution stress local ownership of the process, involving not just governments and donors but also civil society and the poor themselves in a participatory fashion. Such plans would be comprehensive and reviewed regularly on a three-year basis. Above all, producing a PRSP became a precondition to qualify for debt relief or for soft loans under the IMF's new 'Poverty Reduction and Growth Facility' (PRGF), which replaced the Enhanced Structural Adjustment Facility (ESAF), and the World Bank/IDA 'Poverty Reduction and Support Credit'.

To the extent that PRSPs are effective, they may indeed help promote a more poverty-focused kind of development cooperation that addresses social policy concerns. The first systematic formal study of the PRSP process, based on seven African country case studies, was cautiously optimistic. Initial evidence pointed to the emergence of a cross-sector, anti-poverty policy approach emerging in some instances (ODI, 2003). Yet even though it is still early days, potential key problems have been highlighted (ODI, 2003). These include, for example, not gaining the commitment of all official development agencies to the anti-poverty and participatory principles that underpin PRSPs, together with poor donor coordination. In addition, the weakness of the economic macro-framework and growth strategy, lack of attention to micro–macro linkages, high transaction costs and the need to switch to more flexible forms of funding such as budget support are crucial issues. From a social planning perspective, slowness in applying poverty and social impact analysis (PSIA) in appraising concessional loans (PRGF) may be frustrating the desire of participating governments 'for increased ownership of macro-strategies and appetite for opportunities to develop more country specific policy frameworks' (DFID, 2001: 7). There has also been disquiet about the weakness of the State apparatus in many countries and the extent to which civil society is able to participate effectively in the PRSP process, especially as regards effective empowerment in the key areas of priority setting and monitoring of government performance (Whaites, 2000, 2002). Serious doubts have also been cast over the power of international financial institutions to significantly change recipients' policies during the process of economic adjustment (Mosley et al., 1991; Killick, 1998). It remains to be seen whether social conditionality will prove any more effective in terms of redirecting domestic policy priorities in the direction of effective poverty alleviation.

Aid, globalization and social policy

Overseas development assistance has played a significant role in defining, funding and implementing a social policy agenda in the South. Whether social policy takes the form of residual safety nets under adjustment, incremental social welfare service provision or poverty alleviation within a holistic, social risk management and long-term development perspective, external aid has been and still is a formative influence. A perennial question, however, concerns the precise role and power of international financial institutions (IFIs) within a context of growing globalization; namely, the spread of networks of economic, social, political and cultural connections that transcend national boundaries. Have international agencies such as the World Bank, IMF, regional development banks and UN organizations been all-powerful, imposing their will on weak states in desperate need of external assistance? In other words, we must ask whether 'there has been a major shift in structural power and authority away from states towards non-State agencies and from national political systems to global economic systems', as would be argued by the proponents of 'strong globalization' (Yeates, 2001: 11). In the face of such global power, how much autonomy do national governments retain to determine their economic and social policies? From another perspective, are international institutions such as the World Bank and IMF merely the foreign policy tools of those major states that fund them, 'or do they have the autonomy to develop and fashion policy relevant to the global issues they address?' (Deacon, 1997: 59).

If analysis is carried out of the effectiveness of aid in supporting various types of social policy areas, an extremely diverse picture is obtained. Thus, budgetary and balance-of-payments support, technical assistance, institution-building and reform, human resources development and emergency relief, as discussed above, all have social policy implications. Foreign assistance has been disproportionately influential in certain policy areas such as education, for example. Most criticism regarding what might be termed the negative globalizing influence of IFIs has been directed at the consequences of economic stabilization and adjustment policies, which have been associated with deepening poverty and inequality in the South. In terms of social policy impacts, it could be argued that the 'Washington Consensus' package of deregulation, privatization and public spending cuts led to the adoption of a residual, safety net approach to poverty alleviation which failed to address the root causes of current problems. This safety net approach is now slowly being superseded by a risk management perspective and by the introduction of Poverty Reduction Strategies as a precondition for debt relief under HIPC II. As mentioned above, however, it remains a moot point whether international donors actually have the power to enforce such social conditionality unless recipient governments are themselves willing to comply and have the appropriate means of implementation.

Aid organizations have for many years come under fire for their alleged pernicious influence on development, as discussed earlier in this chapter. High-profile bodies such as the World Bank make convenient targets for aid critics, many of these criticisms being entirely justified. However, it is easy to exaggerate the power of the aid machine to influence the development mainstream, either positively or negatively. The importance of aid must be kept in perspective. Firstly, aid is but a small proportion of total expenditures in the South and is declining in real terms. The annual aid budget of some $50 billion is dwarfed by OECD military spending, which is 10 times this figure. Annual agricultural subsidies in the rich countries alone amount to over $300 billion. Furthermore, a large proportion of international assistance flows back to the donor countries in the form of tied aid and debt servicing. Even where aid is part of a coordinated response to poverty there are serious implementation problems. The 20 : 20 Initiative arising from the Copenhagen Social Summit in 1995 committed donors to allocating 20 per cent of ODA and recipients to 20 per cent of the national budget to 'basic social programmes'. Yet this has been frustrated by governments' inability or unwillingness to commit funds to priority social areas in the face of poor institutional capacity coupled with the problems of grasping an often difficult political nettle.

Clearly, ODA will be more influential in some economic and social sectors and in those countries that are especially dependent on external assistance. Yet even if external assistance imposes certain constraints on the freedom of decision-making within government, this does not necessarily signify a total loss of sovereignty or independence, as suggested by the 'strong globalization' school of thought (see, for example, Amin, 1997). The larger and more powerful developing nations are bound to retain greater control over the aid dialogue and policies given their strategic importance in global financial and geo-political structures (witness the cases of Mexico, Brazil and India, for example). In such scenarios there is a large degree of mutual interdependence between donors and recipients that the latter can often manipulate to their own advantage despite appearing to be the underdog. The consensus seems to be, therefore, that the supposed all-powerful influence of international institutions should be seen in perspective and recognized as limited to some extent by the countervailing power of developing countries themselves.

Going back a step, a related question then relates to how far organizations such as the World Bank and IMF are the passive tools of the world's major industrial powers. The international aid machine has arguably furthered major State interests through promotion of the 'Washington Consensus' and the distribution of official assistance on the basis of geo-political interests which do not, as already discussed, always coincide with the most pressing economic and social needs of recipients. However, one major study was more optimistic, concluding that the organizations:

> themselves and particularly their human resource specialists have a degree of autonomy within this framework which has increasingly been used to fashion an implicit global political dialogue with international NGOs about the social policies of the future that go beyond the political thinking or political capacity of the underpinning states.

Thus, in the absence of other major institutional or political influences, the World Bank is increasingly perceived as '*the* locus of global social policy-making' (Deacon, 1997: 61).

Conclusion

International development cooperation has thus had a small but significant and possibly growing influence on the development of social policies in the South. This has been shown in the areas of developing social safety nets, investing in welfare or, more recently, the implementation of a more holistic, cross-sector, anti-poverty approach. Such external assistance is, generally speaking, far more significant and influential in the more strongly aid-dependent nations of sub-Saharan Africa than in the economically and politically powerful developing nations. Bilateral aid agencies, despite restricted budgets and the constraints imposed by national commercial and geo-political factors, are showing some signs of devoting greater attention to social development. The multilateral aid bodies, notably the World Bank, have shown greater sensitivity and funding commitments to addressing social issues.

Major international aid organizations, arguably, do enjoy a substantial degree of autonomy to address development problems in their own right. At the same time, this influence is held in check by the sheer difficulties of implementation as well as by conscious, countervailing power in the South, especially on the part of those wealthier and more strategically placed developing nations. This influence is currently visible in the form of specific social projects and pro-grammes, as mentioned above. However, another area in which official assistance is influencing the policy agenda is in the setting of minimum social standards and in the promotion of a rights-based approach to development. The issue of global standards in social policy has been discussed in Chapter 1 of this volume, along with the gradual linking of human rights to development. Economic, social and cultural (ESC) rights, complementing civil and political (CP) liberties, have been rising up the policy agenda driven by the international development targets focusing on poverty and human development. Although ratification is very patchy, there is wide agreement that the pursuit of CP and ESC rights are mutually reinforcing and assist in the pursuit of social policy goals such as human development and poverty alleviation. Furthermore, a rights-based approach helps to encourage State responsibility and accountability both legally and by other means (ODI, 1999). International aid agencies such as the UNDP and UNICEF have pioneered the rights-based approach to develop-ment while others such as the World Bank are moving far less convincingly in this direction.

Social policy is still overwhelmingly a national concern (Mishra, 1999). However, much more needs to be done by the aid fraternity to prioritize this field as a fundamental building block for sound development. Unfortunately, the rhetoric of poverty alleviation and social development still far outweighs the reality of aid spending in these fields. Donors, especially bilateral agencies, need to make a far more serious commitment to social spending that addresses basic human needs. This must involve not just prioritizing relevant projects and programmes but also investing in the national capacity-building and train-ing that is so essential for effective implementation over the longer term.

Recommended Reading

The following sources provide an overview of foreign aid with specific reference to social development and social policy issues.

- German, T. and Randel, R. (eds) (2002) *The Reality of Aid 2002*. London: Earthscan. This collection provides a comprehensive analysis of aid trends generally, by donors and by sectors. It has various useful country case studies.
- Bennell, P. and Furlong, D. (1998) 'Has Jomtien made any difference? Trends in donor funding for education and basic needs since the 1980s', *World Development*, 26 (1), January: 45–59. This article provides an excellent survey of trends in donor funding for basic education since the Jomtien Conference of 1990.
- ODI (2003) 'Are PRSPs making a difference? The African experience', *Development Policy Review*, Theme Issue, 21 (2), March. Highly recommended as a preliminary survey on the impacts of Poverty Reduction Strategy Papers.
- Sogge, D. (2002) *Give and Take: What's the Matter with Foreign Aid?* London: Zed Books. A readable if sometimes polemical discussion of the driving forces behind foreign aid, stressing that foreign policy objectives often serve to undermine economic and social development goals.
- Deacon, B., with Hulse, M. and Stubbs, P. (1997) *Global Social Policy: International Organizations and the Future of Welfare*. London: Sage. A seminal work that analyses the influence of international financial institutions such as the World Bank and IMF on the globalization process within social policy.

References

Adams, P. and Solomon, L. (1985) *In the Name of Progress*. London: Earthscan.

Amin, S. (1997) *Capitalism in the Age of Globalization: The Management of Contemporary Society*. London: Zed Books.

Arnold, G. (1985) *Aid and the Third World*. London: Robert Royce.

Avila, W.F.R. (2000) 'On the threshold: basic education in Guatemala', in Randel et al. (eds), op. cit., pp. 187–9.

Bauer, P. (1981) *Equality, the Third World and Economic Delusion*. London: Methuen.

Bennell, P. and Furlong, D. (1998) 'Has Jomtien made any difference? Trends in donor funding for education and basic needs since the 1980s', *World Development*, 26 (1), January: 45–59.

Bigio, A.G. (ed.) (1998) *Social Funds and Reaching the Poor: Experiences and Future Directions*, EDI Learning Resource Series. Washington, DC: World Bank.

Birdsall, N. and Sabot, R.H. (eds) (1996) *Opportunity Foregone: Education in Brazil*. Washington, DC: Inter-American Development Bank.

Cassen, R. and Associates (1994) *Does Aid Work?* Oxford: Clarendon Press.

Clark, J. (1991) *Democratizing Development: The Role of Voluntary Organizations*. London: Earthscan.

Colclough, C. and Lewin, K. (1993) *Educating All the Children: Strategies and Priorities for Primary Schooling in the South*. Oxford: Clarendon Press.

Conway, T. and Norton, A. (2002) 'Nets, ropes, ladders and trampolines: the place of social protection within current debates on poverty reduction', *Development Policy Review*, 20 (5), Theme Issue on 'Poverty, Risk and Rights: New Directions in Social Protection', November: 533–40.

Cornia, G., Jolly, R. and Stewart, F. (1987) *Adjustment with a Human Face*, 2 vols. Oxford: Clarendon Press.

Deacon, B., with Hulse, M. and Stubbs, P. (1997) *Global Social Policy: International Organizations and the Future of Welfare*. London: Sage.

DFID (1998) *Learning Opportunities for all: A Policy Framework for Education*. London: Department for International Development.

DFID (2002) *The Case for Aid for the Poorest Countries*. London: Department for International Development and HM Treasury.

DI (2000) 'The state of humanitarian aid', *Development Information Update*, 3.

Fumo, C., de Haan, A., Holland, J. and Kanji, N. (2000) *Social Funds: Effective Instruments to Support Local Action for Poverty Reduction?* London: Social Development Department, Working Paper No. 5, Department for International Development (DFID).

German, T. and Randel, R. (eds) (2002) *The Reality of Aid 2002*. London: Earthscan.

Ghai, D. (ed.) (1991) *The IMF and the South*. London: Zed Books.

Haddad, S. (2000) 'Educational reform in Brazil: market and social inequity', in Randel et al. (eds), op. cit., pp. 186–7.

Hall, A. (2004) 'Education in Brazil under democracy', in M. D'Alva Kinzo (ed.) *Brazil Since 1945: Economy, Polity and Society*. London: Institute of Latin American Studies, University of London pp. 269–87.

Hancock, G. (1991) *Lords of Poverty*. London: Mandarin.

Hardiman, M. and Midgley, J. (1982) *The Social Dimensions of Development*. London: Wiley.

Hayter, T. (1971) *Aid as Imperialism*. London: Penguin.

Hayter, T. and Watson, C. (1985) *Aid: Rhetoric and Reality*. London: Pluto Press.

Holzman, R. and Jorgensen, S. (2000) 'Social risk management: a new conceptual framework for social protection and beyond'. *Social Protection Discussion Paper*, 6. Washington, DC: World Bank.

Killick, T. (1998) *Aid and the Political Economy of Policy Change*. London: ODI.

King, K. (1991) *Aid and Education in the Developing World*. London: Longman.

Lappé, F.M., Collins, J. and Kinley, D. (1980) *Aid as Obstacle*. Washington, DC: Institute for Food and Development Policy.

Macrea, J. (2001) *Aiding Recovery? The Crisis of Aid in Chronic Political Emergencies*. London: Zed Books.

Macrae, J. and Leader, N. (2000) *Shifting Sands: The Search for Coherence between Political and Humanitarian Responses to Complex Political Emergencies*, HPG Report 8. London: Overseas Development Institute.

Madeley, J. (1991) *When Aid is No Help*. London: Intermediate Technology Publications.

Mishra, R. (1999) *Globalization and the Welfare State*. Cheltenham: Edward Elgar.

Mosley, P. (1987) *Overseas Aid: Its Defence and Reform*. London: Wheatsheaf.

Mosley, P., Harrigan, J. and Toye, J. (1991) *Aid and Power: The World Bank and Policy-based Lending*, 2 vols. London: Routledge.

Narayan, D., Chambers, R., Shah, M.K. and Petesch, P. (2000) *Voices of the Poor: Crying Out for Change*. Washington, DC: World Bank.

ODI (1999) 'What can we do with a rights-based approach to development?' *Briefing Paper No. 3*, April.

ODI (2002) *ODI Briefing Paper*, April.

ODI (2003) 'Are PRSPs making a difference? The African experience', *Development Policy Review*, Theme Issue, 21 (2), March.

OECD (2002) *Official Development Assistance Statistics* (www.oecd.org/dac).

Payer, C. (1991) *Lent and Lost: Foreign Credit and Third World Development*. London: Zed Books.

Palacios, M.A. (2000) 'Investment and innovation lacking in Peru', in Randel et al. (eds), op. cit., pp. 189–92.

Pender, J. (2001) 'From "structural adjustment" to "comprehensive development framework": conditionality transformed?', *Third World Quarterly*, 22 (3): 397–411.

Randel, R., German, T. and Ewing, D. (eds) (2000) *The Reality of Aid 2000*. London: Earthscan.

Riddell, R. (1987) *Foreign Aid Reconsidered*. London: Overseas Development Institute.

Sogge, D. (2002) *Give and Take: What's the Matter with Foreign Aid?* London: Zed Books.

Subbarao, K., Bonnerjee, A., Braithwaite, J., Carvalho, S., Ezemenari, K., Graham, C. and Thompson, A. (1997) *Safety Net Programs and Poverty Reduction: Lessons from Cross-Country Experience*. Washington, DC: World Bank.

UNDP (1990) *Human Development Report 1990*. Oxford: Oxford University Press.

UNDP (2000) *Human Development Report 2000*. Oxford: Oxford University Press.

UNESCO (2000) '181 Governments adopt Framework for Action at the World Education Forum', Press Release, 28 April.

UNICEF (1999) *The State of the World's Children 1999: Education*. New York: UNICEF.

Whaites, A. (2000) *PRSPs: Good News for the Poor? Social Conditionality, Participation and Poverty Reduction*. Milton Keynes: World Vision International.

Whaites, A. (ed.) (2001) *Precarious States: Debt and Government Service Provision to the Poor*. Monrovia, CA: World Vision International.

Whaites, A. (2002) 'Poverty reduction strategy papers: participation and change in social policy', *mimeo.*, Department of Social Policy, London School of Economics and Political Science.

World Bank (1990) *World Development Report 1990: Poverty*. Washington, DC: World Bank.

World Bank (2000) *World Development Report 1999/2000*. Washington, DC: World Bank.

World Bank (2001) *World Development Report 2000/2001*. Washington, DC: World Bank.

World Bank (2002) *Prospects for Development*. Washington, DC: World Bank.

Yeates, N. (2001) *Globalization and Social Policy*. London: Sage.

INDEX